DO-IT-YOURSELF ADVERTISING AND PROMOTION

DO-IT-YOURSELF ADVERTISING AND PROMOTION

Second Edition

How to Produce Great Ads, Brochures, Catalogs, Direct Mail, Web Sites, and More!

Fred E. Hahn and Kenneth G. Mangun

JOHN WILEY & SONS, INC.
New York • Chichester • Weinheim
Brisbane • Singapore • Toronto

Library of Congress Cataloging-in-Publication Data:

Hahn, Fred E., 1925–
    [Do-it-yourself advertising]
    Do-it-yourself advertising & promotion : how to produce great ads, brochures, catalogs, direct mail, Web sites and more! / Fred E. Hahn and Kenneth G. Mangun.—2nd ed.
        p.   cm.
    Includes index.
    ISBN 0-471-15442-3 (cloth : alk. paper). —ISBN 0-471-15443-1 (paper : alk. paper)
        1. Advertising—Handbooks, manuals, etc.   I. Mangun, Kenneth G.
    II. Title.   III. Title: Do-it-yourself advertising and promotion.
    HF5823.H187   1997
    659.1—DC21   96-45268
                                                                CIP

Printed in the United States of America

10 9 8 7 6 5

*Dedicated to
America's 8,983 booksellers,
who, if they sell just one copy each per day
for just a very few years
(we'll tell them when to stop),
will surely help make their customers happy,
successful, and maybe even rich!*

| Preface

Like most of you, the author of this book is not a creative genius. Unlike most of you, he has been fortunate in working for three decades with excellent coaches who shared their advertising and promotion know-how with him. It is as a thank you to them that he now shares that know-how with you. It wasn't his to begin with. It's only fair to pass it on.

The first edition of this book began with the words you have just read. So much has happened so fast in small-business (under $500 million in sales) advertising and promotion that I thought it best to add another brain to my personal think tank. Thanks to the President Emeritus[1] of Roosevelt University, I was fortunate to find Kenneth Mangun. Ken's excellent credentials in both the academic and hands-on business communities were invaluable in making this a much expanded and much improved guide.

FOUR NEW CHAPTERS

So much has changed in advertising in just the past four years that major revisions of the existing chapters—plus four totally new chapters, three with their own checklists—are included in this edition. The four new chapters are

Advertising on the Web

While the Internet/World Wide Web is reinventing itself practically every week, its basic applications to sales and advertising remain quite constant.

- The chapter covers what the information superhighway is and isn't as an advertising medium.
- You get a brief introduction of what on-line is, how it works, and how to get on board.
- You get *specific* examples of how to use it for sales and advertising/promotion, as well as things to watch out for and protect yourself against.
- You get *specific* recommendations on current software, for creating your own "Web site" computer advertisement with appropriate warnings about the speed of change.

---

[1]Dr. Rolf Weil is RU's recently retired president and the former dean of its School of Business.

Out-of-Home Advertising

This chapter is an inclusive overview of 18 media, ranging from billboards to bus cards to balloons. You learn how to use them, where to get them, and how much it's likely to cost. Thanks to this new chapter, out-of-home advertising becomes practical for many more members of the small-business community.

Broadcast Fax

Here's a medium that did not even exist when the previous edition was published in 1993. Fax broadcasting is fast becoming the medium of choice for specific kinds of business communication. It's easy to use, inexpensive . . . and even fun. Check it out!

CCREAM™ Media Evaluation

CCREAM is a new way to compare and evaluate competitive advertising media for your advertising dollars. We're truly proud of developing this easy-to-use, practical system and (modestly) expect it to become the advertising industry standard.

MAJOR REVISIONS AND ADDITIONS

Much to my astonishment, despite being published just four years ago, so much has happened that every chapter of the first edition (with the exception of "Finding the Right Advertising Agency") needed and got a major overhaul and update. For instance, this edition discusses:

- What to do about the production of newspaper and magazine advertising, which has been transformed by in-house typesetting and "prepress" production capabilities.
- Whether it's really true—as some experts claim—that direct mail list selection is now so "scientifically" accurate that all you need to test is copy and design.
- How to get anyone to pay attention, with catalog proliferation gone wild, to *your* catalog.
- How to handle the doubling of the number of trade shows and their becoming trade "stores," rather than just "shows."
- How the Internet has affected publicity and public relations and what, if anything, you have to do differently.
- How to take advantage of the new telemarketing capabilities with the likely future of this rapidly growing medium.
- What you can now do yourself in audiovisual (cassette, CD-ROM) promotions, and when it's still better to leave it to the pros . . . no matter how good your desktop equipment.

There's more! *Lots* more! More helpful charts and illustrations . . . 19 additional Insights for a grand total of 87 . . . all new Applications and Case Histories. In addition, dozens of where-to-find-help phone numbers and Internet addresses are included.

My coauthor, Kenneth Mangun, and our individual subject experts, were invaluable in helping to make these revisions, additions—and a few corrections. In addition, thanks to some readers' suggestions, the checklists and their annotations have been improved to make them easier to use.

Every aspect of this new edition is better, stronger, and more valuable to you for your advertising and promotional needs. That's why I wanted to write this preface on my own, to give Ken, too, the credit and thanks his contribution deserves.

Fred E. Hahn
March 19, 1997

| Acknowledgments

WE COULDN'T HAVE DONE IT WITHOUT . . .

This book would not be nearly as valuable to the reader if individual chapters and sections had not been read and critiqued by experts in the various fields. For those whose professional resources are available to the reader, we have given company names and locations.

Chapter by Chapter

Newspaper and magazine advertising design: Susan Jacobs, J-K Art Directions, Milwaukee, WI (414-273-8194). *Cooperative advertising:* Art Sherwin, Advertising Checking Bureau, New York, NY (212-921-0080). *Media research:* Barbara Grahn, SRDS, Des Plaines, IL (847-375-5000). *Direct mail concept and copy:* John Stern, Palos Heights, IL (708-388-3498). *Catalogs:* Morton Levin (Hahn's first employer in advertising and more important, a wonderful friend). *Out-of-home advertising:* Rocco Iacobellis, Outdoor Services, Chicago, IL (312-397-6700); Tom Drouillard, SRDS (847-375-5000). *Telemarketing:* Mitchell Lieber, Lieber & Assoc., Evanston, IL (847-733-9410); Bruce Gollogly, Jr. *Broadcast fax:* Maury Kauffman, The Kauffman Group, Cherry Hill, NJ (609-482-8288). *Advertising on the Web:* Dr. Ralph F. Wilson, Wilson Internet Services, Rocklin, CA (916-652-4659); Sara Fitzgibbons, Acct. Mgmt., DDB Needham, Chicago; Scott Olsen, Academic Computing Sup., Joliet Jr. Col., Joliet, IL. *Public relations:* Carol DeChant, DeChant-Hughes Assoc., Chicago, IL (773-935-7116); Conroy Erickson, Robert Willmot. *Photo duplication:* Peter James, Quantity Photo, Chicago, IL (312-644-8288). *Audiovisual and audio creative:* William Holtane, Sound/Video Impressions, Des Plaines, IL (847-297-4360). *Video/CD/audio duplication:* Allied Digital Technologies (800-846-0123). *Trade shows and conventions:* Devorah Richards, General Exhibit & Display, Chicago, IL (773-736-6699). *Preprint film separation:* Joseph Erl, Tukaiz, Franklin Park, IL, (800-543-2674). *Printing:* Donald Ladin, Sunrise Printing, Inc., Schiller Park, IL (847-928-1800). *Lettershop mailing services:* Lee Enterprises, South Holland, IL (708-596-7900).

The Whole Book

Michael Snell, literary agent, without whom there would not have been a first edition,[1] much less this second. Ruth Mills and Monika Jain, Wiley senior editor and her assistant, gentle authors' hand-holders beyond the calls of duty. Joseph Mills, Wiley associate managing editor, and the people at Impressions Book and Journal Services, Inc., in Madison, Wisconsin. Laurie McGee, copy editor, general secular savior. Shellie Rounds, Ladd, IL (815-894-3207; E-mail: rdps@techinter.com), creator of all the checklists and other wonderful charts. Nancy Willson, Winnetka, IL (847-446-5003), authors' creative director, production artist, miracle worker. Evanston, IL public library research staff who always knew where to find the answer. Alice Hahn, Fred's wife, who outspells SpellCheck™ . . . outgrammars Fowler . . . and tolerates a husband who insists on working at home.

---

[1]Before Hahn began writing this book, he sent a two-page preliminary outline to 15 literary agents who specialized in business subjects. "Would they be interested in representing him?" he asked. All 15 replied! Seven wrote to say they saw no market for the book. Seven wrote to say they liked the concept, but it was not for them. Michael Snell wrote a brief, positive note enclosing directions on how to prepare a book proposal for a publisher's consideration. Six months and six copies of the 137-page proposal later, Snell called Hahn to tell him "Four publishers want to do the book. Keep writing!" He's also called several times since.

| Introduction

This book is a step-by-step guide to the creation or supervision of the most widely used advertising and promotional activities. Four kinds of audiences will find it particularly helpful:

1. The business, corporation, or organization that must do its own advertising and promotion.
2. Persons newly appointed or promoted to positions in advertising, promotion, marketing, or marketing services with little or no experience in those fields.
3. Managers with supervisory responsibility for advertising and promotion.
4. Adult education and in-house training directors who find traditional textbooks unsatisfactory for their needs.

The book works equally well as a blueprint for the do-it-yourselfer, amateur or professional, or as a checklist for managers and supervisors. It is not a complete "course" in advertising. Each chapter covers a specific type of activity or project and is complete in itself. It focuses on just those things you must know and do to accomplish that specific objective—produce an ad, prepare a catalog, supervise a television commercial, and so on. Ordinary English is used as much as possible. When technical terms are introduced, they are defined immediately, in context. Like every other profession, advertising has its own language, and certain "ordinary" words can prove confusing to the uninitiated. ("Light" for "short" in advertising copy was Hahn's first such experience.)

ADVERTISING AND PROMOTION

Since "advertising" and "promotion" are often used interchangeably, even by professionals, some definitions may be helpful.

In ordinary use, "promotion" is everything that is done to help sell a product or service in every step of the sales chain, from the presentation materials a salesperson uses during a sales call to the television commercial or newspaper advertisement that tries to get the customer to think favorably about what is being advertised. Technically speaking, however, "advertising" is responsible for "space" or "print"—that is, newspaper and magazine ads, radio and television commercials, and direct mail and other "direct response" activities, plus catalogs and billboards.

"Promotion" is responsible for everything else in this area except public relations and publicity. These last two may be assigned to an independent department or to either advertising or promotion, depending on the make-up of the company or organization. Since job titles and department designations are quite arbitrary, a detailed job description is highly desirable to avoid turf battles when more than one person or department does any of the above.

Throughout this book, you will find "insights" that are meant to be both aids to memory and actual guidelines to action. Since many of them are applicable to more than one type of project, please browse through these pages and read them all, even if the help and information you need are contained in a single chapter. For example, here are the "Three S's"—the insight that is basic to all of the how-to knowledge you will find in these pages:

INSIGHT 1

Keep it Simple . . . keep it Specific . . . and you're likely to keep Solvent.

You won't go far wrong by sticking to these three!

ADVERTISING, PROMOTION, AND MARKETING, OR "NO, VIRGINIA, THIS IS NOT A 'MARKETING' GUIDE"

Before Professor E. Jerome McCarthy discovered the Four Commandments—or the "Four P's," as they have become known to several generations of students and tens of thousands of marketing professionals—"marketing" was very much in the same state as sex before the Kinsey report. Most people did it sometime, although they weren't sure whether they were doing it right or how it compared with their peers' successes and failures. Marketing, like sex, lacked academic rigor.

Professor McCarthy should probably be credited with codifying the discipline of modern marketing, which focuses on giving customers what they want, rather than limiting their choices to what a supplier wants to produce. It was McCarthy who recognized that marketing consisted of four subdisciplines and categorized them as the Four P's: Product, Price, Promotion, and Place. The last is really sales, but needing a fourth "P," he decreed that how something got to market and where it was sold—the Place—would be accepted nomenclature. And it was so!

Under this marketing theory, Product is the definition or factual description of the product or service, not its engineering or manufacturing. Thus, Marketing might decide that an automobile would look like a Mercedes, have a top speed of 100 miles per hour, sell for $17,500, and pass a standard crash test in the top 10 percent of its class of cars. How this was to be achieved was a problem not for Marketing, but for Engineering, Manufacturing, and Finance. Marketing also determined basic promotional policies and budgets and decided whether a product would be sold directly, through a wholesaler-retailer chain, door to door, by direct response, or any other way it was to find its Place for the final purchaser.

Probably McCarthy's most important insight was that *profit is not a function of marketing.* Marketing designates the quality of an item and the price needed to sell. Considerations of profit must not be permitted to dilute these attributes. Astonishingly enough from the outsider's view, the system works, with America's telephone and computer corporations and Japan's automotive industry just three of the more obvious examples.

The foregoing is a brief distillation of what $40,000 will purchase at one of the better known business schools. Always remember: You read it here first!

Why This Book Isn't "Marketing"

Do-It-Yourself Advertising and Promotion confines itself to the third "P," Promotion, with just enough of the others to provide context where required. Literally hundreds of other books exist—many of them quite good—to help with Product, Pricing, and Sales. For the beginner at creating or supervising advertising and promotion, however, the choice in guides is much more limited. We believe this book meets that need better than any of the others.

HOW TO USE THE CHECKLISTS

The checklists are practical on-the-job help developed by Hahn for use by his clients as well as by his agency. They can be applied by you for in-house advertising, for working with multiperson staffs, for working with advertising agencies and other outside sources, or any combination of all three. Please note that the checklists are suggested models only. Modify them to fit your own work needs.

A Systems Approach

APPLICATION

Every ad or other promotion must have its own checklist to guarantee control and to ensure a final checkoff on each individual project.

Items on each checklist are numbered for ease of multiperson use. ("Let's look at point 8" rather than "Let's find the line about the offer.") Following each checklist, the numbered items are annotated, with the exception of six that would repeat the same annotation throughout (see Figure I.1). To save space and repetition, those annotations are given here.

NEWSPAPER/MAGAZINE ADVERTISING CHECKLIST

Project Title _____ Date _____
Project Description _____ Project # _____
_____ Checklist # _____
Overall Supervision By _____ Deadline _____
Budget _____ Completion Date _____ Start Up Date _____

MANAGEMENT DECISIONS	ASSIGNED TO	DUE	IN	MUST APPROVE	BY DATE	IN	INFO COPY ONLY	SEE ATTACHED
1. Quotations	_____	___	☐	_____	___	☐	_____	☐
2. Budget approval	_____	___	☐	_____	___	☐	_____	☐
3. Project approval	_____	___	☐	_____	___	☐	_____	☐

Figure I.1 The basic format used with minor variations on all checklists.

Six Uniform Annotations

All annotations are written for multiperson use with you *as the project administrator. For one-person, do-it-*all-*yourself items, or total projects, just translate every "we" into a "me" and work accordingly.*

- **Project title.** The *title* is the project's headline or name.
- **Project description.** The *description* is a brief explanation of the project. For instance, "32-item, 2-color Thanksgiving 4-page insert" or "$1/2$-page Shopping News ad."
- **Project supervisor.** Some *one* person has to be in charge. This is the person who assigns to individuals responsibility for each of the numbered items and, when absolutely required, resolves conflicts.
- **Budget.** The *allocated* cost of the project. *How* budgets are set and approved can have a major impact on the time needed for a project. Allow for this in determining the next two items.
- **Completion date.** Since start-up is controlled by when the project must be done, completion dates are set first; then, working backward through the "time lines" (the time required for each step), a start-up can be set. The start-up to completion dates is called the "time frame." What happens within that frame is spelled out in detailed time lines.

APPLICATION

Make all due dates at least three hours before the end of that work day, not—as is normal—one minute before closing. Have the work delivered by the person who did it. This allows time for immediate inspection to check for obvious omissions and errors, and, if necessary, to return it *on the same day it was received* for modification or correction. Since practically no one else works on anything the day they get it, this saves *two* days—the one it would otherwise take to return the material and the day more it would take to get it restarted.

- **Start-up date.** When work *must* begin on the project. In many organizations, multiple projects are assigned at the same time. Depending on the time needed for each, the number of simultaneous start-ups often determines how many outside resources must be used *and paid for.*

Assigning Responsibilities

In any organization where the assignment of working or supervisory responsibility is not routine, such assignment for a group of projects is best done at a single meeting. The advertising director precedes the meeting by preparing and distributing a checklist with all known information and *likely* due dates for each project. At the meeting, objections to scheduling can be raised and resolved. Should one or more persons be unable to attend, the advertising director fills in the missing due dates and circulates to those absent a clearly marked *Preliminary Working Copy* of the checklist, highlighting due dates assigned to that particular person or department.

If any of those assigned dates present a problem, *that person must contact the project supervisor* and negotiate a workable schedule. The project supervisor sets an absolute deadline for when the schedule should be approved or renegotiated by everyone involved. Based on those negotiations and agreements, the advertising director issues a *Final Checklist.*

Five Vertical Checklist Columns

The checklists, as seen in Figure I.1, are divided into five vertical columns:

1. **Decisions.** The first column is the numbered list of individual project subdivisions. The subheads within that column, such as "Management Decisions" and "Creative Decisions," are used to divide the checklists into easy-to-work-with sections. If this causes a "political" problem, take them out!

2. **Assignment.** The "Assigned to" column tells who is *responsible* for getting that item done, not who actually does it (unless they are the same). "Due" shows the due date. The "In" box can be checked when work is delivered. In one company's system it is checked only when material is completed or delivered on the actual due date. A "minus" or "plus" number shows that it was completed early or late. Thus, "+3" means three days early; "−2" shows two days late.

3. **Approvals.** In many organizations, different persons and departments must approve part or all of a project. The more such approvals are involved, the more time must be allowed *for that step.* The "By date" is the due date for these approvals.

4. **Information only.** Certain persons and departments get copies of parts of the project as they are completed. The "Info copy only" column shows who they are and what they get. Such copies are clearly marked as *Information Only.* (A self-inking stamp works wonders here.)

5. **See attached.** *Everything* that bears on a project must be *in writing* and kept in a central file. If there must be telephone information or instruction, the person receiving it puts it in writing ("Phone from JK 3–7. Price changed to $47.55.") and files that, too, sending a copy to the person from whom it originated. A list of all changes is attached to the checklist, with the "See attached" box checked for each change.

INSIGHT 2

In assigning due dates, always assign a specific calendar date. Do not permit completion "ASAP" (as soon as possible). ASAP most often means NEVER.

Make "Final" FINAL!

If at all possible, avoid issuing *revised* "final" checklists; they are an invitation to make all future finals translate to "preliminary." But if you absolutely must do so, be sure that the new checklist is dated and clearly marked as "Revised" and that the original "finals" are equally clearly marked as "See Revised Copy Dated __."

Remind everyone that getting something perfect is no substitute for getting it done!

NOTE: The checklists in this book are copyrighted. They may, however, be reproduced for personal use. For ease of use on standard $8^{1}/_{2}'' \times 11''$ paper, copy them at 135 percent of their printed size.

Contents

Table of Checklists and Key Charts

DO-IT-YOURSELF ADVERTISING AND PROMOTION

1 | Newspaper and Magazine Advertising

The process of preparing newspaper and magazine advertising described in this chapter serves the same function as a blueprint or detailed drawing in the construction of a garden shed. Using identical plans, the professional builder should construct a somewhat sounder and better looking structure than you—but the shed you do produce on your own will be immeasurably improved by following the drawing rather than trying to make things up as you go along.

WHY YOU ADVERTISE

Preparation and Inspiration

When Thomas Edison was asked the secret of his success, he replied, "Two percent inspiration, 98 percent perspiration." You won't have to work nearly that hard. Think of your task as "90 percent preparation, 10 percent inspiration." That preparation starts with a systematic look at why you advertise and what you expect to get out of advertising.

Put It in Writing

Put into writing your reasons for advertising—*all* the reasons—and the results you expect the advertising to bring. You need this list to give a sharper focus to the ads you are going to create and, probably even more important, to have a method of evaluating results. Don't expect any one ad to do ten different things or you'll get one-tenth the results . . . or none at all! Set priorities, then focus on the most important.

How to Set Goals for Your Advertising

In setting goals for your advertising, remember at all times that your *results must be quantifiable.* Depending on your competitive situation and specific business goals, list the expected results as a definite number or percentage—not "more sales," but, for instance, "5 percent more sales during the week following the ad." If you, like many newcomers to a certain kind of business, have no idea what to expect, put down the number that will justify the cost of the ad *if it meets your list of objectives.*

Regardless of the actual results, *whether you like them or not,* keep a record *in writing.* It is your benchmark for future planning and programs. How to use such a record will be discussed shortly.

Typical Advertising Goals

Following are some goals a retailer might set. Analogous goals would be set for a manufacturer or a service organization. The sample percentages are arbitrary and are not based on actual case histories.

Short-Term Goals
- **Increase total store traffic** by 5 percent during the week following advertising.
- **Increase the sale of advertised items** by 15 percent over the previous week. If you are advertising more than one item, you will want to know how each individual item sold, as well as how all the advertised items sold as a whole. This knowledge gives you information for future promotions, even when sales as a whole do not live up to expectations. Be sure to make a special note of purely seasonal successes, such as pumpkins sold just before Halloween. Make a note of the weather—from great to terrible—plus special occasion successes . . . or failures. A traffic-stopping fire can affect business just as a hailstorm can.
- **Increase the sale of nonadvertised merchandise** by 5 percent over the previous week. Advertising is usually meant to increase traffic, and that should be reflected in increased sales throughout your establishment.

Long-Term Goals
- **Maintain an increase in store traffic** of 2 percent in the month following the advertising, as against the previous year.
- **Increase customers' satisfaction** with products and services. Often it is impractical for a smaller firm to afford professional research on customer or client satisfaction. But informal research is always possible. When customers phone, ask about their satisfaction with your products and service, and whether they are getting the information they want from your advertising and promotions. Make certain *you* get and *read* any letters of complaint as well as those of praise. Make sure everyone associated with you *knows* you *are serious about customer satisfaction.* Make it your personal priority and you'll be astonished at the positive results.

Where to Get Help in Setting Goals

If you are a novice in setting advertising goals, here are some sources of help:

1. **Media.** The publications in which you advertise, the media, have expert representatives who often have information about advertising campaigns such as yours. Whether you plan a single ad or a yearlong series, speak with these "reps" about

what you might expect from your ads. But remember that their jobs depend on their convincing you of the effectiveness of their publications, so check their success stories with the people who did the actual advertising—even if they are now your competitors!

2. **Your competitors.** Take your competitors to lunch—one at a time—and ask them what kind of results they get from their advertising. Chances are, they'll tell you. Almost everyone shows off by talking too much.

Analyze your competitors' promotions. Even if your competitors tell you everything you want to know, check.

3. **Trade associations.** Your trade association probably has an entire library of advertising case histories. Call and ask for this and any other help the association might give.

4. **Colleges and universities.** Contact the head of the advertising or marketing department (advertising is usually taught as part of marketing and is also located in journalism and communications schools). Explain what you are trying to learn, and ask whether that information is available from either staff or research materials. Expect to pay a consultant fee. (You don't work for free, do you?) The faculty will help if it can. For example, Mangun served as coordinator of an image research study where students in his graduate research course monitored and evaluated network TV programs and advertising. Mangun and the students received a fee, but far less than what standard research organizations would have charged.

5. **Libraries.** Explain your need to the research librarian at your public or professional library. These are extraordinarily knowledgeable professionals with access to networks of information through computer linkups.

6. **Build your own research base.** If no other information is available, run your ads, set "best guess" goals, and begin to build your own records. You'll quickly have the best database in town and will be invited to lecture to those whom you previously asked for information. But don't disclose too much. Remember what we said about your competitors. You be the one who does know how to keep your mouth shut, even when you'd much rather show off. Brag about your bank statement, not your ad results.

SUMMARY

- Know why you advertise.
- Put the reasons in writing.
- Analyze your competitors' budgets, promotions, and appeal.
- Set goals that can be quantified.
- There's lots of help available. Use it.

HOW MUCH TO PAY FOR ADVERTISING

How to Budget for Advertising

How much you can, will, or must spend on advertising should be decided as objectively as possible; that is, base your decision on reasoning rather than luck or "hoped for" results. To do this, take your advertising goals and calculate, as well as you can, both the "static" percentage-of-sales and the "dynamic" objective way of establishing your overall advertising budget. Both methods are explained below and have devoted followers. After you've become familiar with them, begin by using the one with which you feel most comfortable—*but stay with it only as long as it gives you the expected results!*

A case history. Gaining additional profit by *not* advertising has been attempted by a number of companies and brands, usually with disastrous results. The nonchocolate milk flavoring, Ovaltine, Hahn's childhood favorite, has never recovered from such a decision. Not advertising to gain dollars to fight, or profit from, a corporate takeover is not an "advertising" consideration.

1. **Percentage-of-sales method.** Historically, "percentage of sales" was the way to establish advertising—and most other—budgets. In many businesses it still is. A specific percentage of *last* year's gross sales, often suggested by "industry standards," is allocated for promotional activities. Objectives are proposed but must be modified by the reality of such budgets.

Despite the static aspect of percentage-of-sales budgeting, many managers welcome its protection from unrealistic sales projections. Most of them recognize that it "protects" them from realistic projections as well. They simply prefer the relative safety of the known to the projected.

2. **Objective method.** The objective method is more dynamic and requires a certain daring by management—especially if it's spending its own money. Unlike percentage of sales, which "locks in" budgets regardless of the current year's goals, the objective method expands promotional budgets to meet what management believes are realizable objectives, regardless of previous years' sales.

APPLICATION

Budgeting based on objectives rather than previous sales is especially important in promoting for new business—what direct marketing calls "the cost of buying a new customer." In many businesses, such a first sale will cost 100 percent of the merchandise sold or, in higher-priced items, 100 percent of the regular profit. An objective promotional budget permits even a major effort in this direction without "eating up" the total percentage-of-sales advertising dollars, thereby eliminating a regular adver-

---

Budgeting for Individual Ads

Using some of the advertising goals suggested earlier, an individual ad plan might look like Figure 1.1. It charts four points to consider in planning:

1. Advertisement goal.
2. Percentage of total ad dollars allocated to your goal.
3. The dollar value for achieving the goal.
4. The time allowed for achieving the goal.

Evaluating Advertising Results

In evaluating the success of your ad, as charted in Figure 1.1, the calculation might seem quite simple; however, what if your overall goal is reached but your individual subgoals are not? Does it really make any difference?

Advertising Planning & Record of Results (To be kept with copy of ad)

Subject or Headline: July 4 Picnic Special. 14 "Sale" items; 21 regular   Ad # 51-629/72–97

Media	Size	Date	/	Day	Cost	Coop $	Our $	Coop With
Daily Mail	Tab page	6-29		Thu	$ 600	$300	$300	Frank's Franks
Sunday Mail	Tab page	7-02		Sun	800	400	400	Frank's Franks
Sunday Herald	Tab island	7-02		Sun	1200	600	600	Sandy's Soaps

Production
Art & Design   400
Type   300
                                          $2600 $1300 $2000

Ad Goal: 6-29/7-5	Last Week	Projected $	& %	Actual $	Actual %	% of Goal
Sale Items	$ 35,000	$ 52,000	+50%	$ 53,622	51%+	+1%
50% over last week						
Nonsale Items	165,000	181,500	+10%	177,662	7.6%+	−2.4%
10% over last week						
Traffic for Week	11,859	12,451	+ 5%	12,706	7.2%	+2.2%
5% over last week						

WEATHER: Perfect for picnicking. About 85°

SPECIAL NOTE: Lots of positive customer comments! "Best sale of year," etc.

Figure 1.1 *Spending on advertising.* A typical record combines the advertising goals, the media used, the various costs (including co-op contributions explained on pages 29–32), and the results. In our example, dollar goals are compared to a single time period that makes sense for that particular business. A more complete comparison by week, month, quarter, and year(s) is easy and practical with computerized spreadsheet records. The "Ad #" at the top right shows that the 51st ad of the year (51) ran on June 29 (629) and July 2 (72), 1997 (97). For record purposes, this number must appear in the ad. Try to put it the same place each time.

The answer depends both on the type of establishment you have and the reasons you set your goals. If you are advertising "loss leaders" to bring new customers to your store, and only regulars show up, you're in a different position from having a sale where your inventory costs have been reduced by a manufacturer, leaving profits the same as at the regular price. These and similar considerations should enter into developing your advertising goals. You want sales, of course, but it requires a different perspective to plan advertising for a funeral home or accounting service than for a hardware store or a farm equipment dealership. In fact, without prohibitively expensive research, how *can* you get a short-term fix on advertising that aims at long-term results? Fortunately, there is a fairly easy, practical, and inexpensive way to do just that.

Getting a Preview of Short-Term Results

Where there is high customer traffic, such as shopping malls, individual stores, banks, and so on, place *large-enough-to-read* copies of possible future promotions and track the results. These can be fairly simple "nonadvertised specials" or copies of complete possible ads. The preview "secret" is to give your prospects a benefit for acting *now!* Your reward is immediate positive, negative, or neutral test results. Two examples show how this works.

1. *Ad previewing in a bank.* Three possible ads, offering what the bank believes are benefits wanted by its customers, are mounted and placed in the bank's windows and high-traffic lobby. Each ad offers in-person or written information. Each test produces a clear winner, which then becomes part of the bank's advertising campaign.
2. *Offer preview.* A talk with the sales representative brings a *free* coffee cup personalized with the prospect's name as Executive of the Year. Hundreds of office managers listen to the sales pitch. Far too few buy for the time spent by the sales force. A different offer is previewed and proves a winning success—both in producing sales and in earning a major advertising award.

Getting a Preview of Long-Term Results

Although the need you fill may lie months or years in the future, try for *some* immediate response to your advertising *now.* If you establish a good relationship before the need arises, you're much more likely to get the call when it does. So do what the movie moguls do before they spend millions on promoting a film: Check it out with a sneak preview.

How to Sneak a Preview

Purchase or produce a helpful hints flyer along the lines of "10 reasons why you should meet your banker *before* you need a loan" or "10 things to look for when you're ready to buy a house." The hints should be specific rather than general and be

PISER WEINSTEIN
Menorah Chapels
Gratch-Mandel · Hartman-Miller

Yes, I would like to receive the Piser Weinstein Medical Emergency Information Card. I understand there is no cost or obligation. Please have Donna Feldman call me for the necessary medical and personal information.

Name _____ Age _____

Address _____

City _____ State _____ Zip _____

Phone _____

Best time to call _____

Figure 1.2 The offer of a free wallet-size medical information card reinforces Weinstein Chapels' image as more than just a funeral home, but a neighborhood friend.

directly related to what you do (where to look for dry rot and how to tell it's there rather than "check for dry rot"). The more valuable the advice, the more likely that it will be kept and consulted when a service such as yours is needed. (See Figure 1.2.)

Informational flyers may be available from your trade or professional organization and often are advertised in trade journals. They tend to be inexpensive and may be customized with your name, address, and telephone number at a small additional cost. You can, of course, also produce your own.

If several suitable flyers are available, offer a different one free each time you advertise, to see which one gets the best response. Then use that flyer as long as the level of response continues. If your budget is limited to fewer ads than the number of different kinds of flyers available, ask the supplier which one has gotten the most repeat orders. Then use that, providing that it meets your other criteria. The least expensive, and often the best, research is to learn from the experience of others.

SUMMARY

- Allocate specific dollar amounts to each advertising goal.
- Don't just wait for long-term results to happen. Offer information or use a premium to jump-start results.

No matter how successful your response, vary the offer occasionally to attract a different audience and to check whether what has been your best draw continues its appeal. Take *nothing* for granted if you can test to make sure.

BUT MICE DON'T BUY MOUSETRAPS: HOW TO FIND THE AUDIENCE YOU NEED

Targeting by Building Profiles

Profile building can be critically important for many different kinds of business and the success of their advertising and promotions. If you are a retailer, your customer profile may seem obvious, but there is a simple and inexpensive way to make sure: *Ask your customers why they bought what they did at your shop.* Since they may not want to tell *you,* use the same approach suggested for getting help in defining advertising objectives. Ask the marketing department of a nearby college or community college for help in wording the questions and doing the actual interviews. For instance:

- Did your customers check advertising before purchasing a product or service and if so, in which medium?
- Which publications do they buy and/or get delivered, actually check the ads, read, or just glance at?
- Which publications do they like best? (This is a check against the "which they read" answers.)
- Demographic information, where appropriate, such as age, education, and income, given in approximate ranges. As stressed in the chapter on telemarketing, it is astonishing what people will tell you, when they are asked politely.

Often the answers are not at all what you expected and lead to changes in advertising plans. Perhaps equally important, it never hurts to show professional concern for your customers' wants and needs!

Manufacturing may require more-sophisticated research—and often gives equally surprising results. For example, when a film company produced a series that would explain upcoming surgery to patients, the company knew its customer profile. It consisted of family doctors who make the initial diagnoses and surgeons specializing in those fields. But before the filmmaker's advertising agency did anything about creating ads, it did a routine check to corroborate the customer profiles. It took only a very brief telemarketing survey to learn that the true customer—ready and eager to order, immediately, over the phone—was *not* the doctor. It was the hospitals' senior floor nurses, who were responsible for putting the patients at ease before surgery.

The client saved tens of thousands of dollars in two ways: by not advertising to the wrong audience and through earning profits by advertising to the right target audience. Even more important, the company gained insight into the importance of verifying a customer profile—even when you "know" that you know the result before you begin.

There's much more about profile building and its use in the chapter on direct mail.

So decide to whom you will be advertising before you write a single word. Often, it's not as obvious as it seems. Suppose you have a baby product. Will you advertise to parents, grandparents, pediatricians, toy store owners, supermarket buyers, and so on? Don't work on what to say until you're absolutely clear about two things:

1. **The audience you're trying to reach.** This may, in fact, be a variety of audiences. The question then becomes one of how many different messages you can get into one ad. Generally, you are better off to concentrate your advertising on one specific target—the "rifle" rather than the "shotgun" approach. To repeat: Don't expect any one ad—or any one medium—to do ten different things or you'll get one-tenth the results . . . or none at all.

2. **What you want your audience to do.** Rush to your shop . . . call for an appointment . . . invite you to their office or home . . . send money . . . send for information . . . authorize a trial subscription . . . Vote! Buy! Try! Call! Write! Drive! Fly! Run! Walk! Taste! Imagine! Sleep! And that's just a sampler to get you started.

DESIGNING THE AD

This chapter will guide you in writing a competent advertisement; however, only God can gift you with the talent to be a designer. Therefore, in the hope that we will be forgiven, we do what real designers do. We borrow. Or as a number of great designers are credited with saying: "The art of creativity is not to reveal one's sources."

How to Design Your Ad without Being a "Designer"

Look through the publications in which you expect to advertise, and pick out those ads which you feel are well designed and are aimed at your audience. Equally important, they must be the same size as the ad you wish to produce. Try to find several examples, especially those with different amounts of manuscript—what copywriters call "light," "medium," or "heavy."

Now pick two or three you like best. These will be your models. Everything you do to create your ad will be based on one of them. The reason for choosing several originals is to give you flexibility in how much you say. But whatever the original has—light copy or heavy, large type or small, with a picture or without—plan to do the same. Avoid the temptation to mix and match—to take design elements from several ads and combine them into a new whole. That is what professional designers often do, but those of us who aren't pros usually botch it up.

Eventually, you'll give your manuscript, along with your design model, to a typesetter and ask him or her to *approximate* the original. (You want to avoid lawsuits whenever possible.) This aspect of advertising is called *production* and needs a manuscript as well as a design. That's why writing the ad is next. Production, including the wisdom of setting your own ads, follows right after.

SUMMARY

- When it comes to design, don't. Find a true designer . . . or follow a real designer's lead.

WRITING THE AD: THE IMPORTANCE OF BENEFITS

The key to writing successful ads lies in training yourself to turn features into benefits—and then to use benefits to sell the product or service.

A **feature** is anything inherent in your product or service, for instance, punctureproof tires on a bicycle, large type in an insurance policy, nonpolluting soap in a laundry. In essence, a feature is what *you* have put into your product or service.

A **benefit** tells the potential buyers what's in it for them if they use your product or service. For example:

- Are your bicycle tires punctureproof because they're made from uncomfortable solid rubber, or is the benefit that these state-of-the-art tires are so safe that riders won't need to carry patching kits and pumps?
- Large type in an insurance policy seems an obvious benefit for the elderly, but is it necessary if you're trying to sell to newlyweds? How about "No eye-straining tiny type, but a policy designed to be read and understood!"
- Surely you can develop six additional benefits of even greater value to the person you are trying to persuade, no matter what you wish to sell.

How to Develop Benefits

Even though you want to end up with benefits, begin with features, since they are what you are likely to know best. List each individual feature at the top of a 5″ × 8″ index card. Start with what *you* know, then enlist the help of anyone who has knowledge you may lack or who might catch an item you've overlooked. Once you're satisfied that you've captured all the features, call an old-fashioned brainstorming session and explain your problem. You have all these great features, but the people you're trying to sell keep saying "So what? What's in it for *me?*" It's the answer to these two questions that are your *benefits.*

THINGS TO REMEMBER IN BRAINSTORMING, WHETHER YOU DO IT BY YOURSELF OR IN A GROUP

1. Use a tape recorder so that you can keep note taking to a minimum—even if you have someone who can take shorthand.
2. There are no dumb suggestions.

3. Do not discuss individual answers now; that will inhibit the free flow of thought and force participants to defend something they may not quite understand themselves.
4. Bring in a new feature the moment the benefit stream dries up. Keep the action lively.
5. If someone suddenly suggests a benefit for a feature that's already been covered . . . great!
6. Don't let *anything* negative get in the way of the process.

Once you and your features are exhausted, type each one, along with its suggested benefits, on individual sheets of paper, and distribute copies to the brainstorming participants. Now is the time for critical scrutiny—and for the addition of those benefits that brought you awake in the middle of the night two days after the original session. Ask everyone to criticize, add to, change, edit, or otherwise modify anyone's suggestions and return the lists to you for a final compilation. Whether you'll have another meeting to discuss this final list will be determined by your working situation, but the end result should be a series of 5″ × 8″ cards listing features and their benefits, in order of importance *for specific audiences.* Thus, the same benefit may appear more than once but be given different emphasis, as in details of nutritional value in selling puppy food to veterinarians and careful feeding instructions in selling it to the general public. You will, of course, put the same information into a computer file. But for fast and easy shuffling of information, nothing beats the cards.

On Group Diversity

As a marketing consultant, Mangun has led brainstorming sessions to develop marketing solutions, new product and service concepts, direct mail packages, and so on. Based on his experience, he has found that some mix of diversity within the group is an important factor in the generation of quality ideas. Consider these examples:

- A *major insurance company.* The brainstorming group consisted of ad agency account executives, creative directors, and a nonagency copywriter. The addition of the writer was a major plus. The ideas were on target and generated numerous concepts that were later developed into direct mailing packages.
- A *major natural history museum.* The group was made up of the department head who was a former Smithsonian employee, museum staff, and a Ph.D. in anthropology. All were very productive; the Ph.D. was incredible.

A note of caution: Make sure no one individual dominates the group. As to the importance of diversity, the two "outsiders," the copywriter and the Ph.D., were the major idea stimulators for their groups.

SUMMARY

- Features instruct. Benefits sell!

Features Instruct. Benefits Sell!

Practically no one buys anything solely because of its features—it's the benefits that sell. Thus, you do *not* say, "the world's best seeds," but "the world's best lawn!" *Not* "777-horsepower engine," but "from 0 to 135 mph in 3 seconds!" And ask yourself where and how anyone is actually going to want to speed up like that and what other uses there can be for a machine with that much power. You'll continue to discover benefits that will surprise even you—and delight you with their pulling and selling power.

Beware of Overkill
Make sure that the benefits you claim are actually those *the buyer* gets. You are legally responsible for any claim made in your promotional materials—for *anything* that appears in print or on electronic media and for which you may be assumed to have given approval. There are some exceptions, such as an innocent mistake in a price that is corrected immediately at the place of purchase—although not a price designed to mislead! In case of doubt, consult your attorney, or better yet, change the benefit to something else. Advertising is not a game to see what you can get away with; it's one of the few ways of communicating what you hope to sell to potential buyers. The end goal is *not* to avoid going to jail. It's to make an honest sale from which the buyer will receive genuine benefits and the seller will earn a profit.

Developing Your Offer

Suppose you've listed every *feature* you can possibly discover in your product or service and overwhelmed the skeptic's "so what" question about each with a flood of irresistible *benefits.* Now it's time to consider the *offer*—the agreement between you and your customers, the promise you make when they buy your product or service.

Planning the Offer
In planning your offer, three different factors need to be considered:

1. **What do you want the reader of the ad to do?** For example, go to your store or shop? Telephone for information? Invite you to make an estimate? Send money?

2. **What will the customers get if they accept your offer?** Offers range from discounts (10 percent off) to service (oil changed while you wait) to promises (service with a smile) to guarantees (unbreakable, or your money back). Offers can be implied (Swiss quality) or trumpeted (world's best roofing shingles). They can be limited (offer ends Wednesday) or universal (lifetime guarantee). Whatever the

offer, try to match it to the needs and interests of your particular audience. If you're not sure and have no other good way to find out, run two versions of the same ad at the same time, changing only the offer, and see what happens. How to do this is covered under advertising production's "A/B Split" a bit later in the chapter.

3. **Can you afford it? Can you afford to offer less?** Obviously, you will make your offer as inexpensive as possible. However, the key is not cost as such, but cost effectiveness or cost per sale. So before deciding on what you can afford, get the best answers possible to four more questions:

A. Is this a one-time sale, or are you trying to establish an ongoing customer relationship, and how much is each of these worth?

B. How fast must you get your return on the dollars spent for promotion, and will that return come faster if you make the offer more attractive?

C. What do your competitors offer, and should you match that or make your offer even more attractive? And what are the likely consequences to them—and you—of an "offer war"?

D. What are the immediate costs of these options, what are their break-even points, and what are their payoffs if they succeed?

The chances are that you'll have to make an educated guess at some of the answers to these questions. Do it, but keep your guesses on the conservative side. If there are to be surprises, let them be happy ones.

SUMMARY

- Load up with benefits to hit your target.
- Plan your offer for your customers' wants, not yours.
- When you can't afford the offer, can you afford to offer less?

WRITING THE AD: WHERE TO START

Every ad is made up of four elements:

1. The *headline,* commonly called "the head."
2. *Body copy,* which is everything except the headline and the identifying signature, or "logo."
3. The *offer,* which is part of the body copy but has to be thought out separately.
4. The *logo,* or signature, which identifies you and is generally the same as or very similar to your letterhead.

Hahn's personal way of working is to begin with the offer, go to the body copy, and do the headline last. The offer forces him to understand *exactly* what he is trying to sell and what the buyer gets in return. Chicken at 49¢ a pound, when the competitors are charging 55¢, requires no explanation; but an HMO or the 27th new restaurant to open this month needs a different kind of enticement.

After a "rough" (preliminary) draft of the offer, Hahn does the body copy. His best headlines have generally grown out of a seed planted in the body, which he suddenly realizes would make the perfect "head." Of course, once the headline is in place, the entire ad may have to be fine-tuned to fit it, but that won't matter, as long as you work within the ARM framework, which we will tell you about next.

Where *You* Should Start

Where *you* start really makes no difference. Many writers begin with the headline or body copy instead of the offer and work from there. But no matter where you *start,* the headline is of such crucial importance that we'll treat it in detail first.

The Headline (and Illustrations)

The headline (and illustrations, if any) are your grabbers. They are the way to catch readers' fleeting attention and get them actually to read what you have to say. To do this, your advertisement, as every other marketing communication, must achieve the three ARM factors.

INSIGHT 3

The Three ARM Factors Every Ad Must Have
A Attract attention.
R Retain interest, so that the reader will become aware of your overall message.
M Motivate the reader to take the action your ad is designed to produce.

Think of these as the ARM portion of "I'd give my arm if only they'd buy." So arm yourself with the best headline you can develop to attract attention.

Two things your headline must do are:

1. Attract the audience that will actually buy the product or at least influence its purchase. Buyers and influencers are not necessarily the end users. Young children neither buy nor influence their parent's purchase of cough syrup, but they are a major factor in deciding on purchases of toys, games, and cereals. Know for whom you write . . . and why!
2. Have carry-over power that will get readers from the headline into the ad itself.

Let's assume that you are writing an ad for a bicycle shop that has added a line for senior citizens. In writing your headline, don't try to be clever or funny. That usually fails, even when attempted by professionals. Rather, begin by stating the most obvious fact and let your ad develop from there. For instance, you might try

BIKES FOR SENIOR CITIZENS

This approach will keep you out of trouble, but is unlikely to attract very many from the audience you want, unless you spice it up with some *benefits*. Two of the all-time best benefits are "new" and "free," so let's try to get at least one of those into the ad, perhaps as easily as this:

NEW! BIKES FOR SENIOR CITIZENS

Notice the difference between "NEW BIKES . . ." and "NEW! BIKES. . . ." In this instance, the second version is probably preferable. With a different product—insurance, for instance—"NEW BENEFITS . . ." might well do better than "NEW! BENEFITS. . . ." Always think of what will appeal to your specific audience and write accordingly.

But there is still nothing in the headline to get very many readers from "A" to "R"—to motivate Attention into Readership. So let's strengthen the headline with stronger benefits and, if room permits, more of them, like this:

NEW! SPECIAL OFFER
FOR 50-PLUS BIKERS

or

FREE TEST DRIVE OF SENIORS'
NEW RECREATIONAL BIKES
Free Lessons For Nonbikers Who Purchase

Note the change from "SENIOR" to "50-PLUS" in the first headline, and think about how you might make a similar change in the second. In writing headlines, keep refining, with three goals in mind:

1. **Broaden the appeal where possible, but take care not to lose your targeted audience.** "50-PLUS" may well capture the attention of seniors, plus attract a bonus group in the close-to-senior years. But broaden one step further to "ADULT," and not only have you lost the focus on your real audience, but you've picked up a number of possible meanings of "adult" that will simply confuse your message. In writing your ad, every single word must be considered for the effect it has on the total message, and nowhere is this more true than in the headline.

2. **Get at least one major benefit into your headline.** "NEW" and "SPECIAL OFFER" show benefits in the first example. The offer might well be the test drive and free lessons spelled out in the second sample, or it might be something entirely different.

3. **Fit the headline into the basic design you've elected as your model.** Count the number of letters and spaces in the headline rather than its words, and work within that limitation. Don't cheat.

A Note on Guarantees, Promises, and Offers

If there is to be *any* limitation or qualification on an offer—such as free lessons only to those who make a purchase—state this immediately in conjunction with the offer. Unless qualified, a "free" offer is legally free to *anyone* who requests it.

SUMMARY

- Start writing your ad wherever in the copy you feel most comfortable; you'll get to the headline soon enough.
- Follow the ARM (Attention/Retention/Motivation) rule for successful copy.
- Stick to the basic design of your models in writing—especially in your headline.

WRITING THE BODY OF THE AD

All your hard work in developing benefits will now pay you back, because this part of the ad should just about write itself.

1. Take the benefits you've put on individual cards or sheets of paper, and arrange them *in order of importance to the person you are trying to sell.*
2. Check your design model, and see how much room you have for copy.
3. Within your space limitation, put as many benefits as will fit, using a ☐ small box, • bullet, or √ check for each. This is the "telegraphic" style and gives a feeling of importance and urgency to your ad:

   - Lets you write incomplete sentences.

   - Gets the most benefits in the fewest words.

IF YOUR ORIGINAL USES A STANDARD PARAGRAPH FORMAT

If your models use a paragraph format, count the letters in each line, and then use the same space for the telegraphic style. Copy in paragraph format takes a "writer," just as original design takes a "designer." And in most instances, the telegraphic style will be more effective, regardless of writing skill. So stick to what you can do.

4. Highlight each benefit with its own bullet, box, or check. You want your readers to know how much they will get. Don't be afraid to pile it on!

5. Separate the benefits from the offer by the use of a "subhead," a smaller headline within the body of the ad. (See Figure 1.3).

6. Your offer can be a continuation of the bullet/box/check format, or it can go to a normal paragraph format as in Figure 1.4. Which it does will depend on the room available and the details of the offer. The goal is to make the offer easy to understand and impossible to resist. Always edit yourself with that in mind.

Features, Too!

What does your audience *have* to know about technical specifications, size, weight, colors, materials, packaging, and so on, to anchor the benefits to reality? Consider "Available in blue only" versus "A rainbow of 14 color selections." Or "1/4-hp motor" versus "3/8-horsepower, three-speed motor with reverse option." Or "All standard sizes" versus "20-gallon drums only." Recall how irritated you get when you respond to an advertisement, only to learn that it left out the one key factor that would have told you it wasn't for you (or when you didn't respond and found out too late that it was for you). Benefits, yes! Pile them on. But don't forget the features. They'll help draw the right customers in and, equally important, keep the wrong audience out.

A Sample

Figure 1.3 shows how the manuscript might look for a small ad for this part of *Do-It-Yourself Advertising and Promotion.* Instructions for type sizes are given in the margin. (The actual ad, in three different type styles, is shown in Figure 1.4.)

Check out how this sample is loaded with benefits. The headline contains three (new, secrets, success). Every point begins with the benefit of "how to" and then adds one or two more. Even the subhead offers the clear benefits of a 30-day trial and a guarantee; and what could be a clearer benefit than a no-nonsense, no-quibble guarantee? Aim for that if your product or service permits; if not, come as close as you can. The features are there, too, with the number and size of pages, checklists, illustrations, and an index as in Figure 1.4(c) set in the Futura typeface.

INSIGHT 4

Keep a single, clearly marked master copy of any manuscript. Use it to show all changes and corrections, and hold it along with all supporting documents that show when and where the changes originated. On computerized systems, use a printed (hard copy) manuscript for this purpose. Neatly redone versions will, of course, exist, but the final check is always against the master.

NEW! Ad Pros' secrets for successful copy
Find out the way to write selling ad copy
the way professionals do in the newly revised 2nd Edition of
Do-It-Yourself Advertising and Promotion.
- How to know exactly what to say
- How to get the most sell into least space
- How to work with layouts
- How to get started . . . and keep going!
- How to get results like a creative
genius without being one!
TRY IT FOR 30 DAYS. IT'S *GUARANTEED!*
Get your copy of ***Do-It-Yourself***
Advertising and Promotion directly from the publisher.
Follow the step-by-step directions for 30 days to create your
own ads. If you're not satisfied for any reason,
return the book for full credit or refund. This handbook
works for you or we take it back and refund your money.
345 pages. 19 Checklists.
Illustrations. Index.
only $00.00
Available wherever books are sold
JOHN WILEY & SONS
605 Third Avenue, New York, NY 10158

Figure 1.3   Manuscript copy for advertisement for *Do-It-Yourself Advertising and Promotion* before final price and number of pages is known.

Identifying Yourself: Your Advertising Signature or "Logo"

Somewhere in every advertisement, the advertiser's logo—the particular way you show your name, address, and telephone number—has to appear. No matter how fancy or plain, be sure that your logo does include your address and telephone number. Don't assume that the ad is so appealing that your readers will look them up. They won't. Rather, they'll go to your competitors—the ones who make it easy to do business with them. Always remember that no one *has* to buy from you, so . . .

- Make it simple.
- Make it easy.
- Make it a benefit for the buyer.
- Prepare to laugh all the way to the bank.

SUMMARY

- Use a telegraphic style for the body of the ad.
- Concentrate on benefits, but don't forget the features.
- Let the offer itself determine its writing style.
- Complete your logo with your address and telephone number. Your readers won't do it for you!

Figure 1.4(a)   Example of the Bookman typeface.   **Figure 1.4(b)**   Example of the Optima typeface.

Figure 1.4(c)   Example of the Futura typeface.

Figure 1.4   The ads shown here in three different typefaces were produced on quite unsophisticated desktop publishing equipment to show the effect of using different types. They were not intended for publication. Note the difference between the century-old favorite, Bookman, and a semi-serif face with a modern touch, the popular Optima. Note too the improved legibility of the reverse (white) type, especially in its smaller sizes, when using the Futura sans-serif type. (To see these ads at the sizes indicated in Figure 1.3, enlarge them to 125%.)

The book illustration is a placeholder. The actual photograph is unlikely to be as emphatic as the placeholder unless you photograph it specifically for that purpose. Discuss with your photographer the differences between shooting for "contrast" and "detail."

ONE FINAL CHECK BEFORE TYPESETTING

You know the audience you need to reach, and you have developed a cornucopia of benefits and offers that should make them buy. Now is the time to analyze your finished copy and layout for its appeal to that particular audience. Answer the following ARM questions:

- Does your headline shout for *Attention* from your specific audience?
- Do your benefits *Retain* and heighten the interest of that same audience?
- Does your offer *Motivate* the audience to the action you want it to take?

If the answers are all "yes," and if the amount of copy matches the model ad you've chosen, you're ready to go to production.

PRODUCTION: FROM MANUSCRIPT AND LAYOUT TO FINISHED AD

You've picked a design and written the copy. Now all you have to do is set the type and get it to the media in a form acceptable to them. Fortunately, that's the easiest part, and the next few pages will tell you how.

Typesetting

Now that you have your manuscript and the ad model you wish to follow, you have four options to use to complete the project:

1. **Outside production service.** Turn over the ad to an outside service and let them do everything else. This is by far the easiest way to go, but it's also the most expensive. And you will still have to supervise and approve everything that's done.

2. **Desktop publishing.** If you are very skillful at using your computer to set type, try to typeset the ad yourself. But unless the end result looks as good as professional typesetting, turn it over to the pros. Professional typesetting should be one of the least expensive parts of the project and will give your ad a polished look.

3. **Typesetting by your medium.** If your advertisement will run in a single magazine or newspaper, find out if the publication you have chosen offers a typesetting service and, if so, at what cost. Often, this is a free or low-cost option, and many publications take pride in doing a fine job as part of their overall service. Some of these publications will even permit you to run ads they set in other media, so check on that, too.

4. **Professional Typesetting.** Professional typesetting, which was a thriving industry when our book was first published in 1993, has largely disappeared as a stand-alone enterprise. In just four years, designers and design studios have taken

this business in-house and the remaining "typesetters" now tend to offer design services also. Old-fashioned typesetting does still exist at many quick printing and copy locations, but the majority lack the knowledge of typography that made old-fashioned typesetters such a valuable helper to the do-it-yourselfer.

Whether your type is set in-house or outside, here are a few things you should do and know in dealing with typesetters:

Things You Should Do
- Explain that you are using your sample ad as a model only; it must not be copied so exactly that you might get sued.
- Get a cost quotation. Find out if the cost includes any changes and, if not, how changes are charged.

Things You Should Know
- Mistakes by the typesetter, called typos, are corrected without any charge to you.
- Alterations are the changes you make after the manuscript and layout are delivered and the type is set. They are at your expense. There will be a minimum charge for any alteration—even a single comma.
- The best way to avoid charges for alterations is to make sure that your manuscript is "clean," that is, exactly as you want it. But be prepared to make a few changes even so. Typesetting seldom comes out exactly as we'd like. So make whatever changes you must, but try very hard to make them all at once. That minimum charge comes back each time you request another set of alterations!

Before deciding which typesetting option to choose, you may wish to know more about type itself. What's involved in deciding on a particular typeface and why you might pick one over another are covered in the next section.

SUMMARY

- Use a professional-quality typesetting source. It's the cheapest way to get a professional look.
- Give your typesetter a letter-perfect manuscript. It's the best way to keep your typesetting inexpensive.

Type: Faces, Weight, and Sizes

There are thousands of different styles (faces) of type from which to choose, but there is no need to work with more than a very few. To explore the differences among them, we've taken the sample ad in Figure 1.3 and set it in the three type-faces in Figure 1.4. As illustrated, the ad shows amateur design and amateur computer skills. It does not begin to reflect the full capabilities of desktop publishing. If your ads look anything like this, when you'd prefer them to look like Figure 1.5, get professional design help. Fast!

Major Type Families

Every typeface belongs to one of three "families":

- **Cursive** type imitates script or handwriting. It has little use in the body of an ad but is sometimes used for the logo, as in the name of the publisher in Figure 1.4(b).
- **Serifs** are the small curlicues or fine lines at the tops and bottoms of letters. Bookman and Optima are serif faces.
- **Sans serif** means "without serif" and is any type in that family. Futura is a sans serif face.

The Serif Advantage.   Most adults find serif type easier to read than sans serif, with a group of serif designs known as "reader faces" easiest of all. Of the tens of thousands of books, magazines, and newspapers published in the United States, practically every one uses such a reader-friendly type.

Bookman, Figure 1.4(a), is a face that has proven its utility for more than a century. Its traditional look is more than compensated for by its legibility, so you should feel comfortable in using it, except when you want a very contemporary tone in your ad.

Optima, Figure 1.4(b), is a modern reader face and somewhat of a bridge between the serif and sans serif styles. It is adaptable to almost any ad, and its use is more a matter of personal choice than degree of legibility.

Futura, Figure 1.4(c), is a modern typeface with as much legibility as any sans serif typeface is likely to give. While the serif faces, as a group, are easier to read, you should consider sans serif under certain circumstances.

The Sans Serif Advantage.   Sans serif, too, has its advantages, chief among them the following:

- **Compressibility.** Sans serif "condenses," or compresses, type better than serif does. That is, you can get more letters per inch without distorting the type.
- **Contrast.** Often, it pays to be different. If everyone else is using a serif face, at least consider the alternative. Or you may want to draw particular attention to one portion of your ad, such as a special offer.
- **Everyone else is doing it.** If everyone else advertising to your audience is using sans serif faces, try to find out why. Ask the representatives of the media where the ads run and the advertisers themselves. Better yet, run the same ad both ways and track the results. Unlike designers or authors of books, your interest isn't in typography; it's in sales. Do whatever works!

- **Reverse type.** White or light-colored type on a dark background is easier to read in sans serif than serif (although it is generally harder to read in either typeface than standard black on white, such as what you're reading here). Use reverse type only in headlines, logos, and what ad pros call "violators," those star-bursts or other shapes that highlight a very bold statement, such as in the bicycle ad described earlier. *Never use reverse type for an entire ad,* especially in body copy. It slows down the ability to read.

A "violator"

- **Overprinting.** Using sans serif definitely improves the legibility of type printed on top of ("over") a background color or illustration. However, "improved" does not necessarily make it "good." The key is contrast between type and background. Equally important, when seniors are your target, larger type sizes are needed. Check your ad proofs as explained in Chapter 14, and let legibility be your guide.
- **Subheads.** Many designers use sans serif for subheads, with the rest of the ad in serif type. The authors' personal preference for subheads is a bolder (darker) version of the face used in the body of the ad.

About Type Weight

"Weight" refers to the thickness of type. Practically every face ranges from a very thick, "bold" style to a "regular" version considered the most legible for text body, to a thin or "light" design. All of these weights are also available in italic and bold, especially on more-sophisticated computerized typesetting machines, which can italicize a term or make it bold at the push of a button. The names given to the degrees of boldness or thinness vary from face to face and are not really comparable. One design's "black" may be darker or lighter than another design's "ultra bold." Your typesetter will have samples with the appropriate names. For desktop setting, your computer can print each version in the styles available to it.

INSIGHT 5

Use a single typeface for your ad. Variations in size and weight are almost always preferable to mixing faces. Do it!

About Type Sizes

> Type sizes have a measuring system all their own, called points, with each point being $1/72$ of an inch. This paragraph is set in 9-point ($1/8$-inch) type, but a quick measurement will tell you that none of the letters are actually this size.

Ascenders and Descenders.   Take a good look at this paragraph. Some letters in it, such as "h" and "l," extend toward the top, while others, such as "p" and "g" extend toward the bottom. Yet despite these ascenders and descenders, none of the lines run into each other. Each letter is confined within a theoretical frame that leaves room at the top and bottom, so no matter how close (or "tight") you fit your copy, there is always space between the lowest descender and the tallest ascender. The exact size of this frame varies with the typeface and may appear larger or smaller than it actually is, according to the design of individual letters. Here are some ways to add legibility:

1. Pick the typeface you find easiest to read.
2. Place additional space, called "leading," between lines. This often is more effective than making the type larger. Spacing instructions to your typesetter are indicated in points. For instance, "9/9" means 9-point type with no extra space, "9/10" means one point ($1/72''$) of space between each line, "9/$_{11}$" means two points, and so on. The type in this paragraph is $11/13$.
3. Reduce the type size, but leave the same point differential. For example, going from $10/11$ to $9/11$ often increases legibility, while giving a few more letters per line. But don't set copy smaller than 9 points if you can avoid it. The easier your ad is to read, the more likely it is that it actually will be read. Leave tiny type to very personal classifieds.

SUMMARY

- Serif faces are easier to read than sans serif. Use serifs.
- The fewer typefaces, the better is the ad. Use a single face of varied weights and sizes.
- There's no point in running ads nobody will read. Keep the smallest type for the body of your ad at $9/11$. *Reduce the amount of copy before you reduce the size of the type.*

Production Considerations for Photography and Art

If your model ad includes photography or art, you have a number of options:

1. Take your own photograph or draw your own illustrations. Let your conscience be your guide.
2. Use a professional photographer or artist. Keep in mind that photographers' and artists' fees are often negotiable and that the quality of their work is seldom affected by their price. Be sure to read the section on art and photo ownership, pp. 140–142, before you order or buy.
3. Use existing photographs or art, or use graphic materials from one of your suppliers. They may be overly familiar to you, but they'll be entirely new to your audience.
4. Use stock photographs and illustrations—pictures that can be used by anyone for a set fee. There are numerous sources for these. The suppliers will work with you to find a picture that fits the mood or subject you specify. Usually, they will also send you a variety of pictures from which to choose. These photographs can be "cropped"; that is, only a portion of the photo need be used, for added impact.

Where to Find Stock Pictures

Many large cities have local creative arts resource directories. Ask the chamber of commerce, your public library, or the director of your local advertising club. Also, there's always the Yellow Pages and your very helpful media representatives. The production directors of advertising agencies are probably the best source. Ask them. They'll be able to do a favor for both you and one of their own suppliers. That's two good deeds with a single telephone call. If you're neither in nor near a large city, ask your fellow advertisers what they do. Obviously, they've solved the problem already and may save you much spinning of wheels.

SUMMARY

- Use a professional photographer or illustrator when possible; otherwise get existing or stock art.
- Finding suppliers is the easy part; deciding which one to use is the hardest.

Film for Advertisements

Many publications will accept your ad in hard copy typeset form, with a clear indication of where the illustrations, if any, are to go. However, if your ad is in color, or if the publication will accept only one-piece hard copy art or film, you need the skills and equipment of a "color separator"—even if the ad is black and white only.

What the Color Separator Does

Color separators take all the elements that make up your advertisement—type, art, and photographs—along with your instructions for making them larger or smaller, into one color or several, and against a tinted or clear background. They then produce film to the printer's specifications. If the magazine or newspaper requires "one-piece art," the color separator will use the film to make a photograph called a *print* or *glossy* that is suitable for that medium. This is the same process that is used to provide the "proofs" that accompany the film and that you get to "proof" the fact that the film was properly prepared.

A Record-Keeping Hint.   Underneath every ad, show the ad number, as explained in Figure 1.1, the media in which it ran, and dates when it appeared. Tell the color separator to leave that information as part of the proof. For ads that do not first go to film, do the same thing and make a good copy for yourself. Keep these record proofs in notebooks that will not be used for any other purpose.

There's much more about film preparation, especially for color printing, in Chapter 14.

ABOUT TESTING

When time and budget permit, advertising professionals test everything about their ads to learn the best advertising approaches and media. You do the same, and, like them, rely on your business experience and common sense when you can't. When testing is practical, be sure to structure your ads so that you learn what you want to know.[1]

• **Testing two completely different ads** for the same product or service is fine, provided that your price and offer are the same for both. Otherwise, how will you know whether the result came from the ad, the price, or the offer?

• **In testing one specific item**—a lower or higher price, headline, offer, picture, illustration, typeface, and so on—leave everything else exactly the same and *change the one item being tested only.* If, for instance, you change both the price and the headline, how will you know which produced the result you get? If you increased the price and sales increased, too, or even stayed the same, you won't care. But what if sales fall? Was it because of the new price or the new headline? Decide exactly what it is you want to learn, and test that without changing anything else. For example, suppose you wish to test the appeal of the same product to two different audiences. Figure 1.5 shows how this might be done. In each ad, the headline identifies the target audience. In the body of the second ad, the benefit is modified slightly from the first in accordance with the audience's needs. The rest of the copy remains the same. By placing these ads in media that provide cards for reader response, test results were achieved at very low cost. Note how adding a name at the bottom ("call Alice" for one ad, "call Jean" for the other) would add to the ease of tracking results.

Testing: The A/B Split

Many newspapers and magazines will run two different ads of the same size in every other copy of an issue, usually at a slight additional charge. Note that this is

---

[1]For much more than can be covered here about testing, see John Caples' *Tested Advertising Methods,* 5th edition, edited by Fred Hahn.

Figure 1.5 Produced on a computer by professional designers, these one-half-column ads (2³/₈″ × 4⁷/₈″) tested the appeal of the same product for two different audiences. (Ad design: J-K Art Directions, Milwaukee, WI. Photography by Lucky Curtis, Chicago, IL (312) 787-4422. Copy by Hahn.)

not one ad in the first half off the press followed by a different ad in the second half. Rather, A/B means that, of the copies delivered to houses, apartments, and offices in the same block, or the copies sold at newsstands, every other one will contain ad A, with the rest having ad B. In publishing terms, that's known as a *true A/B split,* and it is just about the easiest, most effective, and least expensive way to test the appeal of different offers, prices, headlines, and so on.

Demographic Editions

Many publications offer not only A/B splits but also *demographic editions.* When you purchase a demographic edition of a publication, you purchase a specific location and/or socioeconomic segment of the total circulation. Large-city newspapers offer neighborhood editions that make it affordable for local retailers to advertise in the "big" paper. National magazines offer everything from over 100 test market locations (*Reader's Digest*) to 1,600,000 top businessmen and women (*Time*). Explore these possibilities with the media representatives, and, *if it makes economic sense for you,* weigh the factor into your final decision regarding your choice of media for your ad.

WHEN TO CHANGE AN AD

No advertisement retains its selling power forever. Even successful ads are often improved by testing different headlines, benefits, or offers—or sometimes by such a simple thing as changing and advertising new business hours. But never change a successful ad simply because you've seen it so often that you're sure that readers are tired of it. The chances are they're not: In fact, an even better chance is that they're not aware of it at all and the ad is just starting to do its best work.

Procter & Gamble celebrated the 50th anniversary of Tide in 1996 and credits a large part of the detergent's sales success to "continual advertising support with a message that's consistent to this day." Slogans remain the same for years, including the early "Tide's in, dirt out" and "If it's got to be clean, it's got to be Tide," in use by 1996 for more than a decade.

One of the more counterproductive mistakes made by advertisers is to stop running successful advertising because they are bored with it. They've lived with the ad from conception through all the birth pangs, to its final arrival as a fully developed promotion. They want to move on to something new and are convinced their customers feel the same way. But their customers and prospects probably haven't seen the ad at all, and when they do, they won't pay it nearly the attention the advertiser likes to believe they will. There are only two valid business-related reasons for changing an ad:

1. The ad is no longer cost effective.
2. A different ad or a different version of the same ad has proven more effective.

The Only Excuse for a Failed Ad

A second common—and costly—mistake made by advertisers is to invent excuses for advertising that didn't work. Of course, if you are holding a tent sale, and a tornado keeps everyone locked into their cellars, you will certainly take that into account. But if you have a proven offer, product, price, and medium, very little else, except the ad itself, is an acceptable excuse for a failed promotion. Always go back to the three ARM basics of:

1. **Attention:** Did you get readers' attention, and how might that have been done better?
2. **Retention:** Did you retain readers' interest through meaningful benefits, and how might these have been enhanced?

3. **Motivation:** Did your offer motivate the readers to act the way you had expected, and how can you improve the offer?

Learning from Success

Learning from success is much more pleasant than learning from failure, so don't forget to do that, too. Keep detailed records. Analyze them to discover what you did right, and then apply it in the future. Avoid developing new ads without feedback when feedback is available. Celebrating your successes is much more fun than being creative about excuses. And following the directions here should give you lots to celebrate. So go to it!

INSIGHT 6

Beware of the bottom-line success available through drastic reductions in or elimination of advertising. The short-run savings may all seem positive, but the long-term consequences are frequently irreversible. It costs much more to regain than to retain your customers, if it can be done at all.

SUMMARY

- Test those things most likely to matter—media, offer, audience targeting, headline, benefit emphasis, price.
- If testing the obvious motivators doesn't point you toward success, think very hard about your product or service.
- Test only one thing at a time, or test totally different promotions. Never change two aspects of the same promotion within the same test; you won't know why you got the results—no matter what they are.
- Continue to use successful ads until something else proves more cost effective.

COOPERATIVE ADVERTISING

Cooperative advertising, generally abbreviated to co-op, is an agreed-upon sharing of specified advertising or other promotional costs among manufacturers and retailers or analogous groups. As an excellent way to expand advertising and promotion dollars, it's a win-win situation for both. As Figure 1.6 shows, such co-op can extend far beyond newspapers, radio, and television. Almost anything goes, providing it's within the agreed-upon and specified limitations of the manufacturers' plans.

What to Agree Upon and Specify . . . in Writing

Whether you are the national or local partner in a co-op agreement, spell out the rules under which you participate. Make sure that you agree upon at least the following:

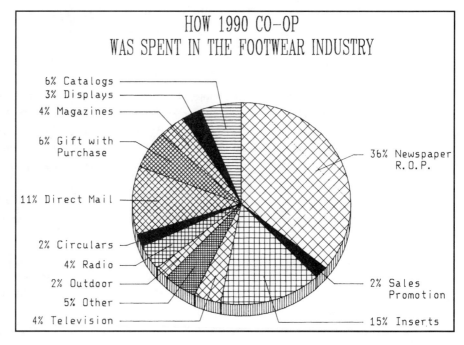

Figure 1.6 Cooperative advertising. (Courtesy The Advertising Checking Bureau, Inc.)

• **Who pays.** How much or what percentage of costs will each of you pay? Specify maximums if any.

• **How co-op accrues.** What goods or services apply to the "accrual"; that is, the amount you get from the manufacturer for your advertising? How is that amount determined? Over what period of time? By law, the accrual must be proportional for all like outlets or participants, regardless of size or volume. For instance, manufacturers may not give retailers 5 percent of sales for a 100-unit purchase and 10 percent for 200 units, thereby rewarding the larger outlets. Thus, the *degree* of co-op must be the same for every retailer, although it can differ or be absent for wholesalers. Co-op may also be regionalized or otherwise limited, as long as it is equally available to *competing* users.

INSIGHT 7

Co-op accruals are "use it or lose it" amounts, not an additional discount automatically credited to everyone. Co-op is distributed for specified promotional use and is forfeited unless earned in that way.

• **What will be promoted.** This need not parallel how co-op is accrued. Often, all of the co-op earned is targeted on a few promotional leaders.

- **When to promote.** Agree upon dates, seasons, or tie-in events and, above all, the final date on which the co-op accrual may be spent. In specifying dates, consider such possibilities as using unspent Christmas co-op for January sales. Try to be flexible, but remember, accountants live by fiscal years.

- **Where and how to promote.** National organizations tend to favor "name" media. But "shoppers," "penny-savers," and similar free media may be a retailer's best buy. Stay flexible. By law, not only must co-op be proportional, but also, it must be functionally available. That is, it may not be limited to what only the largest accruals can buy.

- **Message approvals.** Both co-op partners are responsible for claims about their products and services. Agree on who creates and who approves advertising. To prevent conflicts, many manufacturers prepare advertisements, commercials, flyers, and mailing pieces that are easy and inexpensive to personalize for cooperating retailers. In fact, most of the advertising that appears in newspapers is prepared in just that way.

- **What's not covered.** Many co-op programs exclude all creative or preparatory charges and cover only a specified percentage of the *net* cost of newspaper and magazine space or radio and television on-air time. But see Figure 1.6. The purpose of a co-op program is to promote the product or service better and sell more of it. If what will work isn't in the current agreement, add it. Just remember . . . put it in writing!

Auditing Co-Op: How and Why

Most companies with substantial co-op programs audit retailer or other local charge-backs through an advertising checking service. Local advertisers requesting charge-backs submit tear sheets of their ads—the actual pages on which the ads appeared—or some other proof of promotional activity, with invoices substantiating the cost. But if Hahn's own experience is any guide, the invoices are sometimes the most creative use of the promotional effort.

The Question
While advertising manager for Rand McNally, Hahn was perplexed by how much one of America's leading department stores paid for its newspaper advertising. According to invoices they submitted, ads he assumed would cost around $3,000 for space were invoiced for over double that amount. By coincidence, the same batch of mail that brought the request for charge-back approval also brought him a mailing from ACB, the Advertising Checking Bureau[2]—then, as now, the largest such service in the country. He had not known that such a service existed. Further contact with ACB provided both an answer and a solution to his problems regarding the department store's billings.

The Answer
Billing for almost all publication advertising is based on a projected use of that medium by an advertiser during a calendar year. As distinct from a co-op agreement,

[2]221 W. 41st Street, N Y City 10036. (212) 921-0080

substantial discounts are given to those who advertise more—to the "heavier" advertisers. The true rate is calculated at the end of the year, and adjustments are made at that time. The department store that had sent Hahn the invoice had contracted—and was being billed—for a fraction of the space it would actually use. It got an enormous refund at the end of each year. But in the meantime, it had highly inflated invoices to submit for its share of the co-op, and the newspaper had an interest-free loan that it was happy to repay when actual discounts were calculated.

The Solution

For every U.S. newspaper and hundreds of magazines, the Advertising Checking Bureau (ACB) keeps a running total of the advertisements that appear in it. Other such services track radio and television. All of them can check charge-backs and, where necessary, correct them to their true rate. *In most instances, the corrected charge-back is approved by the retailer.* When the original charge-backs are too high, an audit report specifies actual space or air-time rates and an approved co-op amount. In case of conflict, the service, rather than the manufacturer, becomes a party to the disagreement. Thus, rather than a conflict between a supplier and a customer, you get a debate between accountants. If, as can also happen, charges are too low, notifying retailers about this can hardly be surpassed for creating goodwill. As a matter of record, the department store never questioned the audited, corrected co-op amount.

Many co-op agreements specify that invoices will be checked by an auditing service. Such services are in every major and most secondary markets and can be found in the Yellow Pages. Most of them specialize in local and regional media. A few, such as ACB, operate nationwide. If you are the co-op provider, balance the cost of the auditing against possible savings in charge-back claims. If your co-op program totals $25,000 or more, auditing is probably worthwhile.

WARNING! WARNING! WARNING!

When changing your telephone number *for any reason,* several days later call Information as well as your old number to see what happens. And do it every six months even if you don't change. We repeatedly were given a nonoperating number when trying to contact ACB. It was not the first such misinformation in our experience.

SUMMARY

- Don't limit co-op to the most obvious media; limit it just to those that are likely to work.
- Put co-op agreements into language both sides can understand . . . and make sure that they do.
- As a wholesaler or retailer, expect co-op claims to be audited . . . because they probably will be.

NOTES ON THE NEWSPAPER/MAGAZINE ADVERTISING CHECKLIST

These notes are a supplement to the material presented in this book. They are not *a self-contained substitute for that material.*

1. **Quotations.** The total of all quoted and/or estimated costs accepted from outside suppliers, plus the known or estimated internal out-of-pocket costs. This is the amount given for budget approval in #2.

2. **Budget approval.** The amount either accepted from #1, or otherwise determined as a fair cost to do the project. If lower than the figure in #1, costs may have to be renegotiated with suppliers or the project modified to fit the dollar allocation.

3. **Project approval.** Once the project *can* be done for the amount in #2, a decision on whether the project is worth the cost, no matter how "fair" the individual charges may be.

4. **Target audience.** Determination of the target audience at whom the ad is focused. Usually this is done as part of a total marketing program. Everything else about this ad must then be controlled by that focus. How else will you decide the message and the media?

APPLICATION

Neither the checklist itself nor these notes are a time line. Many of the items must be done at the same time rather than sequentially. For instance, numbers 5 through 8 plus 18 are first decided, then worked on simultaneously.

---

5. **Message.** This tells the writer *what* is to be said, not *how* to say it. The actual wording is the job of the writer in #9.

6. **Benefits.** The benefits keyed to the audience in #4. If none of those benefits seem particularly suited to that group, the choice of *those* benefits and why *that* particular audience was targeted must be reconsidered.

7. **Headline.** The headline's subject, not its wording. Pick the one thing most likely to attract the target audience; usually the key benefit from #6.

8. **Offer.** Make the offer a *major* reason to get the advertised product or service *from you* and to do it *now,* especially if a competitor's options are available. As the advertiser, do not be afraid to echo your competition. If you can't do better, at least stay even. Note that the offer can appear anywhere in the ad as long as the design gives it such prominence that it can't be missed.

9. **Writer.** The checklist shows the person who *appoints* the writer*. If certain things must be said in a specific way, let the writer know before he or she begins . . . and whether this is a legal constraint or a management

NEWSPAPER/MAGAZINE ADVERTISING CHECKLIST

Project Title _____ Date _____

Project Description _____ Project # _____

_____ Checklist # _____

Overall Supervision By _____ Deadline _____

Budget _____ Completion Date _____ Start Up Date _____

MANAGEMENT DECISIONS	ASSIGNED TO	DUE	IN	MUST APPROVE	BY DATE	IN	INFO COPY ONLY	SEE ATTACHED
1. Quotations	_____	___	☐	_____	___	☐	_____	☐
2. Budget approval	_____	___	☐	_____	___	☐	_____	☐
3. Project approval	_____	___	☐	_____	___	☐	_____	☐

CREATIVE DECISIONS

4. Audience Focus	_____	___	☐	_____	___	☐	_____	☐
5. Message of Ad	_____	___	☐	_____	___	☐	_____	☐
6. Benefits Focus	_____	___	☐	_____	___	☐	_____	☐
7. Headline Focus	_____	___	☐	_____	___	☐	_____	☐
8. Offer Focus	_____	___	☐	_____	___	☐	_____	☐
9. Writer	_____	___	☐	_____	___	☐	_____	☐
10. Designer	_____	___	☐	_____	___	☐	_____	☐
11. Colors	_____	___	☐	_____	___	☐	_____	☐
12. Typesetter	_____	___	☐	_____	___	☐	_____	☐
13. Artist	_____	___	☐	_____	___	☐	_____	☐
14. Photography	_____	___	☐	_____	___	☐	_____	☐
15. Camera-Ready Art	_____	___	☐	_____	___	☐	_____	☐
16. Film for Media	_____	___	☐	_____	___	☐	_____	☐
17. Film Shipment	_____	___	☐	_____	___	☐	_____	☐

MEDIA DECISIONS

18. Media Focus/Selection	_____	___	☐	_____	___	☐	_____	☐
19. Ad Dates	_____	___	☐	_____	___	☐	_____	☐
20. Ad Sizes	_____	___	☐	_____	___	☐	_____	☐
21. Space Cost	_____	___	☐	_____	___	☐	_____	☐
22. Media Notification	_____	___	☐	_____	___	☐	_____	☐

MECHANICAL CHECKS

23. Logo OK	_____	___	☐	_____	___	☐	_____	☐
24. Address OK	_____	___	☐	_____	___	☐	_____	☐
25. Phone(s) OK	_____	___	☐	_____	___	☐	_____	☐
26. Editorial OK	_____	___	☐	_____	___	☐	_____	☐
27. Legal OK	_____	___	☐	_____	___	☐	_____	☐
28. Marketing OK	_____	___	☐	_____	___	☐	_____	☐
29. Management OK	_____	___	☐	_____	___	☐	_____	☐
30. Copy of Ad as Run	_____	___	☐	_____	___	☐	_____	☐

MEDIA LIST ☐ If checked, see back for additional media.

Newspaper or Magazine	Cover Date	Date Issued	Reservation Deadline	Deadline for Film	Size	Colors	Cost

decision. If the latter, management should be willing to at least consider alternatives.

10. **Designer.** The person responsible for choosing the designer.* Good designers often surprise, so do not be hasty to say no to what you may not like at first sight. It is the designer's job to know how to appeal *visually* to the targeted audience. All of us, and especially the younger generation, are becoming more visually oriented. Designers are right more often than they are wrong.

11. **Colors.** The use of color in newspaper and magazine ads almost always gains readership. So does size. If dollars are set and you must choose one of the two, ask each media representative for *facts and figures* on which works better in their specific medium. If still undecided, pick color. For low-cost, striking effects, ask about "spot color," the use of any amount of a single color; just so it does not cover the entire ad.

12. **Typesetter.** For advertising that requires design skill, use professional typesetting. Limit in-house desktop typesetting to straightforward flyers, reports, and other simple-to-set projects.

13–14. **Photography/art.** Both who selects the photographer and/or artist and who gives the technical as well as the aesthetic instructions. (Not necessarily the same person!) Unless the person doing or given the assignment is an expert in art *reproduction* for newspapers and/or magazines, discuss this with the filmmaker in #16 before any photography or art is ordered (for instance, to learn about shooting photos for "contrast" or "detail" and what the filmmaker's camera can and cannot "see"). *Much* more about this is included in the Prepress Film Preparation checklist.

15. **Camera-ready.** The all-inclusive term for illustrations, photography, and type put into position as it will be used to create the ad. It is the last chance to change anything at relatively low cost. It includes *every* instruction to the filmmaker *in writing*. If another department or an outside service or agency does this, the person who assigned the project goes over it with them. The filmmaker should be present also. Everyone involved must understand the instructions and understand them *the same way*.

16. **Film.** Film also includes proofs (photographic copies of what the printed ad will look like) for approval, as well as for each publication. The proof is checked against *every* instruction on the original art to make certain it has been followed. It is, literally, checked off so nothing is overlooked. Equally important, the proof is examined to see whether those instructions make sense *in what is seen now*. Newspaper advertisements seldom are as "sharp" (clear) in print as on the proof. If for *any* reason the ad is hard to read on the proof, it will probably be impossible to read when printed. The original instructions must also specify how many proofs and what kind will be needed. Each medium's rate card has this information. Most ask for one proof; some want more.

---

*Here, as elsewhere in these assignments, the person making the appointment and depending on skill and time available, may choose himself or herself, as well as someone else.

17. **Shipment.** Let the filmmaker ship the film to its destination—even if it is across the street from your office. That is part of *their* know-how and *their* responsibility!

18. **Media.** Does the focus of the media match the target audience focus in #4? If not, why this selection—unless it is the only paper in town? If there is no good medium for what you are advertising, use what is available . . . and work on building a mailing list.

19. **Dates.** Differentiate among the four key dates in making magazine selections:

    A. *Closing date.* The date by which ad space must be reserved (ordered) for the ad to appear in a specific issue.

    B. *Mechanical date.* When the material from which the ad will be printed—usually film, sometimes "art"—must be at the publication. If art is required, check with the publication to learn *exactly* what they mean by this term.

    C. *Cover date.* The date printed on the cover.

    D. *Out date.* The dates on which the magazine will be mailed and when it will appear on newsstands. Those may be up to a week apart.

20. **Size.** Have a reason for the size of the ad. Note that it often costs less overall to create a single larger ad and use it everywhere than to pay for the creation of smaller versions for less important *and less expensive* media.

21. **Space cost.** Dramatic discounts are possible when someone advertises fairly frequently in the same medium. Almost all publications combine "space" with "frequency" discounts to make it possible to run more advertising at lower per-ad cost. The media buyer, the person responsible for purchasing the space, should ask media representatives about "rate holders," the smallest ads accepted by a medium, and whether there are any other ways to save. Since media representatives may not be able to negotiate rates other than those given in their rate card, check with the media buying services described in Chapter 2 about *the possibility of negotiated rates!*

22. **Notification.** Notify or confirm orders, including telephone orders, to *each* medium by fax or mail. Use a reservation form similar to the one shown in Figure 1.7. Although reservation on a purchase order or letterhead is accepted by practically everyone, the use of a media form gives a better assurance that all pertinent instructions will be covered.

23–29. **Mechanical checks.** Someone has to be responsible for checking each of these items before anything may be printed. Make sure that the responsible person *does* check them and signs off *in writing*. In many organizations, the logo—the organization's name, address, and telephone number—is preprinted in a variety of sizes and styles and *must* be used from that art. It is an excellent safety measure, providing every such piece is dated and thrown out when there is a change. Experience shows that practically no one really checks logos. Wise advertising directors make themselves the exception.

30. **"As run" copy.** Some *one* person must be responsible for maintaining a file of all ads "as run"; that is, as they actually appeared in each publica-

Hahn, Crane Advertising, Inc.

2035 Hawthorne Lane • Evanston, IL 60201-3002 • Phone/Fax 847-866-9009

SPACE RESERVATION

Date _____

TO THE PUBLISHER OF:

This is authorization to schedule advertising
as specified in:
☐ Rate Card # _____
☐ SRDS Dated _____
☐ Other_____
Ad Size/Colors _____
Space Cost _____
Frequency Rate _____

ADVERTISER_____
Address _____
City_____ State _____ Zip _____
Telephone _____ Fax _____
Authorized Signature _____ Title _____

AGENCY _____
Address _____
City_____ State _____ Zip _____
Telephone _____ Fax _____
Authorized Signature _____ Title _____

AD ID #_____
AD HEADLINE _____
_____
ADVERTISING SCHEDULE
Date(s) _____
_____
_____

☐ Bill to advertiser
☐ Bill to agency
☐ Materials herewith
☐ Materials to follow from:
_____
_____
_____

SPECIAL INSTRUCTIONS
Send 2 tear sheets of printed advertisement with billing.
_____
_____

Figure 1.7 Typical reservation form for newspaper and magazine space. For radio and television, use a "Media Reservation" form.

tion. The printed copies should be used for this file. Normally, only a single copy of the page on which the ad appears accompanies the invoice—even when the advertiser requests two or three. So if accounting must see the *printed* ad before a medium is paid, let them see the original as proof, thank them for their care, and leave with them a reproduced copy "for the record."

2 | Selecting Print Media

WHO READS NEWSPAPERS

The simple, and truthful, answer to "Who reads newspapers?" is "Just about everyone!" Though the trend in newspaper readership is downward, the majority of adult Americans, regardless of income, race, or sex, read either a daily or Sunday newspaper and many of them read both. Furthermore, they read their paper not only for news and features, but, according to an *Advertising Age* study, even more intensely for the paper's advertising, including the classified section.

As of September 1996, 1,533 daily newspapers were published in the United States. Of these, 656 were morning papers, 891 were evening papers,[1] and 868 published a Sunday edition. The six-month average circulation of the daily newspapers totaled 58,193,391. Approximately 80 percent of this total, or 46 million-plus, is made up of morning papers; the remaining 20 percent, or 16 million-plus, are afternoon editions. Sunday papers, though published by somewhat fewer than half the papers, totaled 61,229,292[2] or 3 million more than the combined morning and evening daily total.

This Sunday total is not as surprising as it might at first appear. Papers sell more copies on Sunday, and the larger-circulation papers are most likely to produce a Sunday edition. (The only papers in this top-100 group not to publish a Sunday edition are the *Wall Street Journal* and *USA Today*.) The largest 100, as seen in Figure 2.1, make up 50 percent of the circulation of all the dailies published. Weekly papers, which are equally important in many smaller communities, add about 8 million for an overall daily/weekly total of 65 million-plus.

More than 85 percent of these papers, or approximately 55 million, are delivered to homes, offices, and businesses. The rest are single-copy issues bought from newsstands, retail shops, and vending machines.

Newspaper Readership

Although industry statistics on readership are best taken with a grain of salt, long experience in this field indicates that the vast majority of delivered papers—75 percent seems a conservative estimate—go to homes or businesses with at least two adult readers. This gives a probable readership of about 110 million adults

---

[1]Fourteen "all-day" editions are counted twice in the morning and evening totals.

[2]All circulation figures are from *Editor & Publisher International Year Book 1996* (212-675-4380).

TOP ONE HUNDRED DAILY NEWSPAPERS IN THE UNITED STATES
ACCORDING TO CIRCULATION SEPTEMBER 30, 1995

New York (NY) *Wall Street Journal* ....(m)	1,763,140	Oklahoma City (OK) *Daily Oklahoman*..........(m)	212,382
Arlington (VA) *USA Today*........................(m)	1,523,610	Richmond (VA) *Times-Dispatch* ....(m)	211,589
New York (NY) *Times*..............................(m)	1,081,541	Hartford (CT) *Courant*.............................(m)	211,704
Los Angeles (CA) *Times*............................(m)	1,012,189	St. Paul (MN) *Pioneer Press*......................(m)	208,807
Washington (DC) *Post*.............................(m)	793,660	Seattle (WA) *Post-Intelligencer*..................(m)	204,544
New York (NY) *Daily News*........................(m)	738,091	Cincinnati (OH) *Enquirer* ....(m)	203,158
Chicago (IL) *Tribune*...............................(m)	684,366	Los Angeles (CA) *Daily News*......................(m)	201,239
Long Island (NY) *Newsday*.................(all day)	634,627	Philadelphia (PA) *Daily News* ....(m)	195,447
Houston (TX) *Chronicle*...........................(m)	541,478	Rochester (NY) *Democrat and Chronicle*......(m)	194,677
*Detroit (MI) *Free Press*.............................(m)	531,825	Jacksonville (FL) *Times-Union*....................(m)	194,643
Dallas (TX) *Morning News* ....(m)	500,358	Los Angeles (CA) *Investor's Business Daily*..(m)	193,459
Boston (MA) *Globe* ....(m)	498,853	Norfolk (VA) *Virginian-Pilot* ....(m)	188,678
San Francisco (CA) *Chronicle* ....(m)	489,238	Providence (RI) *Journal* ....(m)	185,014
Chicago (IL) *Sun-Times*...........................(m)	488,405	Memphis (TN) *Commercial Appeal*..............(m)	178,415
Philadelphia (PA) *Inquirer*........................(m)	469,398	Des Moines (IA) *Register*...........................(m)	177,857
Newark (NJ) *Star-Ledger* ....(m)	436,634	Austin (TX) *American-Statesman* ....(m)	177,704
New York (NY) *Post* ....(m)	413,705	Little Rock (AR) *Democrat-Gazette* ....(m)	175,218
Cleveland (OH) *Plain Dealer* ....(m)	396,773	West Palm Beach (FL) *Palm Beach Post*......(m)	173,699
Minneapolis (MN) *Star Tribune*................(m)	389,865	Tulsa (OK) *World*....................................(m)	168,529
Miami (FL) *Herald*...................................(m)	383,212	Riverside (CA) *Press-Enterprise* ....(m)	164,028
San Diego (CA) *Union-Tribune* ....(all day)	379,705	Dayton (OH) *Daily News*...........................(m)	163,187
Phoenix (AZ) *Arizona Republic*.................(m)	365,979	Asbury Park (NJ) *Press* ....(e)	161,052
*Detroit (MI) *News*..................................(e)	354,403	Birmingham (AL) *News*..............................(e)	160,081
Orange County (CA) *Register*....................(m)	349,874	Hackensack (NJ) *Record*............................(m)	156,726
St. Petersburg (FL) *Times*........................(m)	349,874	Fresno (CA) *Bee*......................................(m)	152,554
Baltimore (MD) *Sun*.................................(m)	339,493	Akron (OH) *Beacon Journal* ....(m)	152,211
Portland (OR) *Oregonian*...................(all day)	333,654	Toledo (OH) *Blade*..................................(m)	147,526
Denver (CO) *Rocky Mountain News* ....(m)	331,044	Raleigh (NC) *News & Observer* ....(m)	146,688
St. Louis (MO) *Post-Dispatch* ....(m)	319,990	Nashville (TN) *Tennessean* ....(m)	146,466
Milwaukee (WI) *Journal Sentinel*...............(m)	309,137	Grand Rapids (MI) *Press*...........................(e)	145,521
Boston (MA) *Herald* ....(m)	308,077	Las Vegas (NV) *Review-Journal* ....(m)	142,149
Atlanta (GA) *Constitution* ....(m)	305,457	Allentown (PA) *Morning Call*......................(m)	133,140
Denver (CO) *Post*...................................(m)	303,357	Tacoma (WA) *News Tribune* ....(m)	128,659
San Jose (CA) *Mercury News* ....(m)	286,935	Arlington Heights (IL) *Daily Herald* ....(m)	128,172
Kansas City (MO) *Star*.............................(m)	284,675	Salt Lake City (UT) *Tribune*......................(m)	126,076
Sacramento (CA) *Bee*..............................(m)	279,980	Columbia (SC) *State*................................(m)	126,074
Buffalo (NY) *News* ....(all day)	274,614	Wilmington (DE) *News Journal*............(all day)	125,677
Orlando (FL) *Sentinel*........................(all day)	272,702	Atlanta (GA) *Journal* ....(e)	124,484
New Orleans (LA) *Times-Picayune* ......(all day)	267,397	Spokane (WA) *Spokesman-Review* ....(m)	122,961
Fort Lauderdale (FL) *Sun-Sentinel* ....(m)	264,863	Knoxville (TN) *News-Sentinel* ....(m)	116,429
Tampa (FL) *Tribune* ....(m)	263,674	San Francisco Examiner ....(e)	114,957
Columbus (OH) *Dispatch*..........................(m)	255,390	Sarasota (FL) *Herald-Tribune* ....(m)	114,638
Pittsburgh (PA) *Post-Gazette* ....(m)	242,723	Albuquerque (NM) *Journal* ....(m)	113,031
Charlotte (NC) *Observer*...........................(m)	239,173	Lexington (KY) *Herald-Leader*.....................(m)	112,352
Louisville (KY) *Courier-Journal*..................(m)	236,465	Worcester (MA) *Telegram & Gazette*............(m)	111,836
Seattle (WA) *Times*..................................(e)	232,616	Roanoke (VA) *Times & World-News*.............(m)	110,195
Omaha (NE) *World-Herald* ....(all day)	232,360	Jackson (MS) *Clarion-Ledger*......................(m)	110,059
Indianapolis (IN) *Star*..............................(m)	227,535	Charleston (SC) *Post & Courier* ....(m)	109,520
Fort Worth (TX) *Star-Telegram* ....(m)	225,080	Long Beach (CA) *Press-Telegram* ....(m)	109,029
San Antonio (TX) *Express-News* ....(m)	221,556	Honolulu (HI) *Advertiser* ....(m)	105,624

*Due to the strike in Detroit, March 31, 1995, figures are used for the two Detroit newspapers.

TOP TEN DAILY NEWSPAPERS IN CANADA
ACCORDING TO CIRCULATION SEPTEMBER 30, 1995

Toronto (ON) *Star*......................................(m)	491,411	Montreal (QC) *La Presse* ....(m)	179,523
Toronto (ON) *Globe and Mail*....................(m)	306,260	Vancouver (BC) *Province*...........................(m)	153,758
Montreal (QC) *Le Journal* ....(m)	270,607	Montreal (ON) *Gazette*..............................(m)	148,777
Toronto (ON) *Sun*....................................(m)	240,822	Edmonton (AB) *Journal*.............................(m)	147,060
Vancouver (BC) *Sun* ....(m)	185,535	Ottawa (ON) *Citizen*..........................(all day)	145,952

Figure 2.1 The 100 largest-circulation U.S. dailies. Note that 94 of them are morning or all-day papers with only 6 (compared with 12 four years ago) as evening editions. For those of you who might consider advertising abroad, see Figure 2.2 showing circulation for the top 100 in the world. *Editor & Publisher International Year Book 1996* (212-675-4380).

TOP ONE HUNDRED DAILY NEWSPAPERS IN THE WORLD
ACCORDING TO 1995 CIRCULATION

Yomiuri Shimbun (Japan) **14,573,988**	Nikkan Sports (Japan) **964,285**
Asahi Shimbun (Japan) **12,697,898**	Seoul Shinmun (South Korea) 900,000
Mainichi Shimbun (Japan) **5,947,333**	Xin Hua Ribao (China) 900,000
Bild (Germany) **5,567,100**	Nanfang Ribao (China) 880,000
Nihon Keizai Shimbun (Japan) **4,536,561**	Jang (Pakistan) **820,000**
Chunichi Shimbun (Japan) **4,323,142**	Kyoto Shimbun (Japan) **813,464**
Sun (England) **4,023,548**	Chugoku Shimbun (Japan) **810,506**
Sankei Shimbun (Japan) **2,882,252**	Dazhong Ribao (China) 800,000
Renmin Ribao (China) 2,740,000	Kobe Shimbun (Japan) **799,997**
Daily Mirror (England) **2,568,957**	Washington Post (United States) **793,660**
Chosun Ilbo (South Korea) 2,225,000	Al Akhbar (Egypt) **789,268**
Dong-A Ilbo (South Korea) 2,150,000	Ouest-France (France) 784,463
Al Ahram (Egypt) 2,117,399	Holos Ukrainy (Ukraine) 768,000
Hokkaido Shimbun (Japan) **1,964,774**	De Telegraaf (Netherlands) 751,400
Yangcheng Evening News (China) 1,900,000	Dziennik Zachodni (Poland) 750,000
Eleftherotypia (Greece) 1,858,316	Daily Record (Scotland) **746,861**
Daily Mail (England) **1,815,507**	Daily Star (England) **739,210**
Wall Street Journal (United States) **1,763,140**	New York Daily News (United States) **738,091**
Kerala Kaumudi (India) 1,720,000	Zero Hora (Brazil) 727,188
Joong-Ang Daily News (South Korea) 1,550,000	Diario dos Campos (Brazil) 725,000
USA Today (United States) **1,523,610**	Sabah (Turkey) 722,950
Economic Daily (China) 1,500,000	Jornal da Tarde (Brazil) 709,793
Guangming Ribao (China) 1,500,000	Hubei Ribao (China) 700,000
Kyung-Hyang Daily News (South Korea) 1,478,000	Pusan Ilbo (South Korea) 700,000
Sports Nippon (Japan) **1,445,821**	Thai Rath (Thailand) 700,000
Shizuoka Shimbun (Japan) **1,421,085**	Zhefiang Ribao (China) 700,000
Sichuan Ribao (China) 1,350,000	Il Corriere della Sera (Italy) **691,269**
NRZ (Germany) **1,332,800**	Chicago Tribune (United States) **684,366**
West Deutche Allgemeine (Germany) **1,313,400**	Diaro Insular (Portugal) 684,143
United Daily News (Taiwan) 1,300,000	Granma (Cuba) 675,000
Wen Hui Bao Daily (China) 1,300,000	China Daily News (Taiwan) 670,000
China Times (Taiwan) 1,270,000	Clarin Daily (Argentina) 670,000
Daily Express (England) **1,265,027**	The Times (England) **667,238**
O Estado de Sao Paulo (Brazil) 1,230,160	Al Goumhouryia (Egypt) 650,000
Jang Daily (Pakistan) 1,200,000	Guanxi Ribao (China) 650,000
Jang Lahore (Pakistan) 1,200,000	Kahoku Shimpo (Japan) **636,445**
Akhbar El Yom/Al Akhbar (Egypt) 1,159,339	Long Island Newsday (United States) **634,627**
Hankook Ilbo (South Korea) 1,156,000	El Espectador (Colombia) 632,030
Tokyo Shimbun (Japan) **1,137,727**	La Nacion (Argentina) 630,000
Hochi Shimbun (Japan) **1,081,883**	Hurriyet (Turkey).....................................615,579
New York Times (United States) **1,081,541**	Central Daily News (Taiwan).....................600,000
Times of India (India) **1,071,081**	Fujian Ribao (China)...............................600,000
Malayala Manorama (India) 1,070,465	Guangzhou Ribao (China) 600,000
Daily Telegraph (England) **1,064,717**	Hurriyet (Pakistan)..................................600,000
Tokyo Sports (Japan) **1,045,350**	Liaoning Ribao (China)............................600,000
Nishi Nippon Shimbun (Japan) **1,022,948**	Oriental Daily News (Hong Kong)............600,000
Los Angeles Times (United States) **1,012,189**	Thuringer Allgemeine (Germany) 594,500
Neue Kronenzeitung (Austria) 1,000,480	Indian Express (India)............................576,200
Jiefang Ribao (China) 1,000,000	Nawa-e-Waqt (Pakistan) **573,921**
Tianjin Ribao (China) 1,000,000	Herald Sun (Australia)............................**568,945**

Note: Bold circulation figure indicates audit available for 1995. Russian newspapers excluded.

Copyright ©1996 by the Editor & Publisher Co.

Figure 2.2   Circulation of the top 100 daily newspapers in the world. *Editor & Publisher International Year Book 1996.*

who have paid not only for news but also to let advertisers try to sell them their products or services!

INSIGHT 8

Advertising tends to take up 40 percent of newspaper space, yet has been and continues to be welcome in practically every home. Have you ever heard of *anyone* asking to be protected against receiving "junk advertising" in their newspapers—even if it's the same "junk" catalogs and other "FSI" (Free Standing Inserts) that newspapers write editorials against if it's delivered by mail?

Who Advertises in Newspapers . . . and Why

Newspaper advertising is, overwhelmingly, used by local businesses targeted at local sales, though a surprisingly large number of these businesses have no formalized media plan. While an account executive for an agency specializing in auto dealerships, Mangun helped develop such a plan for one dealer. The new strategy placed full-page advertising in the general news section, rather than in the classified display portion of the local paper where all the other dealers appeared. Since it was the only daily/Sunday paper in this market, it was read by practically everyone interested in buying or leasing an auto . . . and many others who had not realized they were "in the market." Thanks to this media plan, the dealership became and remained number one in its market. It also got more advertising space for its dollars because, as in many other markets, classified display advertising was more expensive than the same size retail ad.[3]

Advertising in all U.S. newspapers totaled over $36 billion ($36,186,000,000) in 1995, a $5 billion increase over 1993! Of this amount, according to *Editor & Publisher*, the three major categories, in thousands of dollars, were:

Retail	General	Classified
$16,652,000	$4,122,000	$11,506,000

Records for general advertising have not been subdivided further since 1984. But using percentages based on the ten-year averages kept from 1974 to 1983, the totals would be:

Retail	Dept. Store	General	Auto	Finance	Classified
51%	6.5%	6.9%	.025%	.035%	35%

This includes national advertisers such as automotive, soft drinks, alcoholic beverages, clothing, and cosmetics. Those firms are willing to pay a higher "national" rate for three reasons:

---

[3]Newspaper advertising is charged by the "column inch." Classified columns almost always are narrower than the rest of the paper; therefore, more columns and more dollars per page.

1. To increase sales of their products in local outlets.
2. To show local retailers that they are supported by national headquarters. (A Hahn-directed campaign aimed at retailers selling the Rand McNally Road Atlas used posters on the outside, sidewalk side of buses where retailers were most likely to see them even while inside their stores.)
3. To make certain that the national advertising message is given exactly as the corporation wants it presented.

WHO READS MAGAZINES

If we consider only those magazines that carry advertising, according to Media Research, Inc., more than 90 percent of all American adults read at least one magazine per month, with the average adult reading two magazines per week and spending about one hour with each.

Magazine Categories

SRDS,[4] a huge database to be discussed shortly, divides magazines into four broad categories:

1. Consumer
2. Agrimedia
3. Business to Business
4. Professional

Scholarly publications, a category that would add thousands of additional titles to the list, are so specialized, and often of such small circulation, that only those specializing in advertising to those fields concern themselves with their rates.

Unlike "scholarly" magazines, "educational" media are the Business category aimed at the preschool through high school market. As an advertising sales representative for *Scholastic* magazines, Mangun became an expert in this field. He received calls from advertisers and advertising agencies wanting to learn about the market. Find out how much of an expert your representative is in *your* field. They often are excellent consultants . . . and free, too!

HOW TO PICK PRINT MEDIA FOR ADVERTISING

The easiest way to pick media is by how well they reach your target audience(s) (TA)—the audience you want to reach. To do this, check on where other advertisers trying to reach the same targeted audience are advertising in a consistent fashion. But don't just look. Do as you did when new to setting objectives. Telephone advertisers. Explain that you are a novice and ask for anything they might tell you

---

[4]Formerly known as The Standard Rate and Data Service.

about the success of their ads in specific publications. Next, call advertisers who use a medium only once or a few times and ask the same questions. Ask, too, which media they would recommend that might be more effective. People love to give advice, so be sure to check whether or not they actually do advertise in the places they recommend.

WARNING! WARNING! WARNING!
BEWARE OF "THE RULE OF TWO"

An often quoted "Rule of Two" states: "See an ad once, it's a test; see it twice, it's a success." Do *not* take this at face value in trying to evaluate where, what, how often, and, most important, why others advertise! Rather, see the "Rule of Three," which follows shortly.

Before using the Rule of Two—or any other rule like it—to evaluate a competitor's advertising schedule, consider the following three points:

1. **Response request.** Is there any response requested in the ad? If the reader is not urged, or at least asked, to do something, as in Figure 2.3, how can your competitor know the ad's results?
   - "⅓-OFF" qualifies as a hint.
   - "BRING THIS COUPON TO GET ⅓-OFF TILL WEDNESDAY!" qualifies as a test.
2. **How to quantify.** Is there an obvious, or subtle, way to quantify; that is, to know responses to the ad? For instance, is there a coupon or reply card that is coded to each medium and issue, or a telephone extension or name for which to ask? (See Figure 2.3.)
3. **Time to quantify.** Before assuming that good results are why the same ad was repeated, check to see whether there was enough time between issues to permit evaluation of results before the next ad was run. In a daily newspaper, that can be as little as three days. In weekly publications, rescheduling an ad even a single day after it appears can mean one to five weeks before it will run again. In most monthly magazines, the wait will be two to four months.

INSIGHT 9

Seeing the same ad over and over doesn't *prove* anything about its results. The Rule of Two is based on the action of direct marketers for whom "advertising" and "sales" are one and the same. Do *not* expect it to be the reason for most other advertisers' scheduling!

Conroy Ericksen
and
Royal Austrian Porcelain

*request the pleasure of your company
at an exclusive bridal event to help
make your wedding planning a pleasure.*

"To Love and to Treasure"
*featuring Christina von Herder
the Royal Austrian Etiquette Consultant,
presenting
"The Art of Elegant Table Setting"*

*Special drawings for fine gifts
in crystal, bone china, and silver.*

Join us for cocktails and hors d' oeuvres.

---

*Friday, May 11th
6:00 P.M.–8:00 P.M.*

CONROY ERICKSEN, LTD.

Conroy Ericksen

*811 West Lexington Avenue
(at the Oxford Hotel)*

Reservations (212) 123-9000

COUPON

$3.00 OFF per sq. yd. with this coupon

Coupon must be presented at time of purchase. With this special sale, save an additional $3.00 per sq. yd. with this coupon. This TREMENDOUS VALUE provides quality carpeting at better than wholesale prices. And at these prices, coupon cannot be used with any other special discounts. Expires one week from date of publication.

L

Figure 2.3   Depending on the target market, just the word "Reservations" will quantify. For most of us, $3 OFF WITH THIS COUPON will be much better.

APPLICATION

"The Rule of Three"

The advertising "Rule of Three" states: "An ad must appear at least three times *in media read by the same audience* before you can expect it to be seen (paid attention to) once." This does not mean before *anyone* will see it once, but before it will be noticed at least once by *the majority* of your target market audience. *In print media, national advertisers consider a range of three to ten exposures as the minimum required for effectiveness.*

The Rule of Three (or "Three Hit Theory") has primary value for longer-term "institutional" advertising targeted at brand recognition rather than the immediate response wanted by many retailers. Note that successful retailers and retail chains—from groceries to computers to autos—often do both kinds of ads.

IF YOU DON'T KNOW WHERE TO ADVERTISE

For anyone, beginner or longtime media professional, *the* guides to the full range of options on advertising to a specific audience or in a particular field are the SRDS directories. They are in many public libraries and practically all professional advertising media departments.

These huge paperbound volumes, frequently updated, give detailed information, field by field, on practically every medium that accepts advertising. Individual SRDS guide titles,[5] as this is written, include the following:

- *Newspaper Advertising Source*
- *Consumer Magazine Advertising Source*
- *Business Publication Advertising Source*
  Includes Card Decks,[6] International Media, much more
- *TV & Cable Source*
- *Radio Advertising Source*
- *Direct Marketing List Source*
- *Community Publication Advertising Source*
- *Interactive Advertising Source*
  The overnight bestseller in the series
- *Out-of-Home Advertising Source*

---

[5]All SRDS guide titles are trademarked. SRDS guides can be purchased from SRDS, 1700 Higgins, Des Plaines, IL 60018. Call them at (847) 375-5000. Look for SRDS on the World Wide Web at http://www.SRDS.com.

[6]Card Decks are packages of postcard-size advertisements mailed on a share-the-cost cooperative basis to a specifically targeted audience. Their primary use has been in business-to-business promotions, but they are beginning to appear as a consumer medium.

- Eighteen away-from-home or office media such as billboards, transit, in-flight, and so on
- *Technology Media Source*
- *Hispanic Media & Market Source*

An additional volume of the SRDS guides covers the mechanical aspects of production, that is, how to get each kind of ad physically ready for a specific medium. But you are unlikely to need that unless you are responsible for furnishing the materials for the ads to many advertising media. The same information is available on an individual basis from any of the media you decide to use.

Understanding SRDS Print Media Listings

Listings in the SRDS guides follow a consistent format of subject, state, and city, ordered alphabetically within each category. Individual listings (Figure 2.4) begin with brief descriptions of the audience and editorial content of the publication. Then they go through a series of uniformly numbered segments of specific interest to advertisers. Thus, categories 4–7 always explain basic costs, and category 10 covers the availability of premium positions for advertising, such as the page opposite the table of contents. Many advertisers believe that these locations get exceptionally high readership and are willing to pay a premium to have one of their ads appear there.

If premium positions are not listed—or present on a rate card—they may be available by request on a "first-come" basis. (One of Hahn's greatest advertising coups was to get ads for a single client on all covers of all programs of their industry's most important trade show by asking, and paying for the space, 18 months in advance of publication. No one had ever asked before—and a special meeting of furious, and much larger, competitors foreclosed the same option for anyone, including themselves, in the future.)

Reliability of SRDS Data

SRDS does not itself research its information but, rather, uses data provided by each publication on an issue-by-issue basis. Many of the publishers supply information on circulation in a standard format that is audited by The Advertising Bureau of Circulation (ABC), an agency very much like a CPA firm.

Whether or not the information is audited is not necessarily an indication of its reliability. The auditing process is quite expensive and unaffordable by some new publications and publications with a small circulation. Other publications have a long history of satisfied advertisers and feel no need to go through auditing. Auditing is, however, a factor you should consider, especially with publications that have multiple audiences, not all of which are your potential customers.

Category 18 gives the basic statistical information about a publication and tells whether or not the information is based on audited data. Thus, for example, in an August 1996 listing, the audited magazine *Art Business News* (see Figure

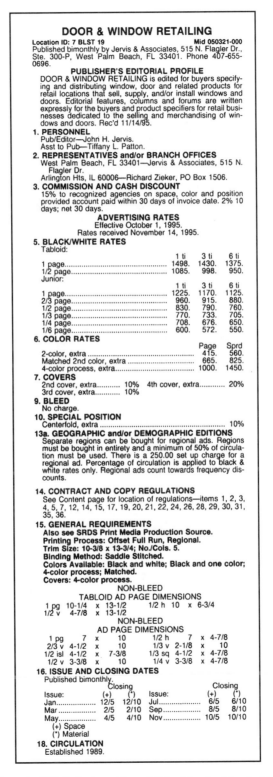

Figure 2.4 Sample SDRD listing. (As published in the March, 1996 edition of *Business Publication Advertising Source,* published by SRDS.)

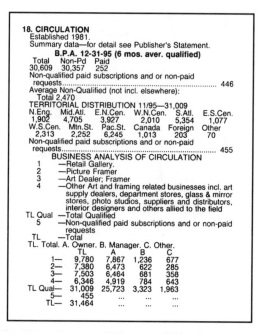

Figure 2.5   Circulation analysis supplied by *Art Business News*. From SRDS, August 1996.

2.5), edited for art dealers and framers, tells us its territorial distribution and that of its 30,000-plus circulation, about one-third are retail galleries while the majority of the others are picture framers. If SRDS does not have this type of circulation analysis, request a media kit from the publication itself. Magazines and trade papers that sound just right from their title may have substantial parts of their circulation that are not your market. For instance, without the circulation analysis, how would you know that *Art Business News* is probably the wrong medium to promote art supplies? Don't trust to luck. *Know* before you buy!

If your interest does lie in reaching galleries or framers or both, find out whether any other publications reach that audience, including those with unaudited circulation.

Before you decide on any of them, however, ask each publication *why* you should use it to reach your specific audience, and then make your evaluation as you would any other investment—including the possibility that you should switch your promotional effort to direct mail or some other medium. Don't fall into the trap of advertising just to see your name in print.

HOW TO RESEARCH A SUBJECT

Though even the SRDS guides can't cover every subject, try them first. Check the classification groupings near the front. If your subject is not there, turn to the index of individual titles and look for a key word. If you still can't find what you need, telephone the SRDS "data acquisition helping hand hot line" at 847-375-5188, and ask them where to look. Ask a few of your larger competitors, too. They want to keep their trade media in existence by finding additional advertisers. It is possible that no specific medium exists for your product or service. In that case, consider a more general publication that's likely to be read by your audience (the Sunday edition of the *New York Times* by college presidents, for instance, or the *Wall Street Journal* by wealthy retirees), providing your reaching them that way has at least the potential of being profitable.

If, as is likely, you do find your category, contact the appropriate media and ask for a Media Kit information package. Request several copies of each publication to get an idea of its editorial content as a "home" for your message. Each medium will probably also wish to meet with you. You can arrange that at your convenience.

WHAT TO DO WITH THE INFORMATION AFTER YOU HAVE IT

The CCREAM™ Analysis for Print Media

The six-area CCREAM chart shown on page 51, with the explanation of each of its points that follows, is an excellent way to gain an objective media analysis. (A filled-in example begins on page 59.) You can get available factual data for chart sections 1, 2, 3, and 6 from your newspaper or magazine media departments and their representatives. Contact the media in which you are interested and ask each for a "Media Kit" information package for use with the CCREAM chart. Be sure to ask for several copies of each publication to get an idea of the contents as a "home" for your message. For sections 4 and 5, you will need to use your own judgment as you check the publications themselves. *An analogous chart can be developed for any medium—radio, television, outdoor, and so on.*

How to Use the CCREAM Chart

Among its most important functions, the CCREAM chart acts as a checklist for what *can* be learned about each medium. Once you know that, you can weight the relative importance of each of these factors, including the importance of personal judgments, in making your media selection. Note the critical importance of deciding a percentage value for each element of the chart. This has three benefits:

1. It ensures a level playing field for *factual* data among competing media. Each medium gets "graded" by the same standard.
2. It permits fast comparisons according to alternative criteria, especially if you put the analysis on a computer database. For instance, changing CPM (cost per thousand) from 50 percent to 30 percent and Target Audience from 40 percent to 60 percent (or vice versa) may give quite different media selections. But don't do this simply to make favorite media your winners. Have a *business* reason for your values.

3. It permits, with minor CCREAM chart adjustments, on-the-spot comparisons among different types of media such as print, radio, TV, and direct response.

When a single factor or a few, such as circulation and cost, control the decision, media selection is easy. But when you need a full analysis of each medium before a selection is made, the CCREAM system makes this practical. How to actually use the chart, with an example of one already filled out, is explained shortly. But, first, you'll want to know what those six major areas and all their subareas are for.

Explanation of the CCREAM Chart Areas

1. CIRCULATION

A. Total circulation. Is this figure verified by the Advertising Bureau of Circulation (ABC), the industry's equivalent of an IRS or CPA review? Note that many start-up and smaller circulation publications cannot afford the ABC cost.

B. Duplications. How much of the circulation of the various publications "overlap"; that is, duplicate each other? This is a plus rather than a minus! As shown in Figure 2.6, the degree of overlap of any publications is exactly the same, whether it is two, three, or more media.

When advertising in two or more publications whose circulations overlap within a targeted audience, the overlapping portions are the

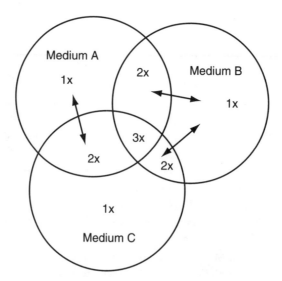

Figure 2.6   Assuming every reader sees every ad, the 1× nonoverlapping reader will see your ad once. However, depending on how many media you use, the 2× overlapping reader will see it twice, the 3×, three times, and so on.

PRINT MEDIA CCREAM™ ANALYSIS CHART

Primary T.A. (Target Audience)

Secondary T.A. (Target Audience)

Medium #1   Medium #2   Medium #3

		Medium 1 Score/Weighted	Medium 2 Score/Weighted	Medium 3 Score/Weighted
1.	**CIRCULATION**	%		
	A. Total Circulation			
	B. Duplicate Circulation			
	C. Paid, Home Delivery, & Mail			
	D. Controlled Circulation			
	E. T.A. Penetration			
	F. T.A. Quality			
2.	**COST OF CIRCULATION**	%		
	A. Total Ad Cost			
	B. Circulation CPM			
	C. T.A. CPM/TA			
3.	**READERSHIP**	%		
	A. Primary Readership			
	B. Secondary Readership			
	C. Pass Along Readership			
4.	**EDITORIAL**	%		
	Quality Analysis			
	A. Writing Quality			
	B. Contemporary?			
	C. Compatibility for Our Ads			
	Reader Involvement			
	D. Letters to Editor			
	E. Other Reader Involvement			
	F. Reader Involvement Studies			
5.	**ADVERTISING**	%		
	A. Number of Competitors Advertising			
	B. Total Competitors' Ad Pages			
	C, Dominating Competitor & Pages			
	D. Advertisements' Quality			
	Editorial/Advertising			
	Content Summary			
	E. Total Number of Pages			
	F. Total Editorial Pages			
	G. Total Advertising Pages			
	H. Editorial/Advertising Ratio			
6.	**MERCHANDISING HELP**	%		
	A. Willingness			
	B. Opportunities			
	C. Comparison to Competing Media			
			Total ____	Total ____	Total ____

most valuable asset. In media terms, overlap gives you additional frequency at no additional cost.

MANAGEMENT PERSPECTIVE

Many advertisers consider overlapping circulation a bonus of increased frequency, providing the publications are wanted by their recipients. Someone interested enough to read two or more publications in your field is probably the best candidate to read your ad. Overlapping circulations give you a multiple chance at that most desirable of prospects.

C. **Paid, Home Delivery, & Mail**

- For newspapers and magazines, how many of each are paid for at a newsstand?

- For newspapers, how many are delivered to a home or office?

- For magazines, how many are received by mail and do they go to a home or office?

    If there are major differences among competing publications, ask each one what makes its circulation better or best.

D. **Controlled circulation.** Is part or all of the circulation "controlled," that is, sent to a targeted audience without being paid for voluntarily by subscriptions? Do *not* decide whether this is a plus or a minus until you have considered point "E."

E. **TA penetration.** Controlled circulation often is the best and sometimes the only practical way to reach *all* of a targeted business or professional group through advertising. For instance, depending on whom you wish to reach, the controlled circulation may be the broadest possible market, such as all licensed pilots, or limited to a specific target audience, such as pilots licensed for multiengine jets, or somewhere in between. If you include publications that are part of membership dues and fees, controlled circulation can always give greater coverage of a targeted group than voluntarily paid subscriptions. And many such publications are of equal or greater interest to the recipients than those for which they pay.

APPLICATION

For controlled circulation publications, ask some of their advertisers—and not just the largest—whether they use them because of the advertising results or for the friendship one may gain with editorial. Usually such subjects are best discussed during a friendly lunch.

F. **Target Audience(s) quality.** Find out not only *where* the publication is send, but *to whom.*

- What are the sources of the controlled lists?
- How was the circulation of each publication determined: to a single individual per organization or several?
- How were they selected?
- How often is the mailing list updated?
- If more than a single controlled list publication originates from the same source, such as association membership, does any one claim to have better coverage and what does it mean by "better"?

Test unfamiliar media, if you can. If you can't, follow the lead of the other advertisers (covered in area 5) aimed at *your* target audience.

2. **COST OF CIRCULATION**

Three factors are involved in evaluating cost of circulation. They are:

- Space cost of the ad.
- Cost per thousand (CPM) of subscribers and/or purchasers.
- Cost per thousand of a targeted audience (CPM/TA), if that's different from CPM. Whether it is or not, the space cost remains the same.

A. **Total ad cost.** What each publication charges. If you cannot afford it, no matter how attractive the medium, consider your alternatives:

- Appear in fewer publications or less often.
- Make the ad smaller.
- Use fewer colors.
- Rather than the "full" circulation, run in regional or local editions where available. If even that is too costly, check the possibility of using a preprinted insert for specific zip codes or other regions. Many newspapers and magazines now offer this.

B. **CPM cost.** To simplify cost comparisons, translate media charges into "CPM"; that is, the cost per thousand of all the copies mailed, sold at newsstands, and otherwise distributed.

In most instances, the same type of publications, in the same field and aimed at *the same audience,* have essentially the same "space" rate; that is, the cost of running the same-size ad. Rates for printing in color or for preferred positions may be slightly different. But competition for advertising, very much like competition for airline passengers to the same destination, keep basic rates the same.

C. **CPM/TA cost.** Cost per thousand (CPM) becomes much more of a factor when the targeted audience (TA) ranges from a comparatively small part to more than half of the circulation. If, as is quite possi-

Magazine	Circulation		Cost	
	Total	*Targeted*	*Page*	*CPM/TA*
A	330,000	61,000	$3,300	$57.70
B	186,500	44,000	1,865	42.37
D	122,000	46,000	1,372	33.15
E	78,000	52,500	1,201	22.88

Figure 2.7   Typical CPM/TA chart.

ble, one magazine has a 26 percent share of your prospects and customers while a second, of much smaller circulation, has 66 percent, the CPM/TA (cost per thousand of target audience) can become critical, as shown in Figure 2.7. Know what you buy. And why.

Note that the Figure 2.7 *complete* circulation page costs hold true to reach the smaller CPM/TA targeted audiences. Thus, the targeted circulation of medium A, though 8,500 greater than that of medium E, costs almost exactly the same as running an ad in *both* magazines D and E, or running in one of those magazines twice. Remembering the Rule of Three and the advantages of circulation overlap (page 50), running in both D and E is almost always the smarter buy.

INSIGHT 10

Media establish certain rates as a fair charge to advertisers. These prices are based on a three-way analysis:
- An established industrywide understanding of what advertising "is worth" in specific media
- Whatever the traffic will bear
- A combination of both

Rates are based on response expected by advertisers targeting the *total* circulation. A page of advertising costs exactly the same whether you target all or just 20 percent of the readership. More important, response by the fraction is unlikely to go up because you paid for the whole. What does go up is the CPM/TA!

3. **READERSHIP**
    A. **Primary Readership.** The persons who get the publication for themselves are the primary readership. *You* must decide how well they match your target audience.
    B. **Secondary Readership.** This group is made up of one or more of the secondary audiences who read the publication in addition to the

primary group. For instance, a newspaper or magazine targeted primarily at 20- to 35-year-olds may also be read by persons aged 36 to 45. Such secondary audiences also exist for radio, television, and all other media.

C. **Pass-along Readership.** This group includes those who read the same publication, but without buying it. Newspapers and magazines in doctors' waiting rooms are examples of such secondary pass-along readership.

To analyze publication "readership," the number of readers claimed by a publication in addition to its circulation, prepare a chart like the one in Figure 2.8. Evaluate the sources and documentation for all such claims. If they seem reasonable, add to your media analysis a CPM and/or CPM/TA cost report for each of the categories *important to you.*

Some publications, as in Figure 2.9, have research showing the number of readers per copy and the amount of time their audiences spend reading their contents. Advertisers believe that a longer reading time leads to a more favorable response to advertising in that publication. This is undoubtedly true for many of them. Do not, however, take "reading" too literally. Many "readers" spend little time on "editorial," that is, everything *except* advertising, but are interested primarily in what is advertised. Think, for example, of women's—and men's—fashion magazines or many business and technical publications. From cover to cover, as far as *their* readers are concerned, *everything* is "editorial." Most readers are somewhere in between. Exactly where that is for larger circulation magazines can be learned from MRI (Magazine Research Institute) reports such as the one shown in Figure 2.10.

4. **EDITORIAL**

A–C. **Quality Analysis.** Even if you think you are familiar with their basic content, do the "Editorial Quality Analysis" shown in the CCREAM chart. Try very hard to be objective. You're working with *your* money!

D–F. **Reader Involvement.** Read the Letters to the Editor to determine reader involvement with what is printed. *As an advertiser,* make sure you are comfortable with having your product or service offered in the *total* publication surroundings. Is *any* of the editorial targeted at your audience? Unless editorial content reflects the "feel" of what you hope to sell, consider carefully whether you'd do better elsewhere.

Many of the better media representatives, in *their* attempts to sell potential advertisers, link their sales efforts to their publications' editorial content, not its ads. So examine

SPRING 1996 SMM	TOTAL AUDIENCE (000)			MEDIAN AGE			MEDIAN HOUSEHOLD INCOME			MEDIAN INDIVIDUAL EMPLOYMENT INCOME			AVG. CIRC* (000)	READERS PER COPY		
	ADULTS	MEN	WOMEN	ADULTS	MEN	WOMEN	ADULTS	MEN	WOMEN	ADULTS	MEN	WOMEN		ADULTS	MEN	WOMEN
POPULAR SCIENCE	7,839	6,264	1,575	40.7	40.4	41.3	44,692	43,582	48,432	29,188	31,922	16,470	1,725	4.54	3.63	0.91
PREMIERE	1,970	1,069	901	30.4	27.1	34.0	53,592	57,421	48,549	21,739	20,794	22,117	580	3.40	1.84	1.55
PREVENTION	12,528	2,998	9,531	49.0	50.1	48.6	40,508	41,623	40,251	22,321	34,295	19,546	3,427	3.66	0.87	2.78
READER'S DIGEST	56,740	24,021	32,719	47.0	47.9	46.3	37,322	39,567	35,633	22,116	29,931	17,520	15,599	3.64	1.54	2.10
REDBOOK	14,341	1,409	12,932	41.4	44.9	41.0	39,211	41,502	38,831	19,086	24,030	18,547	3,223	4.45	0.44	4.01
ROAD & TRACK	5,046	4,428	618	32.6	32.5	35.5	48,379	47,440	55,430	27,108	27,727	19,630	699	7.22	6.33	0.88
ROLLING STONE	8,372	5,273	3,099	28.5	28.7	28.1	46,190	48,207	41,361	19,723	22,381	13,948	1,167	7.17	4.52	2.66
RUNNER'S WORLD	1,870	1,006	864	34.7	34.5	35.0	56,180	52,169	58,784	28,991	34,055	24,344	414	4.52	2.43	2.09
THE SATURDAY EVENING POST	4,038	1,677	2,361	49.9	46.6	51.9	40,687	44,076	37,686	22,379	27,553	19,328	458	8.82	3.66	5.16
SCIENTIFIC AMERICAN	3,609	2,433	1,176	40.3	40.4	40.0	56,501	58,085	49,462	32,001	36,729	20,281	493	7.32	4.93	2.39
SELF	4,994	458	4,536	32.8	34.7	32.4	53,192	63,552	52,213	22,086	34,454	20,772	1,182	4.22	0.39	3.84
SESAME STREET	6,387	1,557	4,830	33.6	35.2	32.8	37,676	42,898	35,768	20,377	32,165	16,841	1,136	5.62	1.37	4.25
SEVENTEEN	8,090	1,131	6,959	28.3	28.7	28.2	38,541	31,078	39,791	13,998	11,587	14,319	2,049	3.95	0.55	3.40
SHAPE	4,159	485	3,674	30.6	34.9	30.2	49,785	57,513	49,377	19,697	35,669	17,526	800	5.20	0.61	4.59
SKI	1,921	1,361	560	32.1	30.5	35.6	60,154	61,395	57,957	27,312	29,347	24,936	433	4.44	3.14	1.29
SKIING	1,686	1,173	513	29.0	29.6	28.2	57,379	57,573	56,845	23,606	26,910	17,421	449	3.76	2.61	1.14
SKY (DELTA AIRLINES)	2,098	1,148	949	42.9	42.8	43.0	61,175	62,746	59,218	32,169	40,616	20,251	477	4.40	2.41	1.99
SMARTMONEY	2,152	1,318	835	40.0	39.3	42.7	57,359	63,279	43,458	33,521	39,824	21,891	593	3.63	2.22	1.41
SMITHSONIAN	9,293	4,119	5,174	46.4	45.4	47.3	48,798	48,542	49,089	25,767	33,327	21,642	2,179	4.26	1.89	2.37
SOAP OPERA DIGEST	8,907	890	8,017	34.9	37.0	34.8	29,859	30,137	29,800	14,870	19,053	14,259	1,288	6.92	0.69	6.22
SOAP OPERA WEEKLY	6,843	633	6,210	34.5	30.7	34.9	28,346	31,254	27,852	13,479	16,967	13,301	442	15.48	1.43	14.05
SOUTHERN LIVING	14,499	3,972	10,527	45.9	45.2	46.3	43,937	48,918	41,312	23,491	37,392	19,613	2,537	5.72	1.57	4.15
SPIN	3,169	1,978	1,190	26.3	25.5	27.9	43,513	47,382	33,215	18,197	19,333	16,208	428	7.40	4.62	2.78
SPIRIT (SOUTHWEST AIRLINES)	1,780	1,045	735	42.1	42.0	42.2	43,681	48,144	35,101	23,232	31,895	15,739	237	7.51	4.41	3.10
SPORT	5,193	4,294	899	34.5	34.2	35.9	39,750	41,514	28,830	23,555	24,729	13,753	724	7.17	5.93	1.24
THE SPORTING NEWS	4,096	3,606	490	33.2	32.0	40.6	44,051	43,890	45,790	24,904	24,931	24,649	578	7.09	6.24	0.85
SPORTS AFIELD	3,303	3,078	225	44.5	44.2	48.1	39,856	40,249	31,949	28,451	28,920	19,189	515	6.41	5.98	0.44
SPORTS ILLUSTRATED	25,377	19,922	5,455	34.7	34.4	35.9	43,205	43,177	43,350	24,256	26,202	19,905	3,234	7.85	6.16	1.69
STAR	10,500	2,723	7,777	38.7	37.2	39.1	28,862	35,503	27,273	15,403	17,942	14,206	2,206	4.76	1.23	3.53
STEREO REVIEW	2,786	2,317	469	31.0	31.3	29.9	45,114	47,475	30,667	20,562	23,562	13,760	447	6.23	5.18	1.05

Figure 2.8   Readership reports are prepared by superb research organizations such as MRI (Mediamark Research Bureau, Inc.) (212-599-0444), Simmons Market Research Bureau, Inc. (212-916-8900), and many others.

1994 SUBSCRIBER STUDY HIGHLIGHTS

READER INVOLVEMENT

Read 4 of last 4 issues	92%
Average time spent with typical issue	I hr., 5I min.
Average number of years reading GOLF WORLD	5.6 yrs.
Average number of readers per copy	3.6

Figure 2.9   "Time spent reading" is one of the three "Reader Involvement" areas in the Subscriber Study section of the *Golf World* 1994 rate card.

the "editorial" portion *from the point of view of the recipients* before you decide where you will put your advertising dollars.

5. **ADVERTISING**

   How readers see you and your competitors

   A–D.   Check carefully on *who* is advertising *what* and *how* in the publications you plan to use. Address the following questions:

   - Does a single advertiser dominate the publication?

   - Is everyone else using full-page ads and might you gain impact by using multiple pages or a preprinted insert, or a series of smaller ads in the same issue?

   - Is everyone else advertising in color and might you gain impact by using black-and-white? Or vice versa?

   Don't be afraid to be different. That is how you get attention and rather often, how you also make sales.

   Editorial/advertising summary

   E.   **Total pages.** Separate the media you consider for advertising into analogous publications *aimed at the same target markets.* For each newspaper or magazine, take the same two or three consecutive issues, plus the "most important of the year," if there is one, and total the number of pages.

   F–H.   **Total editorial/advertising pages.** Use the same issues as 5-E. In comparing media aimed at the same audience, do content analysis; that is, for each one compare the following:

   - The *total* number of pages

   - The *total* pages of editorial and advertising

   - The percentage of advertising in relation to editorial matter

Interest in Advertising

Base: Men

Magazine	Total (000)	Considerable Interest	Some Interest	Not Much Interest	Mean
Business Week	4,341	16.2	41.3	42.2	37
Car & Driver	5,805	39.9	39.0	20.8	60
Esquire	2,282	24.8	40.0	35.1	45
Field & Stream	11,037	28.0	41.5	30.1	49
Fortune	2,831	20.9	42.1	36.9	42
Money	5,761	25.7	39.6	34.0	46
Motor Trend	4,396	34.6	39.5	25.6	54
Newsweek	12,369	16.2	36.0	47.5	34
Outdoor Life	5,760	25.4	44.5	29.9	48
People	12,132	11.8	31.6	56.3	28
Playboy	9,910	29.8	34.2	35.8	47
Reader's Digest	21,087	18.4	31.6	49.5	34
Road & Track	4,466	29.4	41.1	28.6	50
Sports Illustrated	18,397	34.1	35.9	29.8	52
Time	12,993	15.6	37.0	46.9	34
TV Guide	19,144	18.6	31.2	50.1	34

Source: MRI - Spring 1993   EB20

Figure 2.10 Comparative readers' "Interest in Advertising" by men from MRI research data. Other *Ebony* reports show such interest by women and by adults as a whole. MRI (212-599-0444) and Simmons (212-916-8900) are the leading current suppliers of factual readership data for larger circulation media. Data shown are from 1993 and *may not* reflect current research!

Points F–H do not call for an immediate percentage evaluation. Rather, put the page-count totals in each column. Then, knowing the facts in area 5 will give you an insight into how your own and related industries "feel" about each publication *as a medium for advertising.* In advertising, as with editorial content, know the company you'll keep before you join the party.

6. **MERCHANDISING HELP**
   What's offered and its value to you

   A–C.   An increasing number of publications, and not only the largest in circulation, have merchandising programs designed to help their advertisers. These range from mounting ads on handsome "As Advertised In" posters to free premiums. Probably more important, many business and professional media give "most favored" status to press releases from advertisers. Others will send letters to dealer networks or other key customers tying in with ad programs, perhaps even make a "deal" for access to their mailing list. Media representatives make a point of stressing this type of service. But just in case they don't, ask.

INSIGHT 11

The worst of media sins

Thou shalt **not** select media because they appeal to you . . . unless you also are the target audience. Talking to yourself seldom spurs sales!

EXAMPLE OF A FILLED-OUT CCREAM ANALYSIS CHART

Similar Media for Similar Audiences

Before you do anything with the chart itself, separate all the media you will consider by subject matter and audience. For instance, you could find dozens of publications aimed at outdoor activity with audiences ranging from young families to affluent Yuppies to stay-active seniors. Unless you can afford to advertise everywhere, you will have to pick both *among* the various groups and *within* each group. Depending on what you sell, some choices may seem easy. But use the CCREAM chart for them, too. It will make sure that you have the facts, not just what you think you know. Since the importance of many of these facts—such as duplicate circulation, CPM/TA (cost per thousand of target audience), or help in merchandising—will vary with each advertiser, a four-step use of the chart is suggested.

PRINT MEDIA CCREAM™ ANALYSIS CHART

Primary T.A. (Target Audience) _____   Secondary T.A. (Target Audience) _____

Medium #1 _____   Medium #2 _____   Medium #3 _____

			Medium 1 Score/Weighted		Medium 2 Score/Weighted		Medium 3 Score/Weighted	
1.	**CIRCULATION**	50 %						
	A. Total Circulation		101,800			996,450	998,800	
	B. Duplicate Circulation	10	8.0	4.0	8.0	4.0	16.0	8.0
	C. Paid, Home Delivery, & Mail	0						
	D. Controlled Circulation	0						
	E. T.A. Penetration	50	7.85	19.62	6.9	17.25	7.1	17.75
	F. T.A. Quality	40	8.2	16.4	9.018.0	18.00	8.3	16.60
				40.02		39.25		42.35
2.	**COST OF CIRCULATION**	25 %						
	A. Total Ad Cost	0						
	B. Circulation CPM	0						
	C. T.A. CPM/TA	100	17.61		16.05		18.37	
				22.78		25.0		21.8
3.	**READERSHIP**	25 %						
	A. Primary Readership	65	8.5	13.8	8.0	13.0	7.0	11.3
	B. Secondary Readership	25	6.0	3.75	2.0	1.25	9.0	5.6
	C. Pass Along Readership	10	4.0	1.0	4.0	1.0	6.0	1.5
				18.55		15.25		18.4
	Total			81.35		79.50		82.55

© 1997, Fred Hahn and Kenneth Mangun

The Four-Step Approach

1. *Assign weighted value to the six major areas.* As shown in the filled-in example above, it is unlikely that all factors on the chart will be of equal importance for your evaluation. So before you start, as part of a 100 percent total, assign the relative importance to each of the six areas. Place that total in the box to the right of the area name. Then, within each area, rate each point as part of that area's own 100 percent total.

   It's the one way you force yourself to really think about why you are picking the media you do and it's not nearly as complicated as it sounds.

2. *Fill in all obtainable information* on the chart. If you have more than three candidates in the same group, use additional copies of the chart and add columns 4, 5, and so on.

3. *In the scoring area* of each column, assign a 0 to 10 value to each item. That makes a numerical calculation easy. You simply total the items and multiply them by the percentage assigned to that group. How you "score" will, of course, use the factual data about each item available to you.

4. *Total the values assigned* to each medium. Where a clear "winner" emerges, use that newspaper or magazine. Where no winner is obvious, or it is "too close to call," base your judgment on Editorial Compatibility with what you're selling. If even that won't decide, go to Merchandising Help. Someone will outbid the others!

EXPLANATION OF CCREAM ANALYSIS EXAMPLE

Page 60 shows an illustrated example of how the CCREAM chart works.

1. Circulation

- Of the six areas, Circulation counts for 50 percent, while Cost and Readership count for 25 percent each. To keep things simple, we've assumed that Editorial and Advertising turned out to be exactly alike, so they're not a factor. Merchandising becomes our tiebreaker.

- Within Circulation, "Duplicate Circulation" (B) counts for 10 percent, "Penetration of Target Audience" (E) for 50 percent, and "Quality of Target Audience" (F) for 40 percent. Since Total Circulation (A) is almost the same for all three media, our only interest is their circulation among a specific target audience. Points C and D are irrelevant for this analysis.

On a scale of 0 to 10, with "1" showing 10 percent achievement and "10" showing 100 percent, we have scored subcategories B, E, and F as shown on page 60.

- *Point B.* Based on a management decision that a 15 percent duplicate circulation would be worth the full score of 10, a 12 percent duplication (80% of 15) earns an 8. But the *weighted* score takes into account that Circulation is valued at 50 percent of the overall six-area total. So the 10 percent given to Duplicate Circulation can't be "worth" more than 5 (10% of 50) and 80 percent of 5 gives the weighted score of 4.

AN EASY WAY TO CALCULATE

Look at the Circulation percentage column again. Take F as an example. Multiply the percentage given for each lettered item by the percentage in the rectangular box. Now multiply that by the score:

$$\text{(a) } 40 \times .50 \ (50\%) = 20$$
$$\text{(b) } 20 \times .82 \ (8.2) = 16.4$$

It even works for item B in Medium 3. The score of 16 becomes 160 percent of 5 or the weighted total of 8.

- *Point E.* 65 percent Target Audience penetration was assigned the value of the full 10. Since penetration turned out to be 51 percent, the score becomes 7.85 (51 divided by 65 or 78.5% of 65). But here, as in Point B, two more steps are needed:

    Step 1. Point E is 50 percent of Circulation and 78.5% of that gives us 39.25.

    Step 2. But the total Point E is just 50 percent of the six-step analysis and 50 percent of 39.25 gives the *weighted* value of 19.62.

- *Point F.* Target Audience Quality (family income, for instance) is worth 40 percent for the full 10 evaluation. 82 percent of the Target Audience qualify. Evaluation score is 8.2 or 82.0. Using the same two steps as in Point E we find that 16.4 is the weighted total.

The Cost of Circulation Difference

For cost of circulation, take three steps for evaluation. Using our example, for instance, we would:

1. Take the lowest cost of $16.05 and give it the full 25 percent assigned to this category.
2. Divide $16.05 by each higher rate. In our example, divide it first by $17.61. The answer is .9114.
3. Multiply that answer by .25—the percentage assigned to this cost—and enter 22.78. Use the same easy calculation for all the other rates.

APPLICATION

Evaluate how much each CCREAM information point is worth for each new promotion. Spend time, effort, and money only on data you must use, not on what's of no value, even if it's nice to know.

SUMMARY

- Define your audience by what you want it to do about your product or service.
- Find out what that audience is reading and advertise in those publications—not what *you* like to read, what *they* like.
- No product or service is of interest to 100 percent of a newspaper's or magazine's readers. How small a percentage can you afford to reach? How much can you afford to spend to find the answer?
- Lots of help is available. The only stupidity is in not admitting our ignorance!

3 | Flyers, Brochures, Bulletins, and Invitations

FLYERS AND BROCHURES: HOW THEY DIFFER

In standard usage, a *flyer* is made from a single sheet of paper. Figure 3.1 shows just eight of the different formats that a flyer may assume. By contrast, a *brochure,* like the catalogs shown in Figure 5.4, is in booklet format. In working with outside sources, find out what distinction *they* make, so that you both speak the same language. Since different suppliers may have different definitions, keep your *internal* nomenclature consistent and "translate" as you go along.

A BRIEF MANUAL OF PROCEDURES

Procedures for creating flyers and brochures should be the same whether you do everything yourself, are part of an internal team, or supervise outside resources. The procedures apply to everything from simple do-it-yourself projects to the most sophisticated agency-produced materials. As with every promotion, creating a flyer or brochure is a five-step process:

1. Learn, or decide upon, the purpose of your promotion.
2. Establish a time frame and remain within it.
3. Establish and remain within a budget.
4. Write and create the promotion.
5. Produce and distribute the promotion. This is covered as part of Chapter 4, "Direct Mail," and in greatest detail in Chapter 14.

Let's consider each of these points in more detail.

DECIDING ON A PURPOSE

The "Target" Audience

Begin by determining to whom the piece will be addressed. The type and amount of information you include should be guided by its use. For instance, senior management will require a preponderance of financial data, the engineering depart-

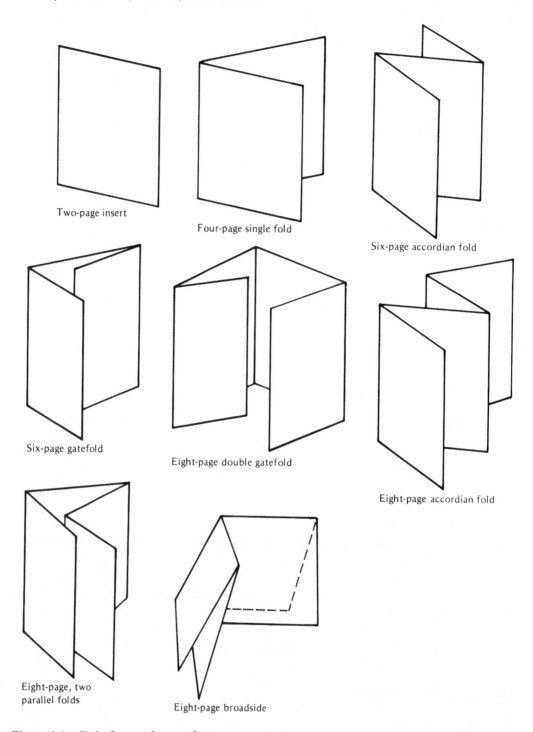

Two-page insert

Four-page single fold

Six-page accordian fold

Six-page gatefold

Eight-page double gatefold

Eight-page accordian fold

Eight-page, two
parallel folds

Eight-page broadside

Figure 3.1   Eight formats for your flier.
Planning a printing project requires a choice of format and paper. The most reliable way to appraise your selection is to have paper samples, called "dummies," made by your printer or paper merchant. These blank dummies give you an accurate example of how a specific paper's substance, weight and surface qualities look and feel in the format you specify. (Formats shown courtesy of James River Premium Printing Papers. Original art for James River by Hyers/Smith Advertising, South Norwalk, CT.)

ment will demand production specifications, and an interior designer will be interested only in size and colors. And that's just for the bathrooms!

If, as is often the case, you must combine information for more than one audience within a single promotion, make it easy for each audience to find and use what it needs. Some simple ways to do this are given later in the section.

How Much to Include

Whether you're a brand new enterprise or long established, don't just guess at how much to tell your audience about who you are and what you have to sell. If you're part of an ongoing organization, accompany several experienced sales representatives as they make their calls. Try to differentiate between sales success based on personality (I like Chuck) and that based on how goods are being sold (I like what I hear and see). If you are a member of an enterprise that is just starting up, you may have to do some or all of the selling yourself.

INSIGHT 12

Always put more detail—whether hard data or a sales pitch—into your printed promotion than into your sales call. There is no way your *readers* can question your flyer or brochure, so give them *everything* they need to make them decide your way.

An extensive guide to what and how much to write begins in a few pages. But don't jump there yet. Though writing comes first, there's a lot more to do before the actual writing begins.

Using the Promotion

Knowing how and by whom the piece you produce will be used is critical to its creation. Will it contain "high" or "low" information; that is, must it generate a sale or produce a lead? Will it be mailed? Placed on the Internet? Distributed by a sales staff? Included in packages? Posted on bulletin boards? Used at trade shows? Or all of these? Let's consider each of these options in turn. (Use on the Internet is covered in Chapter 9.)

Mailing
Mailings can be self-mailers; that is, mailed without envelopes, or mailed inside of envelopes or other containers. They may go by first class or several variations of third class. You may include a coupon or a reply form, or request the recipient to write, call, or fax. These and other mailing options and decisions require a chapter all by themselves and are covered in Chapter 4.

Use by the Sales Staff
Your promotion can be a visual aid during a sales call, a leave-behind reminder, or both. It can be "Let me walk you through this flyer, which illustrates the impor-

tant points about our service," or "Let me just leave you this brochure, which highlights the points we've been talking about. You can look it over with engineering, and I'll call you about an order on Tuesday."

Some "political" points must also be considered. For example, in larger organizations, how will the sales staff react if the only address shown on flyers and brochures is the home office? And conversely, how will the home office react if all the responses go to the field? As the advertising or promotion director, you may be the only person involved in the promotion who works for "the company," so resolve any such conflicts before your creative efforts begin.[1]

Enclosures

Make sure that your promotion piece fits into the package. Is your piece the first thing you want seen or the last, and how can you be certain that it will be seen at all? Join the packaging design team first and the packaging crew later. There's no substitute for hands-on experience in this phase of promotional activities.

Distribution at Trade Shows

If you use "help yourself" literature bins at conventions, meetings, or other events, how much of the promotion piece do the bins show: the complete page, the top half, or the top few inches only? The answer will affect the design of the piece, so do let the designer know.

ESTABLISHING A TIME FRAME AND TIME LINES

A time frame is the time allowed for the complete project. A time line details the time for each of its subprojects, such as researching, writing, designing, editing copy, typesetting, and doing artwork. For any project involving outside resources, your time frame and budget are totally interrelated. Costs are affected by time allocations, and completion dates may not be flexible. The brochure that says "Visit our booth for a special discount" will do you no good whatsoever after the exhibit closes—no matter how creative the excuses are for not getting it done.

Individual time lines are established by working backward from a targeted end date and allocating completion dates and responsibility for each of the following benchmarks:

- **End date.** When the project must be completed and what "completed" means: printed, distributed (how?), or received (by whom?).

- **Distribution.** The dates for each aspect of distribution, including mailings and warehousing of extra stock.

---

[1] W. Edwards Deming, the U.S. "father" of Japan's industrial miracle, believed that a key error made by the United States is to evaluate individuals only for their immediate, isolated contributions. Everyone is thus forced to be "in business for themselves," and practically no one works for the long-run good of the corporation or organization.

- **Printing and bindery work.** The time from the completion of printing film to the delivery by the printer of *usable* printed pieces. For flyers and brochures, a separate bindery may be involved in collating or folding, or the printers may do this themselves. The time line schedules them both.

- **"Prepress" film and proofing.** Almost all contemporary printing, including newspapers and magazines, begins with a photographed image, *on film,* that will be transferred by the printer onto printing plates. The preparation of this film from the camera-ready art may be done by the printer or by an art studio, or a filmmaking specialist called a *color separator.* The time needed for preparing and transferring film will depend on both the complexity of your project and the time the filmmaker is available. Advanced scheduling and written confirmation are highly recommended. Just remember that you, too, must keep your part of the scheduling agreement.

- **Proofing** is the checking of a test picture made from the film, before your project is actually printed. A number of different proofing processes are available. Printing, film preparation, and proofs are so important that they are covered in much more detail in Chapter 14. For scheduling purposes, the thing to know is that the kind of proof you order affects your costs and your ability at quality control rather than completion time. The same original film must be prepared, no matter which process is used.

- **Camera-ready art** is everything that will be photographed or computer digitized to make the film for printing. Specific considerations must be given not only to the time needed for typesetting, photography, and art, but also to who must approve any of these steps and their availability when they will be needed. The process of combining the various approved elements into the most practical format for photography is largely computer generated. Sophisticated typesetting and art is *possible* with many of the newer desktop publishing computer programs. Whether it is *practical* in-house depends on the experience, skill, and artistic talent of the persons using the system. As with every computer use, GIGO[2] rules.

- **Copy, design, and layout.** Who will do copy, design, and layout and who must approve them are often the most flexible elements of the time line, especially if they are done by internal staff. What is sometimes forgotten is that they are also the foundation on which everything else is built. Constructing that foundation is discussed in detail almost immediately in the upcoming section, "Creating the Promotion."

ESTABLISHING A BUDGET

There are two types of budgets, and they must not be confused. Both are fixed, but they are based on different conditions:

---

[2]GIGO: "Garbage in, garbage out."

1. *Administrative budget.* A specific amount is allocated, and costs must not exceed that amount.
2. *Estimate-based budget.* Costs are estimated, and projects are then approved, rejected, or changed based on the estimates.

The budget becomes a time line consideration when it must be approved by someone other than yourself before any work may start. If this is mandated, build in time for getting estimates and quotations, as well as the approval itself.

CREATING THE PROMOTION: AN OUTLINE

The outline that follows is written as if you were the promotional supervisor of a large organization. Exactly the same procedures apply to the one-person shop or any size of organization in between.

1. **Purpose.** The purpose of the piece is the most important reason or reasons for preparing it; for instance: (a) to use ("walk through") during sales calls, (b) to distribute at conventions, and (c) to mail for leads and/or sales. Make an absolute limit of three. (How many can be "most" important?) *Put them in writing!*
2. **Sources.** Determine who will provide the information needed to write and design the promotion and when they will be available. Get a backup source, if possible.
3. **Check and approve.** Establish responsibility for the accuracy of information about the product, legal clearance, editorial clearance (spelling, grammar, the house style), and sales input. Determine who will edit—rather than write—review, and have final approval of the project. *Only one person can have final approval!*
4. **Concepts and presentations.** Depending on how you and your organization work, you may go through a series of concept presentations or go directly to final copy and layout. In either case, the materials must be put through the following steps, whether they be taken mentally while talking to yourself or in formal presentations to others:

    A. **Organization.** Organize all your information in the order of importance to the specific audience that will see the printed piece. After it is organized, you can decide how much of the information will actually be used and the style in which it is to be presented.

    B. **Emphasis.** Decide which points are to be stressed and which is the most important point of all. Make the latter into your headline.

    C. **Illustrations.** Decide on photographs and other illustrations: how many there will be, what kind they should be, and where to get them.

    D. **Response.** Determine what you want the reader to do and give them a reason to do it. This is the most frequently understated element in promotional literature. We tell the recipient everything, except why we want them to read the material. (For their good, yes, but for our good, too!).

E. **Policing.** Policing is neither proofreading nor editing, but a final check against #1, your stated purpose in producing the promotional piece. That's why we put that purpose into writing. It's very easy to get so carried away with our creativity, that we forget what we set out to do.

Once the basic concept has been developed, preliminary or "draft" copy and possible designs are produced. In organizations with several layers of management, these are the versions presented for managerial comments or approval. Note that detailed revisions may be required for draft copy and designs, as some managers can't visualize promotional materials until they see them in quite finished form. During Hahn's years as an advertising account executive, he's reminded his clients—as gently as he knows how—that they are *paying* for all the changes they order. As employees reporting to management, we both have—equally gently—given notice of impending deadlines. As principals of our own firms, we've played both parts simultaneously with schizophrenic delight.

INSIGHT 13

Do not show managers "rough," that is, not professionally finished, design concepts or unedited copy. Despite their insistence that they wish to eliminate the cost of "finished" presentations, in our several decades of presenting things to them, no manager has been happy with anything less.

SUMMARY

- Determine by whom and how your promotional pieces will be used. Make everything fit into purposes consistent with that determination. Put it in writing!
- Time frames control budgets and vice versa. Nothing saves creative and production dollars like adequate time to do the job.
- Some deadlines must be met, and there is *not* always time to do it over, even if someone is willing to pay the extraordinary expense.
- *Plan* who will be your sources for information, reviews, and approvals. Put it in writing!

A case history. Despite repeated warnings from Mangun, because of his client's indecision, a specialty printer reported he could not meet a deadline. The client shifted the project to another printer who agreed to do it at time and a half. Once the job was delivered, the new printer found it was too complex for his equipment. Finally, the job was returned to the original printer who had to charge double-time to finish by working over the weekend.

A BASIC DESIGN CONCEPT

The One-Third Guide

For a one- or two-page piece (each page is one side of a sheet of paper, not the sheet itself), allow *approximately* one-third of the space for each of the following (see Figure 3.2):

- One-third for headlines and subheads, plus information about ordering or a coupon and your logo—that is, the special way you identify yourself. Frequently, your logo is also the way your name, address, and telephone number appear on your letterhead.
- One-third for illustrations, including charts, and captions.
- One-third for general copy; that is, the body of the ad.

For three pages or more, use the two-page guide for the first page and the last page, and then divide the remaining space so that you use half for copy and half for illustrations. Of course, these are suggested guidelines only, but they will give you a balanced approach to an inviting presentation.

Page Size Guideline

Keep your page size $8^{1}/_{2}'' \times 11''$ (letter) or $8^{1}/_{2}'' \times 14''$ (legal size). Either one will fold into a standard No. 10 business envelope and is flexible for multipurpose use.

WRITING THE MANUSCRIPT: THE IMPORTANCE OF FEATURES AND BENEFITS

In flyers and brochures, present features and benefits as nearly equally as you can. Each one needs and supports the other. *What* benefits and features you choose are, of course, determined by your target audience and your purpose in communicating with them.

Remember, a **feature** is what is inherent in your product or service. It is what *you* have put in. ("Our lawnmower bag is reinforced with glass threads.")

A **benefit** is what the potential *buyer or user* gets from your product or service. Benefits answer the question of "What's in it for me?" ("The safest grass-catcher bag on any mower. Even loose pebbles and sharp objects can't fly out and harm your loved ones.")

Features are usually easy to find and put on paper. We all tend to be familiar with what we, singly or as an organization, bring to our products and services. But many writers have difficulty finding and articulating equally impressive benefits—especially when the same feature requires different benefits for different audiences.

The Magic Benefit Generator

Whether you are forced to be a true do-it-yourselfer or can bring others into the process, here's a surefire way to generate benefits. Take a sheet of paper. At the top, list the feature and the audience for whom you wish to generate benefits. Now pretend you are speaking to that audience. Read the feature, preferably out loud, and add: "*And you will love it because*"—but don't stop. What follows "because" is the series of benefits. Don't even stop to write. Get a tape recorder (for as little as $20), and use that instead. Do the same for each audience and each feature. *Now* copy the listed benefits from the tape onto paper and disk. When you finish, you'll have not only a complete list of features, but also a practically inexhaustible encyclopedia of benefits. If there are features for which you just can't find benefits, share the problem with the person who created the feature in the first place. (For example, "Why is our grass catcher bag only 8 mm thick when everyone else's is 9?")

Brainstorming

Discovering benefits and gaining a greater insight into features is a brainstorming experience that just about everyone profits from and enjoys. Whenever possible, bring different areas of expertise together and let them help generate answers to your "because" question. Here are some basic rules pertaining to brainstorming:

- There are no dumb suggestions.
- Don't argue about other people's suggestions during brainstorming; just build on them.
- Switch to a new feature the moment answers stop coming.
- "I just thought of something" half an hour later is . . . great! Accept it with thanks.

Steps in Writing

Now you are ready to write! But rather than go at it in a haphazard way, do it like this:

1. Organize the features and benefits by order of importance *to the audience to whom you are writing.* This will probably give you different sequences for different audiences.

2. Decide on the number of photographs, graphs, charts, and any other art you want to include, and *make sure you can get them.* Words and illustrations must reinforce each other and work together to get the results you want. You really can't do that unless you know what the illustrations will be.

3. Pick the six most important aspects of the product. Make the first of these the overall headline for the piece. Use the other five as subheads—that is, as secondary headlines for individual sections of the copy or to relate it to a specific audience. If you have fewer than six subjects, work with what you have. Divide one or more subjects into subgroupings if that makes sense. But don't force things! What you are trying to

achieve is copy that has a logical flow. Your headline and subheads, as well as the captions for your illustrations, must give the basic story, even if that is all that is read.

4. Within each section, put all of the points *that will fit* into "bulleted" form as was done in the "Brainstorming" copy on page 71. But don't just leave the copy like this. If only one or two points are to be stressed, rewrite them in regular paragraph style, and then use whichever version seems to look and read better.

State your benefits as factual information, just as you do your features. For ease in understanding the nontechnical terms, keep words to three or fewer syllables and the *average* number of words in a sentence to 12 or fewer. One fairly complicated or run-on sentence can stop your readers in their mental tracks.

Keep your writing as straightforward as possible. The format itself will produce the promotional flair that is needed. The unadorned presentation of benefits and features will strengthen rather than weaken their believability. Limit adjectives and eliminate adverbs; you'll get your chance to use them in the next chapter.

Do not try to force in every single bit of information you have available. If material seems too important to be left out, consider increasing the number of pages, rather than going to a smaller type or having fewer illustrations. But consider also that you ordered your materials in terms of importance. How vital can a seventh or eighth feature or benefit really be?

5. Once you have done all of the preceding things, you still have two more elements to think about and write:

- **The offer.** Tell your readers how to order or to get whatever you have to provide. If there are options, explain them. Make it easy. This is not an IQ test for your customers. Make the information complete. Restate the offer, its benefits, and its price. Include toll-free phone numbers and a fax number if available. Give the address to write to. List a specific department for information if there is one. Include *anything* that will expedite a response.[3]
- **Picture captions.** Copy for picture captions must be orchestrated just as carefully as that for any other element. The illustrations are there to help get across the overall message. Like your subheads, pictures and their captions should tell your basic story all by themselves.

INSIGHT 14

Your audience is most likely to read your flyer or brochure in the following order:
1. Headline and subheads.
2. Special offer if emphasized.
3. Illustrations and captions. Put the product's name in the caption!
4. The body copy in any order that happens to interest them.
Thus, you have three chances to sell or lose the audience, even if your general copy is never read. Use each one!

---

[3]Note the telegraphic style in this paragraph. It combines bulleted-type statements with a paragraph format. It works!

SUMMARY

- To find out the benefits of your product, base them on what your features do for customers and prospects. What sells is not what *you* put into your product or service; it's what *they* get out of it.
- Organize before you write, and the manuscript will take care of itself. Brilliant copy won't help if your readers can't make out why you are writing. (You want me to do *what? Why?*)

LAYOUT AND DESIGN

With the guidance offered here, you can produce your own manuscript ("copy"). But few of us are given the skill to create our own professional-quality design or layout—that is, the overall visual impression and detailed specifications that make a flyer or brochure work. Unlike newspaper and magazine advertising, for which you can find an existing model to follow, printed pieces tend to be too individualistic for that approach. So use a design studio if you can afford it. If not, you have several other options. All but one are quite inexpensive. However, the somewhat more costly one will also be the easiest for you and give you more time for other things.

- **Use the basic layouts shown in Figure 3.2.** These models were created primarily to guide you in writing, rather than layout, but they can serve both purposes if nothing more sophisticated—or simpler—is required. While they are functional, they make no pretense of being superior designs.

- **Use an existing promotion as a model.** Do this with great care, as you must make certain that the model really fits your needs. Never follow competitors' highly stylized versions. Not only will your product likely be mistaken for theirs, adding to their promotional impact rather than yours, but you'll probably hear from their attorneys as well.

- Use one of the layouts that may be built into your computer program or that is available on inexpensive disks.

- **Do your own layout.** Let your conscience be your guide.

- **Use a design studio or freelance designer.** No matter where you are located, there are dozens of studios and freelancers close by, eager to work with you if only they know of your needs. For studios, check with your business association and advertisers whose ads you admire. The easiest way to find freelancers is to place a classified ad in the Help Wanted section of your local newspaper, for example:

FREELANCE DESIGN & LAYOUTS for promotional flyers and brochures. Experience in (whatever you do) is helpful but not required. Call for appointment. (YOUR NAME/NUMBER)

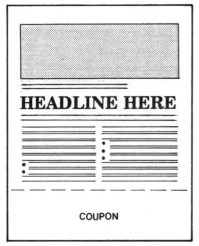

Single-page version
(Use back for mailing)

Front of two pages

Back of two pages

Figure 3.2   Sample layouts for one- or two-page fliers. Put your headline *under* the main picture. And put a selling caption under all your small pictures, too. David Ogilvy, in *Ogilvy on Advertising,* tells us you'll get 10 percent more readership at absolutely no extra cost.

Tell the studios or freelancers what your project is, what your time frame is, and, if possible, your budget for design and camera-ready art. If you have no way of estimating design costs, interview a few of the designers first, and then arrive at a figure based on their quotations. Make sure to *schedule* the interviews. Tell the candidates they will have one hour: 20 minutes to present samples *with their charges for everything they show;* 20 minutes for you to present your project; and 20 minutes for them to ask any questions. An hour should be adequate with the likely candidates. For simpler projects, allow one week for quotations. For more complicated promotions, allow two weeks.

Cost Factors in Working with Outside Designers

Whether you work with a freelance designer, a design studio, or an advertising agency, the following factors will affect your costs:

1. **Time available to complete the project.** Begin by asking potential suppliers their normal time needs for a project such as yours. What you consider a rush project may be their regular schedule.

2. **Quality of manuscript.** Has your copy been given final approval, or will there be repeated copy changes that will require new layouts? Since *you* pay for each new version, find out how they are charged.

3. **Number of versions required.** Many clients want to see two or three (or more) designs from which to choose. For *major* projects, this is a recommended procedure, but get costs quoted in advance. For routine flyers or brochures, get a single design. It will be the one the designer considered the best of the several he or she attempted before deciding on the one you are shown.

4. **Degree of layout "finish."** This refers to how polished the layout must be. There are three generally accepted variations: "rough," "semicomprehensive," and "comprehensive." What these three terms mean varies with everyone who uses them. Have prospective designers show samples of each kind of finish and explain the difference in their costs.

5. **Preparation of camera-ready art.** Most designers prefer to do the camera-ready art. If your budget permits, let them do it. Not only will you get a better end product, but you will have a happier designer, eager to work with you again in the future.

INSIGHT 15

In giving creative or production work to outside sources, have a budget and time line agreed upon in writing . . . and never change those instructions by "client's alterations" without knowing the time and dollar consequences. Ask your suppliers to recommend alternatives. There may be a better way!

TYPE, TYPOGRAPHY, TYPESETTING, AND DESKTOP PUBLISHING

A discussion of type, typography, typesetting, and desktop publishing, as applied to flyers and brochures, is no different from that applied to advertising beginning on page 20.

SUMMARY

If God did not make you into a designer, even such lesser creatures as coworkers and employers will probably notice. For true design, use a true designer. For routine layouts, use or modify an existing model when it is practical to do so. When it is not, get a professional.

NOTES ON THE FLYER/BROCHURE CHECKLIST

These notes are a supplement to the material presented in this chapter. They are not a self-contained substitute for the material.

APPLICATION

Neither the checklist itself nor these notes are a time line. Many of the items must be done at the same time rather than sequentially. For instance, numbers 5 through 8, plus 18, are first decided, then worked on simultaneously.

1. **Quotations.** The total of all quoted and/or estimated costs accepted from outside suppliers, plus the known or estimated internal out-of-pocket costs. This is the amount given for budget approval in #2.
2. **Budget approval.** The amount either accepted from #1, or otherwise determined as a fair cost to do the project. If lower than the figure in #1, costs may have to be renegotiated with suppliers or the project modified to fit the dollar allocation.
3. **Project approval.** Once the project *can* be done for the amount in #2, a decision on whether the project is worth the cost, no matter how "fair" the individual charges may be.
4. **Target audience.** Are you trying to force different audiences' needs and interests into a single piece? You'll probably lose more in sales than you gain in promotional savings. Do this only if you have no way to reach each group individually.
5. **Purpose.** How the item advertised will be used and which use—if there are several—is the most important. Every other item on the checklist must keep the purpose in mind.
6. **Overall focus.** What the message is to achieve as a whole. The general "feel" of the complete piece.
7. **Headline focus.** Based on the benefits keyed to the target audience in #4, the one thing you hope will make the reader stop long enough to learn more about your message. Not the words—leave that to the writer in #10—but the thought!
8. **Subhead focus.** Sell here if you can. But more important, get across the focus message from #6, even if the subheads are all that is read. If #7 and #8 are a ten-second outline that tells your story, you probably have a winner!

FLYER/BROCHURE CHECKLIST

Project Title _____ Date _____

_____ Project # _____

Project Description _____ Checklist # _____

_____ Deadline _____

Budget _____ Completion Date _____ Start Up Date _____

	ASSIGNED TO	DUE	IN	MUST APPROVE	BY DATE	IN	INFO COPY ONLY	SEE ATTACHED
MANAGEMENT DECISIONS								
1. Quotations	_____	__	☐	_____	__	☐	_____	☐
2. Budget Approval	_____	__	☐	_____	__	☐	_____	☐
3. Project Approval	_____	__	☐	_____	__	☐	_____	☐
CREATIVE DECISIONS								
4. Audience	_____	__	☐	_____	__	☐	_____	☐
5. Purpose	_____	__	☐	_____	__	☐	_____	☐
6. Overall Focus	_____	__	☐	_____	__	☐	_____	☐
7. Headline Focus	_____	__	☐	_____	__	☐	_____	☐
8. Subhead(s) Focus	_____	__	☐	_____	__	☐	_____	☐
9. Desired Response	_____	__	☐	_____	__	☐	_____	☐
10. Writers	_____	__	☐	_____	__	☐	_____	☐
11. Designers	_____	__	☐	_____	__	☐	_____	☐
12. Typesetter	_____	__	☐	_____	__	☐	_____	☐
13. Artist	_____	__	☐	_____	__	☐	_____	☐
14. Photographer	_____	__	☐	_____	__	☐	_____	☐
15. Camera-Ready Art	_____	__	☐	_____	__	☐	_____	☐
16. Film OK	_____	__	☐	_____	__	☐	_____	☐
17. On-Press OK	_____	__	☐	_____	__	☐	_____	☐
MECHANICAL DECISIONS								
18. Page Size	_____	__	☐	_____	__	☐	_____	☐
19. Number of Pages	_____	__	☐	_____	__	☐	_____	☐
20. Color(s)	_____	__	☐	_____	__	☐	_____	☐
21. Paper Stock	_____	__	☐	_____	__	☐	_____	☐
22. Film House	_____	__	☐	_____	__	☐	_____	☐
23. Printer	_____	__	☐	_____	__	☐	_____	☐
24. Distribution	_____	__	☐	_____	__	☐	_____	☐
MECHANICAL CHECKS								
25. Logo OK	_____	__	☐	_____	__	☐	_____	☐
26. Address(es) OK	_____	__	☐	_____	__	☐	_____	☐
27. Phone(s) OK	_____	__	☐	_____	__	☐	_____	☐
28. Editorial OK	_____	__	☐	_____	__	☐	_____	☐
29. Legal OK	_____	__	☐	_____	__	☐	_____	☐
30. Marketing OK	_____	__	☐	_____	__	☐	_____	☐
31. Printed Samples	_____	__	☐	_____	__	☐	_____	☐

9. **Response.** What you hope the reader will do after reading the piece. If the answer is "Nothing special," why are you producing the flyer or brochure? Make the offer a *major* reason to get the advertised product or service *from you* and to do it *now*, especially if a competitor's options are available.

10. **Writer.** The checklist shows the person who *appoints* the writer. If certain things must be said in a specific way, let the writer know before he or she begins . . . and whether this is a legal constraint or a management decision. If the latter, management should be willing to at least consider alternatives. Specify whether you want "roughs" or a best effort "finished copy" as first draft. Better yet, ask the writer to produce finished copy, but treat it as a draft. But make sure that you let the writer know you are doing this. Writers tend to get hysterical if it comes as a surprise, after they're done.

11. **Designers.** Will copy be written to fit the design, or will the design be based on the copy? If different persons do #10 and #11, make sure that they can work as a team. Good designers often surprise, so do not be hasty to say no to what you may not like at first sight. It is the designers' job to know how to appeal *visually* to the targeted audience. They are right more often than they are wrong.

12. **Typesetter.** For reasonably simple styling, turn to desktop equipment and set your own type. Give your designer samples of your in-house type faces, so the copy can be marked to match. For pieces that require design skill, use professional typesetting. All other factors being equal, nothing heightens the appeal of your product or service like skillful professional typography!

13–14. **Photos/Art.** Determine who selects, orders, and supervises photography and art. In addition to know-how, it will probably take time. Unless the person doing or given the assignment is an expert not only in art but also in *reproduction* for commercial printing, this should be discussed with the filmmaker in #16 before any photography or art is ordered. *Much* more about this in the Prepress Film Preparation checklist in Chapter 14.

15. **Camera-ready art.** With desktop typesetting, you'll probably create camera-ready "hard-copy" art on your computer. If you are new to desktop typesetting, find out how to make your work practical for your filmmaker to use. For outside production, this is the last chance to change anything at relatively low cost. Put *every* instruction to the filmmaker *in writing.* If another department or an outside service or agency does this, the person who assigned the project goes over it with them. The filmmaker should be present also. Everyone involved must understand the instructions and understand them *the same way.*

16. **Film OK.** You approve the film by checking its proof. Check everything against the instructions on the hard copy, and check the job as a whole. Better yet, if you work in an organization with film and printing specialists, turn to them for help. It's their job. Let them do it.

17. **On-press OK.** Go to the printer for on-press approval. Printers will "hold the presses" for approval and take the material being printed to you—at hundreds, or thousands, of dollars for press and staff waiting time. But what will you do if you want more on-press changes? Wait in your office again . . . and again. *You* go to the printer!

18. **Page size.** Take the original layout to the printer as soon as it is done. Ask your printer if a small decrease or increase in the page size can make

a large difference in savings. If the printer says yes, and the new size is practical, tell the designers. It's easier for everyone if they create the design with the new size in mind.

19. **Number of pages.** Does deciding on the number of pages precede the creative effort or follow it? Why?

20. **Color(s).** While selecting colors is subjective, it's also an art. Accordingly, have it done by an artist if possible. Just make sure that the choices work for sales as well as aesthetics. Not too many of us can read white type inside a light blue background or light blue printed on white.

21. **Paper stock.** Where only a specific stock will do, use it. Where options are possible, check your printer or paper merchant for what they have on hand. For some projects, the use of two different papers may bring dramatic savings. Ask!

22. **Film house.** If someone other than your printer does the film, be sure that the filmmaker knows that printer's needs. Make certain that they speak *with each other,* not only through you.

23. **Printer.** Different printers have different capabilities based on equipment, experience, and expertise. Selection of a printer and film house is best done by an in-house specialist, if one is available. If not, become one by asking your associates in other organizations. Visit their suppliers with them if possible. That's how we learned most of what we know . . . and that's how we continue to learn.

24. **Distribution.** Determine what "distribution" means: How many flyers or brochures will be used for mailing, shipping to staff, warehousing, and so on? Requests and orders for your pieces may come from anywhere. But for approving and filling orders, a single person must be in charge.

25–30. **Mechanical checks.** Someone has been assigned to check each of these items before anything may be printed. Make sure that they do check them and sign off *in writing.* In many organizations, the logo, address, and phone numbers are preprinted in a variety of styles and sizes and *must* be used from that art. It's an excellent safety measure, provided that every such logo is dated and thrown out when there is a change. Experience has shown that practically no one really reads logos. Make yourself the exception.

31. **Sample distribution.** Printed samples generally get wide distribution. Set up a system that won't force you to reinvent the distribution list with every piece produced. As with newspaper and magazine ads, every piece must be coded and a permanent file maintained. Hahn recently astonished a client by still having a mailing the client wanted to re-create that the agency had done 15 years before.

BULLETINS, INVITATIONS, AND INVITATIONAL BULLETINS

Bulletins and invitations are widely—and successfully—used for business-to-business seminars to sell products and services. They are discussed together because, *for advertising and promotional purposes,* their uses are frequently the same. Bulletins are also used for two other purposes with which you may be involved as a creative resource:

1. **Bulletins that must be posted, but that no one reads.** State and federal offices, personnel and accounting departments, and senior management (among others) issue materials that *must* be placed on bulletin boards. However, unless the information displayed has real and immediate application to the audience for whom it was written, it is simply ignored. And if you ask how that audience knows it can, with impunity, ignore such bulletins, the answer is, they just do.

2. **Bulletins that must be posted and that everyone reads.** Often issued by the same sources as in item 1, they give information on newly issued or revised mechanical, safety, or material-handling instructions, on public or private requests for assistance, and many other things. The list is endless. In this case, the audience knows what it must *not* ignore.

The preceding two categories, insofar as they require promotional expertise, can be considered flyers and handled as such. Most often, there are models that can be followed and desktop publishing that can be used to produce the camera-ready art.

The Challenge of Optional Posting

A third category of bulletins is of much more concern to advertising and promotion than the foregoing two. This is the bulletin that no one is *required* to post, although everyone who sees it should *want* to . . . and want to read it, too! Usually distributed by mail, it has to jump the initial hurdle of the mail room or secretarial censor, pass its second barrier of managerial scrutiny, and, most difficult of all, crash through the stone wall of passerby indifference. Since your bulletin competes for posting with all the others received at its destination, the challenge is formidable. Your likelihood of success is directly related to a slight modification of the first insight given in this book, which said, Keep it simple . . . keep it specific . . . and you're likely to keep solvent. Apropos of bulletins, the insight would urge:

INSIGHT 16

Keep it Simple . . . keep it Specific . . . keep it focused on Benefits . . . and you're likely to get posted.

Who Decides What's Posted?

Even if you're sure you know who controls the posting of bulletins at the places to which you mail them, call a dozen of these places at random and ask to speak with the person in charge of putting up bulletins. If the operator does not know, ask for personnel. People will tell you almost anything if asked politely, so remember what you want to learn:

- What happens when a bulletin is addressed to an individual by name?
- What happens when a bulletin is addressed to a title (say, vice president of finance) or a job description (e.g., person in charge of posting financial training bulletins)?
- Does the size of the bulletin make any difference to its being posted? Which sizes are actually used?
- Does how the bulletin is received (e.g., in an envelope, as a self-mailer, hand delivered) make any difference?
- About what percentage of bulletins received actually get posted?
- Why?

Perhaps the single most important insight this chapter has to offer is this.

INSIGHT 17

Take *nothing* for granted. Phone first.

The steps in the posting process will tell you how to address and how to send your mailing, as well as what message, if any, to put alongside the address. Usually, a purely informative message, such as that shown in Figure 3.3, is adequate.

The combination of the right name or title, together with an appropriate "teaser"—that is, an interest-focusing outside message—will very likely get your bulletin posted. Now all you have to do is to get it read and acted upon.

How to Get Your Bulletin Read

For posting on a bulletin board, get all the excitement and information on a single page. Don't force your audience to see the other side to understand your message. You are producing a kind of billboard, not a brochure!

- **Make the benefit obvious.** In Figure 3.3, "additional training" that is of interest to employers may translate into better pay, job security, a quick chance for advancement, or all three for employees. Just don't be too clever or cute. Save that for the section on invitations, which is discussed next.
- **Present the benefit in the largest, boldest, easiest-to-see type.** You want to capture the attention of the casual passerby. So make it easy to read from a reasonable distance.
- **Label everything.** Mention the time, date, place, cost, anything free, what to bring, what the reader will get to take home, how to participate, and so on.

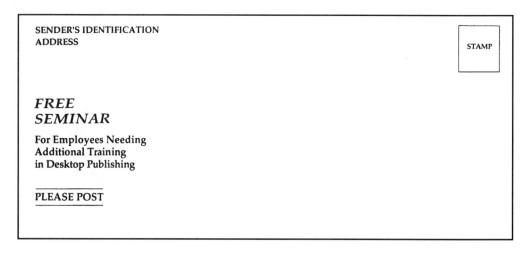

Figure 3.3   The same "teaser" copy and design can be used, as here, for an envelope or for a self-mailer.

- **Sketch a simple map.** Do this for locations away from the home, the neighborhood, or work. Give distances from known locations (e.g., "approx. 3.2 miles west of Exit 89 on State Highway 17").
- **Add a "Take One" as a reminder.** Include the map. Your printer will know a variety of ways to do this.
- **Give a destination phone number.** Do this for people like Hahn, who gets lost going around the block.

Make the information complete, but keep it as simple as possible. Bulletins often are read in passing. Make it possible to do just that. As a safety factor, place a small "Please post" request in one corner. Always tell people what you'd like them to do. Don't make them guess.

Bulletins for Fun Events

Fun events, from puppy beauty contests to the Fourth of July picnic and the Santa Claus parade, may seem exceptions to the rules for getting your bulletin posted on a bulletin board. They're not! It's the *event* that's the fun. The bulletin must still

---

SUMMARY

- In the development of bulletins and invitations, be guided by the Five W's: Who, What, When, Where, Why.
- Don't create bulletins no one will post. Learn who decides what's posted and why . . . then make yours fit in.
- If it reads like a billboard, . . . if it looks like a billboard, . . . if it works like a billboard, . . . you've got a great bulletin!

give every bit of information needed to make the event happen. It's certainly all right to lighten the mood, provided that you don't lose the message.

INVITATIONS

All of us have received invitations to events that made us a captive audience for a sales pitch—from the chance to meet the candidate to hearing an ex-president try to sell time-sharing condominiums. Whether it's Tupperware in your living room or executive jets at the Paris Air Show, the party proves an effective sales tool, and the one thing every party has in common is an invitation.

This section focuses on inviting people together for *business* reasons—specifically, to inform them, persuade them, or sell them—and perhaps all three. It is not concerned with purely social or personal functions, although the suggested method of structuring an invitation is practical for both. How to set up the function itself is covered in the chapter on conventions, beginning on page 282.

A Magical Word

Invitation is one of those magical words, like *free, new,* and *now,* that many prospective and current customers accept uncritically. You are "invited" in magazine and newspaper ads, by radio and television commercials, on bulletin boards, on the Internet, by fax, and in the mail. All of these take advantage of the built-in association of "invitation" and "enjoyment." It is this expectation of a pleasant experience that makes invitations such an effective sales tool and one that could be more widely used. Invitations even let you bring together fierce competitors who have nothing but you in common. Think of fitting new golf shoes to shoe retailers at a golf outing, perhaps as a surprise before teeing off. Or what about a wine-tasting session for wine merchants as they sail along on a moonlight cruise. A bit of imaginative soft sell can do wonders.

A Word About Design

Invitations permit even the least creative among us to become designers. When the event itself has a festive feel, almost anything you develop in typography and layout should work, provided that you include the eight pieces of information from the model that follows. For a more formal feel, look through any stationery store, card shop, or "quick" printer's sample book and pick a model invitation to follow.

Structuring Your Invitation

See Figure 12.1 for an invitation that does just about everything right. The basic invitation has an eight-part structure that adapts to almost any occasion. Although you may not want to use all eight parts, at least consider each one to make sure that it can be skipped. To show how this works, let's produce an invitation to attend a demonstration of a solar-powered car.

1	You are invited
2	to the first public presentation
3	of a truly functional
	Solar-Powered Automobile
4	Saturday, June 24,
	10:00 a.m.
5	Zip-Along Racetrack
	Route 13 at Suicide Drive
6	Champagne brunch
7	Free admission and drawing
	for free test drive,
8	R.S.V.P.

1. **You are invited.** . . . Invitations imply an enjoyable event. The very word "invitation" prepares the recipient to be well disposed toward what comes next, so make that word prominent and the very first thing that's seen.

2. **To the first public presentation.** . . . Generally the single most important part of the invitation. Use your utmost inventiveness to make attending the event a *benefit.* Translate attendance into what the attendees will carry away, and then state that as a promise. For instance:
    *   The most exciting test drive of your life
    *   Your chance to get frank answers from . . . about . . .
    *   A full month of free . . .
    *   Machine tools you will never have to sharpen
    *   Get richer! Get smarter! Get ahead!

3. **Of a truly functional.** . . . Make the description of the event too valuable or appealing to ignore. If a large part of that appeal lies in a guest of honor or a presenter, let your invitation explain who the person is—even if everyone *should* know who he or she is. (For presentations, always use the best presenter rather than the person most knowledgeable on the subject if the two are different. But always have the latter there to help answer questions.)

4. **Saturday, June 24, 10:00 A.M.** . . . Before setting a date and time, make certain that no conflicting activity will keep your most important guests away.[4] Call and ask, then "confirm" later as a reminder just before the meeting date.

---

[4]While developing a marketing plan for the Chicago Field Museum of Natural History, Mangun realized that competing events occurred every day or evening of the year and, in a few instances, the conflict arose without either party knowing of the other's plans.

5. **Zip-Along Racetrack.** . . . Make the location a benefit if possible. Glamorize it (e.g., historic, beautiful, unique), and make it a place that is easy to get to. As with bulletins, provide a map for people who drive and a telephone number for those who may get lost.

6. **Champagne brunch.** . . . Mention food only if it's free or, for longer meetings and events, how it will be made available. Make it sound good, but don't overpromise. Let your surprises be pleasant ones.

7. **Free admission and drawing.** . . . State the charges if there are any. For professional meetings that have a fee, be specific about what is covered and what will be provided. Be generous with the things that cost little (e.g., writing materials and note pads, outlines of presentations, tote bags, door prizes). Be equally specific about what attendees will pay for themselves (e.g., travel and lodging, specific meals, gratuities). Be mindful of possible legal problems with overly generous benefits. For example, a $500 luxury weekend for a $50 fee may raise questions later. Be prepared to document legitimate business necessities and off-season rates, or have advance approval from the appropriate attorney.

8. **R.S.V.P.** Make accepting the invitation easy. Include a reply card (and envelope for privacy). Encourage responses and questions by fax or phone. Have your reply form restate the major benefits, as well as any conditions of acceptance—especially those that favor the respondent. For example, a dieting program might read:

☐ YES! I want to get ready for fat-free gourmet cooking by attending a FREE Oil-No-More hands-on demonstration on Monday, November 9, from 2:00 to 4:00 P.M. at the Ritzy Hotel, Suite 1000. I understand that all cooking materials will be provided without charge and that I must respond before November 1 to attend.

That's one Mangun wouldn't miss for the world, and he's skinny as a rail!

SUMMARY

- An invitation promises something special. Keep that promise!
- In business invitations, tell those who are invited more than enough to get them to come. Your competitors, especially at conventions and trade shows, may be trying to get them, too.
- Follow up on acceptances. Confirm them by phone just before the event to let people know you *really* want them there. *Expect* about 20% fewer than accept, . . . but *prepare* for 10% more.
- The how-to of actually giving a professional party is covered in Chapter 13. Don't miss it!

NOTES ON THE INVITATION/INVITATIONAL BULLETIN CHECKLIST

These notes are a supplement to the material presented in this chapter. They are not a self-contained substitute for that material. This checklist covers the creation, printing, and mailing of invitations. It does not concern itself with who is invited or why, except insofar as that information (#6–7) must be reflected in the invitation.

1. **Event Budget OK.** Invitations generally take up only a small portion of an event's total cost. Has that complete budget been approved, and does it include the number of invitations you plan to use (#14)? If either answer is no, get written approval (#3) before you continue.

2. **Quotations.** Allow a week to get cost quotations and whatever time is required for their approval. On budgeted projects, these quotations should not have to go back to management for another round.

3. **Invitation budget.** If the budget as a whole has not been approved, can you get approval on the invitation portion? Give the decision makers absolute deadlines beyond which invitations are useless.

4. **Speaker(s).** Arrangements for speakers or other attractions or entertainment must generally be made far in advance of an event. Who decides? Who follows up? What's the last possible moment for including changes in the invitation?

5. **Free/charges.** What's free, and what costs, if any, will be charged to the participants?

6–7. **Audience.** Identify the audience to whom you are mailing the invitation and the specific focus of the invitation—the benefits, to the audience, of attending.

8–9. **Copy.** Identify the writer and designer of the invitation. Who follows whom? Who must approve the copy? When must both be done?

10. **Camera-ready art.** Will there be hard copy produced by the typesetter or desktop publishing system?

11. **Art OK.** Approval of camera-ready art is the last chance to make changes before the production of film Give an extra copy to those who must see the original, for their notes and comments. Don't let them write on the original!

12. **Film OK.** Approval of film proofs is a combined design and advertising function, even when both are carried out by the same person. Design makes sure that the work has the quality specified on the original art. Advertising makes sure that *everything* that was on the original is on the proof and that the designer's instructions still make sense when seen in print. If you do both jobs, wear one hat at a time, but be sure that both do get worn.

13. **Printing OK.** For routine jobs, most printers can be left to their own devices. For large, complicated, or otherwise critical projects, be at the printer to give on-press approval. You'll be so bored that it will be the perfect time to read the entire copy one more time . . . and actually call all the telephone numbers and check on the addresses. About 10 percent of the

INVITATION/INVITATIONAL BULLETIN CHECKLIST

Project Title _____ Date _____

Project Description _____ Project # _____

_____ Checklist # _____

Overall Supervision By _____ Deadline _____

Budget _____ Completion Date _____ Start Up Date _____

MANAGEMENT DECISIONS	ASSIGNED TO	DUE	IN	MUST APPROVE	BY DATE	IN	INFO COPY ONLY	SEE ATTACHED
1. Event Budget OK			☐			☐		☐
2. Quotation			☐			☐		☐
3. Invitation Budget			☐			☐		☐
4. Speaker(s)			☐			☐		☐
5. Free/Charge			☐			☐		☐
CREATIVE DECISIONS								
6. Audience			☐			☐		☐
7. Focus			☐			☐		☐
8. Copy			☐			☐		☐
9. Design			☐			☐		☐
10. Camera-Ready Art			☐			☐		☐
11. Camera-Ready Art OK			☐			☐		☐
12. Film OK			☐			☐		☐
13. Printing OK			☐			☐		☐
MECHANICAL DECISIONS								
14. Quantity			☐			☐		☐
15. Mailing List			☐			☐		☐
16. Telephone List			☐			☐		☐
17. Self Mailer			☐			☐		☐
18. Envelope Mailer			☐			☐		☐
19. Components			☐			☐		☐
20. Size(s)			☐			☐		☐
21. Stock			☐			☐		☐
22. Stock Colors			☐			☐		☐
23. Printing Colors			☐			☐		☐
24. Mail Destination Date			☐			☐		☐
25. Mail Replies Due			☐			☐		☐
26. Phone Replies Due			☐			☐		☐
27. Class of Mail			☐			☐		☐
28. Film House			☐			☐		☐
29. Printer			☐			☐		☐
30. Mailing Service			☐			☐		☐
31. Records/Reports			☐			☐		☐
_____			☐			☐		☐

© 1997, Fred Hahn

time, you'll be very glad you did! (Hahn *twice* saved major projects by calling new toll-free numbers given him by clients—in writing—and about to be printed on every page of their catalogs, only to find them wrong.)

14. **Quantity.** The quantity is frequently more than the mailing list. Ask about nonmail distribution to staff and field workers and for last-minute follow-up.

15. **Mailing list.** Who supplies the list, contacts the sources on the list, and checks to make sure that it is reasonably accurate? When using outside lists, responses only, not the list as a whole, become your property for future use.

16. **Telephone list.** Will you phone to issue invitations or as a reminder to those who accept? For initial invitations, what is involved in getting the phone numbers and in getting through to those you call? Test by actually trying to call a dozen potential guests before you commit yourself to getting results.

17–18. **Mail format.** If you are using a self-mailer, skip #18 and #19. If you are using an envelope, check with suppliers of envelopes regarding standard sizes and costs. It's seldom economical to customize envelopes for fewer than 10,000. Before you get *too* creative, check with the post office to make sure they'll accept the mail as designed. They almost always say yes, but check.

19. **Components.** Components include the invitation plus any other elements, such as RSVPs and reply envelopes. Don't be afraid to load up the invitation. If travel is involved, add a map. If the speaker is special, tell why. If the event is extraordinary, tell how. Use an invitation-size sheet for *each* of those items, and watch attendance soar!

20. **Size.** Invitation sizes are determined by the envelope. If the quantity is large enough that you will use a mailing service or letter shop, check with them about the practicality of inserting the invitations into the envelopes by machine. The envelope design is critical. Do this before *anything,* including the mailing list and how it will be addressed, is ordered.

21–22. **Stock/Color.** Not every paper stock comes in every color, especially when you want to match or contrast an envelope. But you can often print the stock into the color you want. It costs practically nothing extra when that color is a tint of a darker ink used on the same page. Discuss this with your film house and printer. You may be pleasantly surprised.

23. **Printing colors.** Use any color paper and ink you wish—as long as the message can be read. If printed in light pink and blue or similar tones, your project may well die before the very eyes of those too nearsighted to see it.

24. **Out date.** The mailing date should be determined by considering the audience to whom you are sending the invitations. How booked up do they get for the time involved? How willing are they to commit their time far in advance? If you're not sure and can't easily find out, telephone a few invitees and ask. They will thank you for your concern!

25–26. **In date.** When *must* you have replies to permit final planning for the event? Telephone (#16) key prospects a few days before the deadline to reinvite them or to confirm their acceptance. There's nothing like an actual human voice to generate response.

27. **Mail class.** Most invitations are sent by first-class mail. Use a stamp or a printed permit that looks like a meter. For larger mailings, don't pre-

stamp the RSVP envelope. But just to play safe, test your level of response by adding a stamp to every tenth reply envelope. Let results guide future invitations.

28. **Film house.** For routine mailing pieces, your printer may wish to supply the film. Whether you agree or use a separate film house, the proofing process (#12) is the same and is a production responsibility rather than an advertising decision. Where the two jobs are handled separately, thank those involved, and let them do their job.

29. **Printer.** Printing is also a production function. For major projects, insist on being kept informed. For others, let those doing the job do it without your help. If you are a printing novice, ask them to help you learn. Don't pretend to expertise you don't have: You do not have to know how to fix something to insist on its being done right.

30. **Mailing service.** Letter Shops work on schedules, too. Don't surprise them with projects out of the blue, or you may be blue indeed when you get the bill. Usually, anything can be done if you are willing to spend the money. Just remember . . . it is *your* money. Plan, stay on schedule, and save.

31. **Records/Reports.** What records must be kept? By whom? What analyses of results done? What reports made and to whom?

4 | Direct Mail and Database Direct Marketing

DIRECT MAIL

INSIGHT 18

Do not confuse "selling by direct mail" with some simple, magical profit generator called "Starting a Direct Mail Business." Selling by mail has all the risks, expenses, and probably all the costs of any other way of selling.

This chapter has three goals:

1. To help you create your own direct response mailings.
2. To guide you in the supervision of mailings done by staff or outside experts.
3. To give you the basic rules and cautions for doing both.

Because of its frequent denunciation as "junk mail," this chapter begins with a brief history and defense of direct mail selling. It then continues with some basic rules and cautions about what is likely to work—and what isn't—in selling by mail. The chapter concludes with specific guidance on how to create a direct mail promotion—always keeping in mind those basic rules and cautions. Four of these will be absolutely critical to your success:

1. The single most important factor in selling by mail is the list.
2. Test whenever possible. Treat every mailing as a retest.
3. Believe the numbers.
4. Know the value of a customer, not just of the order.

Help Abounds

Practically every major city in the United States has a direct marketing association that is able and eager to help you. Check the Yellow Pages. If you are unable to locate the association by this means, contact the Direct Marketing Association, Inc., Dept. DM Clubs, *Association Networks,* 11 West 42nd Street, New York, NY

10036-8096. Ask for the nearest club, and enclose a stamped, self-addressed envelope. Easier yet, call them at (212) 768-7277. Then join your local association. They will help you, even if you're not a member, but the continuing contacts alone are worth the price of admission.

In addition, there is the excellent how-to magazine *Direct Marketing,* published monthly by Hoke Communications. Call the company toll free at (800) 229-6700. In New York, call (516) 746-6700. On a more managerial level, *Direct* magazine is published monthly by Cowles Business Media, (847) 647-0771. For up-to-the-minute news, there's the weekly *DM News,* published by Mill Hollow Corp., (609) 786-4780. Read several issues of each one. Subscribe to all that are helpful. Lots of additional publications exist. As member of a direct marketing club, you'll get information about them, as well as the many new on-line sources.

How the Term "Junk Mail" Came About

In the 1930s and 1940s, a number of syndicated newspaper columnists had a readership and following matched in devotion only by later generations' rock stars and anchor persons. One of those columnists—Hahn thinks it was Westbrook Pegler—became infuriated when his very young daughter somehow was placed on a mailing list of purveyors of suggestive undergarments and nightwear. In his rage, he wrote several columns damning what he called "junk mail."

The story might have ended right there, except for Pegler's syndication. The publishers of several of the newspapers that carried his column greeted the term with absolute delight. They recognized it as the ammunition they had prayed for in battling an opponent that had just become a meaningful competitor for advertising revenue—the growing direct mail industry. Editorials denouncing "junk mail" appeared with increasing frequency, shedding tears for an overworked postal staff—which they forgot to mention also carried their own publications at an even lower rate.

Their attack continues to this day and has gone largely unchallenged in public. Of the dozen or so Letters to the Editor Hahn or Mangun write each year answering print media and talk show attacks upon direct mail, not one has ever been published. And our experience is typical of the industry as a whole. The only thing direct response has going for it in this battle is a history of success. Somehow, calling it "junk" has not been able to erase that fact from its users' business plans. The increased use of direct mail by Top 500 corporations has also improved its image, and in 1996, the Postal Service, as seen in Figure 4.1, has finally come to the defense of its very best customer.

WHAT THE PUBLIC REALLY THINKS TODAY

In mid-1996, according to the Simmons Market Research Bureau,[1] more than 130 million adult Americans—70 percent of the 18-plus population, ordered con-

---

[1]Statistics and figures from *DM News,* June 24, 1996.

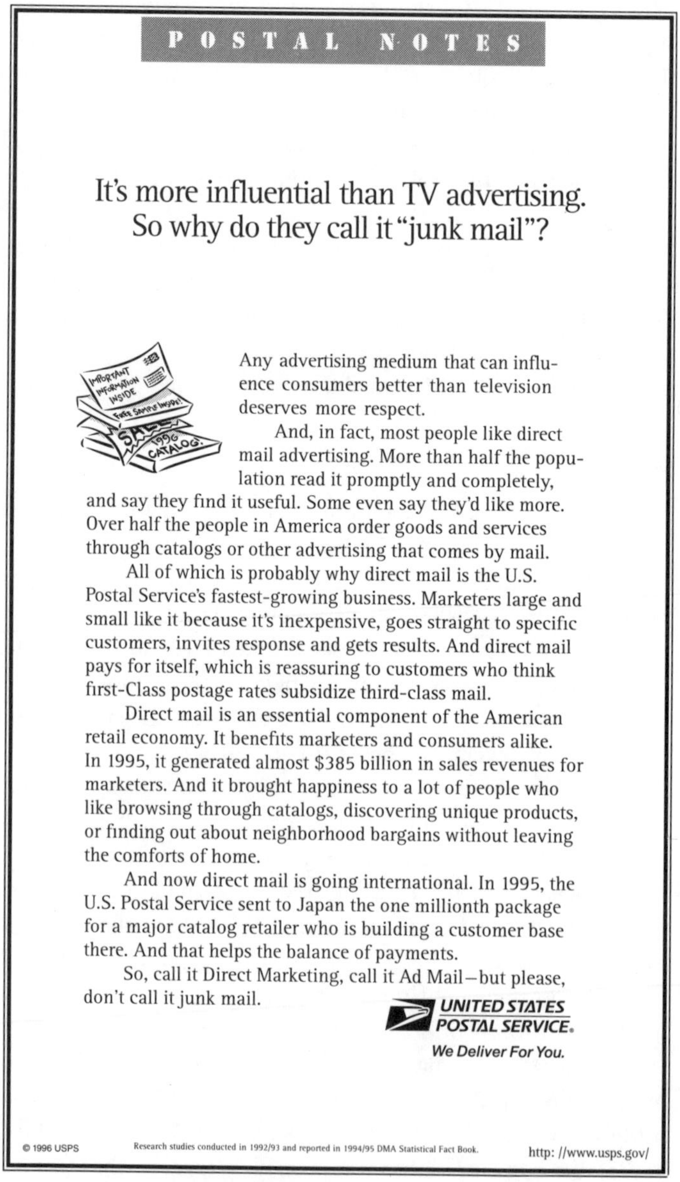

Figure 4.1   The 1996 Postal Service advertising campaign rises to the defense of direct response mail advertising, its very best customer!

sumer goods and services by mail or phone during the past year. That's a 20 million shopper increase over the previous 12 months! In just one category, consumer catalogs, 113 million men and women spent more than $38 billion in 1995, a 20 percent dollar increase in five years. Approximately 40 percent ordered by mail and another 40 percent by phone. Younger consumers are a major reason for the increases. Unlike their parents, they are more willing to give their credit card number by phone. But despite all we hear about direct selling on the Internet, less than one-half of 1 percent ordered *consumer* goods on-line. On-line selling and buying is still a largely computer-related industry.

WHAT YOU NEED TO KNOW ABOUT DIRECT MARKETING LAW

Although it cannot take the place of your attorney, the 1996 *Business Checklist for Direct Marketers* (see Figure 4.2) is an excellent place to begin. The brief, pamphlet form *Checklist* is described as "written for mail, telephone, fax, and computer order merchandisers to give them an overview of rules or statutes that the Federal Trade Commission enforces." Note that each of the 50 states has its own laws and rules, which this pamphlet does not cover! Produced by DMA, the Direct Marketing Association, Inc. in cooperation with The Federal Trade Commission, the pam-

Figure 4.2   Basic must-know law for direct marketers.

phlet is available without charge from DMA at 1120 Avenue of the Americas, New York NY 10036-6700, or by calling 212-768-7277.

TO CREATE OR SUPERVISE: WHEN TO DO EACH

Of course, *any* project may be supervised rather than self-produced, depending on the time, budget, and talent available for it. If you have no skill for doing designs or layouts, employ others for those tasks, no matter how "simple" the project or how much time is available. Whether you do it yourself or supervise, here are some basic rules any design should follow:

- Show and tell the readers what you are selling. If what you say and picture isn't absolutely clear, they won't guess. They won't buy!
- Use type that's easy to read. The less sans serif, the easier it will be to read.
- Keep it simple. The fancier the design, the more costly it will be to print it well.
- "Flow-Channel" your reader; that is, make sure that the mailing as a whole, and *every piece in it,* flows from an attention-grabbing beginning to an action-doing end.

These and other such "rules" are found throughout this chapter. Use them when you do the job yourself. But equally important, insist upon them when you turn work over to others. Do this *before they begin,* as part of your directions, not as expensive, time-consuming "client's alterations" after they've completed their initial copy and design. Make the rules part of your own checklist if they're not already included in the ones presented here.

What You *Must Not* Do Yourself

Two kinds of mailings must be created by direct mail professionals and should never be attempted as do-it-yourself "gifted amateur" projects:

1. A project, no matter how seemingly simple, that determines the survival of your business. (Of course you'll go to a specialist for a heart transplant, but will you try your own simple appendectomy?)
2. True direct mail "packages," such as the annual multicomponent *Reader's Digest* sweepstakes, giant "bedsheet" folded and refolded self-mailers, pop-up or other multidimensional projects. On any mailing that will cost more than $15,000, allow 20 percent for copy and design, and you'll probably be ahead in dollars and results. Good management includes learning to recognize the difference between getting something done exactly as you would do it yourself and having it done competently in some other way.

Doing Your Own Mailings

Help with creating your own mailings begins on page 103, but don't go there yet. The basics of lists, testing, and numbers that you must know for success, hold true no matter who does the mailing or what it costs. The next few pages explain them and how to apply them to what you write, design, and mail.

SUMMARY

- Focus each mailing to generate leads, to sell, or to keep customers sold on you and your product or service. Decide on one of these goals before you start. Let the others happen.
- Selling by mail is sales, not advertising. Budget accordingly.
- If you can't average at least $20 per response, you probably can't do mailings and stay in business.
- If you can't charge *four times* the cost of manufacturing or service time, don't sell by mail.
- When *everything* hinges on a successful mailing, use a professional. If everything hinges on a single, untested mailing, reconsider your options. What if the mailing doesn't work?

MAILING LISTS

The single most important factor in selling by mail is the mailing list. According to a July 1996 Dun & Bradstreet on-line report, other factors being equal, the list contributes 60 percent to the success of your mailing. Offer is given 20 percent; copy, 15 percent; and format (design, envelope, art treatment, etc.), 5 percent. The art and science of selecting lists lie in our ability to match the recipient with the offer—to mail only to those most likely to buy. No matter what we are selling—no matter how appealing the offer—if the recipient is not in the market for our products, nothing else matters. We're not going to sell dog food to cat fanciers; we're not going to sell chain saws to apartment-dwelling couch potatoes. From the *marketers'* standpoint, a mailing—as well as any other promotion—becomes "junk" when it is targeted at the wrong audience or when the quality of the mailing gives the wrong image of the sender. Note that the wrong image may be too rich as well as too poor!

There is no better prospect than a satisfied customer. The most responsive mailing list is almost always made up of your present customers and clients, provided that such a list exists and that they have been well served in the past. That is why so many businesses use such ingenuity to gain your name and address when you pay by cash. You're their best prospect for mail order, too. When, however, even your customer list *seems* to contain little useful information, some basic research is in order.

People with like lifestyles tend to purchase alike. The key to selling is to determine which lifestyles match what you are offering. There are thousands of mailing lists available through list companies and brokers. (Chicago's business-to-business Yellow Pages give 96 such companies.) The more we know about the meaningful characteristics of our current customers or clients, the easier it will be to find likely prospects by matching their customer profiles to ours. What's "meaningful" may not be a matter of common sense, so discuss with several mailing list professionals how they propose to help you find out and what they charge for their service. Then check the advice you get in a test mailing.

- For consumer lists, services exist that can match addresses with socioeconomic census data. Use the *n*th-name system of every 20th, 50th, or 500th name, depending on the size of your list, for a test mailing. You'll get a wealth of information on these people's lifestyles.
- For business and professional lists, existing directories can tell you everything you need to know—from an individual's specialization, age, income, family, and automobiles owned to a corporation's history, profits, officers, and credit rating. If a certain piece of information seems pertinent, it's there for the matching.
- Fewer than 5,000 names is not a statistically valid test. No matter how large the list, a 10,000-name test is almost always adequate.
- A mailing list specialist, preferably experienced with your type of business, can help you analyze your lists. *Before* you request such help, get firm, written cost quotations and current references. Check them out!

A case history. As a marketing consultant, Mangun analyzed the Chicago Field Museum of Natural History membership by zip code. As a result of this analysis, mailing lists, with current members excluded ("purged"), were selected on the basis of membership penetration and tested. This type of analysis works equally well for business and professional mailings, with Standard Industrial Classifications (SIC) replacing zip codes.

For New Businesses

When your business is new, without customers or clients, there are four possibilities regarding mailing lists:

1. Lists exist to fill your needs. Your market is so well defined that available lists are all you need to get started.
2. Your market is hidden within a larger audience for which there are lists.
3. Lists exist, but they are not available to you.
4. No known list exists that will fill your needs.

Let's consider each of these in more detail.

Lists That Fit

With lists that fit, your most important decision may seem to be whether to use the list as a whole or to start in with a test. But before you do either of these, check on the percentage of previous *mail order buyers* in that list, no matter what they have bought or what you are selling.[2] Have the sources of the list give you those proven

---

[2]The most successful initial list for the University of Michigan modern history series was mail order buyers of Swiss Army knives, according to its then sales manager, Henry Fujii.

direct mail buyers only. (Forced subscriptions to association magazines and newsletters don't count.) It's almost always easier to sell such buyers a second time than to sell nonbuyers the first. If no list of previous buyers exists—and you feel that you must sell by mail—test!

Lists That Hide

Let's assume that you have a special racket for overweight, left-handed tennis players, but no mailing list exists for such individuals. A broader "umbrella" list of all tennis players, however, is available. Should you try to sell your submarket within it?

The answer involves the same analysis you should do before any other mailing. Do as little blind guessing as possible. Do a market breakdown; that is, work with what you know or can learn—for instance, the percentage of left-handers in the general population and the degree of overweight seen at local tennis courts and clubs. Although this type of "knowing" is far from certain, it's better than sheer guesswork, and it lets you go to the next step: the calculation of testing costs and the application of test results as a predictor of complete mailings. A number of easy-to-use formulas exist for this purpose (see page 121.)

Lists That Remain Private

Many mailing lists are so valuable to their owners that they are never made available to anyone else. This is especially true of business customers and prospects, such as Collectibles for whom their list is their most valuable promotion property. General consumer lists tend to be less jealously guarded, for two reasons:

1.   Increased use of a mailing list tends to build a larger universe of frequent buyers. As different kinds of products and services are offered, more recipients get into the habit of ordering by mail, making the list increasingly valuable as a source of proven mail order buyers.
2.   For many owners of a list, the income from renting the list is a major factor in their profitability. Suppose a list of 200,000 names generates rental revenues of $25 per thousand 15 times a year. How much of the product would have to be sold to produce the same number of dollars in net income?

The fact that some lists are not generally available tells you that some people have been able to build them for themselves. If you have a list of your own, perhaps you can trade, rather than rent. If not, perhaps you can build your own list, too.

When No List Exists

Even when no list exists for a particular market, it's probable that the names are there if only you can find a way to get at them. It is possible that no one else has previously wanted just those names badly enough to create a list. But it's more likely that gathering the list would have been too difficult or costly. When no list exists, test using other media, including the Internet, to generate leads or sell. When no list exists, think very hard about the *practicality* of making direct mail the key to your selling effort.

Things to Know About Using Lists

Eliminate Duplicate Mailings Where Practical

When using more than one list, the possibility of duplicate mailings becomes increasingly likely. Through a computerized system called Merge/Purge, most of this duplication can be eliminated. But before deciding to use this program, discuss the *process and costs* with both a mailing list expert and a mailing service. Cost alone—lists, printing, mail handling, postage—may not be the key factor: Recipients may become so annoyed at receiving multiple copies of the same thing that they will consider it junk mail and pay no attention to it. Testing here, as elsewhere, will be the best way to discover what, if any, increase in response is achieved—at what cost—by Merge/Purge.

Some Legal Limitations on the Use of Mailing Lists

When using a list other than your own, the rental agreement almost always calls for *one-time mailing use only.* You may *not* copy the list or any part of it, or use it for any other purpose, unless agreed to, in writing, by the owner of the list. After testing, consider negotiating for multiple use of the most successful lists at reduced cost. Do not, however, pay for such multiple use in advance. First make sure the full mailing lives up to the promise of the test return.

Rental lists are "seeded," that is, they include a few names specifically added to discover unauthorized use. *Any response* to your mailing, however, whether it is an order, an inquiry, the acceptance of a premium, or anything else, makes the respondent's name yours to use in the future. With many mailings, you justify their cost by gaining repeat customers, rather than one-time selling of a product or service.

SUMMARY

- Nothing else is as important as your mailing list.
- Your best prospect is a satisfied customer.
- Your best noncustomer prospects are selected from previous mail order buyers with the same buying "profile" in the same price range.
- Predetermine what *you* are buying—customers or one-time sales, or both—and what each is worth.
- Lists abound. They are often very price competitive. Check them out.
- List selection is critical. Get professional help.

Customer or One-Time Buyer

Know what you need to gain from mailing—one-time sales or long-term customers—and evaluate the results accordingly. But beware of paying for customers and then giving them a product or service that reduces them to one-time buyers, or budgeting for customers while having nothing more to sell. Direct response may be the one way of doing business where you *can* sometimes lose a little bit on each sale and then make it up in volume—but only if you also know how to play *that* tune. Know what business you are in and your capabilities!

THE ABSOLUTE NECESSITY FOR TESTING

In direct mail, or any other kind of direct response advertising, the likelihood of getting things just right and most cost effective on the very first try is quite small. We can, of course, and often do produce profitable mailings on just one try. But *most* cost effective is most often the result of testing—*a process that never stops* in many direct mail organizations.

INSIGHT 19

Before performing any test, decide which category will determine the outcome. Will it be percentage of response? Average order? Quantity of response?[3] Cost per response? Quality of response? Something else? No matter which you pick, be sure to record and analyze all of these, especially the "Q Concepts"; that is, the relationship of quality to quantity of the response. Just because we don't get the answer we want doesn't mean that another answer isn't better.

In testing, the version ("package") that does best is called the control. Everything thereafter is controlled by (evaluated against) this package. Most of us tend to use "control" synonymously with "success." Its actual meaning is "the best results *thus far*," which are subject to change with every mailing.

WARNING! WARNING! WARNING!

A word of caution: When a test shows an extraordinary improvement over the existing control, do a retest with a larger portion of your list if possible. Don't hesitate to change to a package that works better. Believe the numbers; just make sure that they aren't a onetime fluke.

Test One Thing Only

Changing one or more factors in our mailings may give us a better response, but it may also have no effect or decrease returns. Even an increased response may have to be balanced against higher mailing costs, and lower costs may have to be balanced against fewer sales. It is quite common to test totally different mailing packages against each other—one or more quite expensive and the others somewhat plainer and less costly. But when testing to see whether *a specific package* can be made more effective, *change only one thing if you wish to understand the results.*

---

[3]One of Hahn's mailings produced only a single order from 6,000 prospects. It totaled $500,000, from the A&P supermarket chain. His client did not object to the paucity of responses.

Structuring a Test

Suppose that you have a reasonably successful package printed in full color (four colors) and offering a specific product at a specified price. You wish to find out if any of the following will be more cost effective:

- Changing the offer.
- Changing the price.
- Changing to a less costly two-color mailing package.

Since it takes a mailing of 5,000[4] pieces to generate fairly predictable results, you will need 12 different mailings totaling 60,000 pieces for your test. The reason we need so many, as Figure 4.3 shows, is that we are testing one specific factor in each mailing, yet testing that one factor against all the other 11:

- Each of the prices is tested against all combinations of offers and colors.
- Each of the color arrangements is tested against all combinations of offers and prices.
- Each offer is tested against all combinations of colors and prices.

Should one of the offers be tested at random—for instance, the four-color offer A at $15.95 against the two-color offer B at $22.50—one will probably sell better than the other. But you have no way of knowing why—whether it was the offer or the price or the color that was responsible for the increased sales. Nor will you know which factor(s) you might change for even better results. You seem to need to perform all 12 tests to get your answer! But don't give up on testing as being too complicated and costly. Help is on the way immediately after the next paragraph.

When to Stop Testing

If you go to Figure 4.3 on page 101, you'll see that adding one more price will add 20,000 units for four more packages. Testing envelopes against self-mailers, or first-class postage against third-class postage, however, will double the number of units needed—from 60,000 to 120,000. We'll soon run out of names or money or both before we run out of tests, so let's take another look at testing.

Five Ways to Approach Testing

1. **Test everything.** Test your product or service in exactly the way that was described in the last few pages. It's what the largest, most successful mailers do.

2. **Decide what might really make a difference, and test just that.** For instance, of the 12 options in Figure 4.3, test only the four-color offers A and B at $15.95. If one is successful, or close to successful, test the other two prices for the same package. Now test what has become your control against that same package in two colors. The result is that you've mailed 5 sets rather than 12. In other

---

[4]Many direct mail experts are convinced that it takes at least 10,000 names, especially for business mailings, when using more than one list and duplicates are eliminated by merge/purge. It is the net quantity that counts—what comes out, not what goes in!

Type of Offer	Test Package	Test Price and Number of Pieces		
		$12.95	$15.95	$22.50
Offer A	4-color	5,000	5,000	5,000
Offer A	2-color	5,000	5,000	5,000
Offer B	4-color	5,000	5,000	5,000
Offer B	2-color	5,000	5,000	5,000

Figure 4.3   Why a Three-Factor Test Requires 12 Mailings

words, you've mailed 35,000 fewer pieces and saved about $6,000 just in postage. For mailings where four colors might be perceived as an extravagance—to non-profit organizations, charities, hospitals, and so on—test two colors or one color first. But do try four colors also. Don't assume; test.

3. **Test fewer than 5,000 names.** When you *really* need to test how a large number of changes will influence results, and restrictions on budget, time, or names make testing 5,000 names impossible, test 2,000 names instead. Then take the top two or three results, and do a "real" test of 5,000 each. If you can possibly avoid it, don't go from a 2,000-name test to a "rollout"—a mailing of a much larger portion of your list or a complete mailing of the entire list. If you do not have time for a real test and results are important, either don't mail, or use a professional—and pray!

4. **Use telemarketing to test before you mail.** If your primary concern is your offer or price, give serious consideration to a telemarketing premailing test. Properly structured, it's fast, accurate, and the way to find out why someone doesn't buy, as well as why they do. (See Chapter 7 for a more detailed discussion of telemarketing for premail testing.)

5. **Use print media to test before you mail.** Find print media—magazines, newspapers, and newsletters—that go to the audience you want to reach. Check with each one to learn whether it accepts preprinted advertisements on postcard-weight stock. You want the best results from your test, and a reply card almost always increases response. That card, in combination with a toll-free number, should give you the best results. If card stock is not acceptable, but regular paper inserts are, consider an order form similar to what is used in most catalogs, preaddressed and, *if publication policy permits,* postage free.

How to Prepare Your Print Media Test
Let's use the 12 variables shown in Figure 4.3. Do the following:

- Check with each publication on the size, format, and delivery date for your insert. Newspapers will probably accept 8½″ × 11″. Magazines not only vary in page size, but usually require extra paper for "trim." If unsure how to handle all this, get help from a print media production pro.
- Prepare each test as an insert with all of the four-color or all of the two-color offers printed together. If you are printing on postcard-weight stock, for easy removal, have the card edges perforated.

- Use a Department Number to code each reply form. Use the same department codes for telephone response and add "M" for mail and "T" for telephone. Keep the system simple. If you're not staffed to handle telephone orders, see telemarketing services in Chapter 7.
- After printing, have the 12 versions separated by your printer or bindery and collated sequentially, that is, into the order 1, 2, 3, 4, . . . , 12. This gives you random, valid testing. What you must not permit is using all the #1's first, then all the #2's, and so on.

Testing Just Two Variables

If only two variables are to be tested, discuss, with each publication, the practicality and cost of running an "A/B split" advertisement with a reply card. (See page 26). This format, especially when also used with an 800 number, gives statistically valid results. If you do not have an 800 number, check with a telemarketing company that offers this service. They're in the Yellow Pages.

INSIGHT 20

Do not expect the percentage of response from a print media test that you would get from direct mail. If print gives you a clear winner and time and budget permit, test the winner in the mail against the two runners-up. Otherwise, use only the winner for the complete mailing. The least that you want to learn is the reliability of your print media testing.

A word of warning: Many professional publications build their circulation by sending multiple copies to the same destination, although not often to the same person. Persons within the same organization will thus get different versions of your offer! If they compare and contact you about the differences, *tell them you are running a test.* They'll understand.

INSIGHT 21

Various laws permit you to test different offers in the same mailing or advertisement. Check with the post office concerning current restrictions—if there are any—before testing. *It is good business practice to fill all test responses at the lowest price being tested, no matter what the final price turns out to be.* If that should be one of the higher prices, write the respondents who purchased with the lower prices in mind a thank-you note, and mention the price at which you will fill their orders in the future. If a lower price wins, congratulate those who purchased at the higher prices on recognizing value. Explain that the large volume of orders now permits a cost saving . . . *and would they like to order some more at the unexpected saving!*

Code Everything!

Create a letter or number code for every variation in response. You want to know where, when, and in what quantity it was used. Change the code for *every* variation, including tests and "rollouts," to check on the influence of mailing dates. It is a critical part of evaluating direct response success. Analyze all results (professionals call this *back-end analysis*), and get professional guidance if you are not sure how to do this.

SUMMARY

- Rented lists permit onetime use only, but responses are yours . . . forever.
- Test! Wouldn't you rather be 98 percent sure *before* you mail?
- Tests are expensive. Use them for what's really likely to make a difference: the list, the offer, the copy, the format—*in that order!*
- For responses to have predictive power, limit each test to one thing only.
- Believe the numbers, but have an adequate statistical universe on which to base your further actions. If not, validate the test results.

CREATING YOUR OWN MAILINGS: THE LETTER

Chapter 3 covered the creation of the flyers or brochures you might include in your mailings. Chapter 4 will concentrate on letters. Just as the list is the most important external factor in determining whether direct mail will be successful, the letter is almost always the most important internal element within the mailing itself. In our experience, which ranges from self-mailers to catalogs to elaborate multicomponent mail "packages," *every* test has shown the cost effectiveness of including a letter. Most of the letter/nonletter tests were used to convince clients who were new to direct response selling. But the most convincing test of all was caused by an accident. It involved a simple, one-paragraph memorandum something like that shown in Figure 4.4.

A mailing prepared by Hahn for Rand McNally offered, in the largest type that would fit on the envelope and cover of the brochure, the biggest discount that company had ever offered on its children's books. The mailing, to those on the publisher's regular customer and prospective customer list, was a resounding flop. Practically no one ordered. Then the mailing service called. Its staff had just discovered the 5,000 letters that were supposed to be included in the mailing and realized that the mailing had gone out without them! Would Rand permit them to duplicate the mailing at their expense, but this time including the memo? Rand McNally agreed. The result was as dramatic a success as the incomplete predecessor had been a failure.

Two case histories. Mangun has designed numerous three-way mail tests of letter/brochure package versus self-mailer versus postcard. For all tests, the letter/

From the Desk of
Bennet B. Harvey

Dear Buyer:

The enclosed brochure offers the biggest
single discounts we have ever been able
to give you on our children's books.
Don't pass up this extraordinary profit
opportunity. It expires on September 1st
and may never come again.

Bennet B. Harvey
Vice President

Figure 4.4   The effectiveness of a simple letter. Testing has repeatedly shown the effectiveness of including a letter in mailings. Above is a simple one-paragraph letter. It worked!

brochure in an envelope usually won. The self-mailer came in second, with versions containing a letter or brief note winning over those without. The postcard always came in third. This does *not* mean that self-mailers and postcards are a poor choice. On a cost-per-order basis, they may well be the best! As a method of testing a wide range of lists, cards usually proved equally effective at by far the lowest cost.

"High" and "low" information. Choice can also depend on what is being tested. For instance, Hahn used postcards to test offers and mailing lists for the *Cricket* children's magazine. While none of the card mailings would have paid for them-

selves, as *tests,* the "winning" offers and lists produced excellent results from a letter/brochure package. Postcards were used to explore lists for which the publisher had "low" (little) information. The much more expensive mailing became justified when "high" (tested) results were available.

SUMMARY

- Letters work!
- Practically everyone likes to get mail.
- Practically everyone looks at the letter first. Take advantage of that fact.

Writing the Direct Mail Letter

Practically anyone can write a good sales letter, provided that they follow the same two-step approach used by most professionals:

1. Decide what you want the recipient to do.
2. Decide what's most likely to get the recipient to do it.

The writing itself is often the easiest part. Where most of us go wrong is that we try so hard to make our letters sound businesslike and professional, that they seem forced and no longer believable. So if you're not yet a direct mail pro, don't write to the person who will actually get the letter. Rather, write to a friend, real or imaginary, who knows *just a little bit less* about the subject than your real audience. The friendship will provide the warmth in tone. The little bit less will keep you from leaving out anything important. Often, we're so afraid of insulting our recipients' intelligence that we leave out those "obvious" facts which show that we know what we're talking about!

The Two-List Approach to Letters

Start out with two short lists that you keep pinned on the wall, in front of your eyes.

List One

- What, exactly, you want the recipient to do.
- How, exactly, the recipient is to do it.
- How, exactly, you will fulfill your end of the deal, especially if the mailing is more of a success than you expect.

Based on a consideration of these three points, you may need to restructure your response to the mailing, especially as telemarketing becomes more important to the sales effort. And in case you can't believe that success can be more of a problem than failure, be warned by the following "success story."

Hahn's own worst direct mail "disaster" involved a business-to-business promotion that promised to "give you the world for 14 minutes of your time." It also promised to deliver the world—a handsome desk-size globe—through a personal visit from a sales representative. The sales manager, who had no faith in premium-induced response, agreed to the mailing only to humor the agency. There were 14 company reps and 28,000 names on the mailing list. There was a 31 percent response. That meant an average of 620 visits per rep and a like number of globes to be given away! It was the agency's first mailing for that client and the last one where they had to plead for permission to test for results.

List Two

- The benefits and features used to create the brochure, now to be used in the letter. If no such list exists, because there is no brochure or because you don't plan to use one, see page 70 and create that list now.
- The three most important benefits from the list. For each of them, find at least three reasons why that specific benefit is more important than the other two.
- A comparison of the benefits, with their supporting reasons, together with a statement of the combination that offers the most *for the audience to whom you are writing the letter.* If you can't decide which combination is best, it may not make any difference, but more likely, you need to learn more about your audience and how *it* benefits from what you are trying to sell.

You now have *the* benefit about which you tell the recipients and at least three reasons they should act to get that benefit *now.* With both of the aforementioned lists at hand, you are ready to write (or supervise the writing of) your letter.

The Three "Tells"

In writing your letter, do not try to emulate the pros, with their cascading cornucopias of compelling reasons for complying with your offer. Keep it simple. Use the "what, why, how" technique:

> What: *Tell* your audience *what* you want it to do. Translate that into a benefit *for them,* not for you.
>
> Why: *Tell* them *why they should do* it. Use the reasons you found to be the strongest *for them.*
>
> How: *Tell* them *how* to do it—*how* easy, *how* fast, *how* safe, and *how* resounding the benefit is if they act *now.*

The sample letters shown in Figures 4.5 and 4.7 can serve as models for applying this technique. They were written not for this book, but to help solve a very real business problem faced by one of Hahn's clients. Some background information is needed to understand the approach.

Background

For two decades, the Lectro-Stik hand waxer grew in annual unit sales. Throughout this time, the manufacturer had sold through retail outlets only. Now, for the first time, unit sales did not exceed the previous year's sales for the same period.

The decline was not attributed to competition, because, although a number of competitors had recently appeared on the scene, their much higher retail price and less sophisticated electronics were felt to keep them out of contention.

Assignment
The agency's assignment was to discover the reason for the decline in sales and return Lectro-Stik to its previous growth pattern.

Approach
It took them four weeks to come up with the plan you have probably already formed just from reading the background. It took another month to convince Lectro-Stik to act on the suggested approach—to *increase* the price, thereby giving retailers the same high profit they were getting from selling the competitors' models.

Because of the industrywide change from "pasteups" to computer-generated desktop art and film, the need for handheld waxers was lessening every day. With a shrinking market, retailers were attracted to the higher profits from the competitors' higher-priced models. At the old price, there was no *economic* advantage to the retailer in recommending Lectro-Stik over the other brands and every economic interest in switching the customer to someone else.

The new plan was as follows:

- **The strategy.** Give retailers and wholesalers an economic reason to push aside the competition and recommend Lectro-Stik.
- **The tactic.** Let them stock up at the current lower $45 cost and then sell at the new $59 price, which basically matched the competition. The $14 difference between the old and the new price was theirs . . . an unexpected profit bonanza—if they acted *now!*
- **The test.** Since the total mailing was less than 5,000, Lectro-Stik tested ten percent of the list with a simple "early bird notice" letter. The purpose was not to test the actual mailing, which had not yet been completed, but to test the appeal of the offer *to potential buyers who were familiar with the waxer.* The final mailing was designed to go to a much broader list requiring a lengthier explanation of the product.

The test was a success, as was the mailing two months later. The following notes explain why the letters were written as they were. Figure 4.6 shows the envelope in which both letters were mailed.

Notes on the "Early Bird" Notice (Figure 4.5)

1. Echoes the message on the envelope.
2. Another echo and the first explanation of "long-range planning."
3. The test went to current dealers only.
4. The first explanation of the new profits.
5. Reassurance that profits will continue into the future.
6. A restatement, for the third time, of windfall profit possibilities . . . explicitly on the envelope and in points 1 and 6, implicitly in point 4.

(Date)

SPECIAL "EARLY BIRD" NOTICE ①

Make $14 more on every Lectro-Stik Waxer ①
—$1 more on every box of wax— ①
you order now to sell after September 1st! ②

Dear Lectro-Stik Dealer: ③

• The list price of the Lectro-Stik Hand Waxer will increase from $45 to $59 on September 1 ④ ..our first price increase in eight years.

• The price of our 10 oz. box of wax will go up proportionately, from $3.50 to $4.50. ④

• Your generous discount percentage will remain the same with slight rounding of prices. ⑤

HOW TO MAKE A MINT! ⑥
ORDER WAXER AND WAX NOW, AT THEIR OLD PRICE,
FOR DELIVERY BEFORE SEPTEMBER 1. THEN, AFTER
THE 1st, SELL THEM FOR $59 AND $4.50. **YOU KEEP THE
DIFFERENCE** OF $14 PER WAXER AND $1 FOR WAX!

Call, write, or FAX your order now as part of your long-range planning.
We will continue to sell through our dealer network ⑦ ..so STOCK UP
FOR PROFITS and order soon!

Cordially yours,

Bill Fisher

Figure 4.5   Test letter sent to regular customers and prospects already familiar with the waxer.

INSIGHT 22

In a direct response, make your main point at least three times in *each* major part of the promotion—in the letter *and* in the brochure, as well as in other pieces that might be included. The *words* don't have to be the same; the *meaning* does.

LECTRO-STIK CORPORATION

STAMP

NOW...
MAKE $14 MORE
ON HAND WAXERS –

$1 MORE ON WAX REFILLS

Special Early-Bird Notice for Long-Range Planners

Figure 4.6 Use of Early Bird envelope teaser. The same envelope was used for both early bird mailings.

7. Additional reassurance to the dealer, because the "early bird" was asked to order so far in advance of the price change. This letter was mailed in May, the full mailing in July.

Notes on the Letter for the Second Mailing

1. Use this box device, called a "Johnson box," in one of two ways: (a) When you have a single point you wish to emphasize—in this case, the extraordinary profit opportunity—but you want more than just a few words with which to do it. The box focuses your readers' attention and tells them instantly whether or not the rest of the letter must be read. (b) When you can use a statement from someone other than the person signing the letter—for example, a note from the CEO of your company telling how important this letter is to the reader, or a plea from a local relief worker hoping we'll listen to the national appeal.

2. All three of your "tell them" reasons are in these three lines:
   - *What* you want is that dealers recommend the Lectro-Stik product rather than the competitions'. In this case, that can be implied rather than stated. Retailers and wholesalers aren't stupid; they know their profit on the waxer won't increase unless they do just that.
   - *Why* they should do it—in addition to profits—is detailed later on. Here, we concentrate on the single most important reason: profits!
   - *How* to gain the benefit is made simple and easy: Order *now!*

3. Personalize the letter—that is, address the dealers individually by name if that is practical. If it is not, note the welcome variation from "Dear dealer."

4. One of the oldest rules in direct mail selling is to make your most important point(s) at least three times. The theme is profits, but while raising prices and profits to match the competition has to be announced, that alone gives dealers no

---

Lectro-Stik
CORPORATION

(Date)

①

MAKE $14 MORE on every Lectro-Stik Waxer, **PLUS**
MAKE $1 MORE on every box of Lectro-Stik Wax
. . .you order now and sell after September 1! ②

③
To Our Valued Dealers :

For the first time in over eight years, inflation has forced us to increase the price of the Lectro-Stik Waxer and Wax. Effective September 1, 1991, the nationally advertised price of the Waxer will be $59 and the 10-oz. box of wax will be $4.50. ④

Order now for shipment *before* September 1st and we will fill your order at the price of $45 per Waxer and $3.50 per box of wax. That's a mammoth increase in your profits now. . .and a huge on-going larger profit from now on. ⑤

YOUR CUSTOMERS WILL PROFIT TOO ⑥
By featuring Lectro-Stik, you give your customers much the best on the market—by far! No other hand waxer gives them more than 2 of these 6 state-of-the-art features. . . *All standard on Lectro-Stik!* ⑦

1. **LEAKPROOF**

2. **TRULY HANDY**. Rolls on an economical strip 1-1/4'' wide vs. bulky waxers that lay down strips up to 3'' wide.

3. **NEW TIRES**   These should last the life of the waxer.

4. **SEE-THROUGH BODY** for instant wax visibility. A Lectro-Stik exclusive!

5. **ELECTRONIC HEATING** for precise control and long life. Won't burn out or fluctuate. . .as do some competitors' thermostats.

6. **"TACKIFIER"** is **NOT NEEDED** and **NOT USED** in Lectro-Stik Wax. Sticky tackifiers make it harder to position the bits and pieces that go into pasteups. . . negating the very advantage wax is designed to give!

⑧ Write, FAX, or phone your order *before* September 1st and let us know when you want delivery (before September 1). It's the profit bonanza of the decade! Do it now. ⑨

Cordially yours,

Bill Taylor

P.S. **TO HELP YOU SELL EVEN MORE, WE'LL BE RUNNING ADS — AS ENCLOSED.** Get FREE reprints with room to overprint or rubber stamp *your name*. Just write or call with quantity and whether to fold. ⑩

Figure 4.7   Letter to prospects not familiar with the product. Follow up to test in Figure 4.5.

particular reason to favor Lectro-Stik. It removes the lower profit negative, but what's needed now is a jump-start to the positive.

5.   That jump is here, a reiteration and amplification of point 2. In writing direct mail letters, all the rules are working at the same time—especially the ones that say to keep it simple, . . . make it easy, . . . and make one point at a time; but, where possible, make it in multibenefit fashion. In three short paragraphs, readers have learned (in points 2, 4, and 5) what you want them to do, what's in it for them (especially in 2 and 5), and how to gain this benefit (also in 2 and 5). Everything else in the letter will reinforce what you have already said.

6.   When possible, use a key word loaded with benefits to add even more value to your message. Dozens of words might have substituted for *profit,* such as "benefit" and "value." But if profit is the theme, be as generous with the term as clearly understood meaning permits. *Don't become cute,* however: Very few businesses find what they do funny.

7.   The six features that follow grew out of a feature-benefit analysis like the one explained on page 70. Notice how they let dealers justify—to themselves and their customers—their recommendation of Lectro-Stik without any mention of price. Note, too, that every point gives both the feature (presenting the dealer as expert) and the benefit (presenting the dealer as the customer's friend), in language that does not demand great technical expertise. When—as sometimes does happen—a feature and benefit are exactly the same, leave them that way. We seldom gain from making things more complicated than need be!

8.   A repetition of the "how to take advantage" information. Always put it just before the signature, no matter how often it's mentioned elsewhere. That's where your readers will look for it. Don't disappoint them.

9.   In the final version of this letter, one sentence was added immediately before this call to action. It said, "A preaddressed order form is enclosed." And don't think you are insulting your readers by statements like "Do it now." Repeated tests have shown that they will; or worse yet, if the exhortation is left out, . . . that they won't!

10.   P.S.s tend to be the best-read portions of letters, so they are often used to give one more repetition of the writer's single most important point. In this instance, the news of a national advertising campaign was felt to be even more important. The additional offer of free reprints is well understood by the industry and needed no further explanation.

Post Office Clearance

For your mailings, get *written* clearance from the post office as a first step, not as the last. Show those in charge at the post office a layout of the envelope or self-mailer with the key words in place, and request approval for mailing the items.

They will date, indicate "OK," and sign that layout. If they refuse, find out why. The reason may be an easily changed technical detail, not the mailing itself. When they approve, ask whether there is any way to make postal charges less costly— from changing the size of the self-mailer or envelope to changing the way it is addressed. Legal clearance is next. But keep in mind that there's little point in asking—and paying for—legal guidance before you've taken advantage of the *free* and generally very able assistance from your postal staff.

Always remember you are *legally bound* to any commitment promised by your mailing. Make certain that you know the implications of what you are offering and what you must do to make good on the promise. Don't guess. Know!

When planning a look-alike simulation, such as a window envelope's see-through "check" or a seeming legal or governmental notice, consider both the percentage you anticipate will respond and the percentage you anticipate will have a negative reaction because they have been "fooled." John Dewey's warning that we are responsible for the foreseeable consequences of our actions applies to business as well as morals. Fortunately, in direct mail, it's easier to foresee the consequences. Test!

SUMMARY

- Include a letter in any mailing you do. It's what transforms mass mail into personal communication.
- Be absolutely clear about what you want the recipients to do . . . and that you can handle the response if they agree to do it.
- Translate your self-interest into benefits for your prospective customers. Don't tell them about your wonderful seeds; tell them about *their* glorious garden.

ENVELOPES AND TEASERS

The "teaser" is the message—actual or implied—by which the sender gets us to open an envelope or to look through a self-mailer. Like the headline in our ads, its job is to capture our attention—to separate a particular piece of mail from all the others and get us to explore it a bit further. The majority of teasers, especially in business-to-business mailings, can be do-it-yourself projects. Others should be attempted only by professionals. *You* may, of course, be responsible for overall supervision.

For Professional Pens Only

Some mailings tease us with offers we cannot refuse, in giant type right on the envelope or the front of the self-mailer. Figure 4.8 is of this variety.

Other mailings tease with the look of important documents, legal forms, or checks, and the simple request:

POSTMASTER: Dated material. Please expedite.

```
SENDER'S IDENTIFICATION
ADDRESS                                          ┌──────┐
                                                 │      │
                                                 │ STAMP│
                                                 │      │
                                                 └──────┘

YOU
MAY HAVE
ALREADY
WON
$10,000,000!

Check Your Personal Entry Number and Other Details Inside
```

Figure 4.8 Sample of type of envelope "teaser" best left for pros. Note how much stronger the message is without the ".00" before the exclamation mark. Try it and see.

The Other 90 Percent

Set aside the mailings you'll assign to the pros: anything to do with insurance, finance, and banking; contests, games, and sweepstakes; clubs (for books, foods, or records), continuity programs, and negative options; fund raising and politics, and almost all consumer direct response. That still leaves 90 percent to get done. Most are business-to-business mailings, and you *can* do those yourself by applying some businesslike techniques.

If you are writing the mailing yourself and are not a direct mail professional, leave the envelope blank. No teaser is almost always better than *any* teaser that is poorly done. Would *you* throw away a plain envelope without any teaser—without even looking inside? Well, neither will your recipients.

If you do decide to use a teaser, here are some guidelines:

• **Make your message instantly compelling.** In larger companies, it's likely that it will be screened by a mail clerk, secretary, and administrative assistant. That doesn't mean it will be dumped. It does mean that the teaser message must offer a benefit *worth investigating* by the person to whom it is addressed. If there's more than a single major benefit, or more than one way to sell it, don't guess. Test!

• **Relate the teaser to what comes next.** Or relate what comes next to the teaser. When your readers open the envelope or self-mailer, continue the message of the teaser. Before you go on to anything else, expand on, expound on, and solidify the benefit hinted at or promised in the teaser. The fastest way to lose your audience is to remove the reason you gave them for paying attention.

• **Make it easy to read.** Be as creative as your imagination and skills permit, but relate the message to your audience. Be aware that art directors and interstate trucking firms *may* require a different approach, but don't take that for granted. Prepare several versions, make copies, and ask a dozen members of the group to whom you are mailing your promotion which version they like best. Then, after they have told you, ask them why they like it best. There is no *statistical* validity in the responses, but you should at least learn whether you are totally off base. You're not trying to eliminate the test; you just want to zero in on *what* to test.

The Response: More Than Just a B.R.C.

Busy readers, especially in the business community, often go directly from the teaser to the "b.r.c."—the business reply card or coupon. Before spending time learning all the details, they want to discover what the offer is going to cost them—in dollars, time, effort, or some other commitment. So many of us now do this from force of habit, that mailers load the b.r.c. with the key benefits. Usually, it echoes the offer, the guarantee, and the conditions, as in Figure 4.9.

The b.r.c. is so important that many direct marketing copywriters do the response card or order form first. It forces them to summarize the offer and turn it into benefits that sell the target audience. Once you can do that, you've solved a major part of the direct response problem.

To Card . . . or Not to Card

The format you choose for your customer's reply, whether a card, an order form, a formal contract, or something else, will depend on what you can get your readers to do and the impression you want them to have about you. For many business mailings, practically no one uses the response form you enclose; they use their own purchase orders instead. But don't eliminate the b.r.c.! It's what gets sent to the purchasing department with instructions to "order this." The more complicated the offer, the more important it is that there's a fully spelled-out agreement for your recipients to copy or to return. Make it easy. Let them Fax!

Lectro-Stik LIMITED TIME OFFER * Expires September 1

☐ YES! We want to get **an additional $14 profit** on every
Lectro-Stik waxer and **additional $1** on each
box of Lectro-Stik wax! Fill the order below
at the current $45 price for waxers and $3.50
for wax, and ship at our regular discount before
September 1. We understand that the nationally
advertised price will increase to $59 and $4.50
after that date and that our orders will be filled
at these new prices thereafter.

Figure 4.9 How to load a reply card with benefits.

• **Use a reply card** when the offer is simple and there's no need for privacy or confidential information, such as credit card or personal telephone numbers. An increasing number of businesses ask us to give our credit card numbers and signature on the back of a reply card. You have an obligation to protect a customer who might not know better, so *don't do this* in mailings you prepare.

• **Use an order form** when the offer is complicated, there is a need for privacy, or confidential information is requested.

• **Use the order form** also to survey customers and prospects. (Yes, even nonordering prospects will respond, if properly motivated.) This is delicate customer relations. Get professional help.

• **Include an envelope** when asking for payment by check or money order or when multiple pieces or order forms need to be returned.

• **With multiple-product mailings,** especially if the items being sold are similar, illustrate them on the order form when possible. (As advertising manager for Rand McNally, Hahn dramatically increased sales of premium atlases by picturing similar-sounding atlases on the order form. Being new to the company, he could not immediately connect product names with the stock numbers then used as the only way to identify them on order forms. Pictures made the connection instantly obvious. His assumption that some buyers might have the same difficulty, especially when a sales representative was not present to assist in ordering, proved correct.)

• **As a multiple-product (or service) supplier doing a single-product mailing,** list your other products on the order form. Doing so can have astonishingly positive results. Feature the subject of the mailing by framing it within a box such as the "Johnson box" used in the letter shown in Figure 4.7, and then list as many other items as you wish. Use very short descriptions if names are not self-explanatory. Thus, if you are a manufacturer of bicycles introducing a new model, you might also list other models and peripheral equipment such as helmets, pumps, and tool kits. If you have not done this before, . . . test! In our experience with a variety of companies, the results have been positive, but each universe of mail recipients is different. Always remember that with direct mail, you do not have to take anything for granted. Test!

Toll-Free Ordering

Give *all* the options you have available. If you do not yet have toll-free capability, use a service bureau for a test. Encourage toll-free phone—and fax—ordering, especially if your competitors don't, and even more important, if they do. The fear that you'll be faxed lots of advertising literature is largely unfounded. Most advertisers are too smart to make *you* pay 800-line charges for something *they're* trying to sell. For outside handling of toll-free orders, check with your direct response association or see the Yellow Pages. Suppliers are becoming increasingly competitive in price and service. Shop before you buy. Put your agreement in writing.

SELF-MAILERS AND REPLY CARDS

Think of your self-mailer as a large sheet of paper on which you are going to print and then cut out an envelope, a letter, a brochure, and a coupon or reply form. But instead of cutting them apart, you fold the sheet in such a way that, when unfolded, they present your message in a logical fashion. Figure 3.1, plus Figures 4.10 through 4.14 show a few examples.

Figure 4.10 uses a basic page size of 8½″ × 11″ or 9″ × 12″. Almost any printer can run and fold the double gate fold format economically. Use this as a self-mailer or as the flyer in a multipiece envelope mailing.

A case history. As marketing consultant for the Chicago Field Museum of Natural History, Mangun found a gradual decrease in response to the educational programs. One of the reasons proved to be the use of the same basic design, with only slight variations, on the announcement self-mailers. The cost savings proved self-defeating. Recipients stopped looking at what they thought was the same mailing. At Mangun's suggestion, designs were changed to reflect each program. Attendance increase more than made up the increased cost.

Figure 4.11 shows the single fold with return flap. It can be a self-mailer, a newspaper or magazine insert, or enclosed in an envelope as part of a multiunit

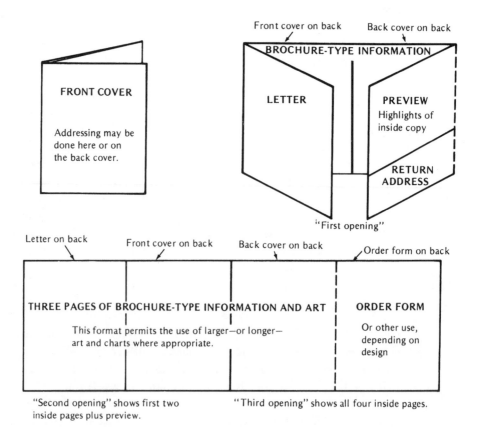

Figure 4.10 Double gate fold format. Use this as a self-mailer or as the flyer in a multipiece envelope mailing.

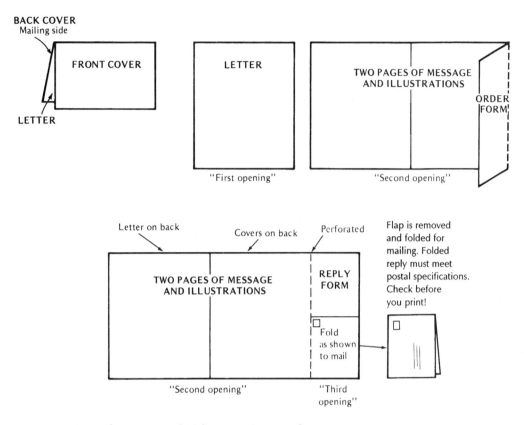

Figure 4.11 Single-fold format with return flap.

mailing. If the stock is less than postcard weight, the flap is removed and folded for mailing. The front cover can be folded as shown (it can even fold down to business letter size) or be used in its full $8\frac{1}{2}'' \times 11''$. The advantage of this format is that the first opening goes to a letter and the second opening to two facing pages—what printers call a spread.

The third opening is a 4-inch flap that can be used as a reply form when folded in the middle. Be sure to get the latest postal specifications on the size and weight of the paper used for the flap.

Self-Mailer Advantages and Disadvantages

The advantages of the self-mailer are its lower cost, the immediacy of its message, and its ability to "stand out in the crowd" of recipients' business mail. *The disadvantages* are that it may be less response efficient than a "standard" mailing and that it is often perceived as junk mail. Do not take any of these for granted, however. Test if possible!

The Triple Postcard

An interesting variation of the single fold with flap is the triple postcard, consistently one of those formats with "the most bang for the buck," in our experience.

To make a "dummy," or sample (see Figure 4.12), take an $8^1/2'' \times 11''$ sheet of paper, fold it horizontally into thirds, and cut along the fold. Tape the shorter ends together to make a single strip. Cut $1/8''$ from one end. Then fold as shown in the figure.

A teaser or brief note can go on the front cover addressing side (A). Currently, postal regulations do not require that this card be sealed, but check for the latest rulings before every mailing.

The back cover (B) may be used for your letter or other supporting materials—professional evaluations, testimonials, or any favorable printed comments. Many recipients look at the back before they check the inside, so use benefit-laden headlines or subheads to create and hold interest.

For easy folding, the reply card (C) is slightly shorter than the other two sections. Note that you do not have to use the entire panel for the reply. Postal regulations give you the option of creating a smaller card (check the latest regulations for exact sizes) with the remaining space—section BB—available for other purposes. When using the "postage-free" reply format, note that there are severe restrictions on what, other than the address, may appear on a postage prepaid return address side (C). With the smaller format for the reply card, area BB can emphasize telephone and/or fax service, deadlines, savings, guarantees, and so forth.

Figure 4.13 shows the second opening of the triple postcard. The messages on all three cards are now visible. Note that area EE may be used for optional mes-

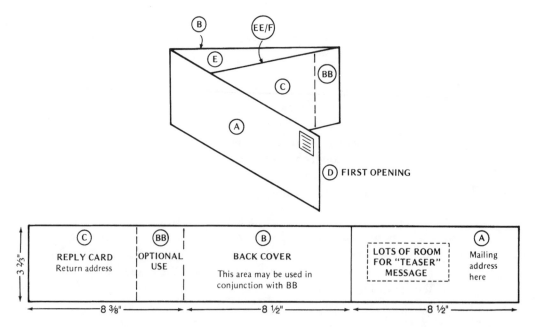

Figure 4.12 "Dummy" of triple postcard, front and back. (A) Front cover, addressing side. (B) Back cover. (C) Reply card. For easy folding, the reply card is slightly shorter than the other two sections.

Figure 4.13   Second opening of triple postcard.

sages even if the ordering side is extended to its full size *and* you use the prepaid return format shown in section C of Figure 4.14.

Use the space in portions D, E, and EE in any way you wish. It does not have to divide neatly into thirds. Let your message create the format!

In designing the triple postcard, it is generally preferable to use panel C for the return address and panel F for ordering or other response information. As the card is opened, the recipient has all the necessary information in one straight-line communication, following our very first insight: "Keep it simple."

Additional Triple Postcard Suggestions

Your triple card does not have to have a removable reply card. Design it to be returned with section C on the outside (Figure 4.14), and two, or all three, of the sections are returned to you. Make certain that the card will refold easily. *Very few optional messages* may appear on side C, the return address side. Check with the post office regarding regulations on such self-mailers. Two advantages of the triple card format are as follows:

• **Questionnaire and other research answers seem less formidable in the triple card format.** For ease of processing, limit answers to the D-E-F interior only. This has proven a particularly successful device when accompanied by a short

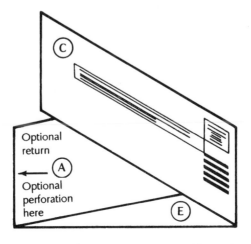

Figure 4.14   Triple postcard refolded to place return address (C) on outside.

explanatory letter and sent in an envelope. It has, however, also worked as a self-mailer. As always . . . test.

• **Lower-cost paper, rather that card-weight stock, can be used for the two- or three-section reply.** Consider allocating the same dollars as for card stock, but purchasing a finer paper for first impression impact. Before you decide, test the paper stock in the mail. Get paper samples from your printer, make dummy copies to size, and send them to yourself. Better yet, send a dozen to people you know across the country and have them returned.

• To make it stand out, use an oversize card. Have the card size somewhat larger than the standard formats. Discuss with your printer the practical aspects of fitting a larger design onto regular paper stocks. Take both a standard size and a dummy of the oversized card, prepared on the proposed paper stock (or stocks), to the post office. Find out the difference in mailing rates, outgoing and incoming, caused by the larger size and its increased weight. If either, or both, are a factor, find out the maximum size or weight that will not cause an increase in cost.

A case history. While a consultant for a direct marketing agency, the agency developed a two-way postcard format for a time-share condominium. The mailings used personalization from a highly desired destination. Analysis by Mangun showed that the high success of the mailing came from the recipients' association of the postcard format with travel.

THE MAILING COST/TESTING AND BUDGETING FORMULA

All calculations for the following formula must be based on firm quotations. The cumulative cost of all test mailings or other premail tests is included as part of the total cost when estimating profitability. Some companies and organizations charge mailing tests to advertising and final mailing to sales. The formula will let you do it either way.

INSIGHT 23

Your pretesting estimates are used to calculate the likely profit from a complete mailing—tests plus roll-out. But once that testing is completed, only the profits it predicts from the roll-out—*without including the cost of the tests*—should control further action. The money spent on testing is gone, no matter what its results! That is why some firms budget testing as "Advertising" and roll-outs as "Sales." The dollars are the same, but management tends to feel better.

The $20 Rule Applied

Earlier in this chapter, it was suggested that profitable selling by mail required a $20 minimum order. To see why, let's apply the formula given in Step 2 of the

MAILING COST/TESTING & BUDGETING FORMULA

Project Title _____   Date _____

Project Description _____   Project # _____

_____   Deadline _____

Overall Supervision by _____   Start Up Date _____

Test Quantity _____ Rollout Quantity _____

Budget _____ Completion Date _____

		TEST	ROLLOUT	
A.	**PRE-FILM**	$_____	$	✔ *These calculations are*
	• Creative Supervision			*required for EACH test*
	• Concept	_____		*or rollout with*
	• Design/Layout	_____		*differences in out-of-*
	• Copy	_____		*pocket costs. Note that*
	• Editorial Supervision	_____		*camera-ready art is*
	• Type	_____		*prepared for the test (A)*
	• Photography	_____		*and has no charges for*
	• Illustration(s)	_____		*rollout. New film may be*
	• Hard Copy/Disk	_____		*needed. Multiple*
				suppliers are less likely
B.	**FILM**	_____	_____	*for a letter shop, but*
				check it out!
C.	**PRINTING/BINDERY**			
	• All Printing	_____	_____	
	• Special Folds/Die Cuts	_____	_____	
	• Bindery	_____	_____	
	• Other _____	_____	_____	
D.	**ENVELOPES/CONTAINERS**	_____	_____	
E.	**MAILING LIST(S)**	_____	_____	
F.	**MAILING SERVICE**			
	• Merge/Purge, if used	_____	_____	
	• Inserting all elements into envelope or container; seal & mail	_____	_____	
	• Mailing service, in addition to the above	_____	_____	
	• Postage	_____	_____	
		$_____	$_____	
	TOTAL			
G.	**COST OF GOODS PER UNIT & OVERHEAD**	$_____	$_____	
H.	**MINIMUM ACCEPTABLE PROFIT**	_____	_____	
I.	**SALES PRICE PER UNIT**	_____	_____	

> ### VALUE OF THE NEW CUSTOMER!
>
> In evaluating returns, do not neglect the dollar value of gaining a new customer. It is a vital part of any evaluation in which getting customers as well as one-time buyers is your goal.

THE 3-STEP CALCULATION

STEP 1. $\dfrac{A + B + C + D + E + F}{\text{Quantity Mailed}}$ x 100 = Cost per 100 mailed $_____   (Eliminate "A" for Rollout)

STEP 2. $\dfrac{\text{Mailing Cost per 100}}{\text{I (including } G + H)}$ = Percentage of return needed for minimum acceptable profit. If more than 3%, check with expert about likely success.

STEP 3. Based on the likely percentage of return needed to justify mailing, modify "I" and/or test various options before deciding on any rollout.

three-step calculation shown and assume a $20 selling price with $4 cost of goods including overhead, a $2 (10%) profit requirement, and a 50¢ per unit mailing cost. The formula now looks like this:

$$\frac{\$50}{\$20. - \$4. - \$2} = \frac{\$50}{\$14} = 3.5714.$$

That translates into 3.57+ orders per 100 mailed to break even. Increase the price to $25 and break-even becomes 2.63 percent; lower mailing costs to 40¢ or increase the price to $30 and break-even is reduced to 2+ percent. Many mailings produce the 2 percent return; few achieve 3.57. Calculate as you plan. Adjust your costs where possible. Test!

NOTES ON THE DIRECT MAIL *CREATIVE* CHECKLIST

These notes are a supplement to the material presented in this chapter. They are not a self-contained substitute for that material.

1. **Purpose.** What the mailing is to achieve. This can include immediate sales, finding long-term customers, building a base on which to sell through personal, telephone, or additional mail follow-up, information gathering, and so on. If more than a single purpose is selected, pick one as key. Where else in life would you devote exactly the same effort to every objective?

2. **Budget.** The budget for direct mail *creative* stops with design (#10) plus outside charges for #11 on. How the total project is budgeted and what must be approved before creative design may begin are decided here. Note that #15 and #16 are for *approvals only*.

3. **Test(s).** What, if anything, is to be tested. Schedule not only the time allocated for the tests themselves but also for analyzing and following up on them. #4 must have this information to build a workable time line.

4. **Time line.** The specific time line for the creative process and how it relates to testing, plus the time required to satisfy all the other check-lists noted at the bottom of this checklist.

5. **Supervision.** Supervision for the creative processes, if such supervision is different from the overall supervision. If several supervisors are involved, decide who may and who may not override whom. Only one person can be "in charge."

6. **Audience.** All we can learn about our obvious target audience(s) and, possibly, new prospects we had not realized were there. (In regard to the latter, body odor [B.O.] was once invented to find a need for a strong-smelling soap practically no one had known they wanted.)

7. **Focus.** The specific focus (approach) of each test in attempting to achieve the purpose in #1. Most often, this is done by giving the copy-writers broad guidelines on which to use their personal creativity.

8. **Research.** If research is wanted or needed, what will it cost? How long will it take? Who will do it? Who must approve? And, most important,

DIRECT MAIL <u>CREATIVE</u> CHECKLIST

Project Title _____ Date _____

Project Description _____ Project # _____

_____ Checklist # _____

Overall Supervision By _____ Deadline _____

Budget _____ Completion Date _____ Start Up Date _____

MANAGEMENT DECISIONS	ASSIGNED TO	DUE	IN	MUST APPROVE	BY DATE	IN	INFO COPY ONLY	SEE ATTACHED
1. Purpose	_____	___	☐	_____	___	☐	_____	☐
2. Budget	_____	___	☐	_____	___	☐	_____	☐
3. Test(s)	_____	___	☐	_____	___	☐	_____	☐
4. Time Line	_____	___	☐	_____	___	☐	_____	☐
5. Supervision	_____	___	☐	_____	___	☐	_____	☐
CREATIVE DECISIONS								
6. Audience(s)	_____	___	☐	_____	___	☐	_____	☐
7. Focus	_____	___	☐	_____	___	☐	_____	☐
8. Research	_____	___	☐	_____	___	☐	_____	☐
9. Writer(s)	_____	___	☐	_____	___	☐	_____	☐
10. Designer(s)	_____	___	☐	_____	___	☐	_____	☐
11. Typesetter(s)	_____	___	☐	_____	___	☐	_____	☐
12. Photography	_____	___	☐	_____	___	☐	_____	☐
13. Art	_____	___	☐	_____	___	☐	_____	☐
14. Camera-Ready Art	_____	___	☐	_____	___	☐	_____	☐
15. Film/Proofs OK	_____	___	☐	_____	___	☐	_____	☐
16. On Press OK	_____	___	☐	_____	___	☐	_____	☐
17. Test Analysis	_____	___	☐	_____	___	☐	_____	☐
MECHANICAL CHECKS								
18. Editorial OK	_____	___	☐	_____	___	☐	_____	☐
19. Legal OK	_____	___	☐	_____	___	☐	_____	☐
20. Postal OK	_____	___	☐	_____	___	☐	_____	☐
21. Letter Shop OK	_____	___	☐	_____	___	☐	_____	☐
22. Logo	_____	___	☐	_____	___	☐	_____	☐
_____	_____	___	☐	_____	___	☐	_____	☐
_____	_____	___	☐	_____	___	☐	_____	☐
_____	_____	___	☐	_____	___	☐	_____	☐
_____	_____	___	☐	_____	___	☐	_____	☐
_____	_____	___	☐	_____	___	☐	_____	☐

Separate checklists cover testing & budgeting, film & proofing, printing & bindery, and letter shop mailing.

© 1997, Fred Hahn

what actions will you take on the basis of the research results? Start with the last point first. If the answer is "none," go directly from #7 to #9.

9. **Writer.** If you are the writer and are new to writing, do just one approach from beginning to end before going on to the next. Then base

the second approach on the first, the third on the second, and so on. Now go back and redo the first—and probably the others, too. You'll be astonished by how much you've learned and how fast you've learned it. This chapter gives you a step-by-step approach. Use it *every time.*

10. **Designer.** Direct mail design is a specialized art, so find and use a specialist, especially if you are a beginner.

11. **Typesetter.** For simpler projects, try desktop publishing—but only if your in-house setting meets professional standards. Professional quality typesetting tends to be the least expensive of outside costs.

12–13. **Photo/Art.** Not just a nice illustration, but a picture that does something—that moves the viewer to share your objective. Would the Sistine Chapel be nearly as much of an attraction if the finger of God were closed into His fist? Generally, use art for emotion and photography for fact. If in doubt, test . . . and always be ready to be pleasantly surprised.

14. **Camera-ready art.** Who prepares it? Who approves it? Who reviews it with the filmmaker? Who, if anyone, may change it, based on the filmmaker's suggestions?

15. **Film proofs OK.** If the designers (#10) are not the only approval required, the designers should at least be consulted . . . and listened to. They'll be the only ones to catch the "obvious" *design* mistakes no one else sees.

16. **On-press OK.** This is often a quite time-consuming process, but it is absolutely essential. If possible, send two persons: a print production expert who knows how—and when—to give on-press approval and one to learn how to do it. There's much more to this part of the job than meets the untrained eye. (See Chapter 5 for Hahn's near disastrous introduction to the approval process.)

17. **Test analysis.** Testing and analysis affect everything the creative people will do if they are given the opportunity to learn about it. Accordingly, share the results, no matter what they are. And be specific: It's hard to do better next time if all they are told is, "It failed." It's even hard to do as well if all they know is, "It's great!"

18. **Editorial OK.** This is the final authority on the mechanics of language, the house style, and the technical accuracy of the text, including stock numbers and prices. The editorial person or department sees and has final approval of the *final manuscript* and checks the *final type* against it, whenever that is ready. Make no changes in either one without editorial approval. Remember, there can be only one "final" version!

19. **Legal OK.** Direct mail and other direct response advertising are regulated by federal, state, and, by the time you read this, possibly even local, laws. (Sales tax collection is just one of the legal issues.) Make yourself knowledgeable, and if in-house legal expertise is not available, use your direct marketing association to lead you to where it is.

20. **Postal OK.** Your post office approved your design in writing, including any message you plan to put on the outside of your package. Right?

21. **Lettershop OK.** Your lettershop mailing service saw dummy samples of your package, told you they could do it, and quoted a price in writing. And the mailing package hasn't changed without their knowing it. Right?

22. **Logo.** Someone has actually looked at every logo, every address, and every telephone number on the mailings. And so have you. Right?

MAIL ORDER, DIRECT MARKETING, AND DATABASE DIRECT MARKETING

Database marketing is based on two criteria: (1) the existence, availability, and use of pertinent information on which you can base your marketing decisions and (2) the modification of that marketing effort as new data become available.

Database *direct* marketing involves exactly the same things. Its only difference is in the way it sells—directly rather than through others. For example, a mailing that urges you to buy by mail and makes it practical to do so is a basic part of mail order direct marketing. Exactly the same mailing that urges you to make the purchase in a retail outlet is mail advertising. Quite a bit more than nomenclature is involved in this difference.

As the introduction to this book noted, marketing concerns itself with "the four p's,"—product, price, place (sales), and promotion. In direct response, what we normally think of as promotion is actually sales—our advertisement and method of selling are one and the same. Promotion, therefore, is best budgeted and utilized for research to find better ways to make sales work. The distinction is arbitrary, but of value in (1) selling the absolute need for advertising to management and (2) keeping the research budget from skewing ultimate sales costs.

Establishing Your Database

Imagine that you are a sales representative with 25 key accounts. In your customer database or notebook, you keep the names of your clients with, as far as you can learn, their business reasons for dealing with you—price, delivery, quality, and so on—as well as such things as their birthdays and favorite places to eat. You'll note others on the staff who are important to the purchasing decision, and you'll note the "politics" involved in the decision. You'll try to discover the key competitors' approach to luring your business away and how you might react to it. This database is for clients or customers. You have an analogous file for prospects. Both of these information-laden resources are your database. The database is invaluable, but only as long as you continually *both* update your information *and* act upon it.

Now, expand this example to thousands or millions of names. The process still holds. But now your data are on a computer, and a whole new set of considerations is required:

• Which department "owns" the computer: Accounting? Order processing? Estimating? Direct marketing? What is the pecking order? Most systems generate data through order entry. Access to that information and to computer time for its analysis is critical to databased marketing.

• What can the computer do? That is, what is its capacity for receiving, analyzing, and acting upon each piece of information? If your sales efforts involve 1,000 different items, how much time and capacity are involved if you want access to everyone who ordered any single item? Any one of 100 different categories? 25 categories? Can the computer do the same for prices? Frequency of orders? Any combination of these? Can it add, remove, and correct data quickly and easily? Can it protect data? What are its limitations, and how does it fit into today's state of the art? Note that *your* computer is not involved with lists you purchase for mailing, but only with supplying in-house lists and handling responses. Purchased lists go directly to a mailing service.

• A Note on Style: Go back and reread the preceding two paragraphs—not for content, but for style. Note the many short sentences and sentence fragments. See how question marks emphasize the need for answers and action. Mentally remove those question marks, and substitute commas. You'll have an instant demonstration of the need to *keep it simple.*

What You Really Have to Know

INSIGHT 24

Limit your data to information you are likely to use. Robert Kestnbaum's widely accepted FRAT formulation suggests Frequency, Recency, Amount of purchase, and Type of merchandise or service as the key components. For psychographic components, consult professional help . . . but get a firm price quotation before you begin.

Determine what you must know, store, and be able to manipulate by computer to improve sales. What would you do with different kinds of information if you had it? Differentiate between "nice to know" and "vital for improved performance." In his autobiography, Sloane Willson, a president of General Motors, tells of seeing a "severely handicapped" person working in one of the plants. In a casual comment to his companions, he wondered how many such employees were at GM. Six months and tens of thousands of dollars later, he got a research report giving him the answer he didn't need to a question he'd long since forgotten he'd asked. Your computer will, if instructed, do the same thing—endlessly store expensively gathered information you thought you wanted but didn't know what to do with once it arrived. *Before* you ask for it . . .

   1.   Determine what will be done with *any* information once you have it.

2. Be open to and welcome unasked-for information, unwelcome information, and inconclusive information. They can be as important to your marketing as actual sales. Believe the numbers . . . but in addition to getting just the facts, consider whether it makes any difference to also know "why".

Database Direct Marketing and the "Four P's"

1. *About the Product (or Service).*

    *   Research for customer needs before anything is produced.[5] Research further when you get conflicting answers. (Yes, we want the lowest price. No, we don't have time for comparison shopping.)

    *   Research for satisfaction after the product or service has been delivered. (Is it what you expected? Are you satisfied? How might it be better?)

    *   Modify the product or service based on what you learn, providing it is practical, cost effective, and in your long-term interest to do so. And remember . . .

    *   Your concern as a marketer is *not* with profit, but with customer satisfaction.

APPLICATION

". . . no firm is going to find the future first if it waits around to get direction from existing customers.

"The goal is not simply to be led by customers' expressed needs; responsiveness is not enough. The objective is to amaze customers by anticipating and fulfilling their unarticulated needs. . . . Companies that create the future are companies that are constantly searching for ways to apply their competencies in novel ways to meet basic customer needs."[5]

---

2. *About Price.*

    *   Database analysis lets you produce a "best" price before more than your test is put into print, on the air, on the Internet, or is used in telemarketing.

    *   You determine that price based on *your audience's criteria.* It is the audience that makes the buy/no buy decisions.

---

[5]For a different-from-the-usual approach to learning and satisfying customer "needs," see Gary Hamel and C. K. Prahalad's brilliant 1994 book, *Competing for the Future,* Harvard Business School Press.

3. *About Place (Sales/Distribution).* Determine how the order will be solicited, how it will be received, and how it will be filled.

- Will you use only mail? Newspaper or magazine print advertising? Radio and TV? The Internet? Telemarketing? Package inserts? Out-of-Home? Sampling? Or some combination of these?

- Will orders be received by mail only? By telephone (including a toll-free number)? By fax (including a toll-free number)? By computer? Or by some combination of these?

- Will everything be shipped from a single location or from regional centers? Which will be faster? Which will produce lower shipping costs?

- How will you control drop shipments sent directly from manufacturers or wholesalers rather than by you?

- Should you do direct response only? Establish your own retail outlets? Sell through others? Use your promotions to help you answer these questions!

  A Case History. When Reliable office supplies changed from in-person selling to 100 percent database direct response, they did something practically unheard of in today's business world. They arranged for their sales staff to be hired by a major competitor, promising to fill no orders from the firms their sales staff had previously sold. The change to direct response was successful, and profitable, from the first year on. They recently moved from Chicago to Schaumburg, IL to handle the need for a much expanded operation.

4. *About Promotion.*

- Test your product, price, and sales approaches as requested by those in charge of each. Note that this testing is *not* limited to mail, but may—and often does—include telemarketing, focus groups, and other types of research.

- Assist the people in charge of the product, price, and sales in evaluating test results.

- Apply specified results in test promotions to validate research.

- Test direct mail or other direct response media continually, from minor revisions to totally new on-line approaches.

- Believe the numbers.

INSIGHT 25

Analyze every direct response effort as if it were a test.

---

5 | Catalogs: A Project for Creative Nitpickers

Producing a catalog is different from any other promotional project you are likely to undertake. It permits, but does not demand, copious creative flair, combined with meticulous mastery of mountains of minutiae, expertise in a half-dozen technical specializations, financial acumen to match that of a dedicated auditor, the human relations rapport of a soother of egos, and the management skills of a mover of mountains. Few experienced catalog producers claim to be able to juggle all of those at the same time during the actual production of a catalog. If you can possibly avoid trying, neither should you.

This chapter guides you, step by step, through the creation, production, and distribution of a *printed* catalog. CD-ROM and other digitized versions follow analogous creative steps, though production requires specialized hardware and skills.[1] Unlike some of the other chapters, it concentrates less on creativity and more on procedures that let your creativity have maximum impact. It tells you *how* to achieve superior copy and design, not *what* to write or draw. It assumes that *you* are the soother of egos and mover of mountains. If, in addition to that, you could take on additional roles, ask yourself whether you really should. In any major catalog with which we have been involved, just those two functions alone have been a full-time job. Where staff is available, assign what you can and do only what you must. And what you must do is assume responsibility for the job as a whole. Management is unlikely to accept as an excuse or explanation that you were too swamped with detail to supervise. No matter how much better you could do it than the person assigned to the details . . . don't! Your function is to manage. Do it!

INSIGHT 26

If you are new to management, it will be hard not to insist that everything be done exactly as if you had done it yourself. But few of us do our best as clones. Force yourself to recognize when proposed solutions, although different from your own, will work. That's what makes you a good manager—and a great soother of egos, too.

---

[1]See Chapter 9 for a more detailed how-to discussion.

DECIDING ON GOALS AND CONSTRAINTS

Management

In most organizations that use a catalog, its budget and over-all purpose must have management approval. Automobile dealers and department stores, as well as other retail outlets that have a sales force, are in a different position from vitamin manufacturers, food-of-the-month clubs, and giftware importers that sell *only* by mail. And what is the purpose of the gift catalog issued by your local art museum? Very much like a magazine competing for readers' interest and subscription dollars, the "mission" of each of these catalogs must be defined at the highest level and then produced with that goal in mind.

Marketing

Marketing is the overall activity that encompasses the creation and production of your company's product or service, its pricing, its sale, and its promotion. Advertising, including the production of catalogs, is only one—albeit important—part of the total marketing mission, which, like the management mission, must be incorporated into your decisions relating to the catalog. The function of the catalog in the sales plan is of vital importance. That is, is it business-to-business or consumer; traffic-building, mail order, or, if some of each, how much? It must be defined *in writing,* to avoid later "retroactive omniscience."

Editorial Matters

Someone must have final approval over the *technical accuracy* of the features and benefits presented in the catalog—that is, over *what* is said rather than *how* it is said. The exact authority of this person and who, if anyone, can override it, must be defined in writing.

Legal Matters

The law is quite clear. You are responsible for anything you claim, promise, and generally say in your promotion. Other laws specify how fast you must ship paid or charge orders, or get customer approval for delay. Get legal clearance while the catalog is still in its manuscript stage, not when it is printed and ready to mail! Learn and keep up-to-date on the rules through your direct marketing club and association news.

Copy

Copy is the preparation of *every word* of the manuscript, no matter who writes it. Assign specific responsibilities for information on ordering and your policy on returns, as well as for product descriptions—for the nuts and bolts as well as for the glamour.

Design

Design is a rendering of the visual impression given by the catalog. The design concept may be presented for approval in rough form or with as much detail and finish as the designer wishes. In either case, it must be finished enough to show how the major elements that make up the catalog merge into a synergetic whole. Among those elements are the catalog's covers, type, descriptions, illustrations, ordering information, and mailing envelope, if one is used.

Layout

Layout is a detailed rendering of how each page of the catalog and every other element of the "catalog package" reflect the design concept. The layout may be prepared by the designer, but it is frequently done by a specialist in turning design into a practical blueprint for writers, typesetters, artists, and photographers. Approval of the layout—not the design—is the signal for the start of the physical production of the catalog.

Production

Everything begins with agreement on a production schedule. This schedule is controlled by the approval process, which follows in the next section, and how that process fits into the catalog checklist. The process and checklist may differ from what is suggested here, but both are needed and best put into writing.

A SYSTEM FOR INTERNAL APPROVALS

The approval process is unique to each organization. Fight, if you must, to organize and limit the number of approvals required. Nothing is as frustrating as waiting for approvals from managers who assign deadlines and then do not find time to meet them themselves.

The approval steps in creating and producing the catalog constitute a process rather than a specific number of persons. Whether you do it all yourself or have a staff, the procedure is the same. No matter how large the staff, the project manager should be the person with the most advertising expertise. Assign this function first, to let that person play a key role in filling the other slots.

Figure 5.1 shows the steps involved in the approval process, from creation to printing of the catalog.

PRODUCING YOUR CATALOG

The production of a catalog involves three sets of activities:

1. Preproduction activities
2. Physical production of the catalog
3. Postproduction activities

Preproduction Activities

Probably the single most important preproduction decision is agreement on the date when the catalog must be ready to mail or otherwise be distributed. Every

Catalog Printing Approval Process	Assigned To:	Approvals By:	Conflict Resolution By:
Step			
1. Initial discussion/assignments	___	___	___
2. Creative suppliers: design, copy, photo, art	___	___	___
3. Production suppliers: type, camera-ready art (CRA), film, printing, die cutting, etc.	___	___	___
4. Design presentation	___	___	___
5. Copy: concept presentation	___	___	___
6. Complete layouts	___	___	___
7. Complete draft manuscript	___	___	___
8. Editorial oversight, proofing	___	___	___
9. Manuscript/Editorial reconciliation	___	___	___
10. Art/photography approval	___	___	___
11. CRA approval	___	___	___
12. Film (proof) approval	___	___	___
13. On-press (printing) approval	___	___	___

Figure 5.1   Approval process for printed materials—creation to printing.

other decision will be driven by that date and the inflexibility of the printing and distribution schedules.

Meetings

The number of meetings required for producing a catalog—or for any other promotional project—depends on the role of advertising and the degree of independence assigned to advertising by management and sales. In most organizations, this is management's decision to make. It reflects the importance of the project, the specifics of the sales message, the amount of time available for their supervision, and, probably most important, the degree of autonomy earned by the promotion department through its own performance.

Approvals

A number of signed approvals are almost always required to start production of the catalog. These include the approvals of management, finance (the budget OK), marketing, sales, and advertising. Other departmental OKs may be involved later on and are designated when the catalog is first discussed.

First General Meeting

Call an initial meeting of all interested parties, including the in-house design, print production, and editorial departments if they exist in your organization.

In the memorandum calling for the meeting, specify what is to be discussed and the decisions required, together with a *brief* outline of data that will help in making the decisions. The meeting should cover at least the following subjects:

- **Budget.** Give the cost of the entire project. Show costs for the most recent similar catalog. Outline reasons why the cost of the new one may be higher, lower, or the same.
- **Objective.** Will the catalog be used for direct sales, by a sales staff, for convention and meeting distribution, for public relations aimed at employees, stockholders, and so on? Other? If more than one of these, rate their level of importance as a percentage.
- **Theme.** Get agreement on the overall sales or marketing themes the catalog must reflect and their order of importance. For instance: Contemporary . . . New . . . Updated . . . Safe . . . Faster . . . Cheaper . . . More personal on-line help . . . Single source . . . and so on. This is *not* an attempt to coin a slogan, but to get direction.
- **Physical specifications.** Specify any general or special considerations that must be followed. Among the possibilities are fewer or more products to be shown, modification of the physical size of the catalog to permit its broader use and the inclusion of more or fewer order forms or enclosures.
- **Due date.** Set the date of the first use of the catalog. Answer the following questions: What use? Where? When? How many?
- **Mail date.** Set the date when catalog is to be *received* (rather than sent out).
- **Special instructions.** Get specific instructions from management, marketing, and sales for items not already covered. Make sure to differentiate between instructions and suggestions. Get the instructions in writing.
- **Approval process.** Determine who must see and approve the items covered on the Catalog Checklist if this is not already established procedure. In what order? Who has *final* sign-off?

INSIGHT 27

For meetings at which senior managers are to be present, ask them to call the meeting. Attendance will jump.

Let us consider six of these subjects in a bit more detail.

Budgeting

You will be starting on either a new creative effort or a revision of an existing catalog. Where only minor revisions are needed, such as updating prices and getting a new cover design, a budget is easy to specify. Even when a major new creative effort is called for, a budget can be estimated. Where similar work was done during the past three years, use that figure, adding 5 percent per year for inflation, except for postage. Get exact current postal rates and use that amount. (Figure 14.1 shows their range. If not knowledgeable about this, get help from a mailing service.) Where no comparable recent costs are available, ask likely suppliers to give you "ball park" estimates. Add 5 percent to those, too. Present both options at the first meeting. Management appreciates—and rewards—that kind of foresight!

A case history. In developing a new mail-order catalog for a security products marketer, a Chicago advertising agency used Mangun as a consultant. Research showed no direct mail-order catalog competitors, though quite a few carried security items in addition to other products. Because of client budget constraints, a minicatalog was developed and tested in both the consumer and business markets. The business market effort proved a success, and ongoing analysis established the small- to medium-size markets as best. *In successful direct response, research never ends; every mailing is analyzed as if it were an ongoing test!*

Objective

If your catalog is to be available on the Internet, do you have the internal know-how to produce—or even supervise—that version and to handle the response? As this is written, practically no consumer on-line catalogs are profitable. How important is it for you to be there? How much are you willing to invest in learning the medium? See Chapter 9 for much more.

Theme

One of the major purposes of the initial meeting is to come to agreement on a theme for the catalog, though *not* on how the theme is to be implemented. The latter is the responsibility of the advertising people.

Every catalog has a theme—that is, it conveys a message to its recipients, whether or not its sender intended to put that message into its pages. The theme can range from "We are better at what we do than anyone else" to "We don't know what we're doing" . . . from "Nobody beats our service!" to "Service? Beat it!" Obviously, some of these themes are implicit rather than explicit and not what the producer deliberately planned. *Some* theme is going to be there, so be sure it conveys what you *want* to say. Do not permit its accidental creation by inattention to *any* detail!

Physical Specifications

The concerns of senior management with the details of physical specification are likely to reflect the importance of the catalog in the marketing plan. The more critical the catalog is to sales, the more intense will be the pressure for direct involvement from the sales department. Unlike some of our colleagues in advertising, we try very hard to not find that frustrating. As we point out to our associates: "If Sales doesn't sell, . . . *nobody* gets paid." The salespeople may actually *know* something that can help. Ask them, and see how quickly they change from interdepartmental adversaries to cooperative friends!

Other Considerations

The other four subjects—due date, mail date, special instructions, and the approval process—are likely to be routine. They are covered at the initial meeting to make certain that the advertising people can proceed without getting caught in unforeseen booby traps, for example, an earlier than expected due date, special instructions you didn't get because you didn't ask, or a new link in the approval chain that you "should" have known about.

The Approval Ladder

Only one person (or a committee) can have *final* authority for any aspect of the production of a catalog. If your organizational meeting does nothing else, have it create an approval ladder to determine who must approve each step and who must resolve or dictate solutions to conflicts. In multilevel organizations, keep senior managers out of these conflicts. That's why the rest of us are around. Do, however, keep senior managers informed—not about the problems, but about their solutions!

SUMMARY

- Begin planning for the catalog with a proposed schedule and budget estimates. Conclude all meetings with a review of the decisions made.
- Issue your own meeting report. Spell out every decision as *you* understand it.
- Have everyone who must approve anything sign off on *your* meeting report.
- Do not begin the catalog until approval is granted or your report is officially corrected in writing.

PHYSICAL PRODUCTION OF THE CATALOG

"Producing" a catalog and catalog "production" have somewhat different meanings. *Producing* is all inclusive. It goes from the first discussion of the project to "back-end" analyses of results and what they mean for future efforts. *Production,* on the other hand, refers specifically to the period from the initial copy and design through printing and distribution.

Assignment and Scheduling

Catalog production involves nine major areas:

- Writing copy
- Design and layout
- Art and photography
- Typesetting
- "Camera-ready" art (hard copy) and/or "film-ready" computer disk
- Film preparation and proofing
- Printing and binding
- Distribution and mailing
- Back-end analysis

Some or all of these will be assigned to outside suppliers. The first order of business will be to find and approve these suppliers and to agree on a schedule for the work to be supplied. In working with either an inside or an outside supplier, the following insight should be your guide:

INSIGHT 28

The Laws of Outside Services
LAW I: Everything takes longer than it takes.
LAW II: Everything costs more than it costs.

Writing Copy

If your products or services require specialized understanding, at least the first draft should be written in-house. Outside writers can and do add their own special touch. Let them provide the sell that dramatizes your data.

The Function of Copy

The function of catalog copy will be to make a sale, generate a lead, and/or reinforce other promotions; that is, one or more of the following:

1. To sell the reader who is unfamiliar with your product or service (the new order).
2. To sell the reader who is familiar with your product or service (the reorder).
3. To generate a lead by persuading the reader to ask for samples or an in-person presentation (major industrial purchases, computer or telephone systems, educational programs, etc.).
4. To reinforce the sales message the reader has gained from a presentation or examination of the product (the auto dealership, trade shows, etc.).

For 1 and 2, the function of catalog copy is, at a minimum, to give enough information to let the purchaser order. This information probably includes an order number, price, and basic "hard" data such as sizes, colors, and materials. In addition, guided by space and policy, there will be descriptions, illustrations, and, sometimes, special inducements to get the reader to buy.

INSIGHT 29

Your audiences remember less from presentations than the sales force likes to believe. They also remember less of the written message than writers like to acknowledge. Therefore, for catalogs that reinforce a presentation, let the written message echo the spoken one, in emphasis if not in exact wording. By reinforcing each other, the messages make the whole become greater than the sum of the parts.

Show Rather Than Tell

For all four functions of catalog copy, show, rather than tell, the reader if at all possible. Today's audience is more likely to be visual and oral, instead of literary. This does *not* mean that the copy must be exceptionally brief; rather, it must be as succinct as you can make it and still do its job.

Train yourself to read your own copy with the mind-set of your most likely audience. Pretend that you have never heard of the product:

- Would you understand the message?
- Would you want to learn more about the product?
- Is there a practical way to give that information—in text or picture— right in the catalog?

Your readers are busy and frequently impatient. Make their lives as easy as you can. Efficiency and consideration always reflect well on your company.

Now read the copy with the mind-set of an audience that has been to a presentation. Have you attended such a presentation yourself within the past six months? Have you videotaped several of them—especially the audiences' positive and negative reactions to the points being made? They may not be at all the points you would assume just from *reading* the presentation back at your office. Nonetheless, the positive reactions are the high points your catalog should echo. The negative are the points your catalog must try to overcome *before they are raised.*

Finally, review your checklist of catalog imperatives. Do you have the correct stock numbers, prices, quantities, colors, sizes, materials, special offers, conditions of sale, and so on. Now look at your copy as a whole, and ask yourself the following questions:

- Does your copy sell the uninformed reader?
- Does your copy confirm the partially committed reader?
- Does your copy make it easy and practical to order?

If the answers to these questions are yes, you've done your job. If the answer is no to even one of them, continue to work on your manuscript until all the answers *are* yes. When it comes to copy, don't settle until you have it in writing!

An Approach to Getting Manuscripts Approved

Throughout the production of printed materials, getting manuscripts approved offers endless opportunities for confusion, delay, and ill will. If more than a single person is involved, the following suggestions will help alleviate all three problems.

1. **Appoint a single *final* approver.** A final authority is needed for each different aspect of the catalog—the factual accuracy of descriptions, numbers and prices, the promotional approach, grammar and spelling, the house style, and legal clearance. Determine who must, and who may, comment on each specific point and who, in case of conflict, will rule. Designate a final authority for resolution of conflicts.

2. **Circulate suggested draft copy.** Circulate the draft copy of the catalog to all designated parties, *except those in charge of grammar and spelling.* Their time-intensive editorial expertise should not be requested until all other revisions have been agreed upon.

3. **Negotiate . . . and settle.** Where conflicting suggestions or instructions are given about the same subject (for instance, differences in promotional approach), have the suggesters negotiate a resolution among themselves. But don't let the process drag on. That's why there's an authority in charge of resolving conflicts.

4. **Create a single master manuscript.** After, and only after, it is agreed upon, clearly marked, and dated, send it to the editorial people. There are likely to be conflicts between what they know is correct and what the promotion people consider necessary. Here, too, negotiation should be attempted, but in most instances, promotion will win. Of course, you do not wish to appear illiterate, but your copy must sell. Editors are not blind to this need; they often have excellent suggestions for resolving promotion and editorial problems. Ask them. Then thank them!

INSIGHT 30

A single master "hard copy" manuscript, as ultimately corrected and approved, becomes the original against which everything else is checked. Only one master may exist, though clearly marked copies may be circulated. Subsequent changes must be added to the master, with appropriate authorization noted. While "clean" (retyped or computer-corrected) copies of the master may be used, proofing is done against the original master, no matter how messy it may become with changes and corrections.

Design and Layout

Design and layout are not the same thing. The *design* of the catalog is the overall visual and aesthetic concept underlying the material presented. The design develops reader flow and gives your catalog sales impact just from its appearance and "feel." The *layout* is the arrangement of words and illustrations within the overall design. The design is analogous to an architect's sketch for a building, with the layout the later detailed blueprints for the construction crew.

Design Sources and Costs

The creation of design concepts is often assigned to an outside source. For important projects, such as producing a catalog, several sources may be commissioned, with the understanding that just one will be selected to complete the project. *Each of these designers is paid an agreed-upon amount for his or her work!*

When assigning this or any other project to a designer, be clear about what the designer is to achieve. Get agreement *in advance* from concerned in-house managers about the goals for the catalog. Since debate inevitably occurs on questions of design, agree on a final arbiter for both the design goals and the results achieved.

When there is more than a single designer, give *exactly* the same guidelines to each. If, as often happens in discussing a project with a designer, you modify your instructions or add to them, inform your other designers of these changes. Keep the playing field level, but remember who could help you think, as well as do.

Whatever the final instructions, you will want to see at least the following:

- The front cover, or the cover "wraparound" where the front and back are one
- The inside front cover and page 1—the first thing the recipient is likely to turn to
- The typical treatment of a single item on a page or spread
- The typical treatment of multiple items on a page or spread
- A one-of-a-kind page, such as the page containing the ordering information, an index, or a table of contents
- The order form or other reply device

These items should be presented in fairly detailed renderings, with major headlines shown in their suggested typefaces and colors clearly indicated. Have your more important projects evaluated by one or more focus groups of typical recipients. This is generally done by a professional Focus Group Research organization. For a less costly and quite effective approach, bring together 10 to 12 typical catalog recipients or users for a social event and have the competing catalog designs simply lying around. Observe your guests' reactions. If you have an obvious winner—and you usually do—you've saved yourself thousands of dollars and rewarded all concerned with a grand party!

The other pages may be presented in rough "thumbnail" sketches, usually one-quarter of the final page size, to show that the designer has resolved the major visual problems without any obvious oversights. To return to the analogy with an architect, you want to be sure that there are windows and bathrooms in your house, as well as a stairway to the second floor.

Bidding the complete job. Most designers will want to bid on the complete job, from original concept through supervision of proofing and printing. Let them do so, but get their bid to specify each of the following, even when the "package" is bid as a whole. *You* want the cost of each component for your own information and for future comparative shopping.

Costs included in the designer's bid
1. Original designs
2. Page-by-page layouts, including type specifications and necessary instructions to artists and photographers
3. Art and photography
4. Supervision of art and photography
5. Typesetting
6. Camera- and/or film-ready art, including all instructions for film preparation

7. Supervision of film and proofing
8. Printing supervision
9. Hourly or a full project rate for revisions and client meetings

A note about profits.   Outside sources cannot work for you unless they earn a profit on your projects. It is important for them to know that you understand this. If their billing structure is such that they make a small profit on each aspect of the total job—from initial concept through printing supervision—and you want less than this from them, be certain that they know this *before* they accept the job. They can then adjust their cost structure to permit a profit. Otherwise, they will adjust their level of commitment to give you "what you paid for."

INSIGHT 31

Once a catalog or other promotion project is well under way with an outside source, there is little opportunity to change suppliers. Think of yourself as a marriage broker who has to make both parties happy with each other for a long time.

SUMMARY

- Differentiate between design and layout before deciding on the same supplier for both.
- Before assigning multiple components to a single source, find out how much the supplier will charge for *each* component if, *for any reason,* you pull (remove) the job. Get the costs in writing.
- Remember the supplier's pledge: "My clients are my friends, and I'll do *anything* for my friends—except work for nothing."

Art and Photography

WARNING! WARNING! WARNING!

Artists and photographers frequently have different charges for outright purchase of their work, versus a one-time or specified limited use. Decide whether you will need more than a single use of their work. It is the least expensive of their charges. Whichever you order, get written agreement about *further use of works by artists or photographers themselves,* except as examples of their own work for presentation. Exceptions *must* have your written approval. Get *everything* in writing!

The conventional wisdom states that for catalogs, photography is better than art. There are some exceptions, however:

- Use art for highly styled treatment when impression is more important than reality.
- Use art where it's better at showing necessary detail, for example, for certain hardware, colorless products, or the interior workings of closed systems such as pumps and people.
- Use art for dreams that have not yet been realized. Unbuilt homes are a typical example.
- Talented artists are comparatively rare and expensive. They do, however, create a "feel" that few on-computer designers can create.

Unless you are an advertiser who uses art as a personalized signature, use photography for everything else. It gives a psychological as well as a visual perception of a "real" product.

What to Specify on Your Purchase Order for Art

- **The cost of the initial concepts.** If, for *any* reason, the project is cancelled or the final art is not assigned to a certain artist, you still have to pay the artist for his or her work. Not liking the concept does not release you from payment; after all, that's why a "concept" is ordered.
- **The cost of final art.** Specify an outright purchase. If that price seems too high, check on the cost of onetime or limited use—if that is practical. Negotiate!
- **The time allowed for delivery** of the concept and for final art after approval of the concept.
- **Any penalties for late delivery.**
- **Any penalties for delivery of final art that does not meet the agreed-upon concept.** (A personal experience may make this clear. An artist was commissioned to illustrate the Robert Frost poem, "Stopping by Woods on a Snowy Evening." Despite the poem's line that "My little horse must think it queer/To stop without a farm house near," the art showed a farmhouse—lighting the woods Frost saw as "dark and deep." The artist explained that he did understand the poem; he just liked his art better and would not change it. He did not get paid for it either. Note that this had nothing to do with the quality of the drawing, which was excellent, but everything to do with following an agreed-upon concept.)
- **Put everything in writing** and have the agreement signed by the supplier. Your verbal instructions alone are not proof that they were received . . . and very little else focuses attention like writing one's name upon a contract.

The Photographer
While there is an astonishingly large number of excellent photographers, not all of them are equally good at the same thing. Check their samples for the *type* of photography you hope to achieve, rather than expecting to find an exact sample. Selecting a photographer is very much like selecting an artist, except that you will want to work with someone whose studio is fairly close to where you work or live.

It's common practice for the client to be present while the photographer works. No one else is as likely to know the products and to keep the photographer from making "obvious" mistakes in what is combined for each scene or shot.

Finding your photographer.   If you have not already established a source of photographers, ask your corporate art director, your designer, or other advertising people to make a recommendation. Visit photographers' studios to get a feel for how you might work together. Ask those with whom you might wish to work to give you their costs on a daily rate, a half-day rate, and a minimum per-shot rate for repetitive photography needing little setup time. Get references and check them, especially for meeting deadlines.

How to order.   Give the catalog layout to each photographer you have selected as probably qualified. Have each quote a price for the total job, including an estimate for the additional cost of film and processing. This quotation is for *complete ownership by you* of all photography, including "outtakes" of film and pictures shot but not used. Specify that the photographer may use any of the pictures in a personal portfolio of samples.

If several photographers meet your criteria, have each one do the same picture for the catalog. Keep the picture simple. You'll be able to tell the difference among them. After reviewing their work with your art director and production director, make a decision on whom to use.

What to specify on your purchase order for photography
- *The cost of the entire project,* including photography, film, and processing.
- *The cost of a photographer-supplied art director or stylist.* You may wish to supply such a person yourself or have one supplied by your design studio. If the latter, get the studio's cost of the charges before giving the assignment.
- *The cost of any props or outside purchases made by the photographer.*
- *The time required to complete the job.* Specify the start-up time and the finishing time, not just the number of workdays. Specify what happens if *you* are not able to start on time or supply materials, as well as if the photographer causes delays.
- *Specify whether photos are to be shot for contrast or detail.* But first, discuss this with your filmmaker and printer.
- *Specify your outright ownership of all photography, including pictures not used.*
- *Put everything in writing.* Have everyone sign before you buy.

INSIGHT 32

There is nothing better than involvement from the beginning to give the feeling of project responsibility and ownership.

Getting Your Production Manager and Art Director Involved
On any project that will involve the purchase of design, art, photography, film separation, and/or printing, go over the project with your organization's art director and production director before it is assigned to the outside sources. Also, go over it with them before the completed art is actually approved. Their contributions can save you much frustration and, frequently, much money. Have the art and production directors:

- Review your *instructions* to suppliers. They will recognize when you've asked for too much . . . as well as when you've requested too little.
- Review quotations from suppliers, as well as their concepts and production layouts. They will know which prices are negotiable without losing quality. They will also alert you to problems a design may cause in the production of film or in printing or binding. You may elect not to follow their suggestions, but you will be wise to obtain them!
- Review the art and photography for their *reproduction* quality, as well as purely aesthetic considerations. Listen to their warnings!
- Accompany you to the printer when major jobs are produced. They will be much more demanding—and get better results at the same cost and within the promised time!

Finally, recognize the contribution of the art and production directors publicly. They will have earned it!

SUMMARY

- To show products, use photography rather than art, unless you have a special reason to do otherwise.
- Artists and photographers get paid whether you like their work or not, so specify what you need . . . in writing.
- Get your experts involved early, before work is assigned. It's easier and cheaper to avoid problems than to fix them.

Typesetting and Desktop Publishing

Desktop publishing, the ability to produce both layouts and high-quality typesetting from a personal computer, has revolutionized much of the production of catalogs. It is now *possible* to do a great deal of typesetting in-house. But before deciding to do it yourself, the following points must be considered:

Reproduction Quality
When hard copy is needed, how good is your in-house typesetting as camera-ready art? How well will it photograph or scan? Unless you can produce professional-

quality work, outside typesetting will be of *unmistakably* higher quality. Discuss with a professional typesetter their fee for producing hard copy from your disk. This often can give you the best of both worlds.

Design Quality

When in-house typesetting fails to meet promotional needs, it is most often because it lacks the qualities a trained typographer adds to typesetting. Some of this lack results from the use of less sophisticated equipment; some is caused by a lack of training. Likely problem areas include the following:

- **Line spacing.** How much room should you leave between each line and between paragraphs? This will vary, depending on the size, density (a lighter or darker version of the same type), style (sans serif or with serifs), and characteristics of each typeface.
- **Letter and word spacing.** How much room should you leave between each letter in a word and between words in a sentence? This will vary for the same reasons mentioned in regard to line spacing, as well as because one has to make a subjective judgment about legibility. Contemporary typography tends to leave little such room; that is, it is "set tight." Your older, 50-plus reader will find a "looser" setting easier to read. Know your audience and act accordingly.
- **Flexibility.** Find the style you want within a given typeface—ultralight to ultrabold, regular, italics, small and large capitals, and so on. With true computer-generated typesetting, this is unlikely to be a problem; most so-called desktop systems, on the other hand, are quite limited. Figure 5.2 shows and explains eight professionally set typefaces used by leading designers for catalogs and other advertising projects.
- **Staffing.** Who can take over when trained in-house personnel are on vacation, ill, absent for some other reason, get fired, or quit in the middle of a rush project?

Some Typesetting Considerations

The more important the project, the more critical is the first impression of its product. Therefore, lean toward outside, professional typesetting.

WARNING! WARNING! WARNING!

Today's technology permits almost anyone to proclaim themselves a typesetter/ typographer. Before using an unfamiliar outside source, ask about their employees' training and ask for references and samples. You want a *typographer,* the typesetting equivalent of an art director or designer. Typesetting without typography can now be done in-house.

This is 10-point Bembo Roman, often chosen for its suggestion of tradition. First designed in Italy in 1495, it was revived in 1929. *As you can see, Bembo Italic projects an image of grace and refinement.* BEMBO IS OFTEN USED WITH SMALL CAPS AND OLDSTYLE FIGURES, SUCH AS 1234567890. It is frequently employed in annual reports and publications of nonprofit organizations.

This is 10-point Garamond 3 Roman, preferred for its classic feel. It was designed in France during the sixteenth century and bears its creator's name. *Garamond 3 Italic, like Bembo Italic, is graceful and refined.* IT ALSO ENJOYS A COMPLEMENT OF SMALL CAPS AND OLDSTYLE FIGURES, SUCH AS 1234567890, IN ADDITION TO THE NORMAL 1234567890. It is frequently used in university and hospital publications that solicit contributions from alumni or philanthropists.

This is 10-point Sabon Roman, which was designed in the 1920s but is based on Garamond, with much of the same charm. *Sabon Italic differs only slightly, yet perceptibly, from Bembo Italic.* Designers often use Sabon as a substitute for Bembo or Garamond for a change of pace.

This is 10-point Bodoni Roman, classified as "modern," with its distinctive slab serifs and sharp contrasts. *Bodoni Italic is dignified and not at all flowery.* First designed during the Italian Renaissance, Bodoni was all the rage in the earlier part of this century and is now making a comeback in annual reports and high-quality newsletters.

This is 10-point ITC Berkeley Oldstyle Book, based on a 1938 design, and often selected for its elegant details. *ITC Berkeley Oldstyle Book Italic is even more detailed, as evident on the Q, & and z.* The face is sometimes used in advertising for a less subdued traditional look, and sometimes in brochures and other shorter publications.

This is 10-point Palatino Roman, a more modern serif face. Its contemporary feel comes from the taller x-height on its lowercase letters and the wider feel of its upper case. *Palatino Italic lends a touch of elegance when needed for emphasis or titles.* Palatino can be used for anything from newsletters to fine art books.

This is 10-point Futura Extra Black Condensed, often chosen for its excessive boldness. Previously thought suitable for headlines only, it is now sometimes used in text to achieve a radically modern feel. At this size, it requires additional letterspace to be readable. The face has been used in invitations to art gallery openings and nightclubs, for example.

This is 10-point Univers 55, often chosen for its sans serif simplicity and its subtle character. That subtle character differentiates it from Helvetica (not shown), whose ubiquity from train platforms to instruction manuals renders it undistinguished. Univers is less blocky than Helvetica, yet just as consistent.

Figure 5.2 Eight currently popular typefaces used by leading designers for catalogs and other advertising projects. (The examples and explanations are from Paul Baker Typography, Inc., Evanston, IL.)

Your less important projects have a cumulative impact that is just as great and just as profit or result sensitive as your most important ones. *Everything* that bears your name represents *you* and is the only messenger of that moment.

✓ Less important? Yes.

✓ Unimportant? Never!

Typefaces

Try to limit the number of typefaces used *in the body* of the catalog to one or two. There are so many variations available *within* each face, that creativity won't suffer. In addition to the obvious changes in the size of the type and the use of standard italics or boldface, computer typesetting systems give you practically unlimited degrees of boldness and styles that can have dramatic impact. Changing the amount of space between lines and between paragraphs, indenting or not indenting paragraphs, making all lines of uniform length ("justified") or letting the margins fall where they may (ragged right; very seldom, ragged left), and the use of capitals for *short* headlines are useful devices.

Serif vs. Sans Serif Type

Sans serif (square) type is harder for most adults to read than type with serifs (the little flourishes at the ends of each letter, as in the type in this book). The more sans serif type there is in a document, the more difficult it is to read. Hundreds of studies on the legibility of type verify this rule, and—to our knowledge—not a single study contradicts it. Many *designers* suggest sans serif because of its design-like, chiseled look. Let what you learn in this chapter guide you before you agree.

Costs

To give quotations on typesetting, your typographer/typesetter must have from you a reasonable estimate of both the length of the manuscript and its degree of difficulty. For catalogs, it is best to wait until you have a completed layout that shows both of these. If you must estimate in advance, find the cost of a similar project and add 10 percent (last year's catalog price, plus 10 percent), plus an estimate for any additional length or difficulty.

Typesetters estimate original setting costs based on the number of lines and the number of changes in typeface and style within a copy block (another reason for keeping it simple!). After the type has been set, they charge for client-ordered changes on either an hourly rate or a rate reflecting the number of lines corrected. There is always a minimum cost just to put the job into production—to take it from storage, set up hardware and software to work on the specified project, make the changes or corrections, and return the job to storage. That cost is there whether you change just one comma to a semicolon or whether you change every other word on the page. Typesetters do not charge for their own mistakes, called typos or PEs (printer's errors), but only for *client* changes and alterations.

In getting quotations for lengthy typesetting jobs, get the costs for setting with no client changes and the formulas for changes in 5 percent and 10 percent of the lines (i.e., 32 pages times 35 lines per page, or 1,120 lines, with 56 lines corrected for 5%), and so forth. Since you will probably have two or three sets of corrections, estimate those costs also. Get the agreed-upon pricing structure in writing before you assign the work.

Chapter 1 also presented a discussion of typesetting beginning on page 20.

SUMMARY

- Typeset in-house only if you have the right equipment and personnel. Either one alone is not enough.
- Find and use a typographer you trust, whether you set in-house or out. (It's OK to battle with your typographers, but usually they should win.)
- Get estimates that include more changes than you know you're going to make. You'll still be too low.

Camera-Ready Art

In nontechnical terms, practically everything that is to be printed must either be prepared or changed into a particular computer format or, as in the case of art, "scanned" (computer photographed) to get it ready for making film and plates. In its simplest form, this "photographing" is an automatic process such as the one used on a Xerox™ copy machine. The Xeroxed copies are the final printed pieces. In more complicated printing, right up to multicolor catalogs, elements from a variety of sources may have to be brought together on a single page. For instance, you may wish to combine drawings, photographs, type, tints, and reverses on a page. This was, until the mid-1990s, created via a montage-type system called a "pasteup." In an almost overnight computer revolution, it is now done with desktop typesetting and picture-scanning and art-creating equipment to produce "Quark-Express Disks" for the filmmaker and "copy board" proofs to let you check what the disks contain.

Copy Board

When disk material is combined with additional art—for instance, when disks have copy only—each copy board shows everything, in position, that will appear on the printed page. An overlay holds the instructions that tell the filmmaker *exactly* how to put all the pieces together. Even when all the material exists in an electronic file, the copy boards accompany it for ongoing checking.

For multipage projects such as catalogs, copy boards are prepared as "double-page spreads" or "facing-page spreads."[2] One important requirement of the copy boards is that they have a system for defining the exact outer limits of each page and that this system be consistent throughout the project. A common way of doing this is through *crosshatches* at the four corners. They look like this:

---

[2]The two terms mean the same thing and are interchangeable. They are also redundant, since a "spread" is defined as two facing pages. Verbal habits die hard—if ever.

There are two reasons for using such a system:

1. When more than a single color of ink is put onto a page, each color is prepared as a separate piece of film and is later transferred to its own printing plate. The crosshatches are the printer's guide for superimposing the colors on top of each other during the actual printing—a task called "keeping the job in register."

2. While the design and production are *prepared* as facing pages (pages 2–3 together, 4–5 together, etc.), no project of five or more pages can *print* that way. Instead, the filmmaker computer separates the filmed pages and rearranges them in the order they will be printed, so that a simple eight-page film may look like Figure 5.3.

In the rearranged sequence for printing, the sum of the page numbers of any two facing pages is always one more than the total number of pages being printed. Thus, the page numbers of each of the facing 8-page spreads totals 9. In a 16-page unit it will total 17, and in a 32-page unit—the largest most printers can produce—it will total 33. That your film agrees with this rule is one more check you can make without having to be an expert . . . and should make, even if you are.

Camera-Ready Art
When camera-ready art is used, instructions are put on a sheet of transparent paper that is fastened *securely* to the edge of each copy board, covering the work to be scanned. Use this sheet to give detailed instructions about colors, the placement or treatment of art and photography, items that need special handling, or problems you wish to call to the attention of the filmmaker with pleas for help or requests to "use your best judgment." *Do not* write directly on top of anything that is to be

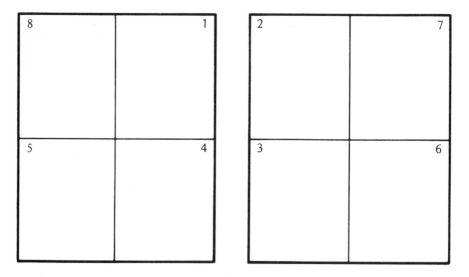

Figure 5.3   Eight-page film may look like this.

scanned. Any impression made by the pressure of your writing will be reproduced on the film! Where possible, place an X in the spot to be noted, circle the X, and draw a line—very lightly—from the circled X into the margin. That's where you write your instructions.

Approving the camera-ready art.   This final art is the last chance you'll have to make changes without adding very expensive film costs. Be prepared for the possibility that a number of your colleagues will want to make changes *now,* so give them *copies* clearly marked "FINAL CHECK BEFORE PRINTING." (No one touches the *originals* except you!) You may need a final FINAL check from the editorial people, with a separate final check on all pricing. If not, at least make certain that no prices have changed since the previous approval. Final legal, managerial, and departmental readings will have been set by policy, as will the need for a statement such as "Pricing guaranteed through (date)," or "Pricing subject to change without notice."

As always, get approvals and requests for changes in writing. This is the time to differentiate between the changes people would like and what they really need!

SUMMARY

- Treat the camera-ready art as if it were a valuable original. It is!
- Write all instructions on the overlay, and then go over *each one* with the filmmaker. It's a great review and a revelation about nomenclature.

Film Separation and Proofing

The following explanation, though somewhat simplified, is essentially accurate. Additional information on film separation and proofing, including a checklist, is given in Chapter 14.

Modern printing is a process in which various colors can be placed on paper in one of two ways:

1. Special colors can be printed one at a time or in combination using inks made up just for the project at hand. Thousands of such colors exist, and others can be created at will.
2. More commonly—especially for the reproduction of materials that were in color as originals—colors are reproduced by combining just four inks that are specific tones of magenta (red), cyan (blue), black, and yellow. These are the "process colors" used in "full-color" process printing. Almost all full-color catalogs and other promotional materials are printed this way.

From Final Art to Film

"Final art" is everything that is used to put together an ad or printed page, including its type and pictures. For multicolor printing until the mid-1980s, film was prepared by special cameras. Today, the same work is done by laser scanners or computer-generated, digitized color separation. They, as with film, "see" the original work as shades of red, yellow, blue, and black. The recombining of those four colors is the printing process. However, depending on the original, some of what the human eye sees may not be captured exactly by this color separation system. This seldom is a problem.

INSIGHT 33

Discuss the capabilities—and limitations—of their separation process with your "color separator" film supplier before art or photography is assigned. It's a lot easier and cheaper than trying to "fix" the material after it's delivered!

Stripping and Contacting.   In "stripping," the filmmaker takes two or more pieces of film and tapes them together. We can think of this as a "film pasteup." Stripping can also be used to move elements closer together or place them farther apart after they have been transferred to film.

"Contacting" means that a film—original or itself a copy—is copied. The "original" for that project is its "first-generation" film. The copy is "second generation." Both these processes are essentially obsolete. But they are still done where the illustrations are available only on the film, or there are other reasons for an exact match of the original.

Digitized Film Duplication

A huge advantage of digitized original art is that you can *always* generate and modify another "first-generation" film. You can even change the appearance of the art to give it a fresh look. And the problem of film storage is moved from warehouses to closets. As with other critical records, be sure to keep a backup copy disk in a separate location. Once a year decide what's worth keeping. Review everything. Have a Dump Party!

INSIGHT 34

Accidents can happen anytime anyone works with film. So don't just check your own corrections—check *everything*. But don't change anything unless *absolutely* necessary. Correcting film is costly and requires equally careful rechecking every time.

The Printer's Guide

The proof provided by the color separator is marked "OK for printing" or "OK as corrected" (note the difference!), signed *by the advertiser,* and dated. This accompanies the film sent to the printer. It becomes the printer's guide against which the printed piece is checked. In reviewing the proof, be mindful that "what you see is what you get." Do not give your approval until you are satisfied with what you do see!

Of course, you will let your print production and art departments take the lead in checking and approving proofs. If such departments are not available, use your designer. It is *their* area of *expertise;* it is *your* area of *responsibility.*

Single-color proofs.   Where only one color will be used in printing, the color chosen and the sophistication of the design will determine how closely the proofs must match the printed piece. An exact match of a specific color done by the Cromalin process is more costly than a routine monotone, but as with multicolor proofs, it is the only way to know what you will see when you get the printed piece.

Folding dummy.   The folding dummy is produced in one color on paper that is light enough to fold easily. This proof is folded or formed by the printer into the exact shape and format of the final printed product. It is the folding dummy that lets you see how facing pages actually look when all the elements are present and that lets you know that all the elements are the way they were specified. The following is a list of things to check in using the folding dummy.

- ☐ Are all the pages present and in consecutive order?
- ☐ Do elements that run across the center of facing pages (across the "*gutter*") line up?
- ☐ Do the index and table of contents reflect where the elements are placed? If not, which one is wrong? Do all cross-references check out?
- ☐ Do all the elements fit together? Do the materials fit into the envelope? Are items that bind together the proper shape and size? Etc.
- ☐ Are comparable elements positioned properly? For instance, are all the page numbers (called *folios*) in the same location on the page? Is the use of section or page headings consistent? If not, is the inconsistency deliberate?
- ☐ Is all mailing information present and accurate? Telephone numbers? Direct dial? Are all legal and self-protective requirements met? For example, is such information as "Printed in USA," "Prices subject to change," and so on, present?

SUMMARY

- The filmmaker's equipment does not see the way you do. Learn its capabilities and limitations before a multicolor project is begun.
- Expect the worst; check *everything* each time you proof.
- The OK'd proof becomes your printer's guide. Don't settle for less than you want or need on the assurance that the printer can fix it. The chances are, they can't!
- Encourage creativity, but check with the post office before you approve anything new and different in size, shape, or format. Post office staff are there to help. Let them!

This is the final chance to see the job as a whole before printing. Take the opportunity—and time—to check *everything*.

Printing and Binding

Printing is a process in which original materials—the copy board or computer-generated camera-ready art—are scanned or photographed and separated onto film. Each film holds one of the colors used in printing. The photographic image is transferred from film onto a printing plate and then printed.

The best advice that can be given about working with printers and binderies is to know what you want to achieve, but never to tell them how to do it. A personal anecdote is illustrative.

Hahn's introduction to advertising ("Why don't you try it for three months and see how you like it?") was with a modest retail chain that paid for an exceptional promotional department by syndicating its stores' catalog. The three months turned into three years, during which he wrote every word of every catalog, as well as the syndication promotions that put their only two competitors out of business. Hahn obviously had a gift for copy. Fortunately for him, his boss, Morton Levin, had a gift for instruction and became the first of his many great advertising coaches.

The Christmas catalog was by far their biggest annual effort. Over a hundred stores used it nationwide, and Levin decided to reward Hahn for his efforts by letting him supervise its printing. Actually, what he really wanted was to go to Minnesota, and the printing schedule conflicted with the short duck-hunting season in that state.

Hahn didn't care. He was in charge!

One week later, he found himself at one of the very first commercial printers to use the then-revolutionary new high-speed "web" presses. It was 3:30 A.M., and the printing staff had spent eight hours trying to produce a printed sheet that matched the proof, continually asking his advice on how to make it better. Foolishly, and out of sheer frustration at not getting what he wanted, he told them. Nothing worked. Actually, he was fairly sure that the problem was not fixable that way. The printed catalogs looked dirty. There was a light layer of ink on areas that should have been pure white. They had lost contrast and sharpness. The real problem, as he later learned, was in the printing plates. The presses should have been stopped and new plates made. But this is exactly what the printer did not want to do. He'd spent hours getting his new press "in register," with colors correctly positioned on top of each other. New plates would mean that he'd have to do it all over again—not to mention the time the press would be "down" while the plates were made.

Somehow—though Hahn really knew better—he became convinced that the printing was as good as the press could make it. He approved the printing "as is," knowing that he had done something wrong, but not sure what. One thing he was sure about. He was going to get fired!

This story has an ending with two parts. In part number 1, he did not get fired. When Levin returned, he took one look at the catalog and—rather than blaming Hahn—totally blamed the printer for taking advantage of his inexperience. Fortunately for Hahn, he didn't equate his ignorance with stupidity. They never did business with that printer again. Part number 2 became one of the few technically correct examples of irony in our experience. Despite its apparent drabness, that catalog proved to be the most successful in the syndication firm's, and their hundred-plus customers', history. Hahn assumed that the products—and, of course, his copy—overcame all else.

Things You Can Do

1.   Get a firm quotation, as well as samples of paper to be used, based on actual layouts and specifications. An excellent safety measure is to show the potential printer a copy of the designer's concept and ask whether printing it will present difficulties. Then act accordingly.

2.   Any unusual folds or combinations of materials or sizes may cause difficulties and increase costs. Check these aspects for possible problems as early as possible—certainly, early enough to change them to something more practical if need be.

3.   Anything unusual in shape or size must be checked with the post office for mailing approval, as well as for special handling charges. Make an exact sample (called a *dummy*), and have someone in the post office permits section *approve it and sign the approval.*

4.   If the catalog, or any other mailing, will be sent by third-class bulk rate, and you mail fewer than 100,000 pieces, a fractional ounce of additional weight should not create budgeting problems, but check for the latest postal rates to make sure. If, however, you will be mailing any materials first class, have your printer give you an exact dummy made from all of the different papers that you expect to use (Figure 5.4). If you are close to any whole ounce in weight, do something to make the project lighter. *The chances are that adding ink to the paper will be enough to put you into the next ounce and a higher postage rate.* Consider making your project $1/_{32}''$ smaller on one side. That's generally enough to compensate for the weight of the ink. But check with your printer and your mailing service to make sure.

5.   Deal with printers and binderies through your print production department. Its staff are the experts in these areas. Ask them to explain what they are doing and why they are doing it. Your job is to *know,* not necessarily to *do.* So join them at the printer and bindery when your projects are being produced. Ask about anything you do not know or understand . . . but remember to insist on what you want to achieve. Questions about "more red" or "less blue" or "heavier black" are turned over to the production or art staff. If you are the only one at the printer or bindery, point to the proof and repeat the magic words:

"That's what we want. I wouldn't begin to try to tell *you* how to get it."

Resist the temptation to claim more expertise than you have.

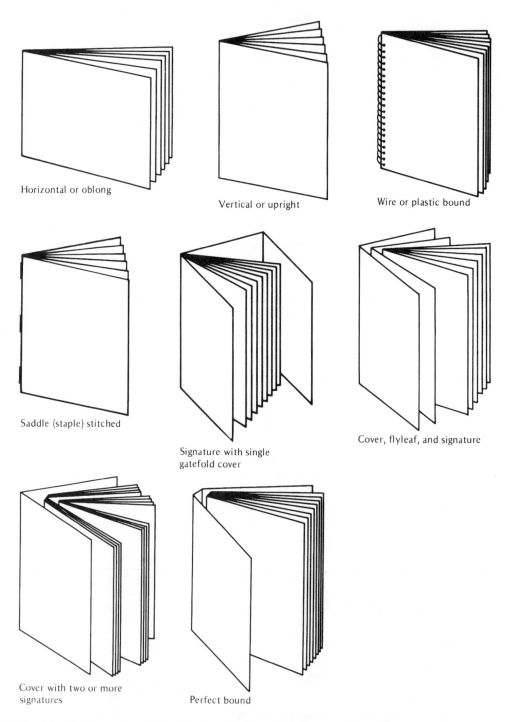

Horizontal or oblong

Vertical or upright

Wire or plastic bound

Saddle (staple) stitched

Signature with single
gatefold cover

Cover, flyleaf, and signature

Cover with two or more
signatures

Perfect bound

Figure 5.4 Catalog and multipage brochure formats. Planning a catalog or brochure requires a choice of format and one or more papers. The most reliable way to evaluate tentative selections is to have paper dummies made by your printer or paper merchant. These blank dummies will give you an accurate way of judging how a paper's substance, weight, and surface qualities look and feel in each of the formats you are considering and how much each of them will cost to mail. (Formats shown courtesy of James River Premium Printing Papers. Original art for James River by Hyers/Smith Advertising, South Norwalk, CT.)

SUMMARY

- Printers know how to print. Don't try to help, even when they ask.
- The proof is your bible. Remain a printing fundamentalist.
- The press run won't get better after you leave. Stay until you are satisfied with what you see.

Additional information on printing, including a Printing/Bindery checklist, is given in Chapter 14.

Distribution and Mailing

Distribution refers to catalogs sent in bulk to outlets and sales staff, to company offices and departments, to the warehouse for bulk storage, and to the mailing facility for handling.

Mailing refers specifically to those catalogs mailed to customers, prospects, and any other groups and individuals specified by management.

Determining Who Handles the Mailing

Postage costs will be exactly the same and the delivery time will be approximately the same, no matter who handles the mailing. Your mailing service should therefore be chosen for the following reasons:

- **Distance from bindery.** What will it cost to ship the bound catalogs to the mailing service? A bindery that has its own mailing department is preferred over one that does not, *other factors being equal.*
- **Cost of service.** Cost is based on the size and weight of the catalogs. Get a written quotation. Be sure the potential mailing service staff sees a layout of the mailing side of the catalog—usually the back cover—while there is still time to make changes. Their equipment may make it impossible to put the address where your layout indicates. That's generally an "easy fix" for you, given adequate warning; it may be an impossible fix for them.
- **Reliability of service.** If you are planning to use a supplier for the first time, get references *and check them.*

Seeding the Mailing List

When using outside mailing lists, add ("seed") the lists with the names and addresses of some of your fellow employees (in different parts of the country if possible), as well as yourself and other in-house staff. Then ask these people to let you know *exactly* when they receive the catalog. This will give you a record of when catalogs are received in various parts of the country and whether there are any likely problems in the mail handling. Do this with *every* mailing, whether you use an outside list or your own.

Paying for Postage

Postage must be received by the post office before mailing. For bulk rate mailing, postage is paid into a special account established by the post office in your or your supplier's name. Find out from your mailing service what bulk rate information has to be printed onto the catalog, to whom the check for postage is to be issued, and when that check must be received. As this is written, the post office does *not* require that such a check be certified.

INSIGHT 35

Do *not* let your printer rush a sample *of anything* to your employer, the chairman of the board, or anyone else. Invariably, it will be one with a glaring mistake, such as a page printed upside down that they later corrected but were saving to show how helpful they were to fix your oversights. *You* deliver the sample, checking it very carefully first. It's *your* project. You do the showing off!

SUMMARY

- Get *exact*, complete dummy samples from the printer as soon as designs are approved. You'll need them to learn the cost of postage and to make final postage-related adjustments. Your post office will help.
- Seed the mailing lists with the names of some people who'll tell you when the catalog arrives. Add your name, too.

Much more detailed information on lettershop mailing services, including postage rates and a Lettershop/Distribution checklist, is given in Chapter 14.

IT ISN'T OVER TILL . . .

Postproduction Activities

Here's a way to close out the current catalog before the next one comes due: Use the items applicable to your situation, modify where necessary, . . . and celebrate when done!

- **What to return.** Get all products used for photography and return them to stock. Make sure that your department is credited with their return, because you were surely charged when they went out. Gather any other materials (such as original art or photo props) that were borrowed for the project, and return them as promised. Anything of value must be insured and return delivery signed for.

- **What to store.** Store the complete catalog copy boards and disk after checking for any missing pieces. Determine who will follow up on missing elements and when they are to report on what they have found.

  Remove photos and transparencies, and file them in the advertising/promotion department. You will want instant access to them for other projects. These photos should be noted "best" and filed with any backup shots.

  Save all price quotations, purchase orders, and advisory or instructional memoranda in a permanent project file.

- **What to throw away.** Thirty days after the catalog has been distributed, notify management and departments that you will dispose of "all manuscripts, proofs, and incidental paperwork" concerning the project, unless they instruct you to the contrary by a certain date (say, 7 days hence). Unless you are ordered to save any of these materials, throw them out!

Recordkeeping and Reporting

The following detailed records must be kept and reported:

- **The actual cost** of the project versus the estimated or quoted costs and reasons for any discrepancy. This report is issued as soon as all invoices have been received.
- **The response** to the mailing. If possible, a detailed record of responses should be kept for at least 60 days after the first response is received. This is especially important if the catalog is used to test lists or the viability of products or a promotional effort. A report on the response is issued at the conclusion of a specified period. Where comparisons to previous similar efforts are practical and pertinent, they are, of course, included. "Back-end analysis" is a specialty all its own. Get professional help if it is needed.

NOTES ON THE CATALOG CHECKLIST

These notes are a supplement to the material presented in this chapter. They are not a substitute for that material.

1. **Schedule.** For scheduling purposes, the most important management decision is the date the catalog must be completed and what "completed" means. If meeting the deadline is impossible under normal time or budgeting constraints, management must decide whether or not to authorize the impossible. (Do *not* present management with an on-time delivery at a cost that is significantly over budget because you "knew" they wanted it that way. Even if they did, it is *their* decision. Some of our best friends have been fired for not understanding this difference.)

CATALOG CHECKLIST

Project Title _____   Date _____

Project Description _____   Project # _____

_____   Checklist # _____

Overall Supervision By _____   Deadline _____

Budget _____   Completion Date _____   Start Up Date _____

MANAGEMENT DECISIONS	ASSIGNED TO	DUE	IN	MUST APPROVE	BY DATE	IN	INFO COPY ONLY	SEE ATTACHED
1. Schedule	_____	___	☐	_____	___	☐	_____	☐
2. Quantity	_____	___	☐	_____	___	☐	_____	☐
3. Budget	_____	___	☐	_____	___	☐	_____	☐
4. Theme	_____	___	☐	_____	___	☐	_____	☐
5. Audience	_____	___	☐	_____	___	☐	_____	☐
6. Report(s)	_____	___	☐	_____	___	☐	_____	☐
7. Project Manager	_____	___	☐	_____	___	☐	_____	☐
CREATIVE DECISIONS								
8. Design Concept	_____	___	☐	_____	___	☐	_____	☐
9. Layout	_____	___	☐	_____	___	☐	_____	☐
10. Copy	_____	___	☐	_____	___	☐	_____	☐
11. Typesetting	_____	___	☐	_____	___	☐	_____	☐
12. Cover Subjects	_____	___	☐	_____	___	☐	_____	☐
13. Photographer(s)	_____	___	☐	_____	___	☐	_____	☐
14. Artist(s)	_____	___	☐	_____	___	☐	_____	☐
15. Insert(s)	_____	___	☐	_____	___	☐	_____	☐
16. Order Form(s)	_____	___	☐	_____	___	☐	_____	☐
17. Envelope	_____	___	☐	_____	___	☐	_____	☐
MECHANICAL DECISIONS								
18. Camera-Ready Art: Cover(s)	_____	___	☐	_____	___	☐	_____	☐
19. Camera-Ready Art: Body	_____	___	☐	_____	___	☐	_____	☐
20. Camera-Ready Art:_____	_____	___	☐	_____	___	☐	_____	☐
21. Film: Cover(s)*	_____	___	☐	_____	___	☐	_____	☐
22. Film: Body	_____	___	☐	_____	___	☐	_____	☐
23. Film: _____	_____	___	☐	_____	___	☐	_____	☐
24. Print: Cover(s)*	_____	___	☐	_____	___	☐	_____	☐
25. Print: Body	_____	___	☐	_____	___	☐	_____	☐
26. Print: _____	_____	___	☐	_____	___	☐	_____	☐
27. Bindery	_____	___	☐	_____	___	☐	_____	☐
28. Mailing Service*	_____	___	☐	_____	___	☐	_____	☐
29. Postage Check(s)	_____	___	☐	_____	___	☐	_____	☐
_____	_____	___	☐	_____	___	☐	_____	☐
_____	_____	___	☐	_____	___	☐	_____	☐

*   Separate checklists are included in Chapter 14 for film work, printing, and mailing service.

2. **Quantity.** If the needed quantity becomes a budget problem, here are a few ways to get more catalogs for the same dollars:

   - Use less expensive paper. Often a slightly lighter weight paper, a somewhat smaller size, or both will save enough on postage to make up the difference.

   - Use fewer (or more!) pages, provided that they give you the least expensive printing. Adding just 4 pages to a 32-page catalog adds appreciably more than one-eighth the cost. The same or even higher costs may be true when printing "only" 28 pages on presses designed for 32. Discuss with your printer the most economical ways to get the job done. If you are unfamiliar with purchasing print, make sure that you learn the whys involved.

   - Give your printer a needed quantity and the budget decided upon. If the printer can't meet it, shop around for another.

3. **Budget.** In estimating budgets, make sure that the suppliers know when the services will be needed. If there are likely increases in union rates, nonunion shops will probably have similar raises. Check with the post office for possible changes in regulations as well as postage. As always, try to keep management's surprises pleasant.

4. **Theme.** Try to keep managers from becoming copywriters. Good luck!

5. **Target audience.** "Audience" relates directly to #2, the quantity needed, and #3, the cost of getting catalogs to each recipient. Remind management of this interrelationship, and, where budgets are limited, get the priorities or some other guidance.

6. **Report(s).** Is there a report needed or wanted beyond the budget, costs, and results? Discuss the practicality of each request if getting the information is not already built into your system. Much of this kind of data is nice to know, but what will be done with it after it's been gathered?

7. **Project manager.** The project manager, if different from the overall supervisor, will be *directly* responsible for the supervision of points 8–28. She or he most often appoints as well as supervises the persons involved.

8–9. **Design/layout.** Who will do each? In some instances, the layout can be done internally, even if a design is purchased outside.

10. **Copy.** How much does the writer have to know about your product or service to do the job? Write technical copy inside, and then give it to an outside writer for review. In accuracy versus sell, settle for accuracy every time.

11. **Typesetting.** Discuss with your outside typesetters the practicality of your producing the manuscript on disk, then having them prepare finished hard copy or film for reproduction. This is often the best solution when the copy is other than standard English or there are numerous last-second changes in numbers, prices, or other data.

12. **Covers.** Who decides? Who assigns? Who approves final art?

13–14. **Photo/Art.** Commercial artists and photographers tend to do best at specific kinds of projects. Get samples. Negotiate for prices. Get a *signed* agreement. Try to give "the kid" a chance.

15.   **Insert(s).** Inserts are a practical way to address specific audiences without adding everything to the main catalog. Use them also for testing, as described on pages 99–103. In using different inserts for different parts of your mailing, discuss controls with your mailing service *before* mailing lists are ordered or anything is printed. Identification codes will be required on each part. Find out where to place them!

16.   **Order form(s).** It often pays huge dividends to have more than a single order form in catalogs that have a fairly long life. Test.

17.   **Envelope.** Few catalogs are mailed in envelopes, unless they are accompanied by a variety of loose materials. Often the latter can be bound in. Check. Save!

18–23.   **Camera-ready art/proofs.** Be sure to build in adequate time for in-house review. Everyone who sees anything will want to suggest changes, so ask for corrections and comments from the fewest number of persons safety allows. Nothing gets reviewers more furious than being asked for comments and then being ignored!

24–26.   **Printing OK.** Use in-house expertise if available; get the designer involved if not. On-press approval tends to be a *very* lengthy job. Allow for that in scheduling and budgeting.

27–28.   **Bindery/mailing.** Two excellent ways to let beginners learn the importance of nitpicking detail is to supervise the bindery and to supervise the mailing operation. Little is likely to go wrong. But everything must be checked—continually—to keep it that way.

29.   **Postage.** The postal service will not accept a mailing without payment in hand. In organizations where payment is sometimes slow, get management to set up a system that won't delay the mail.

6 | Out-of-Home Advertising and Promotion

This chapter describes and gives advice on using the major "out-of-home" media, from billboards to in-store advertising. Few of these are literally do-it-yourself projects in the sense of doing your own ads or direct mail—you'd hardly paint your own billboard or put up your own bus cards! Like the chapters on audiovisual communication (Chapter 11) and information on convention display construction (Chapter 13), we offer guidance to buying, supervising, and using the media, as well as a reminder of the many effective ways you have to advertise out-of-home if someone just calls them to your attention.

For maximum success (and why would you settle for less!), the use of these media demands the integrated marketing approach to your advertising and promotion that we urge throughout this book. As one example, Figure 6.1 shows how a medium-sized 1994 market had a 59 percent increase in message reach when just 15 percent of an original TV budget was switched to out-of-home media.

The major out-of-home media, listed alphabetically within the major categories, follow.

TRADITIONAL OUTDOOR MEDIA

- Aerial/Inflatable Advertising
- Bus Bench Advertising
- Bus Shelter Advertising
- Mobile Advertising
- Outdoor Advertising
- Taxi Advertising
- Transit Advertising

PLACE-BASED MEDIA

- Airport Advertising
- High School/College Campus Advertising
- Hotel Advertising
- In-Flight Advertising
- In-Store Advertising
- Movie/Theater Advertising

<table>
<tr><td colspan="3">**Effect of Adding Out-of-Home Media to a Media Mix**
(Medium-Sized Market; Target Audience: W 25–54; Schedule: 4 Weeks; 30-Sheet Posters)</td></tr>
<tr><td></td><td>Without O-H-M</td><td>With O-H-M</td></tr>
<tr><td>Budget</td><td>$54,104</td><td>$54,104</td></tr>
<tr><td>Television</td><td>100%</td><td>85%</td></tr>
<tr><td>% Out-of-Home</td><td>—</td><td>15%</td></tr>
<tr><td>GRP's</td><td>500</td><td>795 (+59%)</td></tr>
<tr><td>Cost/Rating Point (Prime Access)</td><td>$108</td><td>$68 (-37%)</td></tr>
<tr><td>% Reach</td><td>45.3%</td><td>88.1% (+17%)</td></tr>
<tr><td>Average Frequency</td><td>6.6 times</td><td>9.0 times (+36%)</td></tr>
<tr><td colspan="3" align="right">Source: OAAA</td></tr>
<tr><td colspan="3" align="center">Out-of-Home Advertising Source</td></tr>
</table>

Figure 6.1   How a 15 percent out-of-home budget share gained 59 percent in Gross Rating Point prospect awareness.

- Shopping Mall Advertising
- Sports/Fitness/Leisure Facility Advertising
- Stadium/Arena/Sports Team Advertising
- Truck Stop Advertising

EVENT MARKETING

- Event Advertising and Promotion

PLANNING AND BUYING TRADITIONAL OUTDOOR MEDIA

Traditional outdoor media range from spectacular 48-foot-long lighted "displays"[1] to 46-inch overhead terminal clocks and 21-inch interior rail cards. Many out-of-home media have industrywide specifications that will let you work in a uniform size no matter where they will be used. Others, such as cold-air inflatables, can be practically any shape or size you want.

The Yellow Pages, SRDS, and Your Sanity

Suppliers for out-of-home media are in major city and some smaller community Yellow Pages. But unless you are *very* familiar with a specific medium and market, check the *SRDS Out-of-Home Advertising Source*™ directory[2] before you do

---

[1] What everyone not in the trade calls billboards.

[2] SRDS Directories, 1700 Higgins Road, Des Plaines, IL 60018. Phone: (800) 851-7737, Fax: (847) 375-5001. For additional SRDS Directories, see pp. 45–46.

anything else. Not only will you find national and local suppliers, but you'll see pricing structures (inclusive of discounts) for practically every size community or occasion. Although pricing may or may not be negotiable, at least you'll know the "ballpark" before you decide to play.

Constructing Your Own

Many desirable out-of-home locations are under long-term contract. If the one you want is not available, consider constructing your own. For instance, offer to pay for surprisingly inexpensive bus-stop benches and to even pay rent for its ad. For placements on private land, talk to the property owners, from airports to farmland to zoos, about your need. Given the abundance of unused parcels of property available, you will find very receptive owners who are entrepreneurial in nature and more than willing to lease or sell for the "right" price. Then talk to a local outdoor company about zoning and the cost of construction, maintenance, and the message itself.

Zoning Restrictions

Out-of-home media are controlled or restricted by local zoning laws as to size, placement, lighting, and content—such as advertising alcohol or tobacco in certain locations. Before ordering any outdoor advertising, discuss zoning clearance with your supplier. Whether the responsibility is theirs or yours, get clearance, *in writing,* from the appropriate community zoning and engineering departments. If in doubt, work through your attorney.

BILLBOARD OUTDOOR DISPLAYS

Outdoor advertising, dominated by, but not limited to billboards, works for local and national advertisers by selling goods and services to travelers, commuters, and those living in the local communities.

INSIGHT 36

In outdoor advertising, it is critically important to decide on the "3 W's"—who, when, and what—when dealing with your local or national representative:
1. *Who* you are trying to reach with your advertising
2. *When* you want to reach them (timing)
3. *What* you will spend to reach them (budget)

How to Get the Billboard You Want

Billboards are owned or represented by hundreds of different local and national companies, many of which have groups of billboards in specific markets. For local

Figure 6.2   For ease of contact, the name of the leasing agent is centered underneath the billboard.

use, if just a few of these companies are listed in your Yellow Pages, have each one give you a map or tour of their board locations. If that proves unworkable, scout the area holding the boards you want. You'll find the name of the leasing agent, as shown in Figure 6.2, at the bottom center, hoping to be seen by potential buyers like you.

Billboards and Their Cost

Outdoor companies offer programs in showing levels, from a single panel to 100 percent of the GRP (Gross Rating Point) potential audience. Common showing sizes include #25, #50, #75, and #100 with the number of display pannels relating directly to a market. For instance:

#50 Showing	30-Sheet Size
Market	*# of panels*
Los Angeles	250
Chicago	164
San Francisco	121
Denver	39

In smaller communities, local suppliers may need comparatively few panels to offer a high-frequency audience "100 percent showing"; that is, a billboard on the major roads entering and leaving all four sides of town, with a "50 percent showing" being half of that.

Many businesses that use outdoor advertising are comparatively small and local, with the fastest-growing group of advertisers involved in travel and tourism, automotive, retail, real estate and insurance, and business products and services.

```
┌─────────────────────────────────────────────────────┐
│                                                       │
│          1995 Average Cost per Thousand               │
│                    Adults 18+                         │
│                                                       │
│                                         Average CPM   │
│   Outdoor (Top 100 Markets)                           │
│      Eight-Sheet Posters #50 Showing        $ .71     │
│      30-Sheet Posters #50 Showing           $1.39     │
│      Rotary Bulletins #10 Showing           $3.07     │
│                                                       │
│   Radio (Top 100 Markets)                             │
│      60-second Drive-Time Commercial        $4.70     │
│                                                       │
│   Television (Top 100 Markets)                        │
│      30-second Local Prime-Time Spot        $15.20    │
│      30-second Prime-Time Network           $8.25     │
│                                                       │
│   Magazines (23 Publications)                         │
│      One 4/C Page                           $7.65     │
│                                                       │
│   Newspapers (Top 100 Markets)                        │
│      1/2 Page B/W                           $18.55    │
│      1/4 Page B/W                           $9.30     │
│                                                       │
│   Sources:                                            │
│      Outdoor Planning Systems—Harris Donovan, Inc.    │
│      Marketers' Guide to Media                        │
│      1995 MRI Spring-Rate Card                        │
│      Grey Advertising–1994 Media Modules              │
│                                                       │
└─────────────────────────────────────────────────────┘
```

Figure 6.3 Comparative cost of using outdoor media compared with print and electronic advertising.

As shown in Figure 6.3, outdoor advertising is highly competitive on a CPM (cost per thousand) basis compared with other media targeted at adults age 18 and up. And market-by-market, it is surprisingly inexpensive. In any community, less traveled locations and smaller billboards are much cheaper. Many locations require multiple-month leasing. Others are available for a single month or for special events of a few days or weeks. Considering the impossibility of economically reaching the majority of the billboard audiences in any other way, that's quite a buy!

Production Costs

The cost of producing the visual ad is often included in the space rental. When it is not, production of some of the largest expressway displays, which are either hand-painted or, increasingly, computerized, ranges from $1,500 to $2,500. Displays that require elaborate three-dimensional construction may, of course, cost much more. The smaller displays are usually lithographed (printed) or silk-screened and vary in price depending on the complexity of the artwork.

On Billboard Design

The key to successful billboard design is a message that is seen, understood, and that *motivates* after no more than a quick glance. Here's an example.

A Case Study

Rand McNally had promoted a new line of school maps to be introduced at that year's most important buyers' convention. Unfortunately for the promotion plan, world politics brought last-minute changes in geographical names and boundaries. Revised maps could not be produced in time.

The solution, as in many similar cases, was to pass the problem to Advertising.

A visit by the Advertising Manager to the convention city uncovered five billboards on the main roadway leading to the convention center. Incredibly, all five were available! Soon all five had the same message:

DON'T BUY MAPS
UNTIL YOUR SEE THE REP FROM RAND McNALLY
IN BOOTH 535!

There are two sequels to this story:

Sequel 1.   Company president Andrew McNally received calls from his major competitors, chiding him for use of the negative "Don't buy maps" theme.

"Negative?" he responded. "It was the most successful convention we ever had!"

Sequel 2.   Jack Heimerdinger, The Rand McNally Advertising Manager[3] who created the billboard theme, got calls from the next three occupants of Booth 535. They told him his message was still there and though *they* had nothing to do with maps, they'd never had the kind of traffic—and business—the billboards created.

Basic Billboard Formats

Outdoor billboard advertising has three basic formats:

- *Bulletins.* These huge displays, 48 feet long by 14 feet high, deliver impact in size, placement, color, and lighting. Many are hand-painted. Most are physically moved every 60 days to a new location.
- *30-sheet posters.* "30 Sheet" refers to the number of printed sheets it originally took to fill this 123-inch by 273-inch space. The economics of hand painting versus printing depends on the number of billboards used.
- *8-sheet poster.* This much smaller 130-inch by 130-inch billboard is most frequently used in neighborhoods such as those with local ethnic populations that are hard to reach economically through other print media. In advertising to this audience, be sure you use a creative source that figuratively and literally speaks your target market's language.

---

[3]Heimerdinger is now an advertising/promotion consultant working out of Plainfield, Illinois (815-436-5137).

Many outdoor placement and production companies offer free guidance in billboard design.[4] Take it!

About Hand Painting

The development of full-color, billboard-sized printing on vinyl is rapidly replacing hand-painted poster art. Even the huge 48-foot bulletins can now be preprinted this way. The finished vinyl is fastened to ratchets on all four sides of the display, then stretched tight. Unlike paper or hand-painted posters, vinyl art is practically weatherproof and takes a fraction of the time to install. And unlike hand painting, it is absolutely uniform in color and design, no matter where, when, or by whom installed.

Three Kinds of Mobile Billboards

1. Truck Advertising

Three distinctly different kinds of truck "billboards" are in use:

- *Special events billboards.* These special event promotions, quite literally billboards-on-wheels, take attention-catching, brightly lit messages where ordinary billboards would not be permitted. Many can change messages electronically, within minutes, as often as desired.
- *Mobile billboards.* Billboard posters attached to commercial trucks on regular routes. Excellent for markets that restrict conventional outdoor advertising.
- *Truck self-advertising.* While all large trucks are painted, few carry a real billboard-type selling message as is done by McDonald's™. Here is a medium waiting to be discovered . . . and used.

2. Taxi Advertising

Taxis are increasingly becoming carriers of exterior and interior advertising messages. Depending on local rulings, many have lighted signs; some with computer animation. An excellent medium for restaurants, lodging, entertainment.

3. Painted Cars

A localized phenomenon in some markets. The personal car-billboard, painted in attention-grabbing psychedelic colors and designs, has sales message impact on a younger audience. Ask the driver how he or she became the mobile message, then follow their lead to the medium source.

---

[4]Outdoor Services, the leading agent for billboard rental, publishes an excellent guide to practical—and creative—outdoor design and production, including the use of computer-generated art. For more information, call (212) 473-4141.

TRANSIT AND BUS DISPLAYS

To ease production problems, the transit industry has adopted a system of uniform sizing for exterior "posters" and interior display "cards." Since placement can be ordered for specific routes or lines, these offer a superb medium for socioeconomic and ethnic targeting, with "take-one" cards as an inexpensive—and underused—method of testing promotional appeals. For instance, use six different headlines—one on every sixth display card—and see which brings in the best response.

Production Considerations

Transit advertising materials have rigid production specifications. See the Yellow Pages under "Advertising—Transit & Transportation" for placement services and for the placement companies' recommendations on printing. Get references from both. Check them out!

Seven different formats are available for buses, transit buses, and subway stations and cars. These are all miniature billboards! Limit the copy to what can be absorbed at a glance.

Bus Formats

1. *Super king size.* On street side of the bus. 240 inches long by 30 inches high. Produced in four sections.
2. *King size.* On both curb and street side. Just under 30-inch by 144-inch display produced in three sections.
3. *Queen size.* Just under 30 inches by 88 inches. Produced in two or three sections.
4. *Front and rear displays.* A variety of size specifications depending on placement. Sizes are not interchangeable!
5. *Interior subway and bus cards.* Mounted in frames, they are from approximately 11 inches by 21 inches to 11 inches by 48 inches.
6. *Interior rail car cards.* Available in two sizes: 21 inches long by 22 inches high or 21 inches long by 33 inches high.
7. *Subway and bus station displays.* Available in three sizes: 30 inches long by 46 inches high, 5 feet long by 46 inches high (the most widely used), and 42 inches long by 84 inches high.

OTHER TRAVEL-RELATED DISPLAYS

Bench Displays

These "minibillboards," often within feet of a bus stop, are seen by bus passengers, auto traffic, and pedestrians. Although most are contracted for by local businesses, often for years at a time, some are available for special events, such as a farewell message with which students surprised a retiring teacher at her regular bus stop. For locations and costs, see "Advertising—Outdoors" in the Yellow Pages or check an advertising bench for the name of the display company.

In-Station Displays

Many displays within rail stations, airports, and bus terminals are controlled by national companies; others by the local transportation authority. These displays include interior backlit dioramas and islands, clocks, and exterior bus shelters. For availability and costs, check the SRDS directory, the Yellow Pages, or contact the airport or train station management, or the rapid transit or bus line.

AERIAL/INFLATABLE ADVERTISING

Most—perhaps all—aerial messages are vanity or show-off advertising aimed as much at publicity or public relations as sales accountability. Consider it a short-term aerial billboard aimed at a known target. Employees see their company name overhead as they sit in a stadium. A political or religious group is identified by a banner towed by a small plane. "Cecilia, Will You Marry Me?" floats across the sky as she hopes the one to whom she's saying yes—probably on the local TV news—is really Chuck! Aerial banners, balloons, blimps, and depending on wind conditions, sky writing is used at sporting, political, religious, and other outdoor events. It's all great fun and, with the exception of the true multicrew blimp, surprisingly inexpensive.

Other aerial promotions. Preformed aerial devices, with or without advertising messages, include smaller "blimps," life-size and oversize animals and story characters, and helium-filled, regular-sized balloons that lend a festive feeling to any occasion.

Where to Find Suppliers and What It Costs

Flyovers
It is now possible to do full-color graphics/murals that can be pulled behind planes as was done for some major beverage companies during Spring Break activities in Florida. Many aerial suppliers give national services. Look in the Yellow Pages under "Advertising—Aerial" or in the SRDS directory to find the help you need.

Costs
Expect to pay from $300 to $500, including creation of the message, for a banner flyover. For the most expensive of aerial advertising, a manned blimp, you'll pay about $200,000 per month. To turn a commercial passenger jet into a flying billboard, check the appropriate airline. It's a great stunt, but who will actually see it?[5]

---

[5]*A case history.* Air France transformed a Zurich-Paris jet into a striking black-and-white promotion for *Phantom of the Opera*. Since passengers had to walk at ground level from the terminal to the plane, it got more undivided attention than most roadside billboards.

Inflatable "Cold Air" Advertising

Inflatables, also known as "cold air advertising," are three-dimensional plastic creations that are filled with air or gas. They include large rooftop or ground balloons and children's holiday and seasonal favorites such as dinosaurs, Santa Claus, and Uncle Sam. Inflatables can be custom-made to practically any shape and size for special events.

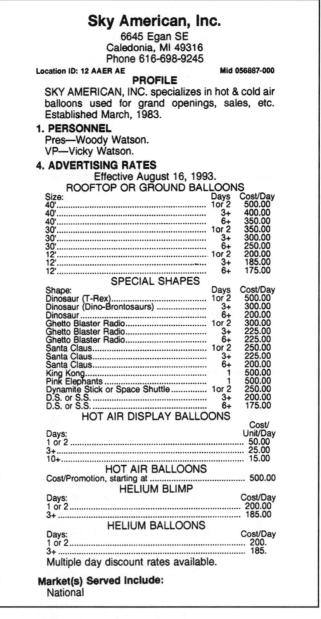

Figure 6.4 A typical range of "cold air" and "hot air" services and products and their costs. *1996 SRDS Out-of-Home Advertising Source.*

Locating Suppliers

Many suppliers give national service. Look in the Yellow Pages under "Advertising—Aerial" or in the SRDS directory to find the help you need.

Costs

Costs for rental of standard, preformed shapes are for days, rather than the fly-by minutes or hours. They range, as seen in Figure 6.4, from less than $200 to $500 and up. Custom-made shapes are more, of course, but also give you ownership of the shapes for future use.

AIRPORT ADVERTISING

Located in airport terminals and their parking lots, these displays include an ever-expanding family of media including waiting area television, backlit structures (dioramas), wall posters, telephone boards, clocks, luggage cards, and so on.

Advantages of Airport Advertising

Few media buys offer so large a captive audience that is frequently bored with waiting or desperate for local information, or both. Use the billboard approach to give them a *benefit-filled* reason to react to your message and you have a winner.

Placement, Production, and Costs

Advertising in more than 90 U.S. airports is handled by Ackerly Airport Advertising, (800) 568-5611. Check them first. Check other airports to learn whether they handle their own or use one of Ackerly's competitors. Pricing seems to have little relationship to passenger traffic, but much more to "all the traffic will bear." That does *not* mean you will be cheated. It does mean—as in all advertising—that you must build in a way of documenting and evaluating what you get from your buy.

IN-FLIGHT ADVERTISING

In-flight advertising, which began as the airlines' magazines, soon expanded to direct response catalogs. It now includes television, movie, and audio commercials and product sampling. Think of it, too, for destination premiums such as entertainment, dining, auto rental, and lodging discounts, especially for business travelers who use the same suppliers from force of habit. Contact any airline's marketing department for current programs and a discussion of innovative new approaches.

SHOPPING MALL ADVERTISING

Don't limit your thinking to posters, signage, and displays in windows and free-standing structures. Think about inside for on-screen showings of each department's fashions . . . to explain the advantages among different model bicycles . . . or to let diners watch the chef prepare their meals. Put the screens in your display windows and see how live action draws a crowd and, almost always, perks up sales.

Computerize Your Mall Directory

Create an interactive mall directory—in effect, a mall catalog—for in-mall as well as Web site use. Younger shoppers especially will love it. Give specific directions to who . . . where . . . when, but also give each mall location a chance to promote themselves. More about this in Chapter 9.

SPORTS/FITNESS/LEISURE FACILITY ADVERTISING

From ski resorts to roller rinks, from health clubs to race tracks, from golf courses to amateur and semipro sports facilities, there are local, regional, and national advertising opportunities. Think, too, about tie-in promotions with sports bars and eating and drinking places near sports facilities. For industrywide or other large-scale advertising, see the SRDS directory. For local promotion, this demands one-on-one contact and persuasion. Begin by creating a benefit *they* will want and your selling job will take care of itself.

HIGH SCHOOL AND COLLEGE ADVERTISING

For the small- to medium-sized company, advertising opportunities include posters on GymBoards and other news and information station bulletin boards, ads in college papers, and messages on newspaper distribution racks. More ambitious efforts include preprinted book covers and class schedule booklets, even custom publications, often tailored to and given free for use in specific courses.

With the exception of college publication advertising, in-school and on-campus promotions probably require permission, or at least following the rules, as to size, length of time, and so on. For just a few locations, call to find the appropriate school officers, then check with them as to clearance procedure. For more ambitious distribution, contact service organizations, such as those described in the SRDS directory. Get *and check* references with both their clients and schools.

MOVIE, CONCERT, AND THEATER ADVERTISING

Theater and Concert Programs

Programs are one of the underused advertising media. They give you a captive audience, almost all of whom will read the program. Furthermore, depending on who is performing and what is presented, the socioeconomics of your audience is known. Theater audiences are new for each performance. For musical occasions other than one-shot extravaganza events, be mindful of seasonal or other repeat attendance ticket holders. Since they generally attend on the same day of the week, the audience is larger than it first appears. Check with each organization's business manager on advertising opportunities and costs.

Movie Advertising

Many movie theaters begin their show with on-screen ads or commercials, often for local businesses. If interested in just one or two theaters, discuss it with their managers. For broader distribution, contact one of the firms listed in the SRDS directory. These are not "TV" commercials, so for production, use someone who knows the medium. Let Chapter 11, "TV, Radio, Video, and CD Creative and Production," be your guide.

HAVE YOU THOUGHT ABOUT . . .

Only our imagination—and pocketbook—limits our use of out-of-home advertising. Here are three more ideas to start your thinking.

Floor Graphics

One of the newest point-of-sale devices. Any image can be placed on the floor: an oversize product picture, as in Figure 6.5, a slogan or offer, a follow-the-footsteps theme . . . *anything.* You'll stop prospects in their tracks, or lead them where you want them to go. Some companies (like 3M Media), produce images on adhesive, easy-to-remove film. Others use graphics floor tiles that temporarily replace the regular floor. Depending on zoning, you may be able to create outside graphics, too.

Figure 6.5   Floor graphics, one of the newest point-of-sale devices, can be placed indoors or out . . . on the floor, wall, ceiling—literally anywhere! Illustration from 3M Commercial Products Division.

A case history. In a floor graphics 20-store test of a new Trident gum and an existing Nestlé chocolate bar, both showed excellent results. Ten stores used standard point-of-sale graphics, 10 others used 3M's "Floorminders."

Results[6] showed that in stores using the floor graphics, sales of Trident brand gum rose 19.2 percent during an initial test period and over 21 percent during a second test. Sales of the Nestlé bar increased even more, 24.8 and 23.6 percent, respectively. Even more important, not only did the floor graphics increase immediate sales, they maintained high sale increases over time.

Painted Walls

Housed in a drab building? Use it as a canvas to paint the striking structure you'd like it to be! Of course, zoning permitting, you can use a blank wall as a billboard, but why not make it something your prospects and customers will not only notice . . . but thank you for, too!

County Fairgrounds, Picnic Grounds, and County Stadiums

Practically every county has public facilities that are busy year-round. Whether it's a stock show or trailer swap, a true old-fashioned fair or a real modern art exhibit, a Fourth of July political picnic or Thanksgiving pumpkin contest—everyone is there for a good time. With that in mind, create an on-site advertisement that promises to make their good times even better. Of course, that benefit approach isn't limited to out-of-home promotions, but it's a great place to start!

NOTES ON THE OUT-OF-HOME CHECKLIST

These notes are a supplement to the material presented in this chapter. They are not a self-contained substitute for that material. The nationwide Outdoor Services media buying association provided much of the information on which this checklist is based.

1. **Purpose.** What is the *one* thing your message is to do? Give directions? Make it simple and exact (Next Exit. Left 1/4 mile) . . . Emphasize a price? Add a benefit (Unconditional 2-Year Guarantee! Only $99.95) . . . Create a product image? Assure a long-term commitment? (Ford's "Job One.")
2. **Client image.** Every out-of-home message shows a "picture" of the advertiser. Make certain it's the image you want portrayed.
3. **Budget.** If out-of-home is part of another advertising or promotion budget, how is each element determined? What has priority?
4. **Testing.** If out-of-home is only a part of the total advertising package, consider testing some of the program without it. Or try out-of-home without the rest. Both together, *use the same TOTAL dollars* and allocate at least 15% for out-of-home.

---

[6]Reported in *Sales And Marketing Strategy & News,* August 1996.

OUT-OF-HOME CHECKLIST

Project Title _____   Date _____

Project Description _____   Project # _____

_____   Checklist # _____

Overall Supervision By _____   Deadline _____

Budget _____ Completion Date _____   Start Up Date _____

MANAGEMENT DECISIONS	ASSIGNED TO	DUE	IN	MUST APPROVE	BY DATE	IN	INFO COPY ONLY	SEE ATTACHED
1. Purpose	_____	__	☐	_____	__	☐	_____	☐
2. Client Image	_____	__	☐	_____	__	☐	_____	☐
3. Budget	_____	__	☐	_____	__	☐	_____	☐
4. Testing	_____	__	☐	_____	__	☐		
5. Project Supervision	_____	__	☐	_____	__	☐		
							_____	☐
CREATIVE/PRODUCTION							_____	☐
6. Timeline	_____	__	☐	_____	__	☐	_____	☐
7. Audience	_____	__	☐	_____	__	☐	_____	☐
8. Copy	_____	__	☐	_____	__	☐	_____	☐
9. Design	_____	__	☐	_____	__	☐	_____	☐
10. Mechanical Art	_____	__	☐	_____	__	☐	_____	☐
11. Client Approval	_____	__	☐	_____	__	☐	_____	☐
12. Physical Production	_____	__	☐	_____	__	☐	_____	☐
13. Media Sizes	_____	__	☐	_____	__	☐	_____	☐
14. Format	_____	__	☐	_____	__	☐	_____	☐
15. Duration	_____	__	☐	_____	__	☐	_____	☐
16. Quantities	_____	__	☐	_____	__	☐	_____	☐
17. Shipping Instructions	_____	__	☐	_____	__	☐	_____	☐
18. Media Notification	_____	__	☐	_____	__	☐	_____	☐
19. Records & Samples	_____	__	☐	_____	__	☐	_____	☐
20. Evaluation	_____	__	☐	_____	__	☐	_____	☐
21. Report	_____	__	☐	_____	__	☐	_____	☐
MECHANICAL CHECKS								
22. Editorial OK	_____	__	☐	_____	__	☐	_____	☐
23. Legal OK	_____	__	☐	_____	__	☐	_____	☐
24. Marketing OK	_____	__	☐	_____	__	☐	_____	☐
25. Management OK	_____	__	☐	_____	__	☐	_____	☐
26. Copy As Used	_____	__	☐	_____	__	☐	_____	☐

5. **Project supervision.** Out-of-home needs special know-how. Give supervision to someone who has it . . . or is willing to learn!

6. **Time line.** Make this step one! Base creative time on your experience with other ads, or on guaranteed art supplier delivery. Rules-of-thumb scheduling exists for production. Check with Outdoor Services or other

industry guides to make sure your time line works in your overall integrated promotion plan. If not, ask your suppliers for suggestions. Budget permitting, the impossible becomes routine.

7. **Audience.** Keep the focus as narrow as practical. Don't try to attract everyone. Do aim for the vast majority of those you really want.

8. **Copy.** Clever wins awards. Direct sells.

9. **Design.** From type selection to colors to word count, you can find out what works best in out-of-home advertising. Ask your creative or production source for the industry association's *documented* guidelines. Follow them!

10. **Mechanical art.** Mechanical art specifications, from giant bulletins to overhead platform clocks to in-flight film commercials, vary with each production company. Do not assume that your creative resource knows what production needs—even when the creative is you. Check to make sure there have been no overnight changes!

11. **Client approval.** Out-of-home advertising will be seen by everyone on the client's staff. But unless they are also the prospects at whom the message is aimed, keep them out of the approval process. Do not make out-of-home a committee project. Make some one person responsible. Let him or her decide!

12. **Physical production.** A three-step process: (A) The physical producer chosen. (B) The reproduction process agreed upon. (C) The schedule fixed.

13. **Media sizes.** Make sure sizes are determined by both market and medium; that is, billboards as well as bus exterior and interior signs can vary in sizes.

14. **Format.** If the same art is used for more than one format, is approval required for each? For the record, code every change in every item!

15. **Duration.** What are the posting dates and the duration of postings? The coding used in point 14 makes a visual record easy to create and maintain.

16. **Quantities.** Almost all media require some extra. Check requirements with each.

17. **Shipping instructions.** If unfamiliar with shipping options and terminology, have both explained ("Best way" vs. "Fastest" vs. "Least expensive to arrive by . . ." etc.). Give shipping instructions to the producer *in a mutually agreed upon format.* Be sure method of shipping and drop-dead due date are included.

18. **Media notification.** Notification to media company(ies) of what is being shipped—including design—tells how, how many, when, and by whom.

19. **Records and samples.** Samples of audiovisual. Picture or photo of each design, with product code and record of use.

20. **Evaluation.** Results, insofar as they are known, of total integrated promotion with out-of-home contribution.

21. **Report.** Presentation of #20 evaluation as required or scheduled.

22. **Editorial OK.** The final authority on the mechanics of language, house style, and technical accuracy of text and art.

23. **Legal OK.** Out-of-home is regulated by federal, state, and local laws and rules. Work with an organization that is knowledgeable in the specifics of what you want to do. Don't guess and hope for the best!

24. **Marketing OK.** The final OK—in writing—from the marketing person or department. Make sure your creative solution still fits the overall marketing plan.

25. **Management OK.** Get this approval if required . . . or if "politics" suggests you should.

26. **Copy/sample as used.** Some *one* person must maintain a permanent file of photographs, samples, disks . . . and an index of where *anything* can be found.

7 | Telemarketing

Telemarketing is the planned use of telecommunications equipment with a set purpose or goal. What it is *not* is simply picking up the phone—whether to answer or call out—with no set directions as to what is to follow. Like audiovisual communication (see Chapter 11), telemarketing is expensive and easily done wrong, with its success depending as much on management commitment as on in-house or outside expertise. Much of telemarketing, such as giving information and taking telephone orders, can be done in-house. More specialized aspects are usually better done by professional telemarketing service bureaus. What is required for successful use of either option is what this chapter is all about.

SCOPE OF TELEMARKETING

Telemarketing was the fastest growing legitimate economic activity of the 1980s and shows every sign of continuing its growth into the nineties and beyond.[1] Just how its dollar totals should be counted is one of the more pleasant industry debates. (For example, do you include the phone call that ordered the Boeing 747, as well as the one that ordered the 79¢ ball-point pen that signed the confirmation?)

Telemarketing Revenues
Whatever the sales totals, there's general agreement that telemarketing had a four-fold increase in revenues in the eighties—from about $70 billion to almost $300 billion, with growth continuing into the nineties at an explosive rate. (See Figure 7.1.)

Telemarketing Expenditures
On a comparable scale, telemarketing *expenditures*[2] grew from $13 billion to more than $40 billion in just five years—from 1990 to 1995—and are expected to reach $79 billion by the year 2000.

Telemarketing Employment
According to a Time, Inc. on-line report, from 1983 to 1993, employment in telemarketing climbed from under 200,000 to more than 5 *million* workers, with telemarketers predicting they will hire 4 million more by the end of the century.

---

[1]Internet and computer-related activities have undoubtedly become the new growth champion of the nineties. How much of this growth has to do with business *outside* the computer industry remains to be seen.

[2]WEFA study for the Direct Marketing Association, reported in *DM News,* 11, 13, 1995.

VOLUME OF U.S. DM-DRIVEN SALES (*Billions of Dollars)				
	1990 (Actual)	1994 (Actual)	1996 (Estimate)	2000 (Forecast)
Telephone Marketing	**$272.8**	**$356.1**	**$385.6**	**$599.0**
Business-to-Business	155.6	205.9	226.3	368.3
Consumer	117.2	150.2	159.3	230.7
Direct Mail	**$250.0**	**$333.1**	**$356.1**	**$517.3**
Business-to-Business	85.4	119.2	130.4	208.7
Consumer	164.6	214.0	225.7	308.6

Figure 7.1 Growth of U.S. telemarketing and direct mail–driven sales. Source: Direct Marketing Association. Reported in *Direct* magazine, January 1996.

Status Report[3]

- Telephone marketing, at 40 percent, is the largest category of all direct marketing.
- At $71 billion-plus in 1995, *business-to-business* advertisers spend more on telemarketing than any other medium.
- Business-to-business telemarketing accounts for approximately 60 percent of all telemarketing sales.
- 43 percent of companies report that they expect to increase their use of telemarketing within the next year.
- 46.2 percent of companies reported increased telemarketing profitability during the past year.

For a peek into the future, see pages 192–194.

TECHNICAL AND PRACTICAL FACTORS

Under the broad categories of "inbound" and "outbound" telemarketing, there are at least a dozen kinds of activities. Before exploring them in detail, let us consider the technical and practical factors that apply to them. These *must* be agreed upon before any telemarketing project is begun. Often, they also control the decision to work in-house or go to an outside service bureau.

- **Time line.** When will the project begin? How long will it continue? How many calls will you get or make? How much time is allowed per call?

---

[3]Based on Direct Marketing Association and *Direct* magazine research. Reported in the magazine's January 1996 issue.

Beware of confusing quantity with success! Would you really rather get 10 calls per hour at $15 in sales each as opposed to 6 calls averaging $45?

- **Personnel.** How will telemarketers *and clerical staff* be acquired, trained, and supervised? How many workers will you need for peak hours? For regular and slow periods? How much will you pay? To whom? On what basis?

- **Location.** Is the location safe before and after standard office hours? Telemarketing is often a 24-hour service. Is there public transportation nearby? Parking? A place to purchase food? Where will telemarketers work, rest, eat, have their coffee breaks, and use toilets?

- **Mechanical.** What equipment must be acquired, installed, and maintained? For how long? At what cost? By whom? If its use is short term, can it be leased? If not, can it be resold? For how much?

- **In-house vs. outside.** For in-house telemarketing, how do you know the answers to all the preceding questions? For outside service bureaus, get written quotations from at least three suppliers. You're looking for the best supplier, not necessarily the cheapest.

- **Management commitment.** Success in telemarketing does not just happen. It demands, from management, a commitment to a plan that permits the costs of learning. It works best—and often works only—when it is integrated into the marketing plan from the very beginning. It is seldom successful as desperate first aid when everything else has failed.

WHAT TELEMARKETERS DO

As defined in the introduction to this book, marketing is concerned with *what* is sold, *where* and *how* it is sold (by mail, phone, radio or TV; in retail stores; through personal calls; etc.), *how* it is priced, and *how* it is promoted. Telemarketing can have a minor or major role in every one of these concerns. Determining your own use of telemarketing is best begun by seeing what outside service bureaus have to offer. Examining them not only opens the mind to new and exciting views of research, sales, and promotion, but also is a very practical overview of what is required to do telemarketing in-house.

Total Service Agencies

"Total" telemarketing service agencies, unlike most telemarketing service bureaus, work as all-around "marketers," rather than specialists. They work on *everything*, from analyzing a client's initial concepts for a product or service through managing the ultimate sales campaign. In this regard, they do exactly what is done by standard manufacturers or service organizations themselves. What they add, however, is their marriage of "tele" and "marketing" to produce a hoped-for synergetic whole. Essentially, they are *multidisciplinary promotion services* that combine product and price testing with electronic, direct mail, telephone, and print selling, plus order fulfillment and collecting. They bring together a half-dozen disciplines that are more often found in-house or at separate outside organizations. Since the vast majority of clients are unwilling to give anyone that much control over their business lives, most telemarketers provide equally expert services, though more limited in scope.

Standard Telemarketing Service Bureaus

Standard telemarketers are "standard" only in that they have a variety of different specialties. Their competitors are each other, not the total service agencies, which do something quite different. The services standard telemarketers provide (see Figure 7.2) can usually be bought individually, as well as in combinations or as "packages." They include the following:

• **Consultation at the marketing plan stage.** What is feasible by telemarketing? What are some alternatives? How long it will take to plan, test, and do, and what will it cost? These are best discussed before a marketing plan is even begun, not after it is set. Many telemarketers will meet for this discussion without charge. Some will have a fee if they do not get the project. Ask!

• **Consulting on what the project is to produce.** Shall the telemarketers do nothing but take the order? Deliver a message? Answer a question? What else, if anything, is practical and affordable? What can you get from the person on the line, once they are there?

• **Scripting, testing, and training.** Writing for telemarketing is an art in itself. But successful scripting is more than that. It is testing to see whether the script works, modifying where necessary, and then training a staff to be suitable for a particular project. In telemarketing, the importance of *how* something is said, as well as *what* is said, is a fact of life. It's also a continuously changing fact that only monitoring and testing will keep current.

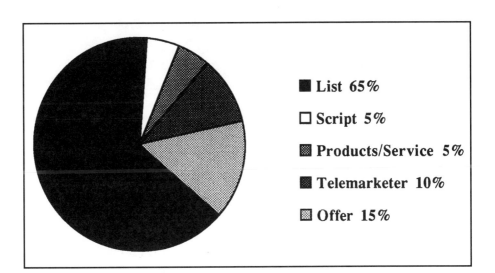

■ List 65%

□ Script 5%

▨ Products/Service 5%

■ Telemarketer 10%

▨ Offer 15%

Figure 7.2   Components of a telemarketing program. (Chart courtesy of Hugh Gollogly, Jr.)

- **Serendipitous supervision.** Some telemarketing operators are better than others. Sometimes it's innate talent. Often it's subtle improvements in the script that the individual operator is not even aware that he or she is making. But *supervisors have to know* that something good has happened, test it with others, and if it works for them, too, give credit to its originator. That is the kind of supervision you search for in building your in-house abilities, as well as evaluating outside services.

- **Continuing evaluation and reports.** Every telemarketing project will become more and more proficient as its operators become more comfortable and efficient with their assignments. Evaluations and reports, however, begin with the first call. On an agreed-upon, often daily, basis, they should tell the following:
  - Number of operators involved, and for how long
  - Number of calls made or received
  - Average time per call per operator
  - Results
  - Operators' comments, both impressions and "hard" facts
  - Service bureau or departmental evaluation and recommendations

- **Standard telemarketing service bureau technologies.**[4] The most important technologies for a service bureau[5] to process are predictive dialing, call handling via an ACD (automatic call distributor), and on-screen script and database viewing. In addition, agencies should accept multiple forms of incoming client data (magnetic diskette, cartridge, or electronic data transfer) and offer various output methods. The agency should also be able to offer remote monitoring, bridge and transfer capability, order verification (tape-recorded or digitized), quality assurance technologies, and extensive information management capabilities. Also look for fault-tolerant systems, backup systems for uninterrupted power, and expandable/flexible technologies that readily accommodate clients' needs.

  A service agency should not only *have* these technologies, but management should be able to *utilize, manage,* and *apply* them *to your specific project.*

How Telemarketers Charge

Telemarketing, in-house or from a service bureau, has three sets of costs. For outside organizations, these usually require partial payment in advance, to help cover up-front expenses. Since telemarketing programs can be—and often are—canceled before even the first call is made, specified cancellation fees are included in most agreements. The three costs are for the following services:

---

[4]Based on a report by Nadji Tehrani, publisher of *Telemarketing* Magazine (800-243-6002).

[5]The terms "service bureau" and "service agency" are used interchangeably within the telemarketing industry.

1. **Planning and consultation.** Know exactly what you wish to discuss, have a written agenda, and make sure that every point is covered. Once a service bureau has been selected, it charges for planning and consultation meetings. If there's a per-person rate for visiting you, ask their charge for your visiting the service bureau instead. Even if that won't be practical for you, it will make them aware of *your* budget concerns.

2. **Writing, testing, and training.** Preparing scripts, testing, revising, and retesting them, and training operators all precede the first call. Just as with preparation of copy and layout for an ad, 90 percent of the planning and creative thinking will have been done and will be charged for, even if the actual program is canceled.

3. **Calling, refining, reporting, evaluating, and recommending.** Most telemarketers charge for their inbound and outbound calling by the hour. The success or completion rate, especially on outbound service, practically demands honor-system billing, with frequent, detailed supporting documentation. If your initial evaluation of a telemarketing service makes you uncomfortable about this, consider other telemarketers until you find the right match. Evaluating, refining, reporting, and giving recommendations on the ongoing projects are usually, but not always, included in the hourly rate. Make sure.

TYPES OF TELEMARKETING

There are several types of telemarketing with which you're most likely to be involved. All can, of course, be given to outside service bureaus. We emphasize the opportunities and problems each brings the do-it-yourselfer.

Inbound Telemarketing

In inbound telemarketing, the inquiries and orders received by phone or fax are increasingly important to direct response selling. Where speed in fulfilling orders is *vital* to business success, the toll-free telephone—and, increasingly, the toll-free fax—has practically replaced ordering by mail.

Simple Product Ordering
Taking orders by phone has always been the most widely used of all telemarketing activities. Simple product ordering, whether from a catalog with thousands of items or in response to a television commercial offering a product that is "not available in retail stores!" *can* be handled in-house. Whether they *should* be depends largely on traffic flow. While you might be able to handle gigantic bursts of telephone activity economically for two weeks every two months, how would you staff for such a contingency? Outside help is unlikely to wait the other month and a half without seeking more dependable employment. Here are some approaches that work:

- **Stagger your promotions,** where practical. For instance, mail, advertise, or broadcast your products to one quarter of your audience two weeks apart. You'll need only a fraction of the staff to handle the responses, and you'll be able to give them all full-time work and decrease turnover, with its recruiting and training costs.

- **Promote the products more often** to the same audience. Even the most successful of promotions leaves the vast majority unsold on *that* item at *that* time. If you can't find new products or services, use what worked before. Run exactly the same promotion twice and even three times. But, of course, test first!

- **Use an outside service bureau.** These organizations *are* staffed to handle sudden bursts of activity with trained telemarketers who'll learn and remember your ordering system the next time it comes on line.

A catalog or other promotion may bring orders for years. Many service bureaus can continue to handle these orders as well as in-house personnel could, throughout that time. Through a system known as automatic phone distribution, callers are given to specific telemarketers who know a particular product line and have become even better at selling it as time goes by.

After-Hours Business
Telephone activity does not stop after "normal business hours," especially not for toll-free calling. Many service bureaus can handle this for you.

Relationship Selling
This is not the illegal "bait and switch," but legitimate and often appreciated "cross-selling" and even "up-selling." Relationship selling works best when the selections are comparatively limited (say, an 80-item catalog rather than an 800-item one) and the conversation is presumed to be with an expert in the field. Thus, a skilled telemarketer might suggest the scarf or glove shown on page 12 to go with the jacket ordered from page 17 . . . brushes or cleaning fluid to go with a specific paint . . . or an additional fall flowering plant when one is ordered for spring.

Supervise relationship selling as if your life depended on it. If potential customers are turned off by it, your business life may cease as well.

Free Information
In offering telephone information about a product or service, a number of factors have to be evaluated on an ongoing basis:

- **How the call will be charged.** Options include a local, regional, or national toll-free service, to accept collect calls, or to have the caller pay.[6]

---

[6]When both paid and toll-free calls are available, practically no one chooses to pay, even for local calls, as Hahn discovered when he used a wrong number in a client's promotion. The number had been taken from a previous brochure. To Hahn's surprise, the client wasn't nearly as shocked as he was. They had not had a paid call since toll-free service began! Hence, toll-free numbers were the only numbers his staff checked before printing. (Hahn did not tell him that, once alerted, he corrected a second wrong number on another brochure. At Hahn's suggestion, the client now uses *only* toll-free numbers in his promotional materials. At least *they* are checked.)

- **Who will get the initial call** and to whom it will be transferred if the first telemarketer can't answer the question.
- **When phone help will be available,** especially to do-it-yourselfers and for products likely to be used evenings or weekends.
- **Limits on types of telephone information** regarding how to *use* a product, rather than the physical product or service itself. This involves both the time you need to spend and possible legal ramifications (for example, telling a caller how to use battery jump cables to start a car). Check your insurance for appropriate coverage.

Charges for Information and Other On-Line Services

Fees for giving immediate telemarketed *services*—though not for information on products—are becoming common. The development of 900-number systems has made it possible to charge practically any amount—from pennies to dollars—to the telephone from which a call originates. Thus, a technical service bureau can charge just enough to keep nuisance calls within manageable limits, a legal or accounting service can cover the cost of an initial telephone consultation, and a children's storyteller (or adult sexual fantasizer) can charge whatever the traffic will bear.

The fact that telemarketing can do all this does not, of course, mean that all of it *should* be done. The resulting conflicts between protectors of the First Amendment and laissez faire capitalists on the one hand and protectors of children's welfare and morality on the other seems certain to grow more heated. Whatever the outcome—and it will vary among communities—*all* of telemarketing, no matter how innocent, will be affected. Consider the long-term consequences before joining either side. Your power to turn off *their* messages may well be their right to turn off *yours!*

Legal Constraints

Laws about what telemarketers may or may not do are growing rapidly, and changed often—usually to make them more restrictive. Whom you may call, when you may call them, and what you must tell them are now a matter of law practically everywhere, especially in consumer contacts. As a do-it-yourselfer, you *must* keep up-to-date. Read the direct response magazines, search the Internet, and participate in the telemarketing group in your direct marketing association.

Outbound Telemarketing

Outbound telemarketing can be simply making your calls in a routine or mechanical fashion. For this, live operators and computer-generated dialing can deliver the same *message.* But very few of the simpler automated dialers have any built-in "judgment." Many of them are operated from a one-person office or a home. The costs are comparatively modest and allow the system's owner to be away, handling leads or projects the calls have brought. But this type of automated dialing has led to annoyances and even dangers; for instance, the tying up of lines by calling every number in a hospital, police, or industrial network. Such automatic dialers have now been outlawed in many communities and some states. More sophisticated—and expensive—systems call specific numbers only and are an important part of true telemarketing.

True telemarketing is much more than mechanical or routine calling. It includes ongoing database analysis on which actions are based. The true telemarketer knows what is being said on both ends of the line—not only what message is sent, but how it is received and responded to. Together with the possibility of ongoing changes and improvements in communication, this knowledge is key to much of telemarketing's success. It also can—and indeed, at times, must—signal failure. When telemarketing will not work—at least, not on a cost-effective basis—the telemarketer must recognize this and be willing to stop the operation. Telemarketing must be used as a self-monitoring tool!

Outbound Sales Calls
Placed as "cold calls," without preparing the prospect, outbound sales calls are the most difficult of all telemarketing efforts. Cold calling requires knowledgeable guidance and continuous, positive reinforcement. When these three factors are kept in mind, it will succeed in many instances. However, don't expect results without professional help.

Requests for Donations
Even when placed cold, requests for donations for community, religious, fraternal, or educational organizations imply a common interest and usually get a friendly hearing. But take care in using professional service bureaus for such efforts. Their fees often absorb the lion's share of what is raised. A volunteer effort may not produce nearly the gross that a service bureau would, but it will probably increase the net amount vastly. Get a pro to help with the message; let dedicated amateurs make the calls.

INSIGHT 37

Make fund-raising efforts and other telephone requests for donations a group effort if at all possible. The group will cheer each other up and on during the inevitable "dry spells" that might cause volunteers at home to give up calling.

Warm-Ups for Mailing
A call to key customers or prospects (or both) lets them know that a very special mailing is coming. It's a proven way of increasing attention to what will be received, but consider these questions before you begin:

- If asked about it on the phone, what can you tell the listener about the content of the mailing? If the answer is "Nothing," why not?
- What if the person called wants a faxed copy of the offer . . . right now?
- What happens after they do get the special mailing? Will they be called again? If the mailing isn't worth a second call, what made it worth the first?

Do *not* use warm-up calls unless the offer is truly special. It's a very expensive way to have your audience disregard your subsequent mailings.

Qualifying Leads

Culling valuable prospects from an undifferentiated group is one of the most valuable services telemarketing can supply. But success in qualifying individuals depends both on what is asked and how it is scripted. It very much demands a skilled hand in both areas with freedom to modify the message and its delivery if the initial response is unsatisfactory. That is, after all, one of the major advantages of telemarketing: the ability to switch approaches midstream. It is imperative to have agreement on the desired results, but also to be flexible on how they are to be achieved. To that end, begin by defining:

- What *exactly* it will take to qualify a lead
- What *exactly* follows when someone does—or doesn't—qualify
- How you will handle overwhelming success—or failure

Qualifying the qualifications

Allow for all possible responses, especially if you are new to telemarketing. Your actual follow-up will show very quickly whether your identification of those who qualified is valid. But don't leave it at that. Give a random selection of nonqualifiers the same positive selling effort. Experienced telemarketers will insist on this as a check on their *real* success. Take nothing for granted. Learn at least *what* works, even if you can't tell *why*. Build a file that can be used as a database. A decade from now you want 10 years' experience, not 1 year's 10 times!

Pretesting Mail

Telemarketing is *not* direct mail. What works *and is affordable* in the one may not work in the other. But the advantages of using telemarketing to *pretest* direct mail offers is proving its worth to many direct marketers.

- Testing by mail gives only yes and no answers. But telemarketing can tell you *why*—both *why* they are *not* ordering and *why* they *are*. The latter especially may not be at all what you expect. It can turn a merely good mail response into a bonanza.
- Testing by mail can take months, from concepts and copy to production, printing, and mailing and then waiting for and analyzing the response. Skillful telemarketers can get their results in weeks!

INSIGHT 38

Consider testing by telemarketing as giving you an expanded instant focus group. It won't work for color or taste, but for many options, it gives a hundredfold increase in participants for about the same cost.

- Skillful telemarketers can change their trial script right in the middle of a message. Properly trained and supervised, they can refine or reposition the offer . . . instantly. Immediate feedback and response can help discover the best target markets, the most likely lists to reach it, and the most persuasive offer to convince it—almost while you wait!

Postsale Follow-Up

Hahn was not surprised when his doctor phoned to make certain that a new medicine had no unwanted side effects. He *was* surprised when the salesman from whom he had bought a washing machine, as well as the dealer to whom he had taken a car for a tune-up, both called to make certain that he had been *completely* satisfied.[7] All of these are examples of postsale telemarketing, one of the easiest[8] and simplest ways to create goodwill and encourage repeat business. Practically everyone is surprised and delighted by such a call. Word-of-mouth advertising— we all like to brag about our importance as customers—is often an additional benefit.

Surveys and Other Research

Why people are willing to speak so freely and frankly on the telephone with absolute strangers has always perplexed us. But they are! Practically any statistically valued information can be gotten this way. Household names like Gallup and Roper, as well as hundreds of other research organizations, provide the expertise needed for complicated research that requires sophisticated analysis. Many *business* surveys, however, can be do-it-yourself projects. Decide what you need to learn, decide who can give you the answer, get a statistically valid list of names, and call. Here are a few things to help bring do-it-yourself success:

- **Have a written script** of the entire conversation, not just the questions. If not, after about the tenth call you'll forget your own name!
- **Tell them immediately the reason for your call** and about how long it will take. (For example, "Good morning. I'm Charlene McCarthy from

---

[7]The mechanic to whom Hahn had gone previously sent a computer generated follow-up. Unfortunately, it was so poorly printed that it was practically impossible to read and hardly spoke well for his attention to detail. (See page 134 for more about messages—subliminal, liminal, and accidental.)

[8]A message from the nurse to the effect that "Dr. Doctor asked me to call . . ." does just as well. The *mechanic* didn't call; his supervisor did—in person.

the Scofield corporation, and I'd appreciate just three minutes of your time to ask about your likely need of toothpaste in the next six months."

- **When calling competitors** who are unlikely to share information, give the project to some graduate students, who can honestly say, "I'm a graduate student at ZLU, and I'm doing a survey of . . ."
- **Establish an in-house research arm** with an identity, address, and telephone that is different from yours. The more important the statistical validity of the responses, the more you will need experience or help in telemarketing, setting up surveys, and analyzing data. For just a general "feel of the situation," do it yourself.

FINDING THE HELP YOU NEED FOR IN-HOUSE OPERATIONS

Setting up in-house, whether business to business, business to consumer, or consumer to business, *must* begin with a telemarketer experienced in *successful start-up operations of that kind.* Just knowing how to run a program is not enough; starting up is the key! This telemarketer is not necessarily the person who can or will run the ongoing operation, so consider a consultant. Here's how to find one:

- **Check with local direct marketing associations.** If you are unfamiliar with where they are, the Direct Marketing Association, Inc., will tell you. Write Direct Marketing Association, Inc., Dept. DM Clubs, *Associations Networks,* 11 West 42nd St., New York, NY 10036-8096. Or call (212)768-7277. If you write, enclose a self-addressed, stamped envelope. Then join your local club. It'll help you even if you're not a member, but the continuing contacts alone are worth the price of admission!

- **Check with local or regional telemarketing service bureaus.** Some may recommend themselves. All will know appropriate consultants. None will want to see you—and telemarketing—fail!

INSIGHT 39

Consider starting up with a service bureau, even if you plan to go in-house. It will give you instant professional telemarketing, plus invaluable research on your work flow and staff needs, while your own facilities and personnel are put into place.

- **Check with telemarketing users, including your competitors.** Every start-up operation needed help. Telemarketing is growing so fast that they may well remember where they got their initial help or know of other sources you can use.

- **Check professional magazines.** Three industrial publications include annual directories of telemarketing products and services: *Telemarketing*® magazine (203)

852-6800, *TeleProfessional*™ magazine (319) 235-4473, and *Call Center* (212) 691-8215. As a comparative novice, subscribe to all three. The resulting flood of mail, and (we hope) calls, will keep you alert to everything new in the field. The *Bacon's Magazine Directory* (800) 621-0561 lists and describes 76 telecommunications publications. For specific needs, check there, too.

• **Find a mentor.** Search for someone whom you can call for advice when disaster strikes—or who can warn you before it happens. Practically everyone loves to find a new audience to hear about *their* pitfalls and how *they* solved them. Your business, direct marketing, and advertising associations are ideal sources. Join. Participate. Learn.

Finding the Right Service Bureau

The process of finding a service bureau is the same as that just discussed for finding a consultant. The problem isn't in the finding; it's deciding on what you need to find. Begin, as always, with a list. Figure 7.3 is an example.

A million names outbound is wholly different from inbound responses to a million catalogs. The first may be completed in 30 days, and you risk comparatively little in working with start-up telemarketers who'll go all out to prove their worth. The second may bring inquiries and orders for 30 months. For inbound service, longevity is all important. Your toll-free number, once published, takes on a life of its own. Consider also what happens when the initial rush of calls tapers off. Can and will the service bureau handle a few calls as well as many? How? For how long? At what cost?

Few, if any, telemarketers can do everything. Define what you need, and then hunt for it with a rifle, rather than a shotgun.

Testing Telemarketers

Elsewhere in this book—for convention displays, catalogs, and major direct mail projects—we suggested a contest among possible suppliers, *with everyone paid for their work.* Telemarketing also seems to lend itself to direct head-to-head testing, but first, consider the following:

• What is the size of the universe you will test, and what percentage of it gives an adequate response? Telemarketers consider 100 to 300 hours of outbound calling a reasonable test. If six of those called can be *contacted* per hour, that's 600 to 1,800 completed calls on which to base your decision. Should you want to match the 5,000 to 10,000 used in direct mail, your hours also will jump into the thousands. (That's 5,000 to 10,000 for *each* competing service!) If there is going to be a major difference in the rate of contact or number of positive responses, it will show up in the smaller quantities. They'll also let you "roll out" (i.e., put into use) your entire list much earlier.

TELEMARKETING SERVICE BUREAU EVALUATION

ABOUT US

☐ What the telemarketer must know or learn : _____

_____

☐ Outbound need : _____

☐ Size/source of lists : _____

☐ Inbound need : _____

☐ Source of calls : _____

ABOUT THE TELEMARKETER

BUREAU_____Date_____

Account executive _____

☐ Experience with similar lists _____

_____

☐ Service bureau age: _____Years of continuous telemarketing

☐ Service bureau specialization

_____ % business to business

_____ % business to consumer

_____ % consumer to business

_____ % other : _____

☐ Maximum number of operators available for project _____

☐ _____years pertinent experience of account executive

☐ $_____guarantee to service bureau

☐ $_____ hourly rate

References:_____

☐ _____

COMMENTS_____

_____

By_____Date _____

Figure 7.3   Sample service bureau evaluation checklist.

• One of the key things in evaluating a test is the type of analysis provided. Is it both quantitative and qualitative? Are the service bureaus making any recommendations as to the market? The product or service? The offer? Or are they simply calling? You really shouldn't do any testing unless you want to learn as well as sell. Telemarketing has the ability to gather vastly more information, and do it more quickly and cheaply, than testing by mail. Determine what you hope to learn. Make a list. Give it to each of the service bureaus being tested. Let *them* decide what's practical. After all, it is a test.

• Where significant differences in success appear, use the winner. More likely, the competitors will be evenly matched. In our experience, even that result has made a decision quite easy. Working with any outside service means forming a partnership toward a common goal. When all other factors seem equal, select the partner who you are convinced has the most to contribute and is willing to give that as part of your relationship.

In an industry as boomingly successful and fast-changing as telemarketing, an expert's look at the likely near future is surely welcome. So here it is.

TEN WAYS TELEPHONE MARKETING WILL CHANGE BY 2001 (BY MITCHELL LIEBER)[9]

Ten evolutionary revolutions are changing the very sounds telephone marketing makes during the final years of the twentieth century and the first few years of the twenty-first.

1. Dialogues

"Dialogues" are replacing "presentations." Instantaneous access to customer databases is enabling real-time individualization of scripts and call guides, based on customer comments and histories.

2. Integration

One-shot calls are being replaced by integrated combinations of mail, telephone, and on-line communication that develop and maintain customer relationships.

3. Modeling/Targeting

Wider deployment of modeling tools and expertise among telemarketers is resulting in better targeted outbound calling and more sophisticated inbound selling.

---

[9]Copyright 1996 by Mitchell A. Lieber, all rights reserved. First published in "Admarks" by the Chicago Association of Direct Marketing in July of 1996, "Ten Ways . . ." was revised by Mitchell Lieber for this book. Lieber's consultancy in telephone and database marketing, and telecommunications technology, Lieber & Associates, is headquartered in Evanston, Illinois (847-733-9410).

4. Computer Telephone Integration (CTI)

Computer Telephone Integration (CTI) is or will be in most business. Instant database "screen pops" and calling number (ANI)-based routing will be commonplace.

Calling number routing automatically routes calls on a *single toll-free number* to the proper department or extension instantaneously, *without human intervention.* It does this by using *ANI (automatic number identification*—caller ID on toll-free calls) together with *CTI (computer telephone integration).* ANI supplies the caller's phone number as the call rings in, and CTI matches it against the database for account status or assignment, and routing instructions.

A case history. For example, four callers to Boars Head Pub Supply's (800) PUB-5899 might be routed to four *different* representatives if the phone system were to consult the account database using this type of routing. The first call, say from Hard Rock Cafe purchasing, rings the major account group, and reaches Allison. The second call, from Sean Guenther, a regular catalog customer who orders English pub glasses for his home, rings the order department and reaches Elizabeth. Unlucky Pete's, the third caller, is a pub in arrears on their account, and is automatically sent to David in the collections department. The fourth call is from Pub Supplies Inc., a wholesaler, and is automatically transferred to Chad at the wholesaler's desk. This is all done transparently to the caller (no touch-tones or special toll-free numbers) by matching their *ANI* against a database using *CTI.*

5. Flexible Technology

Distinctions between the roles of long-distance telephone carriers (such as AT&T, MCI, Sprint), on-site telephone systems (such as Aspect, Lucent/AT&T, Rolm and NorTel), and computers that perform call processing (using Dialogic, Rhetorix, or similar add-in boards with specialized software) are blurring. These three industries are now competing to provide many inbound call processing functions. The underlying technologies that enable this competition are also enabling telephone lines, telephone systems, and computer systems to work together in better ways.

6. Networking

More telemarketing operations are connecting their networks to clients' networks for real-time telemarketing reports and real-time database updates based on telemarketing call activity. Checking telemarketing results is becoming nearly as easy as opening a file on a PC.

Intelligent links between inbound *automatic call distributors (ACDs)* and outbound *predictive dialers* are enabling more call centers to "blend" some staff for both inbound and outbound duties.

Client-server technology is enabling telemarketing systems to access corporate databases on mini and mainframe computers in real time, rather than in daily "batch" downloads. Client-server technology is becoming so commonplace that it will be available (in 1998) on contact-management software, which normally sells for about $250/user.

7. Voice Recognition

More inbound inquiries for hard data such as airline schedules and order status are being handled by voice recognition systems. Customers "talk to" the system. No touch-tones necessary. The system talks back:

> *Caller:* "What time does flight 366 from O'Hare to St. Louis arrive?"
> *System:* "Was that flight 366 from O'Hare to St. Louis?"
> *Caller:* "Yes"
> *System:* "Flight 366 from O'Hare is scheduled to arrive in St. Louis at 4:51 p.m."

Of course, live representatives will handle calls that machines cannot.

8. Interactive Call Centers

Interactive data and video via the Internet, telephone, and cable are transforming inbound telemarketing into a part of interactive call centers. More and more prospects and customers can "click here for a representative"—right on a World Wide Web home page.

9. Labor Costs

Labor shortages and higher wages are helping to drive voice recognition and predictive modeling into the call center mainstream. Further professionalization of telephone staff continues as live reps handle more sophisticated nonroutine calls.

10. Toll-Free

Several new toll-free area codes are joining 888 and 800, and the advent of single number international toll-free calling is shrinking the world. Current owners of vanity 800 numbers are scrambling to retain "exclusives" here and internationally during both "free call" expansions.

NOTES ON THE TELEMARKETING CHECKLIST

These notes are a supplement to the material presented in this chapter. They are not a substitute for that material.

1. **Purpose.** Before deciding on the purpose, suggest a brief professional updating on what the state of the art makes possible. Don't let management limit its options by not having that first.
2. **Budget.** Set specific, though generous, budgets, especially for getting started. Definitely get outside guidance if you are new to this medium.
3. **Time line.** Be specific about dates. Set time lines for management as well as staff: Specify when testing must be done, reported, and evaluated. **No**

TELEMARKETING CHECKLIST

Project Title _____ Date _____

Project Description _____ Project # _____

_____ Checklist # _____

Overall Supervision By _____ Deadline _____

Budget _____ Completion Date _____ Start Up Date _____

MANAGEMENT DECISIONS	ASSIGNED TO	DUE	IN	MUST APPROVE	BY DATE	IN	INFO COPY ONLY	SEE ATTACHED
1. Purpose	_____	___	☐	_____	___	☐	_____	☐
2. Budget	_____	___	☐	_____	___	☐	_____	☐
3. Time Line	_____	___	☐	_____	___	☐	_____	☐
4. In-House/Outside	_____	___	☐	_____	___	☐	_____	☐
5. Project Manager(s)	_____	___	☐	_____	___	☐	_____	☐
INBOUND								
6. Types & Purposes	_____	___	☐	_____	___	☐	_____	☐
7. Toll-free number(s)	_____	___	☐	_____	___	☐	_____	☐
8. 900 number(s)	_____	___	☐	_____	___	☐	_____	☐
9. Regular	_____	___	☐	_____	___	☐	_____	☐
OUTBOUND								
10. Types & Services	_____	___	☐	_____	___	☐	_____	☐
11. Phone Lists	_____	___	☐	_____	___	☐	_____	☐
IN-HOUSE								
12. Location(s)	_____	___	☐	_____	___	☐	_____	☐
13. Personnel	_____	___	☐	_____	___	☐	_____	☐
14. Equipment	_____	___	☐	_____	___	☐	_____	☐
15. Training	_____	___	☐	_____	___	☐	_____	☐
16. Budget	_____	___	☐	_____	___	☐	_____	☐
SERVICE BUREAU								
17. Selection	_____	___	☐	_____	___	☐	_____	☐
18. Script Approval	_____	___	☐	_____	___	☐	_____	☐
19. Schedule	_____	___	☐	_____	___	☐	_____	☐
20. Reporting System	_____	___	☐	_____	___	☐	_____	☐
21. Billing System	_____	___	☐	_____	___	☐	_____	☐
22. Cancellation Option	_____	___	☐	_____	___	☐	_____	☐
23. Budget	_____	___	☐	_____	___	☐	_____	☐
INBOUND/OUTBOUND								
24. Database Records	_____	___	☐	_____	___	☐	_____	☐
25. Evaluation(s)	_____	___	☐	_____	___	☐	_____	☐
26. Reports/ACTIONS	_____	___	☐	_____	___	☐	_____	☐

© 1997, Fred Hahn

"ASAP"![10] Specify when after-the-test decisions must be made, with agreement as to what that involves and on the budget to make it possible.

4. **In-house/Outside.** This is not necessarily an either-or decision. Often, both are required, at least for getting started.

5. **Project manager.** Consider separate managers if *major* in-house staff and a service bureau are both required. Telemarketing—even its supervision—is a totally time-intensive job!

6. **Types and Purposes.** Have *written* agreement on why the inbound services are established and what they are to achieve. Spell out the details against which evaluations can be matched.

7–9. **Call payment.** Decide who pays for each type of call. If different types of calls (routine orders, requests for technical data, simpler how-to questions) require different personnel, will they be available when callers are likely to phone? Who monitors what actually happens? Who's authorized to make it all work?

10–11. **Outbound how-to.** What outbound telemarketing is to accomplish and the data available to help make it happen. Do *not* count on getting usable telemarketing data from *any* computer—especially your own—without first seeing it happen. Don't settle for assurances or promises. Demand a demonstration. For new equipment or software, demand a guarantee.

12. **Location.** Consult your telephone company telemarketing expert—there is one!—before setting up in house. Telemarketing experts may even have solutions to which you have not yet discovered the problems.

13. **Personnel.** Don't start up without a *telemarketing start-up specialist* who's been through it all before . . . several times. This is critical to everything you'll do, from finding people to write the scripts and answer the phones to figuring out who works where with whom on what. Think of them as test pilots . . . there to get you safely launched.

14–15. **Equipment / Training.** Match equipment and training to what you need now. Allow for future expansion in long-range planning, but concentrate on making the present successful first if you want that future to arrive.

16. **Budgeting.** Do as was suggested for direct mail. Separate budgeting for start-up, testing, and ongoing telemarketing. Start-up is probably a capital cost. Testing is advertising. Ongoing telemarketing is sales. Money for start-up and testing is spent no matter what else you do. Don't let it distort posttesting success . . . or failure. Analyze, too, the effect on budgets of changing from in-house to an outside service bureau or vice versa. Keeping within budget is seldom the only reason for such a decision, but it is certainly a major one.

---

[10]See Insight 2.

17. **Selection.** Personal rapport is vital in your working relationship with the account executive, especially during start-up. Let management set parameters for the decision on which bureau to choose. Let the actual choice be made by the project manager.

18. **Script approval.** Read scripts for what they say, not the details of how they say it. Don't try to do the telemarketer's job. It's why you went to an outside service.

19. **Schedule.** Allow for the learning of what works best that can be achieved only on the phone. Discuss needs and scheduling with the service bureau before promising results to management.

20. **Reports.** The frequency and detail of reports, evaluations, and recommendations from the bureau. Who must see everything? Summaries? Only decisions?

21. **Billing.** Have a *written* agreement on how the service bureau bills. What work—if any—they do before payment is made. What adjustments—if any—must take place in your system, as well as theirs.

22. **Cancellation.** Get an unmistakable written agreement. ("Unmistakable" means that both parties understand the same thing the same way.) Establish routine checkpoints for continuation of the service. Set an automatic halt for review if specified goals are not met. Include an option for instant cancellation, with a basis for calculating costs incurred.

23. **Budget.** Most service bureau charges are established as standard costs. Totals are easily estimated for purposes of budgeting.

24. **Database records.** Build customers as well as sales. Meet with data-processing personnel to learn whether and how a database is being built. Take the same precautions as in #10 and #11. Check!

25. **Evaluations.** Much telemarketing is a team effort. It's telemarketing *plus* mailing . . . *plus* space and electronic advertising . . . *plus* selling in person . . . *plus* more and different prospect/suspect/customer contacts. Differentiate here and elsewhere between "prospects" on whom you spend more effort and dollars and "suspects" who are not worthy of that much attention. Relate all this to evaluation, where appropriate.

26. **Reports/actions.** Note especially what has been learned that may apply to future efforts. Check later whether the learning is actually passed on . . . and applied.

8 | Broadcast Fax

TWO NEW MEDIA

The 1990s have seen something unique in the history of communication, the use and acceptance of *two* new media for advertising: broadcast fax and the Internet.

BROADCAST FAX

The appearance of fax revolutionized business communication. Older fax technology took four or six minutes to send a single page with the longer time needed to receive legible copy. It was so little used, the Hahn agency had to give the system to its out-of-town clients for same-day copy transmission.

In the mid-1980s, what is known as "G3" (third-generation) fax gained worldwide acceptance, and the quality became excellent. A page took just 30 seconds or less to transmit, depending on the amount of copy. Within a few years, practically no business could afford to be without a fax.[1] However, its use as a *promotional medium* had to wait for one more communication revolution: the ability to send from ten to tens of thousands individually addressed messages practically instantaneously. The enhanced fax technology known as "broadcast fax" has made that possible.

WHEN TO "BROADCAST" YOUR FAX

If you're a travel agent, you've received messages from tour groups offering huge discounts for not-quite-sold-out travel packages.[2] Experience with broadcast fax has taught them they can still earn a commission the last practical moment offering the empty berths.

Given the right list—we'll get to lists in a moment—almost any special (and even not-so-special) event profits from the same kind of broadcast fax use. For instance:

- Announcement of overstocked inventory or older merchandise *suitable for the audience receiving the message*

---

[1] The 1993 edition of this book had to tell readers where to send and receive a fax if they did not have a machine. By 1997, fax ownership is considered an essential business tool.

[2] If it's a Friday departure, call Monday afternoon and offer to pay 40 percent for the best cabin. The ship leaves whether it's full or not and 40 percent is better than nothing. Prepare to negotiate!

- Business and professional association meeting reminders
- Convention or trade show inducements to visit a specific booth or social event
- Favorable reviews of artistic, musical, and other cultural events sent to likely ticket buyers, especially if they have asked for the information
- Publicity releases to electronic and print media (much more about this in the chapter on publicity and public relations)

Here are somewhat different ways to use broadcast fax:

- Invitation to a seminar or other self-improvement event important to the person being addressed.
- Individualized *next-day* follow-up (see Figure 8.1) to everyone who attended the event. Thank them and offer an action-generating benefit that reinforces the main sales message of your meeting. Always remember that broadcast fax is a *personalized* medium. You're sending one individual message to one man or woman.
- For exhibit booth follow-up, use the same kind of benefit-filled fax. Be sure to give your convention-site visitors a reason to leave their own fax numbers (much more about this in the chapter on conventions and trade shows).

INSIGHT 40

Do not think of broadcast fax as "advertising." It is the most *personal* of *business* promotional media. Business expects to get "advertised at" in person, in print, by phone, on the Internet, and by mail. But not by fax! That is reserved for immediate *business* communication. Make sure your message meets this standard. And make it *personal,* too!

HOW BROADCAST FAX WORKS[3]

Broadcast fax, listed under "Fax Transmission Service" (FTS) in the Yellow Pages and available through big long-distance carriers such as Sprint, must have four elements to be successful for your business needs:

1. *Software.* A communication system that has the software to personalize any number of written messages. The kind of personalization is explained shortly. (It is not available in retail computer stores, as it is too technical.)

---

[3]The technical explanation of how broadcast fax works is found in books like *Computer-Based Fax Processing,* by Maury Kauffman, to whom this section of our book is totally indebted. His nontechnical answer is: "by magic." He is Managing Partner of The Kauffman Group, an enhanced facsimile services consulting firm specializing in the benefits of adding fax to a marketing mix (609-482-8288). E-mail: MKauffman@mcimail.com

Sprint ®

Sprint TeleMedia

Steve Larrick
Marketing Manager - SprintFAX
(913) 661-8005
FAX: (913) 624-2104

FRED   HAHN
FRED   HAHN   ASSOCIATES

I hope you enjoyed the recent seminar. If you have any questions, please call me or
Duanna Matthys at 1-800-366-3297. I look forward to talking with you in the near future.
Thank you.

Sincerely,

Steve Larrick

Steve Larrick

P.S. Don't forget about
the SprintFAX offer of 1,000
Free Fax minutes or 1,000 Free
Fax numbers. The offer is
good for the next 30 days,
so call Duanna at 1-800-366-3297
to take advantage of this
great offer.

I want to express my
appreciation to you for your recent
attendance at our SprintFAX seminar.
We hope that Maury Kauffman's
overview in conjunction with the
presentation of SprintFAX capabilitie
will enhance your marketing mix.

Thanks again for your
attendance. We hope it was
worth your time.

Sincerely,

Duanna Matthys

Figure 8.1   Here's an example of broadcast fax used to its full advantages. Sender and recipient, clearly differentiated by both positioning and individual typefaces, use all six available lines. The brief "Johnson Box"-style typewriter message has both senior management and a local service representative on a single page. And the benefit-loaded handwritten note (printed for legibility!) adds the ultimate in a *personal* touch—even though it's obviously a follow-up message that went to everyone attending the meeting. (For further discussion of the "Johnson Box," see page 109.)

2. *Hardware.* Specialized computer hardware with fax-specific "ports" (telephone lines) to send your messages as scheduled. Several thousand such ports are not at all unusual! The number of ports is critical for large-quantity lists; fewer will be fine for smaller needs. In scouting for an FTS, make the number of ports your first question. Make references the second.
3. *Technical personnel.* Computer programmers and telephony engineers—both are needed—on hand to keep the system operating.
4. *Customer service.* Knowledgeable men and women who can, and will, help you understand, use, and profit from broadcast fax—exactly the same kind of customer service you expect from any other medium.

BROADCAST FAX vs. ELECTRONIC MAIL

Broadcast Fax	Electronic Mail
Best as single page. Two or three pages at most.	Lets you send messages of any length anywhere in the world, practically instantaneously.
Automatic confirmation that message was or was not received.	No way of knowing message was received without action from other end.
Cost of call to local or long-distance destination.	Cost of local phone call to send anywhere in the world. Plus cost for software, modem, and Internet connection service.
Totally private to single-user fax. Tamper-proof as this is written.	No guarantee of privacy even for single-user E-mail terminal.
Can be already on desk when recipient arrives at work.	Recipient must check file, decide whether to read enough to become interested, save, or download as hard copy.
Perfect for promotional use for which it was developed.	Perfect for military, scientific, and other special interest groups for which it was intended and developed.

By 1997 practically every American business-to-business concern uses fax. There are approximately 100 million stand-alone fax machines worldwide and they are growing at some 15 million more per year.[4] That compares with perhaps one-third that number of E-mail users, the majority of whom want no part of advertising messages. Unless promotional data are specifically asked for, E-mail = personal mail = personal; Fax = business mail = business. Where do you think you will find the friendlier business response!

---

[4]"Final Word" column in *Information Week* newsletter.

BUILDING YOUR DATABASE

Someday, hopefully quite soon, every business will have its fax as well as its regular telephone number in the Yellow Pages. Until then, you must gather, collect, store, and keep current your own database. Fortunately, that's easy to do.

- Many business, professional, and membership directories include fax numbers. Some will provide the listing on a disk. Others can be copied from the directories.

When Fax Numbers Are Not Easily Available

- For a small list, call each regular phone number and say, "May I please have your (name or department) fax number?" Few will refuse.
- For larger lists, send the missing fax-number destinations a double, postage prepaid card as in Figure 8.2 requesting the number. Two weeks after receiving the first response, you'll have 90 percent of the likely mail answers. Use a telemarketing service to contact the rest. To increase response, put an offer on the postcard.

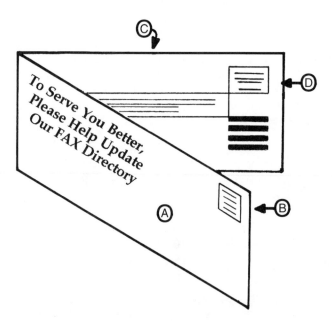

Figure 8.2 A double postcard serves as an excellent, inexpensive way to request—and get—fax numbers and E-mail addresses from a large list. (A) Front cover addressing side. (B) Brief message about use you will make of fax number. Make this a benefit to customer or prospect! (C) Room for fax number fill-in and, possibly, some free offers of "How we can help you with this additional information," described in Checklist point 14. Show small illustration of double card refolded for mailing back. (D) Prepaid return address. You can use much lighter and less expensive stock than having a single card separated and returned.

PERSONALIZING BROADCAST FAX

Broadcast fax can be personalized with up to six lines of 60 characters each, using different type sizes and styles for emphasis, as in Figure 8.3. It cannot, however, add a name or phrase to personalize within the body of a message. That capability remains an advantage of direct mail ink jet printing.

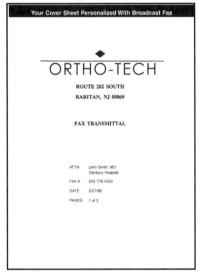

a

b

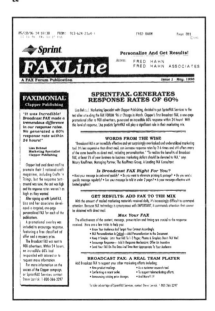

c

Figure 8.3 A full-page cover sheet (Figure 8.3a) certainly adds "class" but is seldom worth the extra cost. The simple "To" personalization in Figure 8.3b works just as well. If immediate sender identification is important, use a regular or modified letterhead as in the newsletter in Figure 8.3c. If you broadcast fax a newsletter, keep it brief and make sure it contains news that offers a benefit to the recipient as well as you. For self-puffery, stick to the mail.

Some Guidance in Personalization

Maury Kauffman, Managing Partner of The Kauffman Group, suggests 12 tricks of the trade to make your fax broadcasting more successful and more cost-effective. They are so valuable, we have made them a special KAUFFMAN'S DOZEN part of this chapter's Broadcast Fax checklist!

SUMMARY

- Almost any event can profit from a broadcast fax push.
- Broadcast fax is a personalized medium. Do *not* make your message an ad! Keep it focused on the recipient.
- Add a simple way to respond to your message. For instance, "Sign and fax back" or "Call toll-free."
- When checking a Fax Transmission Service, check on equipment, personnel, and service. Don't settle for two out of three!

NOTES ON THE BROADCAST FAX CHECKLIST

These notes are a supplement to the material presented in this chapter. They are not a substitute for that material.

1. **Quotations.** The total of all quoted and/or estimated costs accepted from outside suppliers, plus the known or estimated internal out-of-pocket costs. This is the amount given for budget approval in #2.
2. **Budget approval.** The amount either accepted from #1, or otherwise determined as a fair cost to do the project. If lower than the figure in #1, costs may have to be renegotiated with suppliers or the project modified to fit the dollar allocation.
3. **Project approval.** Once the project *can* be done for the amount in #2, a decision on whether the project is worth the cost, no matter how "fair" the individual charges may be.
4. **Target audience.** Determination of the target audience at whom the fax is focused. Everything else about this fax must then be controlled by that focus. Do *not* use fax broadcasting for shotgun marketing or for prospecting. *Do* use it to market to your existing customer base or enclosed groups like tour organizations to travel agents or associations to their members.
5. **Message & Results.** Give the reason for the message and the results it is to produce. This tells the writer *what* is to be said, not *how* to say it. The actual wording is the job of the writer in #9.
6. **Benefits.** The benefits offered in the message, keyed to the audience in #4. If none of those benefits seem particularly suited to that group, the

BROADCAST FAX CHECKLIST

Project Title _____   Date _____

Project Description _____   Project # _____

_____   Checklist # _____

Overall Supervision By _____   Deadline _____

Budget _____   Completion Date _____   Start Up Date _____

MANAGEMENT DECISIONS	ASSIGNED TO	DUE	IN	MUST APPROVE	BY DATE	IN	INFO COPY ONLY	SEE ATTACHED
1. Quotations	_____	___	☐	_____	___	☐	_____	☐
2. Budget approval	_____	___	☐	_____	___	☐	_____	☐
3. Project approval	_____	___	☐	_____	___	☐	_____	☐
CREATIVE DECISIONS								
4. Target Audience	_____	___	☐	_____	___	☐	_____	☐
5. Message & Results	_____	___	☐	_____	___	☐	_____	☐
6. Benefits	_____	___	☐	_____	___	☐	_____	☐
7. Headline	_____	___	☐	_____	___	☐	_____	☐
8. Offer	_____	___	☐	_____	___	☐	_____	☐
9. Writer	_____	___	☐	_____	___	☐	_____	☐
10. Design	_____	___	☐	_____	___	☐	_____	☐
11. Transmission Service	_____	___	☐	_____	___	☐	_____	☐
KAUFFMAN'S DOZEN								
12. Personalization	_____	___	☐	_____	___	☐	_____	☐
13. Response	_____	___	☐	_____	___	☐	_____	☐
14. Interactive Fax	_____	___	☐	_____	___	☐	_____	☐
15. Graphics	_____	___	☐	_____	___	☐	_____	☐
16. Frequency	_____	___	☐	_____	___	☐	_____	☐
17. Legal Limits	_____	___	☐	_____	___	☐	_____	☐
18. Budgeting	_____	___	☐	_____	___	☐	_____	☐
19. Cover Page	_____	___	☐	_____	___	☐	_____	☐
20. Off-peak	_____	___	☐	_____	___	☐	_____	☐
21. Length	_____	___	☐	_____	___	☐	_____	☐
22. Database	_____	___	☐	_____	___	☐	_____	☐
23. Multiple Faxing	_____	___	☐	_____	___	☐	_____	☐
MECHANICAL CHECKS								
24. Record Code	_____	___	☐	_____	___	☐	_____	☐
25. Editorial OK	_____	___	☐	_____	___	☐	_____	☐
26. Legal OK	_____	___	☐	_____	___	☐	_____	☐
27. Marketing OK	_____	___	☐	_____	___	☐	_____	☐
28. Management OK	_____	___	☐	_____	___	☐	_____	☐
29. Hard Copy File	_____	___	☐	_____	___	☐	_____	☐

choice of *those* benefits and why *that* particular audience was targeted must be reconsidered.

7. **Headline.** The headline's subject, not its wording. Pick the one thing most likely to attract the target audience; usually the key benefit from #6.

8. **Offer.** Give the recipient a *major* reason to respond NOW!

9. **Writer.** The checklist shows the person who *appoints* the writer. If certain things must be said in a specific way, let the writer know before he or she begins . . . and whether this is a legal constraint or a management decision. If the latter, management should be willing to at least consider alternatives.

10. **Design.** The person responsible for choosing the designer. This is a fax. Keep it simple and legible!

11. **Transmission Service.** Before hiring your fax transmission service (FTS), get references for the quantity of work you need done. Don't just ask for references. Check them!

KAUFFMAN'S DOZEN

12. **Personalization.** Fax personalization is critical. Name, company, and ID numbers can all be added to a personalized fax. If your database has a field, it can, as in Figure 8.3, be put practically anywhere on the fax.

13. **Response.** Add a response mechanism to your fax. "To get more information (or order), sign here and **fax** back" is just one example.

14. **Interactive fax response (IFR).** IFR, also known as "Fax on Demand" and "Document on Demand," is usually handled by a broadcast fax company. It lets the fax recipient fax or call a toll-free number for frequently requested information. Callers can—*usually within minutes, around the clock*—get a return fax with up-to-the-minute information on product availability and price, order forms, product instructions, training materials, and so on.

15. **Graphics.** Keep the medium in mind when creating a fax. Photos and detailed graphics never fax well. Even fine lines may be a problem.

16. **Frequency.** Do not overuse the fax as a promotional tool. These documents have a sense of urgency that will lose their impact if you send everything by fax.

17. **Legal limits.** Know the limitations placed on fax broadcasting by the Telephone Consumer Protection Act (TCPA). Find an attorney who specializes in this field.

18. **Budgeting.** Allocate 5 percent of your advertising budget to test broadcast fax. Programmed faxing should cost no more—and often less!—than a comparable document send by mail . . . and be delivered in hours, rather than days. Get knowledgeable help. Believe the results.

19. **Cover page.** Whenever possible, limit the use of a full-page cover page. Use a "headline" or Post-it™ note format. Even a half page will do.

20. **Off-peak hours.** Transmit during off-peak hours when possible, especially when sending multiple faxes.

21. **Length.** Send as few pages as possible. A single page is most likely to get read. Single-space most documents. Cut down on white space, but don't jam so much onto a page it becomes uninviting to the eye or hard to read. If you use a typesetting format, make the text at least 12 point in size.

22. **Database.** Establish a system to keep your database up-to-date. Use it!

23. **Multiple faxing.** Use a broadcast fax service bureau with the staff and equipment to do the job right. You'll save countless headaches and countable money.

24–28. **Mechanical checks.** Someone has to be responsible for checking each of these items before anything may be sent. Make sure that they *do* check them and sign off *in writing.*

29. **Hard copy file.** Some *one* person must be responsible for maintaining a hard copy file of all fax "as broadcast"; that is, as they actually appeared.

9 | Advertising on the Web

SMOKE SIGNALS BROUGHT UP-TO-DATE

We have moved in one lifetime through the following:

- Direct response primarily in print
- Direct response in both print and mail (the first revolution)
- Direct response combining print, mail, and phone ("integrated direct marketing"—the second revolution)
- Direct response trying to sell on the Internet. Rather than you hunting for prospects, this "consensual marketing" revolution tries to fulfill every advertiser's dream of getting the prospect to hunt for you!

The Internet as a Medium

The Internet is known to all of us by one of several names, including "The Web," "The World Wide Web," "The Internet," "E-mail," "Computer-based Interactive Communication," and so on. The hardware has been with us for the past few decades. Its use as *both business-to-business and a consumer advertising, promotion, and public relations* medium is new. As this is written, several companies have announced Internet access via television, bypassing the need for a computer. Apparently the use of the Web as an advertising medium is about to skyrocket!

There are two aspects of advertising on the Web: your Web site as an advertisement and advertising your Web site on other sites; that is, having lots of places people can find you. This chapter will be of value to you in both these areas, if you meet one of three conditions:

1. *You have no computer.* You have little or no knowledge of the Internet. You may not have a computer and are going to decide whether it's worth getting one to try and do business on the Web.
2. *You are doing it yourself.* You are in business, have a computer, and are thinking of building your own Web site; that is, making your Web site promotions a do-it-yourself project. This section tells you the minimum of time, effort, and expertise that will be required.
3. *You need an expert.* You have a Web site but hope to make it more effective as a business communication tool. You need help in finding and supervising an outside service that is going to create your Web site. This section will help you ask the right questions and give the key instructions.

The Internet is a medium like print, radio, and TV. Nothing more (maybe less). It begins with a "home page," the first thing your customer or prospect sees. Like all our selling communications, it is "smoke signals brought up-to-date."

In working with the Internet, many of us have spent the past few years working on mechanics, very much like early pilots learning engine repair because they never knew when or where they'd be forced to land. But like much else about computers, that is no longer necessary. Anyone can get on-line and get a home page. The "secret" of success, as in all the previous media, has turned from "mechanics" to "psychology" . . . from how do they work to how to get someone to take action.

YOUR HOME PAGE "TEASER"

Think of your home page as your computer direct response envelope that has to have a "teaser" to get someone inside. No matter how far you get the reader/surfer into your message, until you get some action, nothing happens. No matter what the medium, it is the right psychology that wins.

A Case history.[1] "Our experience shows that four major criteria drive the success of the home page: fast access, frequent updates, rich content, and easy navigation."—Richard Cohn, executive vice president and executive creative director, DraftDirect agency, Chicago (312-944-3500).

GETTING WEB SURFERS TO FIND YOU

How do you get Web surfers (or lookers) to look for you or find you by accident? Some who succeeded include the following:

• A medium-sized city put on a Community Home Web site and gave every business its own page. Some shopping centers have done that also. This could be done for any organization that wants to make its membership public or a portion of whose membership wants to be known as affiliated with it. Think of a hospital and its doctors or a school's faculty open to consultant offers!

• A small chain of home-center stores puts a monthly do-it-yourself project on-line with a plan and a list of what's needed to make it. Viewers download and take this to the store where everything—including helpful advice—is waiting. What a great idea for a sewing machine or fabrics shop. Each month, put on-line some sewing tips and fairly simple children's clothing patterns that can be purchased with the materials at the store. Make your product or service fit a similar *helpful* sales plan, and you should have a Web sales winner.

---

[1]Quoted in *Midwest ADWEEK,* Nov. 4, 1996.

The examples just given work because customers and prospects were told about the Web site. Every communication used by the advertiser included the suggestion to "Check Our Web site: www.success.unlimited.com for New Help Every Month."

WHO MAKES MONEY ON THE INTERNET?

In 1997 and probably for a few years to come, the question of who makes money has three possible answers:

1. *Sales to everyone.* Whether you are selling directly to consumers or business-to-business, most sales are by providers of Internet information, software, and hardware. But "most" is far from "all."
2. *Business-to-business.* Business-to-business sales are probably underreported. Many of them, as shown in Chapter 13, involve "just" giving prospects and customers instant, detailed information needed to make a buying decision. Providing that information in a "selling" fashion undoubtedly helps. Comparatively few businesses will surf the Web looking for suppliers. Rather, they know their suppliers' Web "addresses" and link directly to them.
3. *Consumer sales.* Consumer selling not connected to the Internet itself is both the weakest *current* seller and the strongest *potential* seller in the medium. At-home computer ownership and Web linkup is growing by the millions each year. Practically every major corporation and an increasing number of large and small businesses are doing business on the Web.

Though there is absolutely no way of knowing what will be happening to the Web as a business medium, the only thing we can be sure about is that change will be fast and constant. Think of how much has changed in one lifetime—and how much has changed that we've forgotten about. The one thing you cannot afford to do is to pretend it isn't happening! Your future on the Internet, as your future on every other medium, demands that you learn, Learn, LEARN and test, Test, TEST. Test what is here today and what will be coming. Surf the Internet and see what is going on, then apply what makes sense to your own needs.

WHERE TO LEARN THE BASICS

Practically every community college has courses in the use of computers for personal and business applications. What just a few years ago took complicated programming has become point-and-click simplicity. Decide what you want to learn about selling on the Internet, then take a course to fit your needs. And don't worry about your grade! You are there to learn, whether or not you can find the time and skill to do it yourself, and what someone else must know, if you can't. You'll see that the basics are now fun and easy, but complex tasks are still best left to true experts. Designing the Web page that is your Internet showroom is your first such decision. Like you, we asked a true expert[2] for help. Here it is!

ABOUT "12 WEB PAGE DESIGN DECISIONS"

The "12 Web Page Design" section that follows is an example of a successful Web site; that is, a business that is successful in selling its services on the Internet. Since you are reading a book rather than a computer screen, the copy has been modified slightly to explain things that longtime computer users have forgotten they ever had to learn.

If you are reasonably computer literate and prefer a screen to a book, you will find the same "12 Web Page Design Decisions" section at http://www.wilsonweb.com/-articles/12design.htm. For the rest of us (like Hahn), who have to check whether the Internet and the World Wide Web are really just different names for the same thing[3] . . . read on!

---

12 WEB PAGE DESIGN DECISIONS YOUR BUSINESS OR ORGANIZATION WILL NEED TO MAKE (By Dr. Ralph F. Wilson)

So you're a business owner or organization director trying to design a system of Web pages? Small business? Nonprofit organization? Chamber of commerce? Religious organization? Association? You have unique needs. I'll try to guide you through the process. When you're finished, you'll know a lot more about what goes into Web page design. You'll also have a set of design decisions to guide your own Hypertext Mark-up Language (HTML) adventures, to give to your local Web-page designer, or to send to me so I can design pages for your organization. I'll remind you to print this document at the end of this long page, and you'll be sent a copy of your design decisions.[4]

Together we'll examine these 12 decisions:

- Purpose
- Index Page and Site Organization
- Site and Domain Names
- Main Graphic to Highlight Your Site
- Background Color and Texture
- Basic Page Elements

---

[2]Such as Dr. Ralph Wilson, the source for the "12 Web Page design" section.

[3]Think of the Internet as analogous to all the telephone wires in the world and the World Wide Web (www in all those Web addresses) as all the phone companies *and individual telephones.* Of course, some phone company does have to get paid before your phone works. But just as you can call anyone from any phone, no matter who owns the phone company or line, your computer can call (link) and communicate with any other computer.

[4]Remember, this is a copy of an actual Web site, modified for book format.

- Finishing Touches
- Photos and Graphics
- Forms to Get Customer Response
- Uploading and Testing Your Pages
- Registering and Advertising Your Site
- Maintaining Your Site

Finally, we'll look at cost ranges.

1. Purpose: Why Do You Want to Do This?

You'll save a lot of time and money by being honest with yourself right here at the beginning. Just why are you doing this? What do you hope to achieve? What is your purpose?

☐ "The World Wide Web is hot. Everybody is getting a Web presence. *I'd better do it, too, or be left behind.*" If this represents your thinking, as it does many businesses, you're probably right, but you need more focus.

☐ We want potential customers to learn about our company, and *gain a favorable impression* of us.

☐ We want to *develop a qualified list of prospects* for our goods and services.

☐ We want to *sell products directly* from our Web pages.

☐ *Other,* specifically: _____

Begin with patience and the long-term view. Your business results from the World Wide Web may be immediate and spectacular. Then again, you may not make much of an impact right away. Be ready to soar, but realize that some products and services don't lend themselves to this medium. "Browse" the Web for as many businesses as you can find similar to yours. Of course, anyone can get onto the Web, but being there is no proof of business success. Perhaps your prospective Web-page designer can give your some insight.

Now state your purpose for developing your Web site in one simple sentence:

_____

_____

_____

2. Index Page and Site Organization

Some people call this a "home page." I like to think of it as your "storefront" on the World Wide Web marketplace. It provides an index to the set of pages that describe your business or organization.

Your web-page system will have several main sections, such as:

- **About your organization.** This section may include a vision or mission statement, history of your business, a philosophy of how you do business, and so on. Sell the customer on why he or she should do business with *you* rather than with your competitor.

- **Product lines.** With photos and text, describe the benefits to your customers of your goods and services. You can also show features, applications, or examples. Plan to use several web pages for each major product line. You can also use your Web pages as a catalog, which you can update easily, inexpensively, and often.
- **Technical support.** Some businesses find it useful to provide technical information, specifications, frequently asked questions, parts lists and diagrams, troubleshooting decision trees, etc.
- **How to order.** This will include a form that E-mails your customer's information to you at the click of a mouse. The prospect or customer doesn't need to call or mail. It's instant, automatic, and free.
- **Service section.** This is free information of interest to your potential customers that'll keep them coming back to your site for updates. It might be news of your industry, of a related field, or something unique or interesting. Give some thought to what service *your* Web pages will provide to draw customers to your "storefront" again and again.
- **What's new** section is where you put updates or new copies of a newsletter.

Your Web designer will ask you what you want to display on your site. This will help you be prepared to explain your concept. Take a few minutes right now to sketch out your thoughts in the spaces below.

About our company

Product or service lines

Technical support

Guestbook or order page (See Point 9 on pages 219–220 for an example.)

Services to attract customers to our site

Other

3. Site and Domain Name

Next, you need to determine a tentative name for your Web site. You may just want to use your existing business name. But your Web site focus may be broader or narrower than your organization name implies. In that case, look for a name that is descriptive, unique, short, and memorable. Your tentative Web site name is:

_____

_____

Now give thought to your domain name; that is, your unique Internet address. You may presently be using your Internet Service Provider's chosen domain name. You may be able to select a domain name which is related to your site name, if the best names are not already taken. You can find out which names are still available by trying your proposed domain name at the InterNIC "whois" interface (http://rs.internic.net/cgi-bin/whois/). Check the domain name that you'd like to use against their on-line database to see if it has been taken. You may have to check several variations until you find the right domain name.

How to protect your domain name

You don't have to secure your own business domain name, but it gives your site, like a telephone number, its own identity. Currently, in 1997, the fee for a new domain name is $100 to cover the first two years, and then $50 per year thereafter.

Another advantage of selecting a unique domain name for your organization is that you aren't so dependent upon your Internet Service Provider (ISP). Suppose your ISP raises prices too high, or goes out of business? If you have your own domain name, just have your new ISP send notification to the InterNIC registration center that they are now hosting the address on their server. Your viewer base and links, the way viewers find you, are protected.

☐ I do not plan to get a special domain name at this time.
☐ I would like to try to have a domain name like _____

You need to plan on a few weeks' lead time to register a domain name, so get started with that right away if you're going to do it.

4. Main Graphic to Highlight Your Site

Your "index" or "home" page needs a graphic to look inviting. Think about it as the sign over your storefront that beckons your customer inside.

☐ **No graphic.** Just use headline text. This is the easiest way to go, but dull. If this is a do-it-yourself project, begin but don't end here.

☐ **Clip art graphic.** Perhaps you have access to black-and-white or color clip art from a program such as Corel Draw®, or Word for Windows®, or Microsoft Publisher®. Make sure your image is copyright free; you don't want your company to be sued. Inquire first about copyright ownership! Then convert it to a GIF format image. JPEG format images are often larger than GIFs for clip art.

☐ **Scanned-in graphic.** You may already have a company logo or an artist's drawing. You can scan this in and convert to a GIF image. Use your own scanner, or have a local computer service bureau (or Kinko's®) do this for you.

☐ **Customized type fonts.** These can be developed from programs such as Paint Shop Pro®, L View Pro®, or Photoshop® to save as a GIF or JPEG image.

☐ **Scanned-in photograph with type superimposed.** You can find some great collections of sky photographs on the Internet. Some are free, most are for sale at a reasonable price. Download one of these and superimpose your company's name over it. You can do this by using the Paint Shop Pro® or Adobe Photoshop® program. Or you can let your Web designer do it for you.

☐ **Customized computer art by a computer artist.** This may cost you a few bucks, but the right graphic sets the tone for your site.

☐ **Word and/or image map combined with customized computer art.** Using the image map as guide (see Figure 9.1), the customer clicks on the subject in the graphic that interests him or her. An underlying program compares the position of your mouse cursor with the words or icons on the image and transports you to your selected destination. Image maps are cool, but start to get expensive, since they take more programming skill, and require a special interface with your host computer. You may want to is to leave this one to a professional Web page designer.

A few pointers:

- Try to keep your total images under 40K per page, or your customer may lose interest. I've found that at least 75 percent of a Web site's visitors will come with "auto load images" on, that is, they're waiting for pictures to download.
- Not all your viewers have a monitor with 16 million color capability, or even 256 colors. Many can see only 16 colors. What does your graphic look like with 16 colors? Test!
- Using "interlaced" GIF images helps keep your customer's interest as the graphic gradually displays over four "passes." The total time is about the same for interlaced or noninterlaced images. However, be careful and test extensively!
- The best combination is a single sparkling graphic combined with text.
- The overall look of your "home" page needs to be graphically balanced, pleasing, informative.
- Your "index" or "home" page functions as your storefront. It needs to entice the customer in the door to look at the rest of what you have to offer. This is where a professional writer can help, too.

Okay, let's get back to the hard decisions which face you.

5. Background Color and Texture

You want to set your Web site off from all the rest. One way is with a well-designed graphic. The other is with a background texture and/or color.

☐ **Plain gray.** This is your entry-level color scheme. All browsers can display it. The novice HTML writer can do this without even trying. I don't know why anyone uses gray when they can choose something brighter. Gray is ugly.

☐ **Colored background and lettering.** If you know the RGB codes for your colors, you can easily change the background color. Make the letters a contrasting color. Remember that light-colored letters don't show up well if your visitor wants to print out the page on paper!

☐ **Textured and colored backgrounds** abound on the Web. This is really pretty easy, like the tiled wallpaper used in your Windows® desktop. Both texture and color will make your site special. But you have to be *very* careful that your text is easily readable when you're finished. If they can't read it they won't stay. Don't let the background overwhelm the text, but subtly complement it. Consider white.

6. Basic Page Elements

If you have lots of information, you need to choose between long or multiple pages.

☐ **Long Web pages.** These are good if you expect people to print out or download your pages for future reference (like this document, for example).[5] You can index these to internal "bookmarks" to help your customers find their way to needed information. Netscape's "Handbook" is a pretty long file treated this way. The drawback is that long pages of 40K or more may be more than your customers will want to wait for. Webmasters mutter words like "bandwidth" and shake their heads.

☐ **Multiple shorter pages.** Here your menu links jump to many shorter pages that treat just one subject each. It doesn't take as long to view, but if you think people will want to download or print out ten different pages, think again.

Check below the elements that you want to include on every page:

☐ **Web page title** which displays at the *top line* of your Web browser is *very* important because it often shows up in search engines such as WebCrawler®, Infoseek®, and AltaVista®. Make this descriptive, using key words that people might use to find your page.

☐ **Top-of-page graphic.** A small graphic at the top of each of your pages helps unify your Web pages. You can use a smaller version of your main "index page" graphic. Or perhaps a band at the top of the page with your company name and a small logo. I always call this something like "page-top.gif." That way if I want to change it, I don't have to alter every page. Just upload a new image with that

---

[5]Remember, this is a copy of an actual Web site, modified for book format.

Figure 9.1   Wilson's own image map, leading to additional services his company provides.

name. Choose where you want this top graphic: ☐ centered, ☐ upper left, or ☐ upper right?[6]

☐ **Page background.** Textured and colored backgrounds unify your pages. I call this something like "page-bak.gif" so it can be changed easily. Alternatively, you can specify an RGB color for the background. Many Web sites today use a simple white background for readability by the widest variety of Web browser and monitor configurations.

☐ **Headline type.** Decide what size to use on these "subpages" and use it consistently.

☐ **Text.** Go very sparingly on the headline typefaces. Use the normal typeface instead. It looks more *modest.* There is such a thing as overkill.

☐ **Last update.** If your site features up-to-date information, an update date is helpful. But if you don't do much updating, leave the date off or the site will look untended.

☐ **URL address.** You don't have to include this, but consider including a sentence such as "The URL of this document is http://wilsonweb.com/article/12design.htm" or some such. That way they'll know from the printed page how to get back to your Web site.

☐ **Jump lines.** If you have a complex site, you may want to have one or two-word links that will allow your customer to jump to another section of your Web site. Most common is a "home" or "top of page" jump, sometimes using "clickable images" or "buttons." (See Figure 9.1.)

☐ **Links.** The power of the Web is its ability to link to any other page in the world. But be very careful. You've just got the customer in your store. Don't quickly send him or her away. Resist your impulse to show off your knowledge of cool sites until you've got your customer's name, address, and hopefully the order. This is business.

☐ **Signature.** Sign your pages so the author is apparent (e.g., Designed by Ralph F. Wilson). Alternatively, you may want to include an E-mail address.

☐ **E-mail address,** which when clicked takes your customer to a "mail-to" form that allows him or her to send you E-mail, such as "E-mail feedback to rfwilson@wilsonweb.com"

7. Finishing Touches

☐ **Horizontal rules.** These don't take any extra time to download. They can also be varied in length and width.

---

[6]Remember . . . you are reading a Web site direct response form that asks for reader involvement.

☐ **Colored lines** take a few seconds but can spice up your page, especially if they are coordinated with the color scheme you have designed. Don't overdo it.

☐ **Bullets** are available as an HTML option to set off lists.

☐ **Colored balls, arrows, and pointers** are also available. But be careful. A little color goes a long way. Don't add these just to show off.

☐ **Colorful "new" or "updated" markers** draw your customers' attention to items you may have added recently. How about "Sale" or "Special"? Again, don't overdo it: only one or two per page. More than that defeats the purpose.

8. Photos and Graphics

You'll want to illustrate your products or services to help tell your story. Or you may want to put your whole catalog on-line. Remember to use the `<IMG ALT=>` tag so customers who are not displaying graphics will know what the image shows. Here are a few decisions.

☐ **Black-and-white.** These may be a bit less expensive, and are within the range of most hand scanners using gray-scale. Black-and-white images can easily be tinted slightly blue or brown to give an antique flavor.

☐ **Color images.** Color grabs people. Tell your story through a few pictures. Obtain professional-quality photos of your products locally. Then send your Web designer the photos. You can also obtain stock photography from inexpensive CD-ROMs from Expert and Softkey, or professional stock photographs on-line from PhotoDisc (http://www.photodisc.com).

In my area I can get a color scan of an $8^{1}/_{2}'' \times 11''$ page for about $8.00 (but $8^{1}/_{2}'' \times 11''$ is way too big to display). Keep the size of these down so that your customers don't have to wait all day to be able to see them. They may just click to another site and be gone. 20K to 40K is the acceptable range for people with 14.4K modems. Resize or crop as needed so your photos are sized appropriately for the page, and don't take too long to download. Or hire someone like me to do it for you.

☐ **Clickable thumbnail images** are one compromise. You show the picture in a thumbnail size image. If the customer is interested he or she can click on it to display the larger photo. You can also give the image size, such as 57K, so the customer has an idea of whether to choose this option.

Type of image is important, too.

☐ **GIF images** can be viewed by all Web browsers, and are better for text and simple drawings.

☐ **JPEG images** of photographs compress better and thus load faster.

Here's another decision. Do you want . . .

☐ **A rectangular image** with color to the edges?

☐ **Transparent areas** around your graphics? Your Web designer will know how to make transparent backgrounds that make images appear to "float" over the page. Do-it-yourselfers can accomplish this using L View Pro® or Adobe Photoshop®.

Multimedia is getting more common and more Web browsers and computers support it, so you might want to include:

☐ **Sound**
☐ **Animation,** such as GF animation
☐ **Video clips**

For now, however, the "bandwidth" or modem speed of 14.4K or 28.8 bps is really too slow for most very large files.

9. Forms to Get Orders or Customer Response

You need to connect with your customer. These are options that return information from your customer to you by E-mail.

☐ **Guestbooks.** You can entice potential customers to sign your guestbook (see Figure 9.2), and perhaps receive a free gift. Their answers to key questions help you qualify them as a prospect to pursue by telephone or direct mail (or E-mail, for that matter).

☐ **Requests for information.** Have a place for a customer's or prospect's name, address, phone number, and so on, as well as check boxes to request information on specific products or services.

☐ **Order forms.** Ideally, you take the order right on-line. Since people are still concerned with security of their credit card information on the Internet, consider using a combination of an order form and an 800 number. Former customers could order on the basis of credit information they have previously given you. Or you might have a page that contains an order form your customer can print out, fill out manually, and mail in with a check or a credit card number.

☐ **Shopping cart program.** If you are selling a number of products directly over the Internet, you probably ought to invest in "shopping cart" software, so people can put multiple items in their "cart" from any number of product pages. Upon "checkout," they have a total of their items, as well as tax (if any) and shipping charges included. At http://www.wilsonweb.com/demo, I have set up a complete DEMO STORE to illustrate just how shopping cart software works.

☐ **Secure server.** If you're serious about selling directly on the Internet, invest in the extra cost of putting your pages on an SSL-compatible server, such as the Netscape Secure Commerce Server, which encrypts the information quite well. Perception is the real issue, not stealing of information. The whole blue key at the bottom left of the user's screen provides a symbol of that security and is worth the extra money you'll pay.

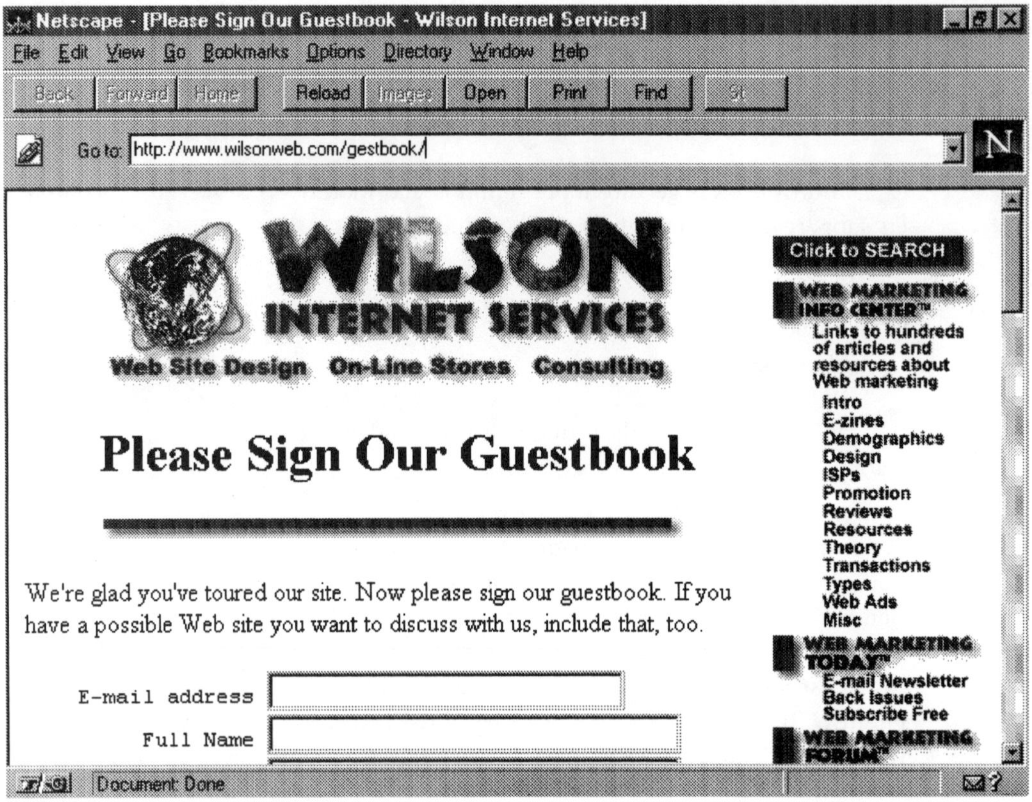

Figure 9.2 Information filled in by your Web site "guests" is transmitted to you, but only if your site is constructed properly. Your guest book can be expanded to include as many check boxes as you wish to add.

Your choices will also include how you get the information sent to you by E-mail. This requires CGI (Common Gateway Interface) programming—that is the really tricky part.

☐ **Access programs** already are on your ISP's computer.

☐ **Adapt CGI programs** that you find on the Internet. This takes a bit of programming savvy. You also need to befriend your host computer's system operator to let you have your own cgi-bin file.

☐ **Write your own CGI programs.** This takes *a lot* of programming savvy.

☐ **Hire a computer science grad student** to write your CGI script for you.

☐ **Employ your Web designer** to take care of this for you. Some Web designers have highly tuned programming skills. Others develop partnerships with programmers to get your job done the way you want it. Your designer will also work with your host computer system operator to set up the program in a cgi-bin directory.

10. Uploading and Testing Your Pages

Once you finish designing your pages, you need to upload or transfer them to your Internet Service Provider's computer. You need to know the basic Unix commands and directory structures (unless your Internet Service Provider is using a Windows NT operating system). You can . . .

☐ **Upload the pages yourself.** You'll need to do this repeatedly as you test and adjust your pages. This isn't too difficult if you already have a tool such as WS_FTP, available in both Windows 3.1 and Windows 95 versions. You can use this shareware to upload files to your Web site.

☐ **Send the pages to your Internet Service Provider on a diskette to upload for you.** They may do this for you once or twice. But when you find the need for repeated changes to correct errors, they won't be happy.

☐ **Have your Web designer upload and test the pages for you.** Designers who are worth their salt will ask for your approval at key stages so you are fully satisfied with the final product. You know: "Delight the customer."

11. Registering and Advertising Your Site

If you build it, will they come? Only if they can find you. There are several ways of advertising your site. You'll want to use all of these approaches, or pay your Web designer to do it for you.

☐ **Signature.** Subscribe to mailing lists and news groups likely to include potential customers. Actively involve yourself in the discussions, but don't overtly "push" your product. Let the "signature" at the end of your E-mail message do that for you. Use something like:

```
========================================================
SUCCESS UNLIMITED, INC.          Joe Schamole, Owner
       Your choice for Advertising Specialties
            Pens - Mugs - Flyswatters -
           Refrigerator Magnets - T-shirts
         Visit SUCCESS UNLIMITED for free samples
========  http://www.success-unlimited.com  ========
```

Participation takes some time and work, but it's worth it, since you are targeting your marketing efforts on those most likely to purchase your product. This is *your* job, though your Web designer can point you in the right direction.

☐ **Web search engines.** There are a dozen or so important Web search engines and directories for the Internet such as Lycos®, WebCrawler®, AltaVista®, and Yahoo®. Register your "index" page with each of these. Or have your Web designer do it for you.

☐ **Links from related pages.** You may find some people in a complementary business who will agree to reciprocal links with your page. Or one-way links for a modest fee. You know your industry better than your Web designer. You need to explore the Internet for yourself.

☐ **Links from industry index pages.** There may be an "advertising" page that links all related pages at no cost. Tell them about yours. Again, this is *your* job.

☐ **Send brief "press release" announcements** to services that announce "what's new" on the Internet. You just might hit it lucky and have hundreds of people see the announcement and flock to your site—if you're selected for the weekly "scout report." You can send these announcements, or have your Web designer do it for you.

☐ **Print your Web site address** or URL on all your display ads, literature, stationery, and business cards. This will attract customers to your site to learn more about your business and your products.

12. Maintaining Your Site

Once you get up and running, after testing all your links and correcting the inevitable errors, you need to keep your Web site current. You'll need to think of how to handle:

- Price changes
- Product changes
- Adding pages to describe other parts of your business
- Updating links which have become obsolete
- Updating images
- Redoing the "look" of your pages when you do not get the response you want or need

You have choices here, too.

☐ **Do it yourself.** If you have developed your pages thus far by yourself, it'll be a snap.

☐ **Have your Web designer train you or a staff member on how to update files.** You might want to write this ahead of time into your agreement with your Web designer, especially if you have some computer talent within your company. With this option, you'll need to use the Web designer in the future only for major changes.

☐ **Keep your Web designer on a retainer to maintain your pages monthly or as needed.** This saves you or your people from having to become experts on HTML. Your Web designer becomes part of your team without being on your payroll; hire him or her as an outside contractor.

Ignoring long-term page maintenance is *not* a realistic option.

DETERMINING COST RANGES

☐ **Do it yourself** is, of course, the cheapest so far as cash outlay. You need a word processor or HTML editor that will code HTML documents. However, the hidden cost is your time. To be any good, it will take you at least 20 or 30 hours of study and practice to get to the basic level. And there is quite a learning curve for the finishing touches. Expect to be constantly tinkering to improve your Web site—or leave your site forever mediocre. Time *is* money! When you finish, will the Web site really look professional? To do a really professional job takes professional-level graphics software and a great deal of experience. The improving HTML editing software makes it look easy, but if you're really serious about attracting business with your Web site, professional sites are worth what you pay for them.

☐ **Small businesses and organizations.** Simple Web pages with modest graphics and a guestbook will probably cost you $100 to $150 per page or more when averaged over the whole job. Many Web designers, however, won't give you a binding estimate, since each project has its own unique challenges. For an outlay of $400 to $1,500, you can get a set of professionally-designed pages. You'll save time up front by sharing this Web Design Decision Sheet with your Web designer, since you will have thought through the basic questions already.

☐ **Medium sized companies** may spend from $1,500 to $25,000 or more on Web page design. They are probably paying for the expertise—and overhead—of an advertising agency specializing in Web page design. Custom graphics, image maps, and CGI programs can be expensive.

☐ **Larger corporations** may expect to spend from $25,000 to a million or more. Sometimes you can see the difference, sometimes you can't. Animation, video clips, and sound can cost a pretty penny—but they can attract people who might be your customers.

You've gotten your feet wet with some Web site design decisions now, but there's a world of information out there you still need in order to develop a successful Web site. A free, triweekly e-mail newsletter, *Web Marketing Today*,[7] edited by Dr. Ralph F. Wilson, is yours for the asking. To subscribe, send an E-mail message containing the words SUBSCRIBE WEB-MARKETING to majordomo@ wilsonweb.com. You can unsubscribe at any time.[8]

---

[7] © 1996 by Ralph F. Wilson, all rights reserved. Web Marketing Today is a trademark of Wilson Internet Services.

[8] This Web page "infomercial" concludes with a detailed order form that can be E-mailed to the Internet "reader."

HOW TO ATTRACT VISITORS TO YOUR WEB SITE[9]
By Dr. Ralph F. Wilson

Too many Web marketers work on the if-you-build-it-they-will-come model. They won't. Once you build a Web site you must give them a *reason* to come. A Web site is a *passive* form of marketing: providing a signboard that points visitors to your products and services. To be most effective, a Web site should be used in conjunction with seven *active* forms of marketing, which we will examine briefly in this section. Just how do small-business people on a limited budget entice visitors to their Web site?

1. Use the Web Search Engines

First, advertise your Web site to Web search engines that index the Web, such as Yahoo, Lycos, WebCrawler, and Infoseek. The actual registration process can be deceptively simple. A service called SubmitIt! (*http://www.submit-it.com*) provides a way to submit information to approximately 15 of the most important indexes. If you do this late at night when Internet traffic is at its lowest, you can transmit your business's on-line address and description to all of these within three-quarters of an hour. Done right, a person who is seeking a consulting engineer in Northern California with experience in large electrical systems will quickly locate your name. Widget customers will be able to pick you out from the increasing crowd of on-line vendors.

The danger is that the untutored can construct a carelessly written 25-word or 200-character marketing description that blows their opportunity to be seen by vast blocks of potential customers. These 25 words must be written to include the chief keywords by which customers would locate you. If you want to change your description in a month or two, it takes much longer than an hour to contact each of the services separately, and then convince or nag them into making changes.

You can pay modest amounts to several services to perform this important task for you. For example, my company, Wilson Internet Services, offers as part of our Web site packages to carefully register your Web site with the most important indexes.

2. Give Them a Good Reason to Come

Second, you must give visitors a good reason to come. A tried-and-true marketing approach is to offer something of value for free. A number of well-financed corporate Web sites offer an entertaining fare that changes constantly. While most small

---

[9]Copyright 1995, Ralph F. Wilson, all rights reserved, used by permission. "How to Attract Visitors to Your Web Site" originally appeared in *Web Marketing Today.* (November 20, 1995), a free tri-weekly E-mail newsletter. You may "subscribe" by sending the message SUBSCRIBE WEB-MARKETING to majordomo@wilsonweb.com.

business Web marketers can't afford to compete, you *can* afford to offer valuable information. If you take the time to provide up-to-date information about your industry, for example, you'll find people returning again and again to your site, each time increasing their chances of doing business with you.

AN EXAMPLE: Wilson Internet Services offers the "Web Marketing Info Center" (*http://www.wilsonweb.com/webmarket*), a constantly updated source of links to Web marketing articles. Because it is so valuable, *Your Company* magazine rated it as one of the top small-business Web sites in the country, encouraging even more people to visit that page, and sending an increasing number of people to consider our modestly priced Web site packages.

3. Find Industrywide Linking Pages

A third approach is to find industrywide linking pages and negotiate reciprocal links to and from their Web pages. Your trade association probably lists members. Several on-line craft centers, for example, offer free links to other crafters. If you are a hotel, be sure to get a link with "All the Hotels on the Web." Consultants may seek links with The Expert Marketplace, or try for a listing in the Virtual Trade Show. The entire list can seem endless, but it is specific for each industry. Surf the net enough to find which are the key sites for your field, and then seek links there.

But be judicious in your use of outgoing links. You've just got those people in your door; don't quickly send them away again.

4. Purchase Web Advertising

A fourth method is to purchase Web advertising—usually a rectangle ad with a clickable link to your site on a carefully selected, high-volume Web site. A certain percentage of their thousands of visitors will explore your Web site, and hopefully like what they find. A whole industry has sprung up to act as brokers for such ads. Small-business people will need to find ways to test the effect of specific ads on the bottom line, perhaps by sending people from each ad to a different Web page "front door" so you can monitor traffic from each ad.

5. Join Internet News Groups and Mailing Lists

A fifth important way to let people know about your Web site is to become active in several of the thousands of Internet news groups and mailing lists. Find the groups that are most likely to be frequented by your potential customers—groups can be *very* narrowly targeted—and join in the discussion. You might find groups that relate to your industry by doing a bit of research with Reference.Com (*http://www.reference.com*), which searches messages about particular topics or companies voiced in thousands of news groups and mailing lists.

"Lurk" for a few weeks so you understand the particular culture of the group you are targeting. Then find ways to add constructive comments to the discussion.

At the bottom of each message include a "signature"—a four- to eight-line mini-advertisement with your product, phone number, and Web address. Every time you contribute to the discussion, your mini-ad is seen by hundreds. You'll find considerable fruit this way, but like anything, it comes in response to hard work and persistence. Resist the temptation to send bulk E-mail messages to dozens of news groups—"spamming" in Internet parlance. People do it, but while it may bring customers, it doesn't offer the solid reputation and respect that will build your business in the long run.

6. Join a Web "Mall"

Sixth, make your Web site part of one or more of the many "malls." Businesses in physical shopping malls benefit from the traffic flow of multitudes window shopping. The same can be true on-line.

Some malls only include businesses who subscribe to a particular Internet Service Provider (ISP) or pay a fee or percentage of their gross revenues. Others take any business that fits their particular criteria. Dave Taylor, for example, developed The Internet Mall (http://www.iw.com/imall/), with tens of thousands of businesses that meet under one roof. The mall is illusory, however, since businesses in the mall are hosted on separate Internet Service Provider sites all over the world. This, the largest mall, charges no fee to its business; instead it sells advertising to companies who pay for an ad in the high-volume entryway to this mall.

7. Include Your E-mail and Web Address on All Correspondence

Finally, include your e-mail and Web addresses on all your company's print literature, stationery, and display advertising. If people believe they can find out more about your products or services by looking on-line, many will do so.

There you have it, seven important ways to increase traffic to your company's Web site. If you use most or all of these forms of marketing, the chances are that two years from now you'll be bragging about your foresight in developing a Web site when you did, rather than trashing Web marketing as just another fad where you threw good money after bad.

14 POINTS TO CONSIDER IN YOUR WEB MARKETING PROGRAM

These "14 Points" are based on material originally prepared by *HotWired* Ventures LCC, an on-line magazine at (415-222-6340) or http://www.hotwired.com.

1. A Text-Based Medium

The present Web is a text-based medium. Given current technology and speed, the Web is *not* about large graphics, video, or sound. It is about text. For casual browsers, if your message takes more than 20 seconds to download, you have lost the prospect.

INSIGHT 41

Text is not as easy to read on screen as in print. Use short paragraphs and big type.

---

2. Your Web Site Is Never Finished!

For most Web marketers, only a small part of the message on your site is about creating traditional passive advertising. It's more about creating a dialog—or even a multilog—in an *interactive* engagement with current or past customers and prospects. It is not about radiating your message toward passive couch potatoes. It's about active seekers in some kind of "discussion." For best results, it becomes a multilog among your current customers, prospects, and you.

3. Your Web Site Is Alive!

Some of what you save in not paying for more print, TV, or radio advertising must be invested in staff to stay engaged with your Web community.

INSIGHT 42

Your Web site is *not* "broadcasting." It is "pointcasting." You are not speaking to thousands or millions of viewers at one time. You are talking to exactly one person, on his or her time!

---

4. Interactivity Is the Key!

For much on-site success, developing involvement with and among your customers and prospects is important. Do they request information, explore your site in depth, and/or engage in discussion among themselves? Discuss with an expert how to learn how your audience interacts when it visits your site.

AN EXAMPLE: At *HotWired,* over 10,000 volunteers are part of a Member Panel. Their participation can identify the psychographics and demographics of an advertiser's target, link behavioral data such as exposure to response, and be recruited for focus groups.

5. About Paying for "Links"

Before you advertise (buy links) on other Web sites, ask for documentation on how involved their audience is with the site. Do they just pass through or is it a destination site? Destinations have strong relationships with their audience. This works to your advantage. But remember, *the Web is a medium.* As with any other medium, know what you pay for.

6. How to Build Relationships Via E-mail

If you have *regular* news, one of the most effective ways to spread it is E-mail. Add a dialog box to your site that lets people ask to be on your "mailing" list.

7. Research! Research! Research!

Research is an investment you can't afford not to make. In an environment where the relationship is personal and change is constant, research is the only way to stay on top and in touch. Update your studies often. Make research the soul of your Web strategy.

8. Test! Test! Test!

The Web is the most cost-effective way to conduct copy testing. On the Web, your ad need never be finished. Depending on response, you can change it daily, even hourly. Do it! Learn what your audience likes and why, then "evolve" your message, your graphics, and overall Web site design. The Web lets you test, learn, change, evolve . . . all in real time. Using this medium, so can your marketing change.

9. Mine the Referral Log's Gold

A Referral log, which shows who visited your site, can tell you how users found you, where they are from, what they see and when they see it, and how they interact with it all. How you design the interaction can result in a wealth of information on users' likes and dislikes. Don't set up your site without it!

10. Customize Your Message

With today's evolving technology, you can, for instance, identify whether or not visitors come from a particular college, what computer platform and browsers they are using, even from what country they are visiting. Soon you will be able to build discrete profiles of individual users—and customize and send your message to individuals, as well as to highly targeted groups.

11. CPM and CPI

The measure of Web efficiency is not CPM. Like direct mail, it is the number of people who open the envelope *and respond.* It is the CPI; that is, the cost per involvement or cost per inquiry. The only valid measure is based on response. The best long-term opportunity is not buying "hits" by the ton. Rather, it is buying qualified leads and sales.

12. Put Your URL Everywhere

Think of your URL, your Universal Resource Locator, as an 800 number that does not need a staff of 24-hour operators. You are always accessible, yet able to manage the communications on your own time.

13. It Really Is a Global Village!

The Web does not stop at the edge of any "marketing area." Your audience is global. You have tremendous opportunities for national, even worldwide, research and sales. But bear in mind that different cultures respond differently to questionnaires in general, and to measurement scales in particular. Use the Web, but use with care.

14. Buying and Selling Web Site Ad Space

Demographics are critical. Whether you buy access to another site or sell access to your own, *documented* demographics and consumer profiles control what is bought. Psychographics count, too. Do you want, or do you have, the people who shape markets or those who follow; and where are the *certified* statistics? Just as in any other medium, know what you are buying—or selling—and why. Even if it isn't *your* own money, treat it as if it were!

ABOUT THE MISSING CHECKLIST

The "12 Web Page Design Decisions," "How to Attract Visitors," and "14 Points to Consider" are so analogous to our annotated checklists, that a regular Checklist seems unnecessary. Please let us know if we are wrong and a regular Checklist will be added in the next edition.

---

10 | Publicity and Public Relations

This chapter aims at helping you generate and disseminate good public relations (PR) for yourself and counteracting any bad PR you may receive. It does not cover the generation of bad publicity about your competitors or opponents—whether they deserve it or not.

INSIGHT 43

Media wastepaper baskets are filled with PR from sources that equate "free" with "too cheap to invest in doing right." Publicity and public relations are *not* "free"! The effort, knowledge, skill, experience, time, and budget needed to prepare effective PR are every bit as great as required for paid advertising. To get such PR, management must understand this and commit the resources that make it possible, because without those resources and that commitment, it won't get it.

Throughout this chapter, certain words and phrases are used repeatedly. Their definitions, as given here, will usually be assumed by your audience. However, it is always safer to confirm such an understanding, rather than take it for granted. Point out that "there are so many ways I've heard (fill in the appropriate term here) used lately, that I'd feel a lot safer if we agreed on a definition in advance." Doing this will save endless grief, without forcing anyone to admit to ignorance.[1]

PR: Abbreviation for "public relations." "Publicity" is generally understood to be part of the total public relations function.

Medium (plural, media): Any method of communication for getting PR made public. Newspapers, radio talk shows, TV, the Internet, and word-of-mouth are all media.

The press: Newspaper and magazine reporters and feature writers; sometimes, depending on the context, the term includes radio and television reporters also.

Electronic media: Radio and television. Sometimes the Internet.

Print media: Newspapers, magazines, and newsletters.

Published: Made public by print media. Sometimes the Internet.

Broadcast: Made public by electronic media.

Aired: A synonym for "broadcast."

---

[1]Do not confuse "ignorance" with "stupidity." Ignorance means we don't know something . . . yet. Stupidity means we're too dumb to learn it . . . ever.

INSIGHT 44

For internal communication, don't fight about what something's called, only about what it is to accomplish and how to get it done. For external communication, you must use generally accepted nomenclature to get across what you wish to communicate.

ABOUT PR ON THE INTERNET

Little PR material is picked up by traditional media from the Internet. Specific Web sites are quite effective in forming single-issue groups to contact legislators or suggest other types of combined action. But the media that are the targets of "business" PR rely on known or trusted sources rather than searching a screen for messages of unknown origin and validity. This is *not* to imply that any of the Internet material lacks validity. It *is* to tell you that PR media expect *you* to do the work. Get the message to them; don't expect them to hunt in the World Wide Web for ways to publicize you!

PUBLICITY AND PUBLIC RELATIONS

How They Differ and Why It Matters

PR professionals can, and do, write and speak endlessly about the differences between publicity and public relations. But, for our purposes, an arbitrary distinction is appropriate.

Publicity: Do good and let the world know. A good product, good cause, good film, or good deed all meet this criterion.

Public relations: Limit harm when it strikes and, where possible, neutralize harm or turn it into good.

This chapter has three goals that relate to these definitions:

1. To help you formulate publicity and public relations procedures agreed upon by every level of management.
2. To guide you in doing your own publicity.
3. To urge you to use professional help—from internal or external resources—in major publicity campaigns and in all public relations.

Your Relationship with the Press

The press and electronic news media are in the business of presenting news and otherwise useful information, not of giving favorable free coverage to whoever requests it. The best way to establish an excellent relationship with the print and electronic press is to make yourself a resource for news and to present your stories or story ideas to them in a "news" or "feature" context. How to do this is shown in the pages that follow. Of course, the more news or features you provide to the press, the more valuable you will become, and the more likely it will be that even your lesser stories will get favorable attention. You may even become a source that the press will contact for interesting filler materials when the "hard" news is "light" (sparse).[2] Much more important, you will want the press to know you as a reachable and, especially, *honest* source of fact and opinion about your organization. That's an invaluable reputation to have earned when raw news, without interpretation, can be harmful to your interests. The opportunity to present your side, in context, when a story *first* appears, is immeasurably more valuable than a dozen after-the-fact correctives (as targets of "dirty politics" have learned to their sorrow).

An Opportunity . . .

Downsizing of in-house news staff at practically every medium makes news- and feature-worthy PR more welcome than ever. But the old rule still applies: The more professional the PR, the more likely its acceptance. Fit the presentation to the standards of the media. Don't expect them to do lots of work to fix it when it's so easy to leave it out.

Be a Pro!

There is absolutely nothing wrong with having your relationship with the media on a personal, first-name basis . . . *provided that it also remains on a professional level.* That media people respect and believe you is much more important than that they like you, although it certainly helps if they do both.

Deciding Who's in Charge

Whether publicity and public relations are assigned to the advertising department or to a separate public relations department depends on both the workload and the experience and PR expertise the departments have. Advertising involves comparatively little direct contact with reporters, on-air personnel, or editorial staffs. As an advertiser, your contact is more likely to be with a sales representative. Your advertising concern is *where* and *when* the advertisement is placed—in which section and on what page of the newspaper or magazine it appears and at what time and in which segment of a series of commercials it runs. You're paying, and your fiddle calls the tune. The ad will appear exactly as agreed on.

Publicity and public relations operate under quite different rules. Unlike paid-for advertising, their goal is favorable coverage by media without payment for space or time. The PR/publicity purpose is threefold. Deciding who will be in charge must be based upon who can accomplish all three purposes:

---

[2]There are many columnists and feature writers whose coverage is as important as news is to companies and organizations. These writers and electronic commentators live on a constant supply of publicity-type information. It takes a long while to build this type of relationship, but once established, it becomes a very nice bonus for both sides.

1. Favorable public notice for what you *do* want publicized.
2. The opportunity to present your point of view on what would otherwise be presented only in a negative fashion. Your hope is to neutralize, in whole or in part, the *approach* to a story, not the story itself.
3. The ability to get instant public notice for certain kinds of news, no matter what the negative consequences to your organization. Tampering with products in a way that may endanger the lives of buyers is a familiar example for which you would want such instant public notice.

SUMMARY

- Your best chance to get published or to get air time is to give the media *news.*
- Your best chance to get trusted is to give the media *truth.*
- The best person to handle publicity and PR is the one who can best do both of these, unhindered by persons or departments who do not understand the preceding two points.

THE NEED FOR AGREED-UPON PR PROCEDURES

As the PR person charged with spreading the news, you'll likely get more help than you really want. Everyone wants to spread good news and be the first to pass off blame for the bad. Where news is widely known or suspected, both of these are bound to happen. Here's an example from our own experience. A young account executive[3] for a public relations agency learned from a client's infuriated PR director that it was not *his* job to reveal the agency's new publicity campaign to the company president whom he happened to meet in the hallway, thereby depriving the director of her moment of glory. Fortunately, his apologetic realization that inexperience doesn't excuse stupidity saved the account.

He never repeated the error, but it's probably impossible to get that kind of self-discipline from nonadministrative employees. They'll spread your news, good and bad, and any attempt to stop them may well be counterproductive. After all, why would you want to hide the story of *their* success and *your* failure? Are you trying to steal all the credit or shift all the blame?

Is It Really a Problem?

The problem with having your news become published through unofficial, word-of-mouth sources is that even when it's reported accurately, you are unlikely to gain the full advantages good news can generate. While bad news can expect ongoing and practically unlimited attention, good news most often gets only a

---

[3]Hahn.

single mention, unless the press is given specific reasons for continuing its coverage. A manufacturing contract presented without an interesting explanation of its civic and human advantages will likely appear on page 37 of the newspaper; a lawsuit will surely be featured on page 1. You may not be able to change that placement, but your PR efforts should get either story to reflect your point of view. The rest of this chapter is a guide both to doing just that yourself and to recognizing whether the PR work done for you by others is likely to get the results you want.

Convincing Management

The first impulse of most people contacted by the media is to feel so important that they tell more than they know. The second impulse is to be so fearful of saying something wrong as to say nothing at all. An agreed-upon, *written guide to media contacts* will guard against both of these extremes.

Since reporters usually try to contact the more senior personnel in an organization, management, too, must agree to follow your procedures in order for them to do their jobs. Here, as in just about every other aspect of organizational life, senior management sets the tone. If the CEO not only signs off on your plan, but actually follows it thereafter, your organization's media problems will be simplified. Since the majority of CEOs reached their position by recognizing the obvious, getting their agreement should present little difficulty. Here's the agreement:

1. **Designate an official spokesperson for PR.** This has the advantage of letting everyone else point to one person as having *all* the facts when, in fact, some of the facts are still in doubt. This becomes especially important when questions contain totally new "information" to which you are asked to react. "(Name) is going to find that out and get back to you immediately" is a perfectly acceptable answer, whether from the president of the United States or the vice president of the local garden society. If your spokesperson is not a well-grounded PR pro, put him or her through a media rehearsal run by professionals and with video playback. Many PR agencies will do this on a fee basis. *Always* do this before known TV or other major coverage. Make your blunders during rehearsal, not during interviews or on the air!

2. **Preplan whenever possible.** Good news is seldom a total surprise—although it may sometimes not be equally good for everyone concerned. "How to maximize good news," a few pages on, alerts you to some of the problems, as well as the opportunities, that good news offers. Whether such problems exist or not, discuss your story options at the senior level, and then put the approved approaches *in writing.* Note that what you are putting on paper is *not* "how we can fool our audience into thinking we're better than we are." It *is* "the very real benefits our audience will gain from this event." Make your media guide something you'd feel comfortable about having "leaked" to the press, and structure it accordingly.

3. **When good news does come as a total surprise.** Occasionally, good news does come as a total surprise. A telephone call from a reporter will ask your reaction to something almost too good to be true—as quite often it is. Be honest. Tell the

reporter that it's the first you've heard of the event, that you want to double-check to get all the details, and that the reporter will be the very first to get your reaction the moment the news is confirmed. Now check the facts. If the story is true, put your media plan into place exactly as if the story were preplanned, and then contact the reporter who broke it to you. If it is untrue, report that even faster. When it comes to *pleasant* surprises, there is nothing wrong with telling the media that you need some time to check out all the great ramifications. But when it is only a myth, do your best to stop it before it can raise expectations that won't be met.

4. **When bad news strikes.** Where possible, leave the handling of bad news to the professionals. When that proves impossible, do as they would. Whether the event is preplanned, such as a reduction in the workforce, or totally unexpected, such as a fire or explosion, the possible legal as well as PR consequences are not for off-the-cuff handling. If management is asked to comment before a PR plan is in place, ask what the media's deadline is and promise to get back to them before then. Whatever that deadline is, keep it! Emphasize that you are trying to get at the facts. Until you do, uninformed comments might mislead the public and unnecessarily jeopardize your organization. Getting the help you need is covered in this chapter.

SUMMARY

- Designate an official PR spokesperson.
- Preplan your media approach whenever your news, good or bad, can be predicted . . . and then follow the plan.
- When good news is a pleasant surprise, admit the fact . . . but check it before you comment.
- Bad news may have unsuspected negative consequences. Leave the handling of bad news to professionals, unless you really have the experience, qualifications, and authority to respond for your organization.

INSIGHT 45

In announcing what you consider good news, be alert to the possibility that it may be less than welcome to some part of your audience. Your news should be worded with that fact very much in mind!

HOW TO MAXIMIZE GOOD NEWS

1. List every audience to whom news about your company or organization may be of interest. Be sure to include the specialized interest groups or "publics" you wish to influence or inform.

2. Imagine yourself in the place of each group that, on hearing your news, asks, "What's in it for *me?*" Try to make your news into a benefit specific to that group, especially if the group's first reaction may be more negative than you would wish. The chances are that by practicing this type of empathy, you not only will foresee the negatives but also will be able to translate them into something positive. *Do not, under any circumstances, lie!* In almost every instance, you will be found out, with consequences more dire than those you face for telling an unwelcome truth.

INSIGHT 46

It is extraordinarily difficult for any person or group to think beyond self-interest. Nevertheless, this is the job of the PR person: to get the company or organization to think that way and to tailor the message to the *media's* needs and interests. Management is no better, or worse, about this than employees; the writers of news than its readers. PR has the challenge of understanding and satisfying them all.

---

3. After deciding how each of your interest groups is likely to react to your news, you can draw some reasonable conclusions to guide further action. Here are some points you'll want to consider:

- **Should there be any official notice at all?** Your news can be announced by a media release, a news conference, or some other official notice. Or it may simply be permitted to happen. Many—probably most—events aren't worth the time and effort needed to make them into a story that's likely to get published. So concentrate on your best bets—the ones that affect the most people or that concern your audience in a very direct way.

- **Who tells your employees?** Decide how, by whom, and to whom to spread the news. Anything that *benefits* employees should be told to them at the earliest possible moment. To avoid distortion, put it in writing. Place it on bulletin boards and mail it to their homes. You want good news shared with the entire family, to help build goodwill toward the employer.

INSIGHT 47

Make the immediate supervisor the first spreader of good news. Resist the temptation so prevalent in politics to have everything good come from the top and everything unpleasant from below. Use the "Army system." The same sergeant who had us dig the latrine also gave us a weekend pass!

- **What to do when it affects the community.** When your news will have a positive impact upon the community (whether it's the neighborhood or the whole state), share that fact *in advance* with the political leadership. Invite the politicos to share in the goodwill the news can generate. If it is important enough, suggest a joint news conference for the announcement. If you're not experienced at gathering the media, they are! Be sure to have a news or media release (see next section) ready for the event. Just as in communicating with your employees, you want to make certain the story reflects your point of view.

If the political leadership is otherwise occupied, find out whether you can gather the press on your own. Offer a personal interview, but don't be hurt if the press doesn't desire it.

Just because a very limited news staff can't pay a personal visit does not mean that your story will be ignored. Get it to them in some other way. Mail and messenger are always welcome. Don't, however, fax or E-mail without making sure that this method is equally well received. Your attorney and accountant will give you the legal requirements concerning what you *must* tell. Your publicity/PR director will tell you what you *should* tell in addition and how to do it.

- **Investors love good news. Give it to them!** If you are a large enough organization to issue public stock or bonds, you are large enough to use professional help for your communication. Smaller organizations, whether financed by family, financial institutions, or venture capitalists, will want to keep their investors informed, too. As with the giants, the advice, consent, and continuing support of these investors largely depends on what *you* tell them. But their wrath at being misled is likely to be even more fierce than that of the public investment community. In financial matters, while the truth may not make you free, the untruth may well send you to prison. Unlike our possible amusement at the politicians' "spin control," your investors' insistence upon financial veracity is likely to be unforgiving and with a very long, very accurate memory!

SUMMARY

- Aim your news to influence a specific audience.
- Put yourself in the place of that audience, and consider how your news will be received. If the answer isn't "Great!" why are you sending it?
- Let your employees know when good news happens. The rumors they hear are usually the opposite.
- Let the political leadership share in your goodwill. You need them even more than they need you.
- Keep your investors informed. Be happy when you can share good news with them and prompt to tell them the bad. Reluctance to share any financial data is a dangerous stance!

THE MEDIA RELEASE OR NEWS ADVISORY

A media release is a story that you (a) hope will be newsworthy or otherwise worthy of attention and (b) want to make public. Notice that being newsworthy is the more important criterion. In most instances, print and electronic media get many more stories than they can use. The importance and interest of each story *to the medium's particular audience* will largely decide what gets published or aired. That's why the news must be in the very first paragraph, reinforced and emphasized by a suggested headline.

What Not to Do

Do not begin your release with something like "President Jane Jones of Acme Motors announces. . . ." A great many releases do begin that way because so many companies and organizations think that *that's* the "news" or the most important words. *The media* never begin *any* story that way—unless it's with the words "President Clinton announced. . . ."

INSIGHT 48

News media are swamped with requests for coverage. They don't have the time or personnel to study long press releases to discover whether each one truly contains some news. So put the heart of your news into the first paragraph, preferably into the very first sentence. If you don't catch them there, you're unlikely to keep them looking.

The news advisory or release is the basic tool in your publicity campaign. It's also a tool you should have no difficulty in learning how to use. By way of example, let's create a release about the same senior citizen bicycle invented in the chapter on advertising:

E-Z-Ryder Bike Factory * 123 East Fourth * Wakenaw, KY (1)

NEWS RELEASE (2)

March 22, 199x (3)
To   For additional information, contact (5)
Charles Smith (4)   Jeanette Miranda O'Keefe
Sports Editor   Information Director
Wakenaw Daily Bugle   E-Z Ryder
                                            789-001-0002

Release date: FOR IMMEDIATE RELEASE (6)

**New bike for seniors hailed by
50-plus test riders** (7)

Warrensville, KY. (8) Twenty-nine volunteers, ranging in age from 50 to 81, today test drove the new E-Z Ryder bicycles especially designed for seniors to give them more mobility for both entertainment and basic transportation. While only 5 said that they currently use bicycles regularly, 27 said that they might do so in the future because of the **E-Z Ryder's special features**. (9)

"I drove the bike around town for over an hour," reported the most senior of the group, retired Warrensville fireman Chuck Quinzley. (10) "I don't know how they made it so easy," he said, "but that's the most biking I've done all at once in the past 10 years."

Ladies version pleases, too (11)
The 11 women test drivers, who were not asked to volunteer their ages, (12) were equally pleased with their bikes. "They must have done something special with the gears to make riding this easy," suggested former science teacher Mrs. Lisa Spengler. (13) "I think it made all of us feel a lot younger to be biking around town just like the high schoolers I used to teach."

New patent to Ryder Company (14)
"Mrs. Spengler is absolutely correct," said Edwyn Ryder, President of E-Z-Ryder, (15) when told about her remark. "The gears have just been granted a patent, and we're going to tool up for a major increase in production right here in Warrensville, (16) though that won't be ready for about another year. (17) Right now, we're going to sponsor some Sensible Junior/Senior Cycling races in which you have to be over 50 or under 15 to compete. (18) Not only are we going to let us seniors (19) feel like kids again," concluded Ryder with a laugh, "we're going to beat them at their own game!"

-30- (20)

Photograph herewith. (21)

Broadcast-quality video available. (22)
Contact J. O'Keefe for details.

There are 22 points highlighted in this story. Just for fun, take a sheet of paper and jot down what you think is the reason for each point. We'll also give you ours, but just because we don't always agree doesn't mean that you're wrong and we're right. More likely, it means that there is more than one good reason for doing something right or for avoiding something wrong. Please send your list to our attention, c/o the publisher, John Wiley & Sons, 605 Third Avenue, New York, NY 10158. We'll credit you (with your permission, of course) for any changes in future editions.[4] A dated postmark on the envelope will control in case of duplicate suggestions.

22 Ways to Get Your Story Printed

1. Make your corporate or association identification clear. Many of us are so used to identifying ourselves with divisions or departments, that we forget the publicity power of our parent organization.

---

[4]This is an example of the "hidden offer" discussed in Chapter 4.

2. "NEWS" is what your recipients want. Promise it with the largest type on the page. Use "Media News Release" when including electronic media.

3. No one wants to publish old news, so make the date of your release absolutely current. If the same release is used for more than a single day, fill in the dates as they are used.

Use typewriter-style type for the entire release. Double-space! Make sure that it's a typeface you can match for filling in the date and the recipient's name. If your releases are preprinted before being personalized, rather than computer generated, tell your printers about your personalization plan. They will control the density of the ink to give the appearance of individual word processor typing.

4. There is nothing more direct and personal than an individual's name and title, even when the recipient knows that it's all done by computer. You will, of course, have identified the most likely sources for publication through personal contacts or telephone conversations. If you're not sure whom to address in larger news organizations, ask the editor most likely to be in charge. (We'll tell how to find them, shortly.) Not only will you get a name, but you may also interest the editor!

5. Give your recipients a specific person to contact, if possible with a telephone number that cuts through the growing computerized switchboard maze. You're hoping for free in-print and on-air publicity, so don't make contacting you a challenge. Your recipients may not have the time or patience to be so challenged.

6. Your story will usually be held—that is, not published or aired—until the date specified by you. (There are occasional violations of hold dates when the news is "hot" enough.) Most stories are distributed "for immediate release." Others have specific release dates, usually to give weekly or monthly publications the chance to break the news at the same time as the daily media. This is especially important when a key writer won't mention your story once it has appeared elsewhere.

In some media, specific individuals are so widely read that they won't consider a story, unless it's given to them before anyone else. When such an "exclusive" is offered, be sure to give it a time limit. Rather than "for immediate release," indicate something like "Exclusive for (name) to (date)." Indicate release after the specified date on all other copies. An exclusive is valuable and should get you a bit more than routine attention in return.

7. Your headline will help determine the kind of attention each medium gives to your story. In this example, we've given the story a human interest rather than a business emphasis. When used, such emphasis should be a well-thought-out part of your overall plan. Note that you can supply several stories with different emphases as part of a media kit and then add another story that summarizes all of them. Add a contents page, and not only will the media be grateful, but you're less likely to omit something.

8. This tells where the story takes place, not necessarily where it was written. When a particular local context is important, tell the story from that point of view. A Kansas wheat grower teaching Eastern Europeans how to use an Illinois-built combine typifies both the challenges and opportunities PR faces every day.

9. Note how packed with information this first paragraph is. Make *your* first paragraph tell the story in such a way that if nothing else is published, you will still have made your main point. You'll be happy to find that many releases are printed in their entirety, exactly as they are written, especially by smaller publications with limited editorial and rewriting staffs. But most media will use only a portion of the release. Under the "all the news that fits" rule, stories are written to be cut (shortened) from back to front, so load the beginning. Readers, too, pay more attention to initial paragraphs. Whether they are consciously aware of it or not, they know that scanning just the headlines and first paragraphs will give them the overview that determines whether reading more is worth their time.

Everything after the first paragraph is an expansion on what's just been read. It's our job to make this material so enticing or important that the reader can't resist learning more.

INSIGHT 49

In writing the first paragraph of a news story or feature item, picture an individual whom you most want to inform or influence. Within the format of the media that will get your release, write the initial paragraph so that *that* individual will want to know more. Relate your story or feature to the specific interests, wants, and needs of that special reader, and you will also capture the much broader audience for whom you are looking. You may hope that what you write will be read (or heard or seen) by vast numbers of groups, but groups don't read—individuals do. You'll succeed when you make it worth the while of each separate reader.

---

10. Take the story from the abstract to the personal as soon as possible. Chuck is someone to whom readers, as well as a radio or television audience, can relate. And note how he gives the product a believable testimonial, a fact that will be reinforced a bit later in the story. Remember that you are writing *news,* not advertising. Keep the plugs for the product soft sell!

11. Your headline and subheads serve two purposes:
- To "highlight" the main points of your story
- To let the readers spot their own specific interests. No one has time to read everything. Use subheads to make it easy for readers with different interests to find the parts of the story that are important to them.

12. Beware of sexism. Beware doubly of humor. That the female test drivers were not asked to reveal their age may bring a chuckle to some readers, but it would be

resented and found not at all funny by many women. It's placed here as a warning of things to avoid, rather than to include. Attempts at humor, unless quoted or put into a totally humorous context, are best left to the professionals.

13.   Featuring women and minority groups in a positive manner is permitted and often encouraged. (Be careful, however, not to create resentment by appearing condescending—"Why do you have to point out that *we're* just as good as others?") A photograph usually works well in this regard. Provide a picture that shows the science teacher and gear-guru as African American or Hispanic and you've made your point—without saying a word. Religious affiliations, unless absolutely required by the story, are best left unmentioned.

14.   This subhead and the text that follows could easily have been the major focus of the story. They are put here to show how a subhead can signal a change in the direction of the story, even as it downplays the content that follows, by placing it last. It's a handy device for forestalling wild rumors through your own official version.

15.   The introduction of the senior corporate officer's testimony signals a change to a more serious emphasis.

16.   Note the calming of fears about a possible negative local impact, placed here to minimize the likelihood of such fears. The president *immediately* answers the universal questions, "What's in it—positive or negative—for me?"

17.   When promising good things for the future, leave some flexibility as to specific dates. "About another year" is a good deal safer than "One year from today." Notice also that this statement invites an ongoing series of progress reports, with continuing interest and excitement for everyone involved.

18.   The story can stop after the previous sentence or continue with a return to the lighter tone with which it began. The media using the story will make that decision.

19.   Ryder's identification of himself as a fellow senior—the group to which the major headline is addressed—is an effective way of returning the story to the human interest tone with which it began. It is generally better to maintain one tone throughout a story. However, if, as in this story, you do switch, it is best to return to the tone with which you began, very much as in a symphony or sonata, where the opening and concluding themes most frequently echo each other and a middle section is given more freedom to wander—though not to get lost.

20.   The notation "-30-" is a standard way of showing the conclusion of a story and signals that the writer is in the know about even the trivia of his or her craft.

21.   When including a photograph with your release, it may be in color or in black and white. The important things are its degree of contrast and its degree of

detail. A photograph or other illustration that you hope to have shown in color must, of course, be that way in the original. Standard size for the originals is 8 inches by 10 inches, a format photographic duplication services are set up to handle economically. When ordering duplicates, note that it is customary to give the horizontal size first. Make sure that here, as elsewhere, you and your suppliers are speaking the same language.

About Quantity Photo Reproductions

In a quantity photo service, black-and-white and color copies have different systems of reproduction. Black-and-white photos are made from an 8″ × 10″ print, rather than from a negative. If practical, give the service that print instead of your film. It will be cheaper, and copies should be practically indistinguishable from the original. For color reproductions, give the service your negative or transparency along with a print that shows how you wish the photograph to look. If no print exists, tell the reproduction service what the basic colors in the print should be, and then have them make a proof. The cost is nominal and permits you to "color correct" for final duplication. But discuss this with your service if cost is a factor. Almost anything is possible; you must decide whether it's practical.

Quantity photo services are in most major markets. We have used the aptly named Quantity Photo (312-644-8288) in Chicago for more than two decades with superior results.

Type a suggested caption onto a regular sheet of paper, and tape that sheet to the back of the photo. Be sure the caption includes the name of the product! Be sure that both the caption and the illustration can be seen at the same time, as shown in Figure 10.1. For shipping, fold the caption over the photograph.

22. Consider the creation of television-quality video only if TV coverage seems assured and worth the considerable investment. You may, of course, gain even more important advantages from your video in financial, zoning, and other face-

Figure 10.1   Captioning a photo. Tape the caption to the back of your photograph. Make sure the message and picture can both be seen at the same time.

to-face presentations. A more detailed discussion of electronic media is presented in Chapter 11.

MEDIA KITS

A media kit is a package of materials that both includes and expands upon your news release. It *may* contain an expanded news story or feature article. It *will* contain photographs, charts, and other pertinent illustrative materials for print media. Less often, it also holds audio and video materials for radio and television. It may contain a variety of background materials about your organization, including human interest stories about the people you want mentioned.

INSIGHT 50

Do not load your media kit[5] just to impress the media with the importance of the sender. More likely, you'll simply try the patience of the recipient. Check for and take out material that duplicates anything else or that is not essentially tied to the story. Your problem, as always, is to get attention and interest, so make the kit complete, but concise. The media will contact you for more background when they do a story that needs it.

HOW TO GAIN LOCAL COVERAGE

For the majority of us, gaining truly national attention, through, for example, an article in *Business Week,* the *Wall Street Journal,* or *Time,* is unlikely. But don't despair. Send your *major* news releases to them anyway. They may surprise you! More likely coverage, however, lies in your local media—including major cities' neighborhood newspapers—*INC.* magazine, and your regional or national professional and trade publications. They not only want your news; they need it!

In larger communities, such as New York, Chicago, Denver, or Seattle, news of local interest competes for publication with all the news in the world. In smaller communities, including big cities' neighborhoods, you *are* the world. When Hahn was growing up in Chicago, the neighborhood *Hyde Park Herald* told what was really important—in local schools, local politics, and the local business community. He now lives in Evanston, a city of 70,000 bordering directly on Chicago. Here, too, as far as the community's 120-page weekly newspaper is concerned, the world at large hardly exists. Local firms and organizations get the attention that the *Chicago Tribune* neighbor lavishes on Toyota, IBM, and AT&T. Equally important, the local publishers, editors, and reporters live right next door. Since every-

---

[5]The term "media kit" is used in two ways: In public relations, for the package in which you send information to media. In advertising, for the package in which media send information about themselves to you.

one who tells them anything has a "vested" interest in how it will be reported, local "real" news is not only needed, but welcomed.

THREE WAYS TO GET NATIONAL COVERAGE

Essentially, there are three ways you may attain national coverage.

1. Have Fame Thrust Upon You

Practically every day, businesses, corporations, and organizations achieve instant, often unexpected, fame. *People* magazine lauds a product its producer thought would be limited to schools . . . and the phone "rings off the hook." Cold fusion ignites a nationwide debate . . . and a university finds itself in the middle. An auto is downgraded by *Consumer Reports* . . . and a manufacturer's nightmare becomes reality.

The examples range from a small start-up business to a Fortune 500 corporation, from an enterprise that is not yet profitable to one that is nonprofit to one that is desperate for profit. But all have one thing in common: the need for expert response. In two of the three examples cited, that expertise was already on staff. In the third, the plug from *People* so totally overwhelmed its recipient's efforts to capitalize on it himself, that he forgot he had expert help on retainer for just such an emergency!

Fame does strike in most unexpected ways. Just don't panic. Do what *you* are good at. Treat a PR emergency—good or bad—exactly as you would a legal or medical crisis. Stay calm. Get help.

2. Find National Media That Want Your News

Trade media are magazines, journals, and newsletters devoted to a specific interest, trade, or profession. They are the most likely national publications to welcome your news, provided that it will appeal to their readers. So many of these publications exist, that even PR professionals need special directories to keep up-to-date on them. For instance, the SRDS directory *Business Publication Advertising Source,* lists 58 magazines and trade papers devoted to metalworking, with cross-references to several hundred more in 17 related fields. Other topics in this directory have from 6 listings to 650—and that covers only the English-language periodicals from the United States plus selected magazines from Canada.

For PR purposes, the annual Bacon's media directories and *The Editor & Publisher International Year Book* are the most widely used references. Though somewhat overlapping, each has exclusive—and valuable—PR content, and most PR professionals get both. An industry bible, *Editor & Publisher* gives practically encyclopedic newspaper information worldwide, of which PR contacts are only one part. There is also extensive information on newspaper suppliers, news services and syndicates, newspaper organizations, and schools of journalism. Bacon's print media directories (Vol. I, *Magazines,* and Vol. II, *Newspapers*) covers U.S. and Canadian print media and includes midyear updates. An example for the same newspaper from *Bacon's* and *Editor & Publisher* is shown in Figures 10.2 and 10.3.

Portland – 437,319; County: Multnomah; DMA: Portland, OR; (25)

THE OREGONIAN (OR-D160)
1320 S.W. Broadway
Portland, OR 97201-3499 **(503) 221-8327**
FAX: (503) 227-5306
News Phone: (503) 221-8100
E-Mail: oreeditors@aol.com
Circ: (m)350,978, (S)446,296; **Coverage:** Oregon & Southwestern Washington; **Owner:** Newhouse Newspapers; **Wires:** AP, NY Times, Knight-Ridder, Newhouse; **Online:** Compuserve, Dialog, Lexis/Nexis, Dow Jones; **Sub Rate:** $156; **Ad Rate:** $126.90.

Management/News Executives:
Publisher	Fred A. Stickel	(503) 221-8140
Editor	Sandra M. Rowe	(503) 221-8400
Managing Editor	Peter Bhatia	(503) 221-8393
Editorial Page Editor	Robert Landauer	(503) 221-8157
Op Ed Page Editor	Glenn Davis	(503) 221-8174
News Day Editor	John Green	(503) 294-5031
News Night Editor	Dan Hortsch	(503) 221-8223
News Sunday Editor	Diana Colvin	(503) 221-8456
News Copy Editor	Jerry Sass	(503) 294-7602
National News Editor	John Harvey	(503) 221-8149
National News Assistant Editor	Gwenda Richards	(503) 294-5912
National News Day Editor	Howard Scott	(503) 221-8192
State News Senior Editor	Jacqui Banaszynski	(503) 221-8510
Regional News Editor	Rick Bella	(503) 221-8536
City Editor	John Killen	(503) 294-5044
City Editor	Jerry Boone	(503) 221-8255
City Regional Editor	Janet Christ	(503) 294-5032
Local Government Reporter	Greg Nokes	(503) 221-8409
Urban Affairs Reporter	Bryan Smith	(503) 294-4000
Community News Editor	Norm Maves Jr.	(503) 221-8204
Special Sections Editor	Gayle Karol	(503) 221-8331
Photo Director	Serge McCabe	(503) 221-8412
Advertising Director	Dennis Atkin	(503) 221-8279
Circulation Director	Pat Marlton	(503) 221-8183

Editors/Reporters/Columnists:
Automotive Editor	Bob Hill	(503) 294-4103
Book Review Editor	Ellen Heltzel	(503) 221-8066

Business:
Business:
Editor	J. Douglas Bates	(503) 294-5014
Assistant Editor	Patrick Chu	(503) 221-8142
Advertising/Marketing News Reporter	Jim Hill	(503) 221-8262
Banking Reporter	Jeff Manning	(503) 294-5950
Economics Reporter	Ken Hamburg	(503) 221-8429
International Trade Reporter	Rich Read	(503) 294-5135
Personal Finance Reporter	Julie Tripp	(503) 221-8208
Small Business Reporter	Fred Leeson	(503) 221-8532
Stock Market Columnist	Mike Francis	(503) 221-8542

Computers/High Tech:
Reporter	Jim Barnett	(503) 294-5016
Reporter	Fran Gardner	(503) 221-8505
Education Editor	Jack Hart	(503) 221-8229

Entertainment/Arts:
Editor	Karen Brooks	(503) 221-8230
Assistant Editor	Roger Anthony	(503) 221-8430
Assistant Editor	Bob Hicks	(503) 221-8369
Listings Editor	Rosemarie Stein	(503) 221-4358
Movie/Film Critic	Tim Appelo	(503) 221-8332
Theater Critic	Barry Johnson	(503) 221-8589
Music (Classical) Critic	David Stabler	(503) 221-8217
Music (Popular) Critic	Marty Hughley	(503) 221-8383
Environmental Reporter	Peter Sleeth	(503) 294-4119
Farm Reporter	Fred Leeson	(503) 221-8532

Fashion:
Reporter	Michelle Trappen	(503) 221-8538
Beauty/Grooming Reporter	Michelle Trappen	(503) 221-8538

Features:
Senior Editor	Mark Wigginton	(503) 221-8054
Assistant Editor	Judy McDermott	(503) 221-8063

Food:
Editor	Ginger Johnston	(503) 221-8599
Assistant Editor	Naomi Kaufman	(503) 221-8493
Restaurant Reviewer	Karen Brooks	(503) 221-8230
Garden Reporter	Kym Pokorny	(503) 221-8205
Home Reporter	Kym Pokorny	(503) 221-8205
Legal/Legislation Editor	Dave Austin	(503) 221-5383
Religion Reporter	Mark O'Keefe	(503) 294-5039

Medical/Health:
Editor	Therese Bottomly	(503) 221-8434
Assistant Editor	Vicki Martin	(503) 221-8330
Political Editor	Michele McLellan	(503) 221-8439

Radio/Television/Cable:
Editor	Stan Horton	(503) 221-8596
Columnist	Pete Schulberg	(503) 221-8562
Real Estate Reporter	Jim Hill	(503) 221-8262
Science Reporter	Richard Hill	(503) 221-8238

Sports:
Editor	Dennis Peck	(503) 221-8164
Deputy Editor	Paul Gelormino	(503) 294-5046
Assistant Editor	Ron Jenkins	(503) 221-8137
Assistant Editor	Ron Olson	(503) 221-8077

Outdoor:
Editor	Gerry Ewing	(503) 221-8173
Reporter	Bill Monroe	(503) 221-8231
Transportation Reporter	Gordon Oliver	(503) 221-8171
Travel Editor	Sue Hobart	(503) 221-8191

Women's:
Editor	Mark Wigginton	(503) 221-8054
Society Reporter	Beverly Butterworth	(503) 221-8386
"Managing Your Money"	Julie Tripp	(503) 221-8208

General Columnist:
General Columnist	Margie Boule	(503) 221-8450
General Columnist	Jonathan Nicholas	(503) 221-8533
General Columnist	Steve Duin	(503) 221-8597
Sports Columnist	Julie Vader	(503) 221-8070

Figure 10.2 Typical *Bacon's Newspaper Directory* listing (1996© Bacon's Information Inc.). A two-volume set, including *Bacon's Magazine Directory,* covers U.S. and Canadian newspapers and magazines. Separate volumes, available individually, cover U.S. radio and TV/Cable. Editorial calendars for major magazines and dailies are in *Bacon's Media Alerts.* Business and financial editorial contacts for all media are in *Bacon's Business Media Directory.* Print media in Western Europe are covered in the annual *Bacon's International Media Directory. New York Media* and *California Media* are new for 1997. Newspaper, Magazine, Radio, and TV/Cable are available on CD-ROM. Contact Bacon's Information Inc., 332 South Michigan Avenue, Chicago, IL 60604 (800) 621-0561.

Use Regional and Local References
As of March, 1997, *local* references seem plentiful. Ask any local media representative whether one exists for your community.

Check 'em All. . . .
Only the larger PR departments are likely to need both *Bacon's* and *Editor & Publisher.* Their publishers offer excellent descriptive literature. Ask for it if you are unfamiliar with a guide. Be sure to request an *actual-size* sample page, too. This will make it much easier to compare styles for their case and thoroughness of reference.

Local News Welcomed
With endless pages to fill, trade publication editors welcome your local news and features related to their special interest. To the specialist, "local" may have broader

The Oregonian

(all day-mon to fri; m-sat; S)

The Oregonian, 1320 S.W. Broadway, Portland, OR 97201; tel (503) 221-8327; fax (503) 227-5306; e-mail oreeditors@aol.com. Advance Publications group.
Circulation: 333,654(a); 323,478(m-sat); 441,086(S); ABC Sept. 30, 1995.
Price: 35¢(d); 35¢(sat); $1.50(S); $12.00/4wk.
Advertising: Open inch rate $126.90(a); $126.90(m-sat); $131.69(S). **Representative:** Newhouse Newspapers/Metro Suburbia.
News Services: AP, LAT-WP, NYT, NNS, KRT. **Politics:** Independent. **Established:** 1850.
Magazine: Parade (S).

CORPORATE OFFICERS

President	Fred A Stickel
Vice Pres	Theodore Newhouse
Treasurer	S I Newhouse III
Asst Treasurer	D W Palmer
Asst Treasurer	Richard E Diamond

GENERAL MANAGEMENT

Publisher	Fred A Stickel
President	Patrick F Stickel
Controller	D W Palmer
Manager-Credit	Betty Kirk
Manager-Human Resources	Tom Whitehouse
Director-Public Affairs	Stephanie Oliver
Purchasing Agent	James Brown

ADVERTISING

Director	Dennis Atkin
Manager-Retail	John Mannex
Manager-General	Debi Walery
Manager-Classified	Gayle Timmerman

MARKETING AND PROMOTION

Director-Marketing Service	Steve Hubbard

TELECOMMUNICATIONS

Audiotex Manager	Marsha Davis

CIRCULATION

Director	Patrick L Marlton

NEWS EXECUTIVES

Editor	Sandra Mims Rowe
Asst Editor	Richard C Johnston
Managing Editor	Peter Bhatia
Recruiting Director	George Rede

EDITORS AND MANAGERS

Audiotex Editor	Jeff Wohler
Books Editor	Ellen Heltzel
Business Editor	Patrick Chu
Columnist	Steve Duin
Columnist	Jonathan Nicholas
Columnist	Margie Boule
Copy Desk Chief	Jerry Sass
Editorial Cartoonist	Jack Ohman
Entertainment Editor	Karen Brooks
Editorial Writer	Nanine Alexander
Editorial Writer	Phil Cogswell
Editorial Writer	Larry Hilderbrand
Editorial Writer	David Reinhard
Editorial Writer	David Sarasohn
Editorial Writer	Wayne Thompson
Editorial Page Editor	Robert J Caldwell
Food Editor	Virginia Johnston
Graphics Editor	Michelle Wise
Librarian	Sandy Macomber
Photo Director	Serge McCabe
Public Editor	Bob Caldwell
Senior Editor-Enterprise	Jacqui Banaszynski
Senior Editor-Features	Mark Wigginton
Senior Editor-Production	John Harvey
Senior Editor-Spot News	Dennis Peck
Senior Editor-Training	Jack Hart
Suburban Editor	Quinton Smith
Sports Columnist	Dwight Jaynes
Sports Columnist	Julie Vader
Sports Editor	Dennis Peck
Systems Director	John Hamlin
Team Leader-City Life	John Killen
Team Leader-Crime	David Austin
Team Leader-East	Kathleen Glanville
Team Leader-Environment	Jacqui Banaszynski
Team Leader-Family/Education	Sally Cheriel
Team Leader-Government	Michele McLellan
Team Leader-Health	Therese Bottomly
Team Leader-Living	Michael Rollins
Team Leader-Nation/World	John Harvey
Team Leader-North	Beth Erickson
Team Leader-Presentation	Galen Barnett
Team Leader-South	Michael Arrieta-Walden
Team Leader-West	Wilda Wahpepah
Travel Editor	Sue Hobart
Television Editor	Stan Horton

MANAGEMENT INFORMATION SERVICES

Director-Computer Service	Carol Howard
Manager-Production Systems	Dick Rickman
Manager-Communications	Arthur Dummor

PRODUCTION

Manager	Ed Hagstrom
Manager-Ad Service	Larry Wilson
Asst Manager-Ad Service	John Bailey
Superintendent-Plant	Joe Crawford
Superintendent-Composing	Richard Dorr
Superintendent-Mailroom	James Holman
Superintendent-Platemaking	Dan Tucker
Superintendent-Pressroom	Dennis Russell
Asst Superintendent-Mailroom	Ed Spencer
Asst Superintendent-Mailroom	Will Sousley
Asst Superintendent-Pressroom	Herman Etzel
Coordinator-Quality	John McKinney

Market Information: Zoned editions; Split Run; TMC; Operate audiotex.
Mechanical available: Offset; Black and 3 ROP colors; insert accepted — preprinted; page cut-offs — 22¾".
Mechanical specifications: Type page 13" x 21½"; E - 6 cols, 2 1/16", 1/8" between; A - 6 cols, 2 1/16", 1/8" between; C - 10 cols, 1¼", .07" between.
Commodity consumption: Newsprint 90,470 short tons; widths 55", 41¼", 27½"; black ink 1,774,000 pounds; color ink 451,200 pounds; average pages per issue 84(a), 164(S); single plates used 470,000.
Equipment: EDITORIAL: Front-end hardware — 4-CCSI/CPU, DEC/PDP 11-70, 2-HI/Pagination; Other equipment — 213-CCSI/112 BS, 22-HI/2100. CLASSIFIED: Front-end hardware — 4-CCSI/CPU, 3-DEC/PDP 11-70, 1-DEC/PDP 11-84; Other equipment — 100-CCSI/CT97. AUDIOTEX: Hardware — Brite Voice Systems. DISPLAY: Adv layout systems — In-house; Front-end hardware — Cx; Other equipment — 14-Cx/Sun Breeze. PRODUCTION: Typesetters — 1-MON/MK IIi, 4-MON/Express, 4-III/3850; Plate exposures — 2-WL/III; Plate processors — 2-WL/38-D; Electronic picture desk — Lf/AP Leaf Picture Desk; Scanners — 2-ECR/Autokon; Production cameras — 1-C/Marathon; Automatic film processors — P; Film transporters — LE; Digital color separation equipment — CD/646, Lf/Leafscan 45, Nikon/3510.

Figure 10.3 Typical listing from *The Editor & Publisher International Year Book* (© 1996 Editor & Publisher International Year Book). About 20 percent of this listing, giving technical details on printing presses and other mechanical details, is not shown here. Contents cover U.S. and Canadian newspapers in detail, plus basic information about newspapers worldwide. The *Year Book* is also available on CD-ROM and with listing capabilities that let you create your own mailing lists based on multiple criteria. Contact Editor & Publisher International Year Book, 11 West 19th Street, New York, NY 10011-4234 (212) 675-4380.

implications than even we, the senders of the news, realize—and which of us doesn't enjoy being in the know about *everything* in our field. After all, that's what makes us experts!

For stories that are more than routine, call the editor of the most important publication in your field (probably the one most widely read in your own organization), and offer an exclusive. Of course, you'll put a deadline on their acceptance, one that will permit you a wider distribution if the publication says no to your offer. And do thank the editor for considering the offer. You want his or her goodwill for your nonexclusive releases, too.

INSIGHT 51

Publicists at companies and organizations should do telephone follow-ups with trade media. Get to *know* them. With this group, calling is more important than writing.

---

3. Use National Release Services

What National Release Services Do

Several services provide the nation's media with a constant stream of stories, articles, features, and cartoons of such broad interest that they can appear almost anywhere, yet be of local interest. Depending on the season, these items may include stories on gardening or snow blowers, June wedding dresses or Thanksgiving turkey stuffing, or child safety seats in automobiles or new gears for seniors' bikes. The subject list is endless.

Unlike news services that employ reporters and charge media for the use of their stories and features, release services get their materials from public relations offices and get paid to distribute them for free use by the media. But don't be alarmed. The media hasn't sold out. Everyone involved knows the sources and the rules. Release services accept only materials that have wide appeal. Otherwise their primary audience, the editors looking for interesting "fillers," will stop considering what they submit. Release service customers, the companies paying to have their stories distributed, will remain customers only if the materials they distribute actually appear in print. What you, as a customer, are paying for is a combination of professional preparation, specified distribution, and a reasonably friendly reception in editorial offices. You eliminate the expense of an up-to-date mailing list and the duplication and distribution of your individual stories or features.

Where to Find a Release Service

Look in the Yellow Pages under "Publicity Services" for local and regional release services. They'll know that territory best. For national services, check the major city directories. Chicago's Associated Release Service (312-726-8693) is a well-established firm typical of the national group.

Who Uses Release Service Materials

Some release service materials find their way into electronic media and newspapers of major cities, especially in specific interest sections, such as gardening, homemaking, automotive, and cooking. The most widespread use of these materials, however, is in smaller communities. There they are appreciated not only for their content, but because they can be used exactly as received, without new typesetting or editing—a considerable benefit in a budget-conscious office.

How to Learn Where Your Story Appears

Clipping services are in the business of reading practically every newspaper and magazine and, for specified fees, "clipping out" items that mention a specific subject. When you receive from them the stories you've ordered clipped (some 10 days to 3 weeks after they're first published), each has attached the name of the publication in which the story appeared, its circulation, and when the story ran. For organizations that wish to document the local, regional, or national success of their PR efforts, these services, listed under "Clipping Services" in major-city Yellow Pages, are about the only way of keeping track of those efforts. Analogous services also exist for radio and TV.

INSIGHT 52

Remember why you want national media PR:
1. To serve a specific purpose beneficial to your firm or association;
2. To have *national* material to duplicate and distribute to the audience you hope to influence;
3. To let the market for your product or service know it is there or is coming.

GETTING MORE PR FROM YOUR PUBLICITY

- Any mention about you in a national publication—even a trade journal—will get reported in your local press . . . provided that you make it known to them. Do it!
- Employees love to read about themselves and their successes. Post such stories prominently on special "Good News Bulletin Boards" . . . then invite everyone to post their personal good news there also—weddings, births, graduations, anniversaries, divorces, or whatever. Let them decide!
- Mail copies of your national coverage to persons important to you or your organization. Be sure to include local political leaders, the financial community, and your employee and union newsletter.

INSIGHT 53

Few publicity stories have truly national appeal. Don't sink your time and dollars into expectations that just won't be realized. Feeding an ego as big as the world is an appetite few of us can—or should—afford.

SUMMARY

- Local media want and need your news, especially when you give it a local angle. Your audience is always interested first in themselves and second in everything that affects them.
- Think of your trade media as another local market, with the "locality" being its specialized interest. Then write accordingly.
- For national coverage, use the rifle rather than the shotgun approach. Get to know specific media contacts, and then translate your news into a story or feature that meets *their* needs and preferences. Trust hard work and creativity rather than luck.

WHEN NOT TO DO IT YOURSELF

We began this chapter by defining the task of public relations as being "to limit harm and, where possible, to neutralize harm or turn it into good." That "harm" is the way we are viewed by a specific part of the public and the actions they might take because of that perception. Thus, PR has two tasks. One is to forewarn its own company or organization against, and possibly prevent, harmful PR consequences that can be foreseen. The second and more frequently called upon task is to neutralize the public's perception of something—foreseeable or not—after it has occurred. Notice that the focus is on "something," rather than "us." An aircraft failure caused by a usually harmless lightning bolt may cause the same wreck as poor engine maintenance, but the public's perception of mechanics, the flight crew, and the airline affected will be markedly different in the two cases. And if you think this is too radical an example to apply to *you,* consider the fact that it is the expected PR emergency for a specific industry. For an airline, public relations surely should not be handled by amateurs—just as the PR critical to *you* demands equally expert attention. So when you are in need of PR:

- **Consider the stakes.** Are you trying to climb from a 60 percent to a 65 percent market share or halt a precipitous decline?
- **Consider the personalities.** Is the CEO more likely to accept PR guidance from an "objective" outside pro than from inside staff . . . especially when the results are painful as well as necessary?
- **Consider the location.** Will an outsider raise suspicions, whereas local expertise would gain a friendly welcome?
- **Consider your own abilities.** Balance what you can do, and do well, against what *only you* can do, and direct yourself accordingly.

But let's not be "firefighters," waiting to be summoned to PR disasters. Public relations and publicity can and should be used to create goodwill—among employees, customers, clients, and the community as a whole. This may mean sponsoring or helping to publicize a golf tournament, a health fair, a scout outing, a contest for kids, and so on. It may also involve, depending on policy, making public your charitable contributions or involvement by management in public service. You probably do much more good than anyone suspects . . . so let the world know!

YES, YOU CAN DO YOUR OWN PR . . . SOMETIMES

Doing your own publicity can be both rewarding and a great deal of fun, and nothing we have said here should keep you from it.[6] There are, however, times when your expertise should concentrate on finding PR professionals who can handle a project better than you can and then making sure that that's what they do.

---

[6]For a much more detailed treatment of do-it-yourself PR, get *The New Publicity Kit* by Jeanette Smith (Wiley, 1995).

The biggest mistake made by firms when hiring outside PR professionals is not to tell them the *whole* story. Usually, professionals are called in to help overcome a bad image, a falling market share, or unfavorable publicity. Many firms think that they won't get a good job out of the pros if they really tell them *all* the "bad news." So they send them into battle unaware. Of course they do learn—the hard way—from the media! They wind up looking foolish, and their employers look worse. Think of the pro as your good-guy hired gun. Don't arm him or her with blanks!

INSIGHT 54

When assigning any task, search for someone who's better at it than you. And don't worry about being shown up: Organizations are desperate for managers who recognize talent and tend to reward that more liberally than just doing a good job yourself. Good managers get promoted. Good workers get more work.

NOTES ON THE PUBLICITY/PUBLIC RELATIONS CHECKLIST

These notes are a supplement to the material presented in this chapter. They are not a substitute for that material.

1. **Audience.** The audience(s) you want to reach and which—if any—to address specifically, rather than as part of the whole. Differentiate between the same message keyed to different interests and different messages.
2. **Focus.** Decide both what the message is to say and what it is to accomplish. Set realistic PR goals, not those for advertising.
3. **Projects.** Link the project(s) to #1 and #2. Define the media for each audience in relation to the "cash value" of achieving each goal. Not only dollars, but staff and staff time are limited, too.
4. **Time line.** Almost anything can be done—given that nothing else is needed. If due dates demand an absolute concentration of effort on one particular project, make sure that management knows that no other project can receive attention.
5. **Cost control.** This is the centralized budgeting control, especially for multimedia projects such as items 12 through 18. This is not budget setting (that's supposed to be done), but deciding how expenditures are tracked and monitored. Don't do these projects without such a system!
6. **Supervision.** Note here if this is different from the overall supervision and how both work in developing items 1–5.
7. **Components.** Spell out each project's components. Not, for instance, just "Media Kit," but every detail. This includes the type of outer envelope along with its size and message; the color of the pocket folder and the number of pockets it has; any special design or standard format; and what each pocket contains and in what order. Mention also any addi-

PUBLICITY/PUBLIC RELATIONS CHECKLIST

Project Title _____   **Date** _____

Project Description _____   **Project #** _____

_____   **Checklist #** _____

Overall Supervision By _____   **Deadline** _____

Budget _____   **Completion Date** _____   **Start Up Date** _____

Project Focus (Mark A–Z in order of importance): ☐ Managers   ☐ Other Employees   ☐ Immediate Community
☐ Broader Community   ☐ Stockholders   ☐ Other Financial   ☐ Suppliers   ☐ Customers   ☐ Clients
☐ General Press   ☐ Trade Press   ☐ Financial Press   ☐ _____   ☐ _____   ☐ _____

MANAGEMENT DECISIONS	ASSIGNED TO	DUE	IN	MUST APPROVE	BY DATE	IN	INFO COPY ONLY	SEE ATTACHED
1. Audience(s)	_____	___	☐	_____	___	☐	_____	☐
2. Focus	_____	___	☐	_____	___	☐	_____	☐
3. Project(s)	_____	___	☐	_____	___	☐	_____	☐
4. Time Line	_____	___	☐	_____	___	☐	_____	☐
5. Cost–Quotes/Actual	_____	___	☐	_____	___	☐	_____	☐
6. Project Supervision	_____	___	☐	_____	___	☐	_____	☐
PRODUCTION								
7. Components	_____	___	☐	_____	___	☐	_____	☐
8. Copy	_____	___	☐	_____	___	☐	_____	☐
9. Layout	_____	___	☐	_____	___	☐	_____	☐
10. Type	_____	___	☐	_____	___	☐	_____	☐
11. Duplication	_____	___	☐	_____	___	☐	_____	☐
12. Camera-Ready Art	_____	___	☐	_____	___	☐	_____	☐
13. Printing	_____	___	☐	_____	___	☐	_____	☐
14. AV Practice	_____	___	☐	_____	___	☐	_____	☐
15. Audio Creative	_____	___	☐	_____	___	☐	_____	☐
16. Video Creative	_____	___	☐	_____	___	☐	_____	☐
17. AV Duplication	_____	___	☐	_____	___	☐	_____	☐
DISTRIBUTION								
18. Phone Contacts Assigned	_____	___	☐	_____	___	☐	_____	☐
19. Phone Contacts Made	_____	___	☐	_____	___	☐	_____	☐
20. Media Kit Packaging	_____	___	☐	_____	___	☐	_____	☐
21. Lists Ordered (mail/phone)	_____	___	☐	_____	___	☐	_____	☐
22. Shipping Assigned	_____	___	☐	_____	___	☐	_____	☐
23. Postage OK	_____	___	☐	_____	___	☐	_____	☐
24. Personal Contacts Assigned	_____	___	☐	_____	___	☐	_____	☐
25. Personal Contacts Made	_____	___	☐	_____	___	☐	_____	☐
26. Mailing Lists Checked	_____	___	☐	_____	___	☐	_____	☐
27. Phone Lists Checked	_____	___	☐	_____	___	☐	_____	☐
28. Legal Clearance	_____	___	☐	_____	___	☐	_____	☐
REPORTS								
29. Quotes/Estimates	_____	___	☐	_____	___	☐	_____	☐
30. Actual Costs	_____	___	☐	_____	___	☐	_____	☐
31. Checking Bureau Assigned	_____	___	☐	_____	___	☐	_____	☐
32. Results Received/Distributed	_____	___	☐	_____	___	☐	_____	☐

tional enclosures—both new and existing—and the order in which they appear. Specify *everything*. Give every item an ID code and use it on that item.

8. **Copy.** Writing for PR is a specialized skill. Frequently, it can be found or developed in-house. Since its message is most often aimed at print and electronic media, experience even on high school or college newspapers, and/or radio, or TV, is invaluable.

9. **Layout.** When PR requires layout or type, treat them with the importance given to everything else that represents your organization. If it's not worth doing right . . . why do it at all?

10. **Type.** Most PR projects can be produced by desktop publishing.

11. **Duplication.** This is for the simpler quick-print projects and office duplication. For more ambitious outside printing, use #12 and #13.

12–13. **Camera-ready art.** When PR requires the creation and production of major new printed pieces, use the separate checklists included for such projects in Chapter 14. Their use is determined not by the quantity printed, but by the complexity of the work.

14–17. **Radio, TV/Cable.** Practice for likely contacts with electronic media with a *realistic simulation,* especially if you are new to radio and TV broadcasting. Unless you're a pro, do not do this cold! (For creating and producing your own taped materials, use the information and checklist from Chapter 11. Don't even think of doing it yourself without reading that chapter first.)

18–19. **Phone contact.** Most PR telemarketing involves in-house invitations or follow-up on news material. When the list or effort seem overwhelming, use the information and checklist in Chapter 7. That's why they're there.

20–27. **Must-do reminders.** These are a project reminder more than a personnel assignment in most instances. Save personal contact (#25) for something really worthwhile and for media who ignore everything else. If you're a beginner, ask colleagues who in the media that is. It's never a secret.

28. **Legal clearance.** Consider every claim and promise a legal commitment. If in doubt—and even when not—get legal clearance.

29–30. **Cost OK's.** Official report on estimates and decision on approvals. Due dates for this are established as part of #4.

31–32. **Results.** Consult with several checking bureaus regarding what it is possible to learn about results. They're most often the only way to check on PR *distribution* and its *use.* Gauging PR *effectiveness* is beyond the scope of this book.

11 | TV, Radio, Video, and CD Creative and Production

FINDING AN AUDIOVISUAL "PARTNER"

If, like most of us, you're a novice at purchasing audio and video services, you'll need someone at the creative and production end who will become your "partner[1]"—someone whom you can trust to give you your money's worth, especially when you have no way of knowing what that "money's worth" is. Selecting such a person has to be based on finding an organization that can demonstrate a consistent level of results over an extended period of time within an established price range. Shopping by cost is easy: You can always find someone who will do it for less. But not knowing whether you can *use* what you'll be buying is where disaster awaits. An advance deposit with progressive payments is standard practice. You seldom can allow time to do a project over. You have little recourse if you do not like what you get.

The Boutique Factor

Downsizing, especially in corporate audiovisual (AV) departments, has led to much "outsourcing," frequently to former employees at new one- or two-person AV boutiques. Without in any way disparaging their creative abilities, their business know-how is often somewhat less. When working with such a boutique, make sure your working agreement states that you own all videotapes and audiotapes shot for your project. After they have finished your job, take physical possession of the tapes. Store them in a cool, fire-resistant location, perhaps the same place you store your disks of backup computerized records.

The Longevity Factor

Don't hesitate to work with a start-up company that can demonstrate its ability at a lower than expected cost, *if what they produce won't be changed in the future.* Many new audiovisual suppliers have underchanged themselves out of business before they learned the true cost of what they were doing! For long-term projects, work with suppliers who've shown their ability to survive a few years.

---

[1]William "Bill" Holtane, president of Sound-Video Impressions in Des Plaines, IL (847) 297-4360, became Hahn's "partner." He not only helped guide Hahn from ignorance to competence, but is largely responsible for the wisdom in this chapter.

The Basic Skills

Your audiovisual or audio projects require four distinct skills. Each of them has both a *mechanical* and a *quality* factor. Synergy happens when you get a happy marriage of both.

1. **Preproduction.** The script with sound (such as a slamming door) indicated and a cartoon-style storyboard visual concept.
2. **Production.** Videotaping or recording the project—on location, in the studio, or both.
3. **Postproduction.** In-studio or do-it-yourself editing.
4. **Duplication.** As required.

Each of these four skills can be, and often is, provided by different organizations, especially when overall supervision of the project lies with an advertising agency experienced in audiovisual production as well as creativity. As an in-house supervisor, look for an audiovisual "partner" company that can provide all three of the creative functions, from scripting through editing. Duplication, like printing, is quite a different specialty, best given to experts in that field.

The Do-It-Yourself Quality Factor

Video editing requires computer equipment with a *huge* memory; that is, definitely *not* a typical home or office desktop computer. In mid-1996, "amateur" editing equipment costs from $15,000 to $20,000 start-up; professional equipment from $60,000 up ... up ... UP! Excellent quality not only costs more, it demands the skills and experience to use it. You would not expect a $200 bicycle to provide the same ride as a $20,000 automobile. Well, the same is true of video editing equipment ... no matter what the ads say.

Finding Suppliers

In larger markets, if no other guidance seems available, begin with the business Yellow Pages under "Audio-Visual Production," "Recording Services," or "Video Production Services." In smaller communities, you're unlikely to find the same level of experience or sophisticated equipment, but you will be able to find *someone* who can help. Begin by deciding how "big city" you really have to be. Your commercials will actually be seen on television. Instructional and informational "infomercials" are shown on monitors using the same screen. Your audience, without consciously realizing it, expects the technical quality they get from that screen every day in regular programs, other commercials, and feature films. The ability to approach that quality within your budgetary and creative restrictions is what your initial search is all about.

A Wealth of Suppliers

Video and audio production facilities are practically everywhere. Community colleges, some high schools, many hospitals, local radio, TV, and cable companies, and, of course, local video and audio production companies all offer their services.

And look for special promotions in which radio or TV stations—including some in the largest markets—offer to create and produce your commercial without additional charge, provided that you purchase a specified amount of broadcast time. You may even get to use their work on another station! In all probability, though, their end product, while competent, will be very packaged—one of a limited number of set solutions to any promotion problem. If what you want is some variation of "Good morning! We're so and so. Here's our address. Come in or give us a call," this may well be all you need. Much local automotive, home builder, and retail promotion is done exactly that way.

The use of on-air personalities in audiovisual projects requires quite different considerations. Broadcasting—especially local television—demands mechanical skills. Its expertise lies in sending a signal to listeners, subscribers, and viewers. With the exception of some news and sports, few television broadcasts originate locally. Local staff have neither the need nor the talent for much creativity. Radio's call-in and disk jockey personalities do tend to be excellent sales "voices," especially on their own programs. Elsewhere, however, use local talent with caution.

Selecting by Budget

As a novice purchasing audio or video services, begin with the Yellow Pages of a major market. Call several suppliers with the largest ads, several more with medium-sized ads, and several with simple listings. Ask all of them which of the writing, shooting, and editing services they offer. When they tell you "all three," ask for their typical budget. You do *not,* as yet, know enough to work with someone who answers "Anything you wish to spend." You do want to see samples from several suppliers who work within defined ranges, to learn what specific budgets can buy. The $5,000, $15,000 and $75,000 end products should be obviously—perhaps even dramatically—different. Which one you need may be a pleasant surprise. (A little more than the $5,000 one? A lot less than the $15,000 one? Find the suppliers of the $10,000 products, and check them the same way.) If your budget is in the $50,000-plus range, don't go to the $15,000 supplier because they offer a seeming bargain. You won't be satisfied, no matter what the results. Don't look for "just transportation" when you really want a competition sports car, and don't expect to get the latter for the price of the former, no matter what you're told. Search for two things: the best creative ability to understand audiovisual problems and the technical know-how to produce the solutions *within your budget!*

For "Infomercials"

For longer "infomercials," that is, informational programs or commercials that delve deeper into your product or service, you must use people who are, first and foremost, creative. You need a true video or recording production company, preferably one that specializes in the infomercial field. Thousands of producers can hold an audience for 30 seconds. 30 *minutes* is a quite different skill. For TV home-shopping-type selling, infomercial producers who specialize in this field *may* work on a percentage-of-profit basis. If they make such an offer, take it! But have your attorney read the contract before you sign, and realize you will have to relinquish some creative control over both product and packaging.

Tape vs. CD vs. CD-ROM

Commercials and infomercials are produced according to set standards. They do not require *your* decision on tape versus CD. However, before deciding to produce your sales presentation, point-of-sale, or other AV materials on CD or CD-ROM rather than standard tape, consider all of the following:

- You are not producing a music or movie disk. You are producing a commercial message for computer reproduction.
- Before creating and distributing a CD or CD-ROM, survey the recipients' computer capabilities to make sure they can use it.
- Many older computers do not have CD capabilities.
- Even with newer equipment, CD does *not* have a uniform system for computer reproduction. Unless you have a one-to-one fit, your CD message may not work well, if it works at all.
- Here's why there is no uniform standard format for computer CD-ROMs. By the twenty-first century, if not before, the computer industry expects the physical CD-ROM to be replaced by Internet transmission and instant ("real-time") access to the most complicated messages. Until then, work with what you have.
- Editing for CD costs two or three times as much as tape.
- CD-ROM requires an immense amount of computer memory for end user access. The more enhanced your message with sight, sound, and motion, the longer it takes to appear. "Rendering" takes time! If you want to give your end users access to your information, how long do you expect them to wait?

SUMMARY

- Much audiovisual production works on the honor system. Find suppliers who will act as "partners," guarding your interests as well as their own.
- If you are unfamiliar with costs, preview work by suppliers in various price ranges. Establish your budget *after* you see what different dollars can buy.

THE CLIENT AND AUDIOVISUAL CREATIVITY

Begin with introspection: Let the producer or production company know how the clients see themselves, especially if the client is you. Are the clients so serious about what they do, that the least touch of whimsy is out of character? Do they feel branded as stodgy and want a lighter image? Generally, senior managers don't review anything until it's completed. The last thing your audiovisual supplier wants to hear *from them* is "but that's not *us*." There has to be a knowledgeable person from the client's side directly involved in *ongoing* creativity, not to tell the producer how to run the train, but to help redirect it when it's on an obviously wrong track.

What Audiovisual Creativity Is All About

In low- to medium-priced audiovisual organizations, the writer, director, and producer often are one and the same. But whether there is one, two, or a team, audiovisual creativity is the ability to use *media* to tell a story. It begins with the ability to create a script—to write the words that are spoken while sound effects, music, and visual images are received by the audience. It demands from the producer and director technical expertise in acting, filming, and editing. It requires visualizing what the entire project will achieve as individual segments are produced and then making it happen.

For on-location shooting, the writer and producer visit the site to learn whether filming there is practical, both for reasons of safety and to remain within the budget. Once reassured, they put their imagination to work. Immediately, they start seeing shots, hearing words, and visualizing action. Suggested scripts from the agency or the client are actually helpful at this stage. Far from hindering the writers, they tell them what the client wants and how they see themselves in relationship to that project. It focuses creativity within specified limitations, rather than letting it expend time, energy, and costs on efforts that are sure to be rejected.

INSIGHT 55

Give your audiovisual producers suggestions, directions, and even scripts as a base on which to build. If *their* creative ability can't improve on *your* efforts, ask yourself whether you are really that good or whether someone else should decide between the two of you.

Openness to Criticism

No audiovisual professional expects a first script to be accepted without change or comment. It's for discussion. Both client and scriptwriter are like chefs given the same ingredients. One may not recognize the full possibilities, while the other may take them a bit too far. The key is to be open to each other's tastes. Argue, and even fight about the scripts, but just don't forget the audience for whom you are "cooking."

Amateur vs. Professional Talent

How and where your video or audio product will be used may well determine whether amateur talents are an option. Not only do amateurs tend to get frustrated quickly, but contractual obligations for professional talent may be a factor. Your producer, charged with finding the talent, will be aware of these factors.

When the option to use amateurs does exist, you can screen them from among actors, musicians, singers, and dancers in colleges, local drama and music groups, and fraternal organizations. Often, it's not a question of talent as much as it is of a client's wishes and priorities.[2] Keep in mind that what does make the professional different is the ability to follow directions: To a professional, doing or saying the same thing 10 or 20 times or more isn't deadly boring; it's part of the job. The result doesn't deteriorate with repetition; it gets better.

INSIGHT 56

Amateurs require inspiration. Professionals do it with a headache.

SUMMARY

- Differentiate between producing your idea and being open to alternatives. Be honest with yourself, and let the producer know *before* they begin.
- Be candid about how you see yourself. Be open to achieving your aims in unexpected ways.
- When either professional or amateur talent is an option, let the producer decide. "Talented" relatives tend to cost most of all.

ON-LOCATION SHOOTING

A sound stage set and modern video techniques can put you on top of Mt. Everest or lets you battle a shark 3,000 feet under water without leaving the comfort of the studio. But if you are to show your earth-boring machine inside a coal mine, or the vast inventory of a department store or supermarket, video equipment must go where they are—and probably inconvenience a great many people to get the job done.

Management Commitment

Production within a studio is comparatively easy. However, for on-location shooting, management must be absolutely committed to the project. Thanks to the new "chip cameras," true colors now can be shot without an immense amount of lighting, specially placed for shooting. However, distracting extras, whether people or things, still must be removed from the picture. Work, traffic, and possibly sound

---

[2]Try not to impose talented relatives on your producer. One of Hahn's more costly commercials needed a quartet for which he had not budgeted to outsing a client's daughter attempting to turn a simple radio spot into grand opera.

must be stopped or redirected. Electrical cables must be permitted in strange places, and imperfect strangers must be allowed to give orders *to everyone,* whether they're in the video or not . . . and get their releases if they are.

INSIGHT 57

Consider asking employees for a written release at the time of employment, granting permission to picture that person in promotional materials. Many organizations do this. However, check with your attorney first.

Without on-the-scene cooperation, on-location shooting can become literally impossible. So be committed, and make that commitment known!

Endless Shooting

On-location shooting for the average piece, no matter what its length, will be from one to three days. Generally, there's a minimum crew of three: the producer/director, the camera operator, and an expert all-around assistant.[3] Their task is not only to shoot the project, but to *overshoot* everything—the clock on the wall, the view from the window, the notices on the bulletin board, the receptionist's smile, the loading clerk's wave, the office, the hallway, the factory sweeper, and the jeweler's polishing—whether it seems to have a connection with the final piece or not. Though seemingly random, this shooting is far from haphazard. It provides a wealth of raw, "cutaway" footage to be found and inserted wherever there is a need for a smooth transition between scenes. (Lack of such footage becomes obvious only when transition shots are missing or the same ones are endlessly repeated.) For the postproduction editor, there is never too much variety in *good* raw footage.

A Do-It-Yourself Option

In video projects that include location shooting, the two most costly elements are (a) the actual location shooting and (b) later, editing. For fairly simple projects— and for fairly simple shooting only—discuss with your production company the practicality of doing it yourself. For instance, for a wine commercial that calls for some mood scenes of growing and picking grapes, pressing and bottling, taste testing and smiling happy tasters, do-it-yourself video probably will work. For anything more complicated, leave it to the pros. The cost of editing poorly shot video will outweigh any savings from do-it-yourself, up-front shooting.

---

[3]If cost is no object, or the project demands it, a crew can expand to include makeup artists, hairstylists, carpenters, and electricians—indeed, almost any specialist you can name. The reason movies often list a hundred or more credits is that every single person named was *needed* to do *that* film. What "that" means for your project will determine *your* crew and *your* cost.

- Get instructions from the producer on using the camera.
- Use a tripod! Leave handheld video to the pros.
- Shoot three times as much as you think you'll need. You'll need it.
- See the next WARNING box.

THE ART AND CRAFT OF AUDIOVISUAL EDITING

It is in postproduction editing that your project is actually created. The process involves a series of steps, some mechanical, some judgmental, and some both.

Time Code

Most often, video editing begins with the placing of a small time-code "window" onto each frame. The window shows the hour, minute, second, and frame for that video and looks like this: 03:16:32:05. Video is edited to 1/30 of a second. That is, there will be 30 frames *for each second.* But first comes the decision to edit for picture or sound. If the visual is the important thing, make the sound match it. If, on the other hand, you begin with a script that must be followed, tune the video to the sound track. Either is equally possible, provided that the postproduction editors know what is needed.

WARNING! WARNING! WARNING!

Video editing requires a frame-by-frame time code. This is produced automatically while shooting and only becomes visible on editing equipment. But different cameras have different time codes and less expensive equipment probably produces none at all. Check with your production company on the compatibility of their editing equipment with your camera. It's much cheaper to rent the right camera than to retime all your shooting!

Sound Editing

The sound of your project—especially the spoken words—demands the same attention and skill as the picture. Decisions must be made on using the sound from the location or from studio recording. Everyone speaking on camera will require a teleprompter, a device that lets them *read* a script on camera, just as TV news broadcasters do. Teleprompters and tiny lapel microphones that ensure good sound take a bit of practice but have made in-house stars out of many an unlikely candidate.

Sound editing involves first finding the best available sound from on-location shooting and then knowing *and using* sound-quality techniques to improve, or "sweeten," what your location gave you. Incidental, ambient sounds, such as a door closing or footsteps approaching, almost always require "sweetening." Fortunately, they're also the easiest sounds to fix. Voices have fewer options, unless in-studio "lip sync" recording was planned and allowed for. Music, if any, can wait for the final combination of words and pictures.

Visual Editing

As in sound editing, in visual editing all the steps are determined by the producer. Generally, it is the producer/director who views raw footage and determines which sections fit the script best, how to handle transitions, and when to add special effects or enhancements. The client can, and often does, work along with the producer/director but must recognize that the job is immensely time consuming. It begins with viewing *all* the raw footage to eliminate technically unusable shots or those for which superior versions exist. Suppose you start with 10 hours of film. This first assessment, with stops and starts to make notes, review some sections, take personal and meal breaks (although few AV editors actually stop for lunch, rather than eating a sandwich while working), will take at least two days. Now, having eliminated what is obviously unusable, the really creative editing begins. Everything that remains is viewed twice—or three or four times. In audiovisual editing, as in much advertising and promotion, "Everything takes longer than it takes!" But it does get done.

Final Editing

Final editing almost demands the presence of both the producer and the client. Audiotapes for radio commercials or information and training are easily edited and changed by simple cut-and-splice techniques. Video is different, however: Once the sound and picture are brought together in final form, any change, no matter how seemingly trivial, may require starting from scratch. Audiovisual editing is not done on actual film; rather, it is done digitally, with electronic impulses, from which a final film is created. To make changes, sound and pictures must once again be synchronized from a dozen different sources. You must make synchronization decisions during editing, not afterward, or else not only will everything take longer than it takes, but it will surely also cost more than it costs.

INSIGHT 58

About animation: Disney-type animation costs about $2,000 per *second* for the animation alone. That's $7,200,000 for a one-hour feature film, a comfortably low cost by film standards. For a 30-second commercial, it's $60,000, and perhaps twice that by the time the project is done. Don't try and do it for less. If budget is the problem, stick with quality and do something else.

SUMMARY

- On-location shooting is invariably disruptive. Management must make its commitment known and enforced *before* the crew appears on the scene.
- Editing is often more costly than shooting. Keep it in control by being there when it happens, not correcting it after it's done!

THE ART AND CRAFT OF DUPLICATION

The majority of audiovisual production companies do not have facilities or equipment for duplicating large quantities. Where only a few copies are needed—perhaps a dozen or fewer—these companies can undoubtedly do the work. Many producers will provide such duplication as a low-cost service. Others have much higher pricing—from two to ten times more, in our experience—than regular duplication companies. So check all of the following costs before you decide:

- **Setting up.** Preparing tapes and equipment before duplication can begin.
- **Video & CD/CD-ROM duplication.** Make certain that your duplication company knows how the finished product will be used and can provide that service. Anyone can duplicate for a VCR. For anything else, from installing antipiracy protection to knowing TV requirements abroad, find and use specialists.
- **Audio duplication.** The duplication processes for audiocassettes and CDs (compact discs) are so different that each must be handled as a separate project. As this is written in December, 1996, because CD replication (copying) uses digital processes while cassettes use linear techniques, they require a somewhat costly "submaster" to reproduce from the same original master. Before you consider a compact disc because it's the contemporary thing to do, consult a CD replication service. Be sure you learn about the process before you begin.
- **Labeling.** Preparing camera-ready type and art, if any, plus duplicating labels both for the cassette itself and for individual audio- or videocassette containers.
- **Containers.** Boxes for audiocassettes. Use softer "albums" or more sturdy "library cases" for videocassettes.
- **Handling.** Putting everything together as a finished package.
- **Shipping.** Be sure to specify how the complete packages are to be shipped. Many duplication companies routinely ship air express, unless instructed *in writing* to use a less expensive method.
- **Scheduling.** Your responsibilities, as well as theirs, should be specified in writing. And what happens if either one of you is late?

Finding the Duplication Service You Need

Video/CD and audio duplication services are either small- or mass-quantity suppliers. Unlike printers, a middle size hardly exists. Since they may seem much alike to the uninitiated buyer, here are some guidelines:

1. Have your video or audio producer recommend a duplicating service (perhaps itself). Get a quote on the project *based on your producer's specifications* before production begins. If quantities and dollars are low, you can probably stop right there. For large quantities or large dollars, get additional quotations.

2. When evaluating new video or audio duplication companies, have them produce a sample copy from *your* original if time permits. Let them know that you

will compare it with one or two other suppliers and that you will use it as you would a printing proof to check the complete run.

3. In our experience, videocassette/CD duplication services repay the evaluation effort. An obvious "winner" has always been easy to determine. When cost has been a factor, less expensive labels and containers have produced major savings. Consider purchasing them yourself only if your suppliers' sources fail to give them an obvious price advantage. (They're not purchasing just for you; they should get larger quantity discounts.)

4. In our experience, audiocassette services are fairly comparable to one another for *voice* duplication. If music is a critical part of the sound, however, get help in the evaluation. But keep a perspective on what it is that you are producing and the extraordinary cost of perfection when a good product will do!

5. For mass duplication—from thousands to millions of copies—go to a major national company. Before 1990, videocassettes had to be duplicated in real time; that is, a two-hour tape took two hours to copy. Larger producers had to have thousands of duplication machines to handle this. After 1990, high-speed duplication of videocassettes (as had been the case for audio and CD) was finally perfected, with quality every bit as good as the previous real-time system. If quantities warrant, ask your producer to recommend such sources, or check Allied Digital Technologies Corp. (847-595-2900). This firm has offices and facilities from Florida to California.

SUMMARY

- For small quantities, the cost of a new setup may be more than the cost of duplication. Check with your production service before you go elsewhere. Get *total* costs from both—for the finished package, not just the tape or CD.
- To evaluate audio or audiovisual duplicating ability, comparison shop by having *your current project* copied. It's worth the extra cost and will give you a proof against which to check the production run.
- Mass duplication needs a mass producer. Check several, not just the one closest to home.

NOTES ON THE AUDIOVISUAL/AUDIO CHECKLIST

These notes are a supplement to the material presented in this chapter. They are not a substitute for that material.

1. **Purpose.** The purpose of the project from management's point of view—especially *what* it is to achieve. *How* that is to be accomplished is best left by management to the pros.

AUDIOVISUAL/AUDIO CHECKLIST

Project Title _____   Date _____

Project Description _____   Project # _____

_____   Checklist # _____

Overall Supervision By _____   Deadline _____

Budget _____   Completion Date _____   Start Up Date _____

MANAGEMENT DECISIONS	ASSIGNED TO	DUE	IN	MUST APPROVE	BY DATE	IN	INFO COPY ONLY	SEE ATTACHED
1. Purpose	_____	___	☐	_____	___	☐	_____	☐
2. Client Self-Image	_____	___	☐	_____	___	☐	_____	☐
3. Budget	_____	___	☐	_____	___	☐	_____	☐
4. Project Supervision	_____	___	☐	_____	___	☐	_____	☐

CREATIVE

	ASSIGNED TO	DUE	IN	MUST APPROVE	BY DATE	IN	INFO COPY ONLY	SEE ATTACHED
5. Focus	_____	___	☐	_____	___	☐	_____	☐
6. Audience(s)	_____	___	☐	_____	___	☐	_____	☐
7. Desired Response(s)	_____	___	☐	_____	___	☐	_____	☐
8. Supplier Selection	_____	___	☐	_____	___	☐	_____	☐
9. Client Script Ideas	_____	___	☐	_____	___	☐	_____	☐
10. Client Contact/Supervision	_____	___	☐	_____	___	☐	_____	☐
11. Script/Storyboard Approval	_____	___	☐	_____	___	☐	_____	☐
12. Suggested Length	_____	___	☐	_____	___	☐	_____	☐
13. Creative/Production Time Line	_____	___	☐	_____	___	☐	_____	☐

PRODUCTION

	ASSIGNED TO	DUE	IN	MUST APPROVE	BY DATE	IN	INFO COPY ONLY	SEE ATTACHED
14. On-Site Contact	_____	___	☐	_____	___	☐	_____	☐
15. Production Supervision	_____	___	☐	_____	___	☐	_____	☐
16. Editing Supervision	_____	___	☐	_____	___	☐	_____	☐
17. Actual Length	_____	___	☐	_____	___	☐	_____	☐

DUPLICATION

	ASSIGNED TO	DUE	IN	MUST APPROVE	BY DATE	IN	INFO COPY ONLY	SEE ATTACHED
18. Supplier Selection	_____	___	☐	_____	___	☐	_____	☐
19. Supplier Contact	_____	___	☐	_____	___	☐	_____	☐
20. Label Copy with ID	_____	___	☐	_____	___	☐	_____	☐
21. Label Design	_____	___	☐	_____	___	☐	_____	☐
22. Distribution	_____	___	☐	_____	___	☐	_____	☐
23. Duplication Time Line	_____	___	☐	_____	___	☐	_____	☐
24. Report(s)	_____	___	☐	_____	___	☐	_____	☐
_____	_____	___	☐	_____	___	☐	_____	☐

2. **Client Self-image.** Be open about the self-image you wish to project. If there are different suggestions within management, rank them. More than one may fit in.

3. **Budget.** Be certain that management knows what its proposed budget can actually buy. If the budget is too limited for the quality desired, rethink your audiovisual needs.

4. **Project Supervisor.** The project supervisor is charged with managing everything from #5 on. Where supervision is delegated, the project supervisor makes the assignments.

5–7. **Basic approach.** How the purpose of #1 is to be addressed to a specified audience to achieve a specific response. Put #5 through #7 into writing before evaluating suppliers. If you are unsure about focus—soft sell or hard sell, for instance—leave it until after #8. Just be sure which options do exist for you. Not everything will work.

8. **Suppliers.** It's not a question of which suppliers are best at what *they* do, it's who's best at what *you* need done. Evaluate your potential supplier from that perspective! (A teen-ager's rock group that's best for his friends may be a disaster as a dance band for parents.)

9. **Client's script.** Nothing presents the client's self-image more clearly than his or her ideas for scripts. The more detailed, the better they are. Urge management to participate, perhaps in a brainstorming session. Most of us know we're not scriptwriters. Keep it informal.

10. **Client's contact.** The client's one contact person—and keep it at one only!—with whom outside services may deal. Audiovisual production is just too difficult, time consuming, and costly to fix to permit uncoordinated instruction.

11. **Script approval.** Who *must* be involved? Who *may* be involved? Surely, not everyone who *wants* to be involved!

12. **Length.** This is primarily an "infomercial" decision that's often determined by the needs of the sales department. For on-air commercials, determine all the likely uses (say, 60-, 30-, or 15-second spots) before writing begins. It's much easier, and much less costly, to plan now, rather than as an afterthought during editing.

13. **Time line.** This time is determined by the client's needs, the supplier selected, and the variety of the end product. (A 30-second commercial made from a 30-minute infomercial may take as much time as the infomercial.) To reserve duplication time, order duplicates to be made by #18 *now,* based on the #13 schedule, and notify everyone if there are delays. Everything in AV generally takes longer than you expect.

14. **Authorized contact.** Designate who is authorized to act for the client during on-site shooting, especially at the client's site. Also, appoint a backup. Audiovisual or recording producers get paid by the day . . . whether you make it possible for them to work or not.

15. **Production contact.** Designate a project supervisor for management who makes on-the-spot filming and taping decisions. Others may have to be consulted, but the management's project supervisor *decides.*

16. **Editing contact.** After filming and taping, editing achieves the final project. A number of product specialists may be present, but, again, only the management's project supervisor speaks for the client.

17. **Length.** For "infomercials," the actual length is determined during editing. Do not, however, let this vary by more than 10 percent from the projected length in #12 without approval. Sales personnel, for instance, may not be able to use something twice as long, no matter how good it is. Even public service announcements often must fit set time slots. Don't just do. Check!

18. **Supplier.** Hold final approval of the production and duplication suppliers until you know that they are mechanically compatible with each other. Have them speak to one another. Make them explain what they decide.

19. **Purchasing.** This standard purchasing procedure is best left to the purchasing department. Of course, the management project supervisor retains approval on all aspects of quality.

20–21. **Labeling.** Duplication suppliers from #18 are generally the best source for labels and labeling. If special designs are wanted, let your duplicating service know. But find out the effect on production time. Consider routine, but quick, labeling for immediate needs, with customized labels thereafter.

22. **Distribution.** When the duplication supplier also ships the goods, find out the supplier's routine way to distribute them. Many send everything by air express, unless ordered to do otherwise in writing.

23. **Time line.** Don't spare the details for larger projects or multiple shipments. Something will be forgotten if it isn't specified here.

24. **Reports.** Note especially what has been learned that can be applied to future efforts. Put it in writing so that others may learn, too.

12 | Sales and Marketing Presentations

To gain visibility and business for your company, presentations are used in-house, at conferences and meetings, and in prospecting and selling. Although selling as such is not the subject of this book, we do want to share some tricks of the trade that we have used in "selling" ourselves to management as their employees, and our companies as their consultants and their agencies. There is nothing tricky, secret, or underhanded about this. The techniques are taught in presentation classes and many in-house seminars. Those of you who have not had the opportunity to participate in either should find this chapter of exceptional value.

INSIGHT 59

Practice your presentation! Put it on audio—even video if lots of movement is required. You won't look or sound nearly as bad as you feared. Listen and correct any problems that you detect. Do this as often as is required. Don't try to remember your dialog word for word; you're not in a play. Instead, get the concepts and flow of the presentation. *Always* listen to the tape one final time, just before the presentation. We've given hundreds. It works!

SOLUTIONS FOR ASSIGNED PROBLEMS

Start with an Agenda

Start your presentation with a timed agenda that everyone can see. Leave it unobtrusively in view throughout your presentation, or distribute it before you begin. Almost every presentation has a time limit. The agenda permits the control you must have to cover all three parts every presentation should have:

1. **Review the Problem.** When a problem has been assigned for solution, review the assignment for your audience. Be very specific about this. While the problem has received *your* total attention, some of your audience may be hearing about it for the first time. Even those who assigned it to you have been occupied with other matters and can use the reminder. You may also find—and this *has* happened—that the problem has changed, but they forgot to tell you. ("We didn't tell you that our cross-country bike was changed to a senior citizen model?") To avoid this, request a preview of any group presentation with a key insider. You'll learn what is

"obviously" wrong in time to make necessary changes. Of course, you may choose not to make them, but at least you'll be forewarned on *what* you have to sell.

INSIGHT 60

Preapproach your approach! You can learn an astonishing amount about your audience, if you work at it. Depending on the location (an office, a conference room, a convention), there's usually a key person you must convince. Half your success lies in knowing that person's likely objections. The other half lies in answering them before they are asked. It isn't work when it works!

---

2. **Present the Proposed Solution.** But don't just jump into your show and tell. First tell the members of your audience *why* you are presenting your solution to *them.* Tell them the decisions you will ask *them* to make based on the presentation. For instance, are you going to ask for approval of copy and layout? Of media or direct response plans? Of tentative or final budgets? Of time lines? Of all of these? Some of them? Just one? Something else?

Remind everyone of what has already been approved, by whom it was approved, and what they will be asked to decide today. Do *not* make the last of these a surprise at the very end of your meeting, or you may find that they've concentrated on something quite different. ("You mean we're supposed to OK the layout? I thought all we were here for was to OK the budget. You'd better leave those sketches, and we'll get back to you next week.")

3. **Ask for Approval!** Ask for *formal* approval of the decisions that have been made—generally those previewed in Point 2. In any presentation, the presenter is a salesperson. Failing to ask for approval, for "the order," is the most common error made in selling. Don't *you* suggest that you'll come back for a decision next week. Ask for that *positive* decision *now.* Say "As you can see, the layout does exactly what you asked us to prepare, so if we can get your approval on that today, we can have the copy and definitive budget at our next meeting in two weeks," *not* "You'll probably want to think about this and discuss it amongst yourselves." If they can't or won't approve now, let *them* make that suggestion, not you!

Handouts vs. Leave-Behinds

Hand out, in advance, anything that will let participants follow the presentation *without tempting them to jump ahead.* Give everyone an agenda, a pad, and a pencil.[1]

---

[1]Pads, pencils, or pens imprinted with your company name are inexpensive and available from hundreds of quick printers and suppliers of premium goods. Check the Yellow Pages.

Pass out copies of anything *visually* complicated just before you discuss it, but only if you want them to study it right then. Leave behind, for key personnel, a complete copy of your presentation, and any other materials that will help you keep it sold.

INSIGHT 61

Many managers are more comfortable making financial decisions than esthetic judgments. So give them some alternatives on the budget. In promotional matters, present options only when they are requested. Then explain which one you expect to work best. Tell why; managers appreciate that kind of help. Try to base your explanation on fact—your experience *is* a fact!—and they will almost always decide your way.

LOCATION AND VISUAL AIDS

Where to make a presentation and what visual aids to use are important considerations. The following techniques work equally well for the advertising director "selling" management and the sales representative selling the ultimate customer. The emphasis here is on advertising and promotion, but it can easily be adapted to any sales presentation for a product or service. The mechanical and technical considerations especially are exactly the same.

Location

1. **Whose turf?** Where you give your presentation determines much more than the obvious mechanical choices between, for instance, a slide projector and a flip chart. It can also determine the comfort level of your audience, especially when that audience numbers fewer than the presenters. The very reason we would like to invite our audience onto *our* turf—the fact that we feel more comfortable there, rather than in alien prospect, customer, or in-house "executive country"—should warn us against doing so. Perhaps the executive feels just as uncomfortable surrounded by us strange creative types. What back on the executive's own turf would become a careful consideration of copy and art might well turn into an abrupt "I don't like this. Do it over." Outnumbered and outspecialized, the best defense is offense. Why invite that!

INSIGHT 62

Make your presentation where your audience—and not you—feels the most comfortable. When your audience does want it on your turf, suggest a preview by a key person first. You may still get the same "No," but at least you'll learn why.

---

2. **What space?** If at all possible, inspect the physical location where your presentation will be held. For an audience of one, or a small group meeting in some-

one's office, a prior inspection may be impossible. But you can still ask how the audience would like your materials presented. For larger audiences, you need either fairly exact specifications or, preferably, a personal visit to check on the following:

- **Comfort.** Decide what your audience will be doing, if anything, other than just listening and watching. Is there some practical way to get the audience involved, and what will you need to do it: Tables? School-type chairs? Writing materials? Samples? How you handle this without stealing your own thunder is covered shortly.
- **Lighting and visual aids.** How much control will you have over outside and inside lighting? Where are the electrical outlets and what is their capacity? (Beware of extension cords that are an invitation to tripping/falling/breaking/suing.) What projection equipment is available? What is its condition? Should you take your own? And what about a spare bulb in either case! Where will the presenter stand, sit, and move, and is that practical? Are the site and equipment available for rehearsal? Rehearsal—lots of it—is an absolute necessity if a new presenter is involved. You can't remember *everything*. Use our checklist or make your own!

3. **Which audience?** Suppose you have a 20-person conference room, an audience of 5, and a flip chart that can only be seen close up. Their favorite chairs are scattered throughout the room, and they're not about to move out of them. Now suppose you have a meeting room set up for 100, but only 10 of your invited audience show up. Both of these situations are, unfortunately, all too common. Fortunately, you can be prepared—with slides and a projector for the first audience and a more personal flip chart for the second.

INSIGHT 63

Before any presentation, consider the worst case scenario, as well as some that are only bad. Be prepared to turn them into best. When it comes to *your* abilities, make all your surprises pleasant ones!

---

4. **How about sound?** Now that your audience can see you, can they hear you too? Consider and check the following:

- What are the amplification requirements for the presenter and the audience? Play a tape of the presenter's voice, and then wander around the room, listening for spots where it can't be heard. Will you amplify the sound there or block off that spot?
- If sound is a problem, appoint someone to monitor it during the presentation and play conductor for the presenter. Who? How?
- Check on outside sounds, including house music, paging calls, and telephones. Can they be turned off during your presentation? Be sure *you* know how, if you may do it.

- In locations with several halls, can your neighbors blast you out? Play the same tape next door and be forewarned.

Visual Aids

In making a presentation, you have a choice of one or more of at least ten different visual aids. Their advantages and disadvantages should be part of every presenter's personal hands-on experience.

1. Desktop "card" presentation
   - *Advantages.* Of notebook size and often in notebook or small flip-chart format, desktop material offers the most personal of standard-ized presentations. Catalogs, flyers, and fact sheets also fit into this format—as will anything that can be examined by prospects and buyers from the comfort of their own desk.
   - *Comments.* Desktop material may be difficult for several people to see at the same time, so have additional copies available if the prospect wants to share the presentation. Better yet, have a somewhat larger version of the same presentation with you for just that situation. You retain more control and gain extra points for foresight.
2. Actual samples or models
   - *Advantages.* Nothing sells like a hands-on demonstration. It's how we are convinced to buy anything from cutlery to cars to computers. If it's practical to show and try—they'll buy. Do it!
   - *Comments.* If samples or models of multipiece promotions are taken to the prospect's turf, Murphy's law will surely take hold. Whatever can go wrong will. So don't go armed with explanations and excuses; go with the ability to fix the problem before the prospect finds fault with you or your product.
3. Larger flip charts
   - *Advantages.* Flip charts serve as a prompt or script, since what they say *must be* read exactly as it is written. You can point to a chart or illustration and talk about what it means, but if textual matter is to be read by the audience, *read it aloud.* Do not expect the audience to read a written message while you are expanding upon it with a spo-ken message. The reason we can read subtitles in a foreign-language film is because we *don't* understand the somewhat different vocaliza-tion. There, the sound is merely background; it conveys emotion, not comprehension.

INSIGHT 64

In any presentation where words are seen and heard at the same time, make both sets of words *exactly the same.* Showing one message while speaking another is a sure way of losing both.

- *Comments.* Almost all flip charts have too much material—too many words in a typeface that is too small—to be read or understood. Keep it big and simple. In wide rooms, you cannot get enough distance from your audience to let *everyone* see your presentation. Get there early, try various locations, and then make sure that the key people sit where you and your message are visible.

INSIGHT 65

Keep eye contact with your audience! Look at *them* while you're speaking, not only at the chart or screen you're talking about. If the room must be dark for projection, keep some light focused on you, perhaps at a podium, and/or stop every two minutes, turn on the lights, and summarize. Keep the audience contact; you're a salesperson, not a human TV.

---

4. Individual pages
   - *Advantages.* Unlike a bound flip chart, individual pages can easily be added or removed, arranged into any sequence, and left in view to build an increasingly dramatic visual presentation. They can be moved and shown to the entire audience, no matter how it is seated. Placed on a lightweight board, they can be circulated for closer viewing and tactile reinforcement.
   - *Comments.* Pages left in view must have a place to stand, hang, lie, or otherwise be visible.[2] Be sure that your location makes this possible—that you're not at a podium surrounded by empty space, standing illustrations on a stage only the first row can see. Plan ahead to avoid having to improvise.
5. Chalkboard and other on-the-spot creations
   - *Advantages.* These are excellent when a presentation can be built on audience participation that is limited to *brief* statements. Responses to the presenter's question, "What are your most important considerations in awarding this contract?" are usually predictable. But elicited, noted, and considered on the spot, they have a personal relevance that many types of visual aid lack.
   - *Comments.* Using a chalkboard requires an ability to "tease out" participation without creating ill will. This is probably not a good method in multilevel corporate presentations, where participants may be bashful about appearing too smart . . . and fearful of seeming too dumb. Use it with care!

---

[2]Stikky-Wax Sure Clips,® available at stationery stores, hold papers on practically any surface without harm to the surface or what is held. Instantly affixed and removed, they are an excellent solution to many presentation problems.

6. Slides
   - *Advantages.* Slides make a brilliantly lit statement or illustration that forces focused attention. They are one of the least expensive of all presentation devices, are easily portable, and are practical for almost any size audience. Slides are easily keyed to a prerecorded vocal accompaniment, too.
   - *Comments.* Slides are most effective in a dark or dimly lit room, which is not always available. Also, with computer-generated full-color slides, there is a tendency to confuse audiences with information overload through an overuse of colors, words, and typefaces. Slides *that are to be read* are best shown with a frame drawn around them or as reverse type (white or yellow surrounded by black or a very dark background). Keep individual slides to 12 words or less. Read them to the audience *exactly as they are shown.* Change text slides at least every 10 seconds. Illustrations and charts can remain in view as long as they are being discussed. (See Insight 65 for eye contact.)

7. Overhead transparencies
   - *Advantages.* Overheads are similar in effect to slides but have definite advantages in specific applications:
     - Overheads can be shown in fully lit rooms.
     - The image can be written on or otherwise modified as it is being projected.
     - Blank overhead originals can be used for on-the-spot creations.
     - For onetime or limited use, overheads can be produced instantly on standard office copy machines, including full-color copiers. Copies for repeated use are best when done by copying or photographic duplicating services.
   - *Comments.* Overheads are an excellent projection device for those who prefer not to work in the dark. They make multimedia presentations practical without turning the lights on and off repeatedly. For assured excellence in projection, use your own machine or double-check a rental model. Have a *correct* spare bulb on hand, and make sure that you know how to change it. Single-color overheads made on office copiers cost less than slides; full-color copies may cost more. *True* full-color projection, which is seldom necessary, may require originals produced on photographic film. Compare it with the less expensive process. For your use, it probably won't matter. With outside production of overheads, get a sample made from *your* original, not theirs, to check quality.

8. Video and CD
   - *Advantages.* Video and CD are surely the best way to demonstrate action and motion, present individuals who couldn't make it to the presentation, preview new TV commercials, and generally demonstrate that you're at home with current technology for today's audience.
   - *Comments.* Video and CD are by far the most expensive method of presentation. Chapter 11 discusses them in more detail.

9. Computer-generated presentations
   - *Advantages.* New desktop—even laptop—computers allow practically unlimited access to information and the creation of inexpensive presentations that rival video in action and impact. For presentation, use the computer itself, or through digital technology, switch your presentation to video, slides, overheads, oversize sheets, desktop cards, leave-behinds, or all six.[3]
   - *Comments.* Direct computer-to-screen projection is possible, but precheck on its quality at your actual presentation site—the room, not the building! Getting on-line as part of a presentation is frequently (usually, in both our experiences) a disaster. Have a backup, such as an overhead projector, to prevent waiting. Resist the temptation to make the computer presentation show off rather than sell . . . unless you are selling computers or software. The warnings and selling how-to in this chapter apply, no matter what the medium!

10. Talking heads
    - *Advantages.* Besides using the preceding visual aids, there is the plain old-fashioned method of "talking heads"—just you, speaking to an audience of one or hundreds. You have no props, no visual aids, no distractions, and no other helps, except your words and your ability to convey them. As in the most elaborate of multimedia presentations, the three "tells" are your best approach:
    - Tell them what you're going to tell them.
    - Tell them.
    - Tell them what you've told them. (And tell them why. Surely your job is to sell something—even if it's only yourself!)
    - *Comments.* In purely verbal presentations, limit the things you're "going to tell them" to no more than three. That's about the most things audiences can keep in mind as you proceed.

NOTES ON THE PRESENTATION CHECKLIST

These notes are a supplement to the material presented in this chapter. They are not a substitute for that material.

> This checklist has been prepared for a presentation organized by you. If you are an invited presenter rather than the host, learn who your audience will be, what they expect you to present, and where the presentation will take place. Also check #6 and #7, then go to #15-on.

---

[3]For any or all of the above, check the Yellow Pages under "Color Separation." The specifics won't be listed, so ask.

PRESENTATION CHECKLIST

Project Title _____   Date _____
Project Description _____   Project # _____
_____   Checklist # _____
Overall Supervision By _____   Deadline _____
Budget _____ Presentation Date _____   Start Up Date _____

PROJECT SUPERVISION	ASSIGNED TO	DUE	IN	MUST APPROVE	BY DATE	IN	INFO COPY ONLY	SEE ATTACHED
1. Project Supervisor	_____	___	☐	_____	___	☐	_____	☐
AUDIENCE								
2. Selection	_____	___	☐	_____	___	☐	_____	☐
3. Invitations	_____	___	☐	_____	___	☐	_____	☐
4. Telephone Contacts	_____	___	☐	_____	___	☐	_____	☐
5. Badges	_____	___	☐	_____	___	☐	_____	☐
6. Handouts	_____	___	☐	_____	___	☐	_____	☐
7. Premiums	_____	___	☐	_____	___	☐	_____	☐
LOCATION								
8. Find Location	_____	___	☐	_____	___	☐	_____	☐
9. Price Approval	_____	___	☐	_____	___	☐	_____	☐
10. Inspect/Approve	_____	___	☐	_____	___	☐	_____	☐
11. Confirm	_____	___	☐	_____	___	☐	_____	☐
12. Decoration/Materials	_____	___	☐	_____	___	☐	_____	☐
13. Food/Drink	_____	___	☐	_____	___	☐	_____	☐
PRESENTATION								
14. Presenter(s)	_____	___	☐	_____	___	☐	_____	☐
15. Transporation	_____	___	☐	_____	___	☐	_____	☐
16. Lodging	_____	___	☐	_____	___	☐	_____	☐
17. Script/Script OK	_____	___	☐	_____	___	☐	_____	☐
18. Create Visuals	_____	___	☐	_____	___	☐	_____	☐
19. Produce Visuals	_____	___	☐	_____	___	☐	_____	☐
20. Create/Produce Audio	_____	___	☐	_____	___	☐	_____	☐
21. Projectors (specify)	_____	___	☐	_____	___	☐	_____	☐
22. Audience Materials	_____	___	☐	_____	___	☐	_____	☐
FOLLOW-UP								
23. Who/What	_____	___	☐	_____	___	☐	_____	☐
_____	_____	___	☐	_____	___	☐	_____	☐
_____	_____	___	☐	_____	___	☐	_____	☐
_____	_____	___	☐	_____	___	☐	_____	☐
_____	_____	___	☐	_____	___	☐	_____	☐

1. **Project Supervisor.** If the supervisor will not be at the presentation itself, delegate on-the-spot supervision to one other person only. Don't wait until you get there. Do this in advance and let *everybody* know.
2. **Selection.** Which is decided first, who is invited or the number the location can accommodate? Decide before the selection of guests begins.
3. **Invitations.** For repeated presentations, prepare a standard invitation. But remember, "standard" is *not* a synonym for "plain": Old Faithful showers us with standard wonders several times a day.

INSIGHT 66

Include a map as in Figure 12.1. Depending on the location, make it a map that is *not* totally dependent on reading city street signs. Give *exact* mileage and local landmarks, and mention the nearest gas station. Do not leave guests lost in a wintry Wisconsin storm, with every sign hidden under an inch of ice.

Figure 12.1   A "presentation" postcard invitation that does just about everything right! (A good thing too, since one of your coauthors is a graduate and former RU lecturer and the other is an RU associate professor. Though neither had anything to do with producing the card, they suspect the person who did read the first edition.)

4. **Phone contact.** Telephone contacts make responses to written invitations jump in number. Don't rely on either one alone. Synergy works!

5. **Name badges.** Have name badges. Make sure that the presenters use them, too. It's the best way to get everyone on a first-name basis. Of course, make sure that that's what the audience wants too!

6. **Handouts.** Have the timed agenda, translated into a benefit-loaded schedule, on chairs or tables before the presentation begins. Distribute copies of the complete presentation when the presentation is completed.

7. **Premiums.** Give out as premiums a tote bag in which to carry everything home . . . writing materials to use at the presentation and later . . . something special to key into the event—all with your name and logo. That way, they'll still be reminded of you even when they're at home. Better yet, offer to mail everything to their home or office. Have large envelopes, with shipping labels already affixed, ready to distribute while they are still sitting. Make it easy; don't pass them out to a crowd wanting to get out the door!

8. **Location.** This item works in conjunction with #2. Is there knowledgeable local staff to find and inspect a particular location? Hotel and motel floor plans are generally available. Use them.

9. **Price OK.** Price is often negotiable, especially in facilities that include other services, such as food and drink. Ask also for special signs, a reserved parking area, special service, and so on. Make a list!

10. **Site inspection.** For major presentations, have the project supervisor visit the site, even when it's the only location available. The best of floor plans may not forewarn you of *avoidable* hazards to your presentation!

11. **Confirm dates.** Get specific, written agreement on dates required to confirm, change, and cancel your presentation. Phoning is fine, but make sure to get written or faxed confirmation that your order was received.

12. **Decoration.** Get advance approval for anything you'll attach to walls, ceilings, windows, or floors. Often, the house rules (such as requiring the use of specific fasteners) make sense . . . and are easy to follow, too!

13. **Food/drink.** Schedule *coffee* breaks. Do *not* provide alcohol at events from which people will have to drive away. Get legal advice even for a wine tasting!

14. **Presenters.** Use the best presenter(s) to give the presentation, one with drawing power and high visibility, if possible. Use the most knowledgeable to answer questions. If one person must do both tasks, the project supervisor will decide who it is to be.

15–16. **Transportation/Lodging.** Take care of travel and lodging arrangements from where your presenters are, to where they'll stay, to where they're going. Even if no one stays overnight, they'll need a place to freshen up before and after the presentation. Make that part of your negotiations in #9.

17. **Script.** Personalize your talk where possible. Review it with someone who'll know whether you've got it right, especially the pronunciation of

names. For anything other than the routine, rehearse on location, even if you have to get there while others are just waking up.

18–20. **Audio & Visuals.** Will you create new visuals? New copies of existing materials? Special sound effects or music synchronized to sound tracks? Make a list. Find out how long each takes (and costs?) before it is approved.

21. **Projectors.** Use your own equipment. Have a spare—and a *long* extension cord.

22. **Collaterals.** For materials distributed during or after the presentation, in addition to #6 and #7. Who decides what materials to use? How do the materials get there? What happens to materials that are not used?

23. **Follow-up.** They came. They saw. They listened. They left. Have a form for followup that must be used, to note attendance and verbal and non-verbal feedback. (For instance, if audience members leave during, rather than after, the presentation, have someone outside the room to note how many and to ask them why. Was something else scheduled that they had to attend? Had they already learned what they came for? Was the presentation not what they expected? Was the presentation not worth their time? Have an evaluation form for all who stay, too. Be sure to ask how the presentation might be of more value to them . . . and do that next time.) Who is in charge of follow-up? To do what? To report to whom? If the answer is "No one," why were you there?

13 | Conventions, Trade Shows, Consumer Shows, and Meetings

HOW THEY DIFFER AND WHY IT MATTERS

This chapter is about exhibiting[1] at conventions, trade shows, and meetings. In industry jargon, they're all called "shows," but they do have important distinctions.

Conventions

The main purpose of a convention is to advance skills, to increase knowledge, or to promote a cause, and sometimes all three. Heart surgeons, political parties, and associations tend to have "conventions."

Many conventions include exhibits. Your evaluation of such conventions will depend on the interest shown in the exhibits by those attending the convention.

Trade Shows

The main purpose of a trade show is business-to-business—that is, to bring together exhibitors with a preselected audience of customers and prospects. Manufacturers of office equipment and T-shirts, as well as breeders of horses and dogs, have trade shows.

Many trade shows also include convention-type activities such as seminars, but the primary focus is still on the exhibits.

Consumer Shows (for the General Public)

Auto shows and the larger home and garden shows are examples of exhibits for the general public. They almost all charge admission, and many of them sell products directly from their booths. While the information in this chapter is applicable to consumer shows, it does not deal with them directly but concentrates on trade shows, conventions, and meetings.

---

[1]The terms "exhibit" and "display" are used interchangeably by just about everyone concerned with either. The traditional distinction of "display" as a verb and "exhibit" as a noun (e.g., to display at an exhibit) is still found in some dictionaries as the primary definition but is ignored in current practice. Thus, a leading company in the field is called "General Exhibit and Display."

Meetings

A meeting may be a convention, a show, or neither. Check the description in the meeting prospectus before you attend.

WHY YOU CARE

As a new exhibitor or one unfamiliar with a specific show, you don't care what it's called. You want to know what such shows do and how much importance is placed on the exhibits. (See Figures 13.1 and 13.2.) So check the descriptive literature, and then speak to the sponsoring organization—always remembering that they make money only if you decide to go. You'll want answers to at least two questions:

1. **Exhibits-only time.** What times are set aside exclusively for visiting exhibits? (Be aware that many shows which are successful for exhibitors have no such set-asides. Those attending make time. But it's one factor you'll want to consider.)
2. **Conflicts.** What special events by the sponsoring organization, other exhibitors, or anyone else are scheduled? If they do not know, ask for the

Figure 13.1   A ten-booth island display designed by Hahn from modular units originally designed and custom-built by General Exhibit & Display of Chicago, (773) 736-6699. Note how the placement of overhead signs dominates the immediate surrounding exhibit space.

Figure 13.2 Detail of the island display (Figure 13.1) shown during show hours. Prospects listen to a four-minute presentation at six different stations, then, at each station, receive a "Good readers are made, not born" bookmark, pin, or other inexpensive premium that echoes the exhibition theme. They receive a handsome canvas tote bag for answering a brief questionnaire for exhibit evaluation and follow-up.

previous year's final schedule. This type of activity tends to follow similar patterns each year. For instance, if noon to 2:00 P.M. is set aside to visit exhibits, is someone enticing away your prospects with a two-hour buffet, or will they gulp a cup of coffee and rush to the exhibits . . . and how can you know?

TRADE SHOW MARKETING

"Doing business" at trade shows is an increasingly important part of many integrated marketing programs. "Shows have emerged," according to David Kaminer, a widely published, nationally recognized expert in the field,[2] "as an increasingly significant component in companies' total marketing and selling strategies and budgets, as well as places where information is exchanged and major buying decisions are made within given industries. Trade shows today are a major way compa-

---

[2]David A. Kaminer is President of The Kaminer Group, White Plains, New York, a PR and consulting firm specializing in trade shows (914-684-1934).

nies doing business in America—or wanting to do business in America—position themselves and seek to establish and increase their share of market."

Reasons for Increased Importance

"Cost efficiency," according to Kaminer, "is *the* major reason companies are participating in more trade shows, as well as stepping up their profiles at the events. Shows have proven to be three times more effective than a sales call—over 50 percent of trade show leads don't require a sales call to close. And well over 80 percent of the visitors have buying influence for their companies or organizations."

Attendance

The days when low-level managers were sent to trade shows are gone . . . if they ever existed. Research in the 1990s by the Center for Exhibition Industry Research[3] (formerly The Trade Show Bureau) shows predominant attendance is by business leaders with buying power . . . who can and do buy at shows.

- 25 percent-plus of attendance is by top management—presidents, owners, partners, vice president, general managers.
- 50 percent-plus of attendance is by middle management.

Marketing Media

Trade shows ranked number 2 as the "most useful" marketing media according to American Business Press research.[4] The seven leaders, ranked in order, were:

76.4%—Specialized business publications
67.6%—Trade shows
67.1%—Salespeople
61.4%—Conventions, seminars
56.4%—Direct mail
46.8%—Business directories
35.7%—General business publications

INSIGHT 67

When you exhibit, have your own key executives there to meet with comparable key customers and prospects one-on-one. Don't expect this to just happen! Schedule the meetings. Keep them brief. Have a top salesperson there to answer questions . . . and sell.

---

[3]Check them on the Web at http://www.ceir.org/ceirpres.htm

[4]Reported in *Business Marketing* magazine.

Information-Driven Growth

The demand by customers and prospects for instant, detailed information has brought about both an explosive growth in the number of trade shows and in the services they are expected to provide their audiences. Customers and prospects want the shows taken to them, rather than having to spend extra time and dollars traveling cross-country to attend. That's why the number of shows has more than doubled since 1980—from under 5,000 to more than 10,000, with the majority of the growth in a local or regional format. Equally important, computer access to their "at-home" databases by *both buyers and sellers* makes on-the-spot purchasing practical.

- Buyers can *immediately* match or modify exact needs to best offers without returning to check in-office files. Thanks to the laptop and increasingly the Internet, the "files" either travel with them or are only a modem away.
- Sellers can *immediately* match their capabilities against buyers' needs and, often within minutes or hours, propose solutions, including pricing and delivery time.

INSIGHT 68

The computer revolution demands that information requests be met with immediate answers. Staff your booth with salespeople totally at home with your on-computer files. At a successful show, "cold calls" are thrust at staff dozens of times each hour. Over 50 percent of these walk-in leads require no follow-up sales call to close[5] . . . providing you have the information and the staff to sell it!

IS IT WORTHWHILE ATTENDING?

Despite the explosive growth in trade show exhibiting, few exhibitors attend *every* convention or trade show in their field. Before exhibiting at a meeting of unknown value, ask the sponsoring organization to send you a copy of the previous year's program and, if separate, the list of that year's exhibitors. Call a few exhibitors with interests similar to yours and ask for their evaluation. Are they going back? If so, is it for business or "political" reasons? You'll know whether the same reasons apply to you.

When you've decided where to exhibit, you can start planning what will happen before and after you get there. Industry research shows that one-third of trade show leads can come from your own preshow promotion! One thing is absolutely certain: It won't happen if you don't plan.

---

[5]Center for Exhibit Industry Research

SUMMARY

- Conventions focus on knowledge.
- Trade shows focus on product information and services.
- You care not about what it's called—only about what they do.
- Ask previous exhibitors for their evaluations. They paid the bill.

INSIGHT 69

The First "Secret" of Successful Exhibits: "Lack of resources" is an invitation to invent excuses. Forget resources and remember goals. In planning your exhibit, keep your focus on your goals and make the resources fit them.

WHY YOU AND THEY ARE THERE

The planning of your exhibit begins with a search for the answers to two questions:

1. Why are they—my clients and prospects—there?
2. What can I gain from being there with them, and how do I do it?

Figure 13.3 summarizes some appropriate answers to these questions.

In all probability, a trade show held in Las Vegas in mid-February will get less *display* attention than the same show held in Iowa City in August. But less is far different from none. Many of the most successful conventions and trade shows are very deliberately held in seemingly distracting locations. That's how they draw such huge attendance. Taking advantage of that attendance despite the attraction of outside interests requires detailed planning. Especially important is the setting of specific goals that will focus your efforts.

HOW TO FOCUS YOUR EFFORTS AND THEIR ATTENTION

Success with trade shows and conventions is mostly about focusing attention—yours and that of the people you hope to attract and persuade. To demonstrate the problem, imagine yourself at the annual New York or Chicago Premium and Incentive Show. Of the more than 1,000 exhibitors, some 27 specialize in T-shirts and caps, 27 more in watches and clocks, 31 in pens and writing materials, and 19 in some kind of food. In addition, 60 exhibitors have a combination of one or more of those products. If you are a buyer deciding among T-shirts, pens, watches, and edibles as a premium, how do you decide with whom to spend your time? Conversely, if you are one of those exhibitors, how do you get that buyer to spend time

Why Clients and Prospects Attend	How to Turn It to Your Advantage
To make a careful evaluation of exhibitors' and competitors' products and services. Increasingly, to buy.	Your customers aren't the only ones who have competitors. Get out of your booth long enough to see what your competitors are doing. Take photographs of their displays and any others that seem especially interesting, to learn what they do right.
To learn.	Make your displays a learning opportunity by helping *your* customers look smarter to *their* colleagues, employers, and/or customers.
To meet with friends and colleagues.	Become a friend by being active in the organization sponsoring the meeting. The very fact of your being there makes you a colleague.
To get a tax-deductible vacation.	Don't wine and dine guests without a specific purpose in mind. Their goal may be a fancy, free meal; yours has to be more business centered.

Figure 13.3   Why Clients and Exhibitors Attend Conferences

with you when he or she can't possibly evaluate every single display? The answer lies in one word: *focus.*

Focus on Focus

The single most effective way to succeed as an exhibitor is to aim for a particular type of prospect and to give them an instantly recognizable reason for thinking that you can solve the problem that took that prospect to the show. If all you want is to draw a crowd, just give a crisp, cool, delicious apple to anyone who comes to your booth. You'll be inundated with visitors. That may be your goal if you are the leading supplier in your industry and are exhibiting to retain and build on goodwill. But if you are new or one of the lesser players, you don't want *visitors,* you want *prospects.* Make that your focus.

Focus on Prospects

It is, of course, possible that everyone attending a trade show or convention is a prospect for your product or service. Booksellers viewing exhibits from publishers or hardware retailers given their choice of different brands of nails seem likely examples. But no bookseller can stock every title, and few hardware stores have more than a few brands of nails. How you bring attention to *your* titles, *your* nails, *your* brand of ice cream, *your* microwaves, or *your* earthmoving equipment depends—often at first sight—on your prospects' view of you. Focusing that view so they see you as a solver of their problems is the key to your success.

Focus on Customers. They're "Prospects," Too!

Your existing customers are almost always easier to sell than the new prospect . . . if they give you the chance. Don't take them for granted. Treat them as your most important prospects that still have to be sold. Decide what is most helpful to your existing customers and how to attract them to your display when they think they already know all about you. Make this a key part of your planning. There's much help in the pages that follow.

Focus on Your Prospects' Problems—and Solve Them

Think of your prospects as buyers who, in turn, must please a specific kind of customer. This is true whether their "customer" is within their own organization (seeking new furniture for the offices or new locomotives for the trains) or outside (buying a new line of children's shoes or a new line of lawnmowers). Pleasing these ultimate customers should be the focus of everything your prospects do at a show. Your success lies not in appealing to them as a buyer, but in assuring their success as a seller. Convince them that you can make them look good to their ultimate customers, and you'll turn prospects into customers, to your benefit . . . and theirs.

"Trade show selling is extremely fast-paced and highly competitive," reports trade show sales trainer Keith Resnick.[6] "The average sales opportunity lasts only 3 to 5 minutes. And the prospect often leaves your booth to visit with your biggest competitors."

To make those few minutes work to your best advantage, Resnick urges a consistent eight-step approach:

1. Immediate contact. Let your entire "body language" invite and welcome the visitor.
2. Open the sales call with a handshake, a smile, and an introduction.
3. Identify the prospect's company. Make sure you are spending your invaluable time with a prospect, not a competitor!
4. Qualify, as time permits.
5. Present just enough to arrange a follow-up call. If visitors want more, they'll ask.
6. Arrange the next step, from an appointment to a demonstration to buying right there . . . whatever the prospect wants.
7. Close the sales call with a pleasant thank-you and a smile.
8. Record results *immediately,* perhaps on a micro tape recorder, before spending time with anyone else.

Failure to Follow Up

Center for Exhibit Industry Research statistics indicate that 80 percent of trade show leads are not followed up, despite the fact that higher-level prospects are

---

[6]Keith Resnick, president of Creative Training Solutions, Gibbsboro, New Jersey (609-784-3468), conducts workshops and seminars on trade show selling throughout the country.

attending. The problem lies in a combination of poor lead-form design ("What do I do with this garbage?") and lack of a system to ensure lead follow-up ("I don't have time to make my regular calls now. Which ones do you want me to drop?"). The solution, suggests Resnick, lies in getting lead forms designed by the sales representatives who get them after the show, plus establishing a system that makes follow-up practical—and financially rewarding—for everyone involved.

INSIGHT 70

Decide who your real prospects are by focusing on what they want from the show and on whether you can provide it. Then look at your display through their eyes. If it doesn't trumpet you as the best answer to their needs, you're looking at either the wrong prospects or an ineffective display.

SUMMARY

- Discover and fill your customers' and prospects' needs. It's the most likely way to fill your own.

THE BILLBOARD APPROACH TO SUCCESS AT EXHIBITING

No one has learned better than the producers of billboards how to focus fleeting attention. Just think of the problems of selling *in print* to drivers whose lives depend on keeping their eyes on the road! Here's how it's done:

1. **Use one simple message only** . . . the simpler the better. If ever there was a time for the KISS principle (Keep it simple, stupid), this is it.
2. **Keep it single.** Let everything reinforce the same message. Products, words, visuals, colors, and design all work together to achieve a single goal. Make *integrated* marketing communications work for you!
3. **Keep it short.** The fewer words and images you have, the better off you are. Keep it focused. If you can get along without it, do.

What This Book Can Do to Help

Neither this book nor any other guide can design, stock, or staff your exhibit. But it can give you a method for applying the billboard technique to your display from its original preshow concept, to every step along the way, and to your postshow evaluation. Here's how.

1. Assume that you will be placed in the middle of five exhibitors showing what appears to be a product or service identical to yours. To make things easier, assume that you all have the same amount of space.

2. Assume that a temporarily blinded prospect goes to each of you and asks that you tell her *just one thing,* on the basis of which she'll decide whether or not to return after her vision clears up later that day. That one thing is your "billboard"—the featured words that are part of your display and that tell your prospects that you know who they are and that you can solve their problems.

3. Now assume that a temporarily deaf prospect goes by each of your displays. He'll also return to one of you when his hearing clears up. He sees your signs, but he also sees your entire exhibit. Do they both send the same message? Do they reinforce each other? Or do they contradict or ignore each other, as if different persons with different goals had been in charge of preparing your display? You have a one-in-five chance of getting the prospect back if you leave it to luck and if your competitors do the same. Since they're unlikely to do that, however, you'd better not count on it either.

INSIGHT 71

Use the billboard technique. Don't be fuzzy, and hope for the best. Be focused and plan for the most.

SUMMARY

- Think of your display as a billboard with room for a single, simple message.
- Know what you want to say and to whom you want to say it. Then make everything send the same signal: "Your problem solved here!"

When You Are Limited to Saying Just One Thing, Make It a Benefit

The Theme

The key to finding the right theme for your "billboard" is to focus on the audience that your prospects need to please, rather than on the prospects themselves. If your prospects don't know what's in it for them, you'll certainly want to tell them, but only after you've established an even more important point—that a greater chance of their success lies with you than with the exhibitor next door.

Think of your prospects as bees, yourself as a flower, and the entire show as a garden. Bees are attracted to certain flowers not because they are going to gorge themselves, but because they're shopping for the nectar that will satisfy the need of the entire hive. Other creatures are attracted to different plants, but you don't care about them. In fact, you're better off if they ignore you and let you concentrate on attracting and satisfying your target audience.

Since, in reality, you hope to attract prospects rather than bees, your nectar is your products or services, plus words that single you out for attention. To make the entire process work, use those words to turn the focus from features to bene-fits—from what *you* hope to *sell* to what *they* want to *buy*.

The Words

The key to finding the right words for your "billboard" is to translate features into benefits. If you remember that your prospects' success lies in selling your product or service to someone else, you'll find that those words come much easier.

Again, remember that a **feature** is what you have put into your product or service. It's what you know best, so there's a natural temptation to make it your point of focus. Thus, at a Ready-Wear trade show, "hand stitching of every button-hole" and "worsted wool" are both features. Good features, too. Just don't leave it at that.

Benefits are what the ultimate buyer gets from what you sell. They are what your prospect tells that buyer to prove that he or she did a good job.

The best way to develop benefits is the "So what?" test. Just ask "So what?" about every feature. Your answer will be the benefits. You'll be astonished at the range of benefits you discover, so be sure to put them all in writing. You don't want them to get lost. "Tailor-made details at half the tailor-made price" and "New worsted fabric that practically never wears out" are benefits. But wait! Remember the "say one thing only" rule! Well, that may be so, but there's no rule about having more than one benefit. The more the merrier, and you'll certainly have literature and subordinate signs that bring out *all* the benefits—and features, too. It's your basic "billboard" that must give one instantly grasped, impact-filled message. Your task is to find the best pollen that will attract the most bees to your flower. Don't confuse them with 31 flavors. They know what they need.

Here are a few more examples to guide you in translating features into bene-fits. You might find it helpful to check the current literature on your product or service and see whether it is feature or benefit based. You'll want to make sure it's the latter when you use it at your next show.

Examples

- *You* develop a larger computer screen.
  Your prospects want greater productivity through less eye fatigue.
- *You* offer biodegradable paper.
  Your prospects want packaging materials they can brag about.
- *You* offer frozen gourmet dinners for restaurants.
  Your prospects want four-star meals with a nonstar chef.

INSIGHT 72

Features are what you put in. Benefits are what they get out. Features explain and instruct. Benefits attract and sell. Use benefits.

SUMMARY

- Concentrate on learning the real reasons your prospects are at a show, and focus your presentations on meeting that need. (Yes, we said this before, but it's worth repeating.)
- Think of your exhibit as a billboard. It will focus everything you do.

TARGET YOUR PROSPECTS FOR PERSONAL ATTENTION, BECAUSE THERE'S MORE TO EXHIBITING THAN EXHIBITS

How much personal attention you give to specific customers and prospects will depend on five factors:

1. **Identify your targets.** Know the key customers and prospects who are likely to attend. The easiest way to find out is to ask them in advance.
2. **Make two lists.** List one has the clients and prospects you have targeted for special attention, with the reasons they should give it to you (what you have to offer) and what you hope to get out of it. List two has the persons from your company who will attend the show.
3. **Decide what "special attention" means** for everyone on list one.
4. **Focus.** Assign your staff, if any, to specific individuals on list one, with detailed instructions about focusing and goals. Give everyone, including yourself, *objectives you must document!*
5. **Invite the targeted men and women.** Invite them to your booth and to any "special attention" events. Call, then follow up in writing. Do it well in advance of the show, and then confirm their acceptance just before the date. (Don't say, "You can make it, can't you?" Say, "I'm really looking forward to our lunch.")

If You're Few and They're Many

If there are just too many customers and prospects to give all of them personal attention, invite them to a grand breakfast in the centrally located hotel. You'll want a private suite or dining room decorated with your products and literature. But don't give them a hard sell. It's breakfast time, and how would you like a sales talk with your cereal!

Since lunch and dinner invitations abound, your "Breakfast Club" is likely to be more appreciated—and remembered—than something fancier and more expensive later in the day.

Breakfast is also a great way to give a second invitation to anyone who can't join you at a different time. ("I'm really sorry you can't make it for dinner, but perhaps you can join us for an informal breakfast at the Savoy Drop-In Suite. Anytime between 7:00 and 9:00 A.M. on Monday and Tuesday. I'll send you a reminder before the show.")

INSIGHT 73

You and your staff are *not* there to have breakfast! You are there to meet specifically targeted individuals, introduce them to senior management (if that's other than you), generally make them comfortable, . . . and set up a specific time to "do some business" later.

It Doesn't Have to Have Food

The wooing of customers and prospects doesn't *have* to be centered around a meal. Be inventive! Consider a sports event, a play, or a disco. They'll relax with colleagues and entertain each other. When they are back home, drop each one a note by mail or fax. Broadcast fax, described in chapter 8, is perfect for this. Tell them how much you enjoyed their company and how *they* helped the group have a good time. That will remind them who was their host, something often forgotten in the rush of parties at many trade shows and conventions. Of course *you* use the event to focus on your business goals and obtain specific objectives you can document.

There's Always Lunch or Dinner
When the ultimate in individual attention is called for, that usually means lunch or dinner. Here are some suggestions to make those meals more effective as *business* events:

- **Make reservations in advance.** Check a standard guide of restaurant listings. Since the more desirable places fill up early, make your reservations two months in advance of the show dates. If you are unfamiliar with the location, ask for an approximate time and distance from your hotel. You'll want to remain fairly close for lunch.
- **Fewer is better.** Have a maximum of six persons per table. Invite fewer people, rather than use larger tables. When there are more than six per table, comfortable conversation is limited to the persons seated next to you. As host, you lose control of the table as a whole.
- **Be "guest wise."** Generally, a ratio of one host to two guests is preferable to the reverse. There are, of course, exceptions, and your own good sense will tell you when they apply. In assigning guests to hosts, weigh the difference between flattering your guests with attention and intimidating them by sheer weight of numbers.

It is a fact, overlooked at our peril, that much business is done over lunch and golf. That's not because customers or prospects are being "bought." Rather, other things being equal—as they often are—we'd rather do business with our friends, and few things seem to build business friendships faster than a shared activity or a relaxing meal.

INSIGHT 74

NEVER let staff socialize with each other at an event attended by customers and prospects. It is insulting to your guests to have "the help" find itself more interesting than the men and women they invited!

Focus for Individual Attention

Most of this chapter is concerned with your exhibit and you as an exhibitor. But some of your most valuable exhibiting contacts can be made through individual and small-group "business socializing." Like everything else about exhibiting, this requires careful advance planning. You pick the shows to attend because they bring your key customers and prospects to the same location. It's your chance to meet with them individually or collectively, formally or socially, briefly or extensively, as your schedule and theirs permit. Don't pass up the opportunity to cement a business relationship with some personal attention.

INSIGHT 75

Your best prospects and customers are your competitors' most likely key targets. If you don't go courtin' . . . they will.

SUMMARY

- Plan for personal contacts, and then follow them up to make them happen.
- Hold staff—and yourself—responsible for specific targeted results from social events. *Your guests go* to parties; *you* produce business-based events.

YOUR EXHIBIT SPACE

As an exhibitor, you have quite a variety of options for developing your display, but no matter which one you choose, there are certain rules of thumb about the space, generally referred to as "floor space," your exhibit will actually occupy.

Booth Size

Exhibit space is made up of units called "booths," with one booth the minimum space available. At most shows, booths are 10 feet long by 10 feet deep, but always check for variations. If you're attending more than one show and will provide your own exhibit, plan it around the smallest space and build from there.

Booth Height

Almost all standard booths have a maximum height of 8 feet at the back of the booth and then drop rather quickly to a 30-inch table height, to permit visibility along an entire row of displays. The object is to keep exhibitors from blocking their views of each other by erecting "fences" between their booths. The height rule is often different for "peninsula" and "island" displays, as explained shortly.

Aisles and Visibility

The aisle between rows of booths is generally 8 to 10 feet wide. This width becomes an important factor in planning signs and determining what your audience can actually take in when they see your booth from the middle of an aisle. Work with your display company or other professionals to determine the best size and colors for the signs and their lettering as well as how high they should be placed. (As a general rule, make the top row of letters no more than 6 feet off the ground . . . but there are lots of exceptions.) If local sources for signs seem inadequate, check the nearest major city Yellow Pages.

Exhibit Space Configuration

Exhibit space is available in three configurations (see Figure 13.4):

1. **Back wall.** These in-line configurations are any number of booths lined up next to each other. The booths are usually 10 feet wide by 10 feet deep. Occasionally sizes differ, so be sure to check the show guide. The height of the booth is generally limited to 8 feet at the back and table height or 30 inches at the front.
2. **Peninsula.** Peninsula displays have aisles on three sides. Different rules and restrictions apply if they abut another peninsula, versus if they abut

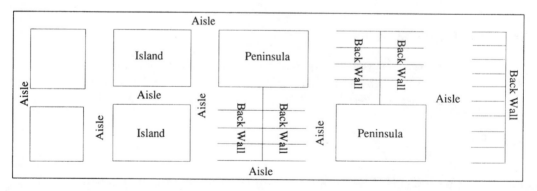

Figure 13.4   Sections of floor plan showing three types of booth configurations.

two rows of back wall booths. Check the show rules for what is permitted. The management will often create a larger size peninsula space upon request by borrowing from abutting back wall booths.

3. **Island.** An island, as the name implies, is surrounded by aisles on all four sides. Special rules apply to islands, but they tend to be quite liberal, as islands are the most expensive spaces to rent and management wants to encourage their use. Height limitations are often highest for island displays, making them the space of choice for tall products or exhibits. Regardless of the height of the ceiling, there are always strict limitations on space you may use. Check before you plan and before you ship your booths.

Hanging Signs

Many shows permit signs that hang above a display. Exhibitors use them to call attention to themselves from locations where their display cannot otherwise be seen. Hanging signs are controlled by show rules and fire regulations but are very effective additional exposure. (See Figures 13.1 and 13.2.)

Space for New Exhibitors

Unless you purchase a major island or peninsula area, prime space goes to regular exhibitors. Newer exhibitors, through repeat exhibiting, must earn their way to the more desirable locations. But don't get mad. Increase the number of visitors to your booth with better preshow promotion. Here are some suggestions:

- Over 25 percent of trade show visitors go to specific booths to which they have been invited.
- Write a month before the show and give your prospects *a reason* to visit you. Prizes, contests, a key to open "Treasure Island" all are proven winners.
- Write two weeks before the show, reemphasize the benefits a visit to your booth offers, and enclose a $3'' \times 5''$ map to your location.
- Fax a reminder three business days before the show. Use broadcast fax for a large list.
- Make sure your booth signage and display reemphasizes your promised benefits the instant they are seen. If ever there was a need to make the right first impression, this is it!

SUMMARY

- Check the show rules for any display you plan to use. Do not assume that last year's rules still apply. Try to limit surprises to pleasant ones.

YOUR DISPLAY

As an exhibitor, you have five options for developing your display. Which one you select—and many exhibitors use more than one kind—should depend on your goals, budget, and availability of staff, probably in that order.

Custom-Built Displays (Option 1)

Custom-built displays are generally designed, built, and maintained by companies specializing in that field. They (and their cousins, the rental display companies, described shortly), are almost always the most impressive exhibits at a show. The most successful displays are designed with a specific goal in mind, and that is their strength, as long as the exhibitor's focus remains constant. A new focus may require a new display. Generally, displays wear out physically in about five years, so the likelihood of their outliving their usefulness is slight.

Modular Design

For displays longer than 10 feet (a single booth), consider a modular design that is organized around 10-foot or 20-foot units. This gives you flexibility in case of budgetary contraction or expansion: You can subtract or add units without rebuilding an entire exhibit. The display shown in Figures 13.1 and 13.2 consists of eight modular 10-foot display units used individually for smaller shows.

What Display Companies Do

Exhibit Design.   Display companies can design your exhibit or consult with you in its design. They are architects, as well as builders, of exhibits. A display company should always be consulted before any design for an exhibit is approved, because of the company's knowledge of exhibit rules and pitfalls.

Exhibit construction.   Display companies construct exhibits and, equally important, the customized, padded containers for shipping your display with minimal damage. Anyone who has ever watched a display being delivered to an exhibit site knows that "no damage" is but a dream.

Show planning.   A display company will act as your agent in all contact with the exhibit site, *except for ordering the actual floor space.* This space is always paid for in advance and then assigned on a first-paid basis. Payment is the responsibility of the exhibitor. Any question as to the size or height of your display, electrical hookups, furniture or other rentals, shipping, setting up and tearing down (dismantling) the display, and shipping the display to the next show or returning it for storage can be handled by the display company as your single "turn key" source of supply. You will want to know what the charges for these services are, and you might decide to do some of them yourself. However, ask yourself what *you* get paid for (even if it's by yourself), then use *them*.

On-site supervision. The display company can send an in-house expert to supervise set-up—the on-site assembly of your display. You are charged for the supervisor's time, transportation, and living expenses while there, but the ability to expedite the assembly of the display and make on-the-spot modifications and repairs often actually saves the additional cost. And the peace of mind of knowing that supervision is being done by the original construction company is priceless. This same degree of supervision may not be required for dismantling the display, depending on the complexity of its construction, on whether the same crew did the setting up, and on whether the crew was made aware of any repacking problems.

Provide storage. A major function of display companies is to ship and store displays between shows. With so many parts and pieces to manage, good inventory control is critically important.

Repair. Display companies refurbish, repair, or modify displays and shipping crates as required.

ABOUT SPECIAL EVENTS

In addition to working on displays, many display companies have become their clients' resource of choice for handling special events. Rather than use their own time and staff, companies use their display company to arrange trade show and convention meetings, dinners, and festivities, and to set up sales meetings, board presentations, employee's picnics, and so on. What began by doing a client a favor has, in many display companies, become an additional successful business.

Costs Involved in Using a Custom-Built or Rental Display

For the purpose of establishing costs, a rental display will go through the same steps to get ready for a show as a custom-built unit. The costs involved in this process may actually be higher than the cost of the floor space the display will occupy. Savings are, of course, possible by using fewer booths. In fact, many displays are unitized—that is, made up of modules that can be assembled into various configurations and sizes, depending on the importance of a show. However, there are always some start-up costs, and the savings may not be proportional to the number of booths used. Your display company can give you accurate estimates to help you decide.

A Dozen Cost Factors

1. **Planning meetings.** Take advantage of your display company's expertise by getting it involved at the earliest stages of planning. While it is

possible to produce almost anything by using the JTWGCHD system ("Just think what God could have done if He'd had our money"), a conscientious representative will forewarn you about costs, time requirements, and other constraints.

2. **Final agreement** on the display and on modifications, if any.

3. **Removing the display from storage,** unpacking it from its crate(s)—for their own protection, displays are stored in their padded shipping crates—and inspecting, repairing, and modifying the display. Since display graphics—the art and signs—are seldom used the same way twice, a detailed inspection is not done until all modifications and new graphics are agreed upon.

4. **Assembly for inspection** of the complete display as repaired and modified. This is an optional, fairly expensive step. Usually, only the new graphics and major modifications need client approval.

5. **Repairing** the shipping crate and packing the display.

6. **Contacting the trucking firm** and reserving space for a guaranteed arrival time. Depending on the number of days and routes available, the display will be shipped one of two ways:

    • **Direct van.** This refers not to the size of the truck, but to the method of routing. Direct van shipments remain on the same truck from pickup to delivery, minimizing handling and the resulting damage. This is usually the fastest way to ship and, if required, the easiest to trace. It is more expensive, however, than common carrier, the next method to be discussed.

    • **Common carrier.** The shipment may be transferred to a different truck to combine materials going to a common destination. While this is the less expensive way to ship, it generally results in more handling, with possible costly damage.

7. **Shipping the display and unloading it at the destination.**

8. **Assembling the display.** At most shows, the exhibitor's own staff may NOT assemble major displays. This work may be supervised by the exhibitor, a display company representative, or an on-site supervisor. Work rules vary widely in right-to-work states. Check before you do anything yourself!

9. **Making on-the-spot repairs and adjustments.**

10. **Preparing for return shipment.** The bills of lading and labels for shipping the display to its next destination or its return to storage are prepared. This paperwork is usually completed in advance by the display company.

11. **Tearing down the display.** The display is disassembled and repacked into the original crates.

12. **Arranging for next use or return shipment.** The crates are checked against the number in the original shipment and, if there is no discrepancy, are sent to their next destination(s) or returned to storage. If returned to storage, repairs are not made at this time, but await possible modification with the next use of the display.

Rental Displays (Option 2)

Many display companies have displays that can be rented and customized to meet an exhibitor's needs. These displays range from impressive island exhibits to single-booth units. They can be very effective where you wish to make a one-shot impact without taking on the cost of designing, constructing, and storing your own display—especially one with limited use.

Off-the-Shelf Displays (Option 3)

Dozens of companies, including many exhibit builders, have standard off-the-shelf displays that can be personalized at little cost, usually by adding the exhibitor's name and some simple graphics. (See Figure 13.5) Many of these displays are truly portable in that they disassemble into suitcase-size units that fit into the trunk of most midsize or larger cars . . . but measure the trunk before you buy. You'll find the names of the manufacturers in any major city's Yellow Pages, under "Exhibits and Displays." Ask several to send you their catalogs.

Pipe and Drape Displays (Option 4)

A curtained backdrop draped from a pipe and holding a sign with the exhibitor's name is supplied by the show as part of your contract for exhibit space. There is no fancy backdrop. There is no special lighting and no unique graphics—just the exhibitor and the products or services. Sometimes a table and/or chairs is also part of the package. Some of today's major exhibitors started just this way.

Although pipe and drape is the least costly booth space, there is no limit, within show rules, to the enhancements that you may put into the area. Off-the-shelf and smaller-space customized displays, or one or more modular sections from large-space displays, are used in many pipe-and-drape booths. Your only limits are your imagination and your budget . . . and with the display suggested in Option 5, even budget should be no problem. Read on!

The One-Show, Leave-Behind Display: An Invitation to Adventure (Option 5)

With a custom-built or rental unit, much of the cost is made up of fees for storage, shipping, assembly, dismantling, reshipping, repair, and general maintenance. Constructing a leave-behind display that is of low weight and bulk, easy to assemble, and sturdy and attractive is not an impossible assignment for an imaginative designer. Since the display will always be brand new, you eliminate the cost of repair and maintenance. Since it's light and compact, you save a major portion—if not all—of the cost of storage, shipping, and handling. And since it's left behind, you save the total cost of return shipment and subsequent handling. You may, depending on exhibit rules, have to use show personnel for assembling the display, but that would also be true of a custom-built display. You will want to tear down or disassemble your display before you leave, or there's a very good chance that show personnel will repack it and ship it to you at your expense. Just tear it apart, and put a few signs reading "Throw Away! Do Not Ship!" where they can't be missed.

Figure 13.5   A portable display transportation and storage case and examples of three off-the-shelf displays with individual art designed and produced by the manufacturer, Skyline Displays, Inc., Burns-field, MN. For their FREE 70-page, illustrated "Trade Show Marketing" Idea Kit, call toll-free at (800) 328-2725. (Many other companies manufacture similar excellent units.)

Figure 13.6 Example of a one-show, leave-behind display. Original concept and design by Jack Heimerdinger, Plainsfield, IL (815-436-5137).

Constructing Your One-Show Display

Triangular Columns

The triangular column, shown in Figure 13.7, is made from a standard sheet of ³/₈-inch-thick, 4 × 8-foot Foamcord.™ This exceptionally strong, yet light, display material is stocked by many sign suppliers. Keep the wording on the columns and signs to an absolute minimum. The fewer words, the more likely it is that they will be read and noted.

The one-show, leave-behind display seen in Figure 13.6 cost less than 25 percent of just the shipping charges associated with using the company's custom-built display seen in Figure 13.1.[7] The entire leave-behind display was produced on site, where the show took place, eliminating storage and shipping costs. Only two suppliers were needed: one made the columns and signs and the other was a "home store" retail outlet. Both were found in the Yellow Pages.

To give the columns of the display stability, use the design shown in Figure 13.7. The original board is 8 feet tall, but you need use only 6 feet for the column. That leaves 24 × 48 inches that you can use to make a sign. (See Figure 13.8.)

---

[7]To be fair, lightweight construction materials used in newer displays have reduced dramatically the cost of shipping.

Figure 13.7   Triangular column design.

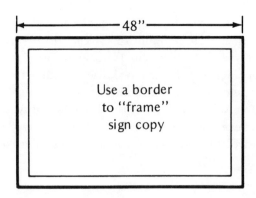

Figure 13.8   Use a border to "frame" sign copy.

Shelved Cases

Not every exhibitor can make use of the easily assembled bookshelf-type cases pictured between the columns in Figure 13.6, but if you can, they are available at low-cost home furnishings stores for about $100 each. Check the Yellow Pages for a source. When ordering, specify cases with or without doors, and ask how much the cost will be to deliver the units assembled. The supplier can probably also provide inexpensive gooseneck lamps and extension cords for lighting. Use the same delivery instructions as for the columns. Everything is an off-the-shelf retail item.

Tables and Chairs

If tables or chairs are needed, rent them from the show. Chairs can also be purchased from the outlet that provides the cases. Purchasing is slightly more expensive, but may have greater eye appeal.

A REMINDER: THROW IT AWAY!

Avoid the temptation to save the columns and signs. Unless you can use them again immediately, they will get damaged or frayed or simply be in the way. Throw them out, even though it hurts. The cases, lamps, and—if purchased—chairs are another matter. Before the show is over and you have to rush off, contact a local charity that can use these items and have them picked up. You'll get a tax write-off that will make you proud!

SUMMARY

- Explore all your options, from purchasing custom-built to leave-behind displays, for the shows your attend. There may be a variety of "best" solutions to your display needs.
- Work with an exhibit company if your budget permits. It will let you concentrate on the selling for which your display is just the background.

ORDERING A NEW DISPLAY

The purchase or rental of displays is one of the most exciting projects for any promotion manager. Here, in outline form, is a basic schedule for this project. A special checklist is provided at the end of the chapter.

1. **Getting in-house agreement on the basics of the display.** Get agreement on the following items:

   - Type of display: custom built, rental, tabletop, modular, leave-behind, and so on.

- Number of booths or running feet of display space.

- Budget. (Get advance cost and time estimates from several possible suppliers, and then add 10%.)

- Materials and services to be featured.

- Purpose of the display, beyond showing materials or services. For instance, will there be conference or sales areas and/or a safe storage section?

- Visual impact desired, such as high tech or warm and friendly or both.

- Frequency of expected use of all or of portions of the display during a three-year period. Will smaller modular units be used more often than the whole? How many? How often?

- Expected life of the display.

- Approval procedure. Who must be consulted and who will give final budgetary and design approval? When will they be available? Who has approval authority in their absence? (There is little point in waiting till March 9 to approve an exhibit for a show that was over on March 8.)

2. **Putting it in writing.** Put the display basics in writing, and get approval of this description from all concerned. If there are disagreements about your description of what was decided on, resolve the difficulties before going any further.

3. **Finding an exhibit company for custom-built or rental.** If you have never before worked with an exhibit company or are unfamiliar with those in your area, ask for recommendations from your competitors (this is not a noncompetitive industry), your colleagues, trade associations, or media representatives (they know a surprising amount). Or simply check the Yellow Pages.

Send each candidate a copy of your display basics from No. 1 and your New Display Construction checklist from page 309. Ask for a *written* response, by a specified date, including the following information:

- The candidate's experience with the type of display you have outlined. Have them include pictures you'll return, costs of displays shown, dates of construction, and persons to contact for recommendations.

- Design and construction personnel. Are they employees or outside contractors and designers? The latter is not necessarily negative, but you will want to take it into consideration.

- Where, and by whom, the display will be stored.

- Basic storage charges, with costs for removing the display from storage or returning it after a show.

- Estimated maintenance charges.

- Who the candidate's account executive will be and that person's experience in the exhibit field.

Make absolutely clear that you will not accept a personal presentation in place of the information you have requested, but that you are prepared to answer by phone any further questions the candidate may have.

4. **If you have an existing display.** For most companies, purchasing a new display is such a large expenditure that multiple bids are mandated, even when they have an excellent relationship with a particular display house. If your company is in such a position, have lunch with your account representative and break the news as gently as possible. No one lives a business life of more threatened security than an account executive, so assure the AE that his or her firm will get "most favored nation" consideration. But ask for exactly the same information you're requesting from everyone else. Few decisions that are at least partly aesthetic can be totally objective, so it is best to begin with a level playing field.

INSIGHT 76

If you are dissatisfied with your current display house or its account executive, try to resolve the problem by going to the senior management of that display house, rather than leaving them out of the picture. Account executives for any kind of supplier sometimes become apologists for their employers, rather than expediters and problem solvers for their clients. That is an excess of loyalty only employers can solve—as they will, but only if you let them know a problem exists. You don't want your account executives fired. You do want them working for YOUR best interest.

---

5. **Narrowing the field and final inspections.** Narrow the number of candidates to a reasonable number, and then arrange for a personal visit to each. Take along the New Display Construction checklist from this chapter with the candidates' mail, fax, or phone responses already filled in. You won't mind their having put their best foot forward, but reality mustn't be too far from what you've already been told.

Satisfy yourself about the ability of the firm you ultimately choose to work together with you. Be prepared to answer some questions about your firm, your credit rating, and your promptness in paying bills. Designing and constructing displays involves such a preponderance of up-front, out-of-pocket costs for the exhibit company, that it customarily gets a one-third down payment before beginning a job, a second third at a specified time during construction, and the final third upon its completion.

Select the finalists—probably three, usually no more than four—and invite them, individually, to visit you for a turnaround inspection in which they will get answers to any questions they may have about you and your project, plus a final project specification form that includes the following:

- General directions, with any modifications from the original version already seen by them.

- The schedule for presentation of their design concept, plus time for at least one revision before a final rendering. Do not discuss the competing presentations with the competitors. *Exhibit design is the intellectual property of the exhibit company until you buy it!* It is unethical to show a design or even discuss its approach with a competing exhibit company.

- The date for the presentation of the final rendering and a scale model. The production of a model is customary and, like the customized shipping containers, is included in the overall cost. The model becomes invaluable in visualizing different configurations and the relationships of various elements to each other. Have each presenter specify the following:

  - The date when all copy and graphics to be used in the actual display must be given to the exhibits house.

  - The date when the display will be ready for a first inspection, with adequate time for modifications before shipment.

  - The presentation date for all concerned—the final show and tell.

  - The date of shipment of the display to the first show. Certain suppliers may wish to trade a shorter production schedule for more time to prepare a presentation. Don't do this. It's unfair to you, as it forces a faster decision-making process, and it's equally unfair to other candidates who prefer a normal work schedule. Extraordinarily fast production is an invitation to shortcuts and shoddy workmanship. Avoid it wherever possible.

INSIGHT 77

Get at least three bids for creating your display, and pay each company an agreed-upon amount for its presentation. Few of us do our very best work "on speculation."

The three companies chosen for the competition that produced the display shown in Figures 13.1 and 13.2 were authorized to charge up to $5,000 each for their presentation designs. Each was given a maximum budget of $200,000 for a completed 100-foot display. Actual cost estimates from each supplier were not a part of management's decision. To management's surprise and delight, the winning display, unanimously agreed upon, proved to be $50,000 less than they had budgeted. (Hahn had told the competitors that within budget, price would not be a factor.)

SUMMARY

- Put everything in writing.
- Get in-house agreement on basics of the display and the assignment of responsibilities—and don't go further until you do.
- Personally visit likely candidates to inspect all aspects of their operations. Insist on the "show" part of the show and tell.
- Prepare a workable schedule for all concerned, and monitor it continually. When all has finally gone well and your new display is a success, put your thanks to all concerned in writing, too.

A BIBLIOGRAPHY: LOTS MORE HELP!

The growth in trade show exhibiting has seen a comparable growth in helpful related magazines for both meeting planners and exhibitors. Check the descriptions to see where you fit. For a more complete annotated list, see *Bacon's Magazine Directory*, 332 S. Michigan Ave., Chicago, IL 60604—(800) 621-0561.

The three largest-circulation magazines in the field

Meeting News. Industry trends, ideas, and methods for corporate and association meetings. (212) 714-1300

Meetings & Conventions. For corporate travel planners. (201) 902-1700

Successful Meetings. Written for management personnel. Includes budgeting outlines and agenda planning tips. (212) 592-6414

More of Equal Interest

Convene. Help in developing educational programming and coordinating conventions of all sizes. (205) 823-7262

Corporate Meetings & Incentives. For senior-level managers involved in meetings and incentive programs. (212) 338-9124

Creative Exhibiting Techniques. Quick-to-read tips, tactics and how-to information for trade show marketing. (507) 289-6556

Exhibit Builder. Technical aspects of design and fabrication of exhibits. (818) 225-0100

Exhibit Marketing Magazine. How-to information for novice or pro exhibitors. (201) 514-5900

Exhibitor Magazine. For individuals responsible for trade show and event management and marketing. *Generally considered the leading magazine for exhibitors.* (507) 289-6556

Exhibitor Times. For those involved with designing, creating, and setting up corporate displays at shows. (602) 990-1101

Expo: The Magazine for Exposition Management. Targeted to exposition managers and association executives. (913) 469-1185

Facilities. New products. Industry news. (212) 532-4150

Ideas. Information for exhibit pros about trade show marketing success. (703) 941-3725

The Meeting Manager. Furthers the professional development and education of meeting industry personnel. (214) 712-7752

Religious Conference Manager. Ideas and suggestions for successful meetings. (508) 897-5552

Special Events. For those involved in planning, staging, and supplying special events. (310) 317-4522

Tradeshow & Exhibit Manager. Topics include security, boothmanship, actual and potential legislation. (310) 828-1309

Tradeshow Week. The "Advertising Age" of the trade show industry. All the news—and gossip—show managers and suppliers need (or want) to know. (310) 826-5696

NOTES ON THE NEW DISPLAY CONSTRUCTION CHECKLIST

Unlike the other checklists in this book, this one needs no annotation. The following notes may, however, be helpful:

- Use a separate copy of this checklist for each potential supplier. Fill in #2–14 for each kind of project. Duplicate as needed.
- The type of display (#1) can be determined in advance or by the information provided in #2–14. Be prepared to make some modification from what you want to what is more practical and less costly, even when the display is custom built or left behind and thrown away.
- You'll need #16–31 primarily for custom-built and major rental displays. That's where you require the most detailed knowledge about your supplier. You ask #17 because you do want that company there a month or a year from now, when it's time to use the display again!
- Modify #15 in accordance with the type of display you order. You certainly won't need it for the pipe and drape display, which comes with the show.

NOTES ON THE CONVENTIONS/ TRADE SHOWS/MEETINGS CHECKLIST

These notes are a supplement to the material presented in this chapter. They are not a substitute for that material.

1. **Exhibit focus.** Determine why you are at *that* show at *that* time. The answer must determine everything else you do . . . every other point on this checklist. It therefore comes first.
2. **Total budget.** The complete-for-everything show budget. If the cost of a new display, whether rented, purchased, or custom built, is included, use the checklist on page 309 for that amount. (See point #10. Custom-built construction is generally a *capital,* rather than a one-show cost. Determine which before including it here.) *Do not let final budget approval delay action on #3 and #4!*
3–4. **Booth space/location.** Unlike real estate, "location, location, location" may not be the most important factor for display booths, but it certainly helps. Find out the why's of space assignments. Just ask! Then be the first to follow the rules and meet the deadlines.
5. **Space reserved/confirmed.** This refers to official notification from a show that specific space has been assigned to you. If you plan something unusual in size, shape, traffic flow, or electrical or other service requirements, don't wait for that "official" notification. Make sure to get approval far enough in advance to change if the answer is "no." The show organizers want you to attend and will try to help. Give them the chance!

NEW DISPLAY CONSTRUCTION CHECKLIST

Project Title _____   **Date** _____

Project Description _____   **Project #** _____

_____   **Checklist #** _____

Overall Supervision By _____   **Deadline** _____

Budget _____   **Completion Date** _____   **Start Up Date** _____

---

1. **STYLE:** ☐ Custom Built   ☐ Rental   ☐ Portable   ☐ Pipe & Drape   ☐ Throw-away
2. **DATE NEEDED:** _____ 3. **QUANTITY NEEDED:** _____ 4. **BUDGET:** $ _____
5. **SIZE:** _____ Booths/ ____ Running feet   6. **MODULAR:** ☐ Yes   ☐ No
7. **BASIC CONFIGURATION:**   ☐ Back Wall   ☐ Island   ☐ Peninsula
8. **MATERIALS TO BE SHOWN—RUNNING FEET OR DIMENSIONS:** _____
   _____
   _____
   _____

9. **STORAGE SPACE NEEDED:** _____
   _____

10. **LITERATURE BINS & OTHER GIVE-AWAYS:** _____
    _____

11. **EXPECTED FREQUENCY OF USE:**
    (Indicate all or part of display. Be specific.) 1-year _____
    3-years _____

12. **SEATING/HOW MANY & WHERE:** _____
    _____

13. **OTHER REQUIREMENTS:** _____
    _____

14. **OVERALL "FEEL":** ☐ Contemporary   ☐ Traditional   ☐ VERY High Tech   ☐ User Friendly
    (Check all that apply)   ☐ Male   ☐ Female   ☐ Other

---

15. **APPROVAL PROCESS: DESIGN AND BUDGET**
    First Presentation   _____
    Second Presentation _____

    Signatures   FINAL DESIGN OK _____ Date _____
                    FINAL BUDGET OK _____ Date _____
                    CONSTRUCTION OK _____ Date _____

---

16. Exhibits Co. Candidate _____ Contact _____
    Address _____ Phone _____
17. Years in business _____ 18. ☐ Own Designers   19. ☐ Outside Design   20. ☐ Own Construction
21. ☐ Outside Construction   22. ☐ Own Storage   23. ☐ Outside Storage
24. ☐ Photos Received   25. ☐ Cost Information Received   26. ☐ Recommendations Checked
27. AE & Experience _____
28. Other _____
29. Date Visited _____ 30. By: _____ 31. Recommendation (+5/–5) _____

See Attached Concerning Nos. ____ ____ ____ ____ ____ ____ ____ ____ ____ ____ ____ ____

© 1997, Fred Hahn

CONVENTIONS/TRADE SHOWS/MEETINGS CHECKLIST

Project Title _____   **Date** _____

Project Description _____   **Project #** _____

_____   **Checklist #** _____

Overall Supervision By _____   **Deadline** _____

Budget _____   **Completion Date** _____   **Start Up Date** _____

	ASSIGNED TO	DUE	IN	MUST APPROVE	BY DATE	IN	INFO COPY ONLY	SEE ATTACHED
EARLIEST DECISIONS								
1. Exhibit focus	_____	___	☐	_____	___	☐	_____	☐
2. Budget approved	_____	___	☐	_____	___	☐	_____	☐
3. Booth space/configuration	_____	___	☐	_____	___	☐	_____	☐
4. Booth location	_____	___	☐	_____	___	☐	_____	☐
5. Space reserved/confirmed	_____	___	☐	_____	___	☐	_____	☐
6. Display company notified	_____	___	☐	_____	___	☐	_____	☐
7. Hotel reservation requested	_____	___	☐	_____	___	☐	_____	☐
8. Direct billing requested	_____	___	☐	_____	___	☐	_____	☐
BUDGET DETAIL OK								
9. Booth $	_____	___	☐	_____	___	☐	_____	☐
10. Display $	_____	___	☐	_____	___	☐	_____	☐
11. Travel $	_____	___	☐	_____	___	☐	_____	☐
12. Product $	_____	___	☐	_____	___	☐	_____	☐
13. Collateral $	_____	___	☐	_____	___	☐	_____	☐
14. Lodging/Food $	_____	___	☐	_____	___	☐	_____	☐
15. Hospitality $	_____	___	☐	_____	___	☐	_____	☐
PERSONNEL/HOSPITALITY								
16. VIP list	_____	___	☐	_____	___	☐	_____	☐
17. VIP responsibilities assigned	_____	___	☐	_____	___	☐	_____	☐
18. Hospitality plan OK	_____	___	☐	_____	___	☐	_____	☐
19. Hospitality ordered/reserved	_____	___	☐	_____	___	☐	_____	☐
20. Hospitality invitations creative	_____	___	☐	_____	___	☐	_____	☐
21. Invitation printing	_____	___	☐	_____	___	☐	_____	☐
22. Invitation mailing/distribution	_____	___	☐	_____	___	☐	_____	☐
23. Hospitality confirmed/cancelled	_____	___	☐	_____	___	☐	_____	☐
24. Personnel attenting OK'd	_____	___	☐	_____	___	☐	_____	☐
25. Personnel notified of plan and assignments	_____	___	☐	_____	___	☐	_____	☐
26. Hotel confirmed/cancelled	_____	___	☐	_____	___	☐	_____	☐
EXHIBITING DETAIL								
27. Display design for setup	_____	___	☐	_____	___	☐	_____	☐
28. Signage ordered	_____	___	☐	_____	___	☐	_____	☐
29. Product ordered	_____	___	☐	_____	___	☐	_____	☐
30. Product shipped	_____	___	☐	_____	___	☐	_____	☐
31. Collateral ordered	_____	___	☐	_____	___	☐	_____	☐
32. Collateral shipped	_____	___	☐	_____	___	☐	_____	☐
33. Physical display ordered	_____	___	☐	_____	___	☐	_____	☐
34. Physical display shipped	_____	___	☐	_____	___	☐	_____	☐
35. Show services & rentals	_____	___	☐	_____	___	☐	_____	☐
36. Service & rentals ordered	_____	___	☐	_____	___	☐	_____	
37. Set up/Tear down	_____	___	☐	_____	___	☐	_____	

6. **Display company order.** One person at your end deals with one person at the display company's end. Put everything in writing. Get it confirmed. Get the work schedule. Check to make sure that it's being followed.

7. **Hotel space/tentative.** Request reservations *the day they may be ordered.* Find out when is the last moment they may be cancelled. *One* person deals with both of these points.

8. **Direct billing OK.** Who is authorized to charge what to your company? What control is there, if any, on those authorized to charge?

9. **Space $ OK.** Display *space* tends to be the least costly of items 9–15. Add more space and place your display within it, perhaps in an island configuration, for extra impact. Even a single extra booth can work for smaller budgets.

10. **New display $.** See the separate New Display checklist for ordering or building a new display. Treat the costs involved as a capital expense, or add them under the total budget in #2. Use #10 for costs associated with maintenance, modification, shipping, setup and dismantling, and reshipping of the display, as well as returning it to storage. For record keeping, separate routine items and one-time costs to make future planning easier.

11. **Attendance/tentative.** Who goes? Who gets them there? How is it paid for?

12–13. **Product/collateral.** If at all possible, send product samples and promotional materials with the display. For both control and huge savings, a single shipment is by far the best thing.

14. **Lodging/food $.** Limitations or rules regarding the cost of daily meals. Lodging is handled under #7, but must be recorded here for purposes of budgeting.

15. **Hospitality $.** Estimated or quoted costs for items 16–23. Have a single person *in charge* of hospitality though any number of individuals may have specific responsibilities.

INSIGHT 78

16–23. **Hospitality details.** Have a reason for hospitality. If you can't justify entertaining the persons in #16, . . . *STOP!* Don't give a party. Go to theirs.

INSIGHT 79

Schedule rehearsal time for *everyone* attending to ensure familiarity with their responsibility, the display itself, the sales message(s), and the location of products and collateral materials. Do role playing, including actual filling out of follow-up reports.

24–25. **Attendance assignments.** Are your personnel attending the show determined by hospitality or other needs? Have a reason for everyone's being there—a cash-effective reason!

26. **Hotel confirmed.** The decision in #24 may be someone else's. The confirmation or cancellation is done by the same person as in #7. Make sure that everything is in writing and everything is confirmed.

27. **Space design.** Exactly how will the display look, and where will the products and collateral materials go? If possible, code every carton or item by number, keyed to a specific location.

28. **Signage.** What do the signs say and where do they go? Ship them with the display.

29–32. **Products/collateral ordered & shipped.** Who is responsible? If this person is different from the one responsible for #27, let #27 know if anything is not available. Don't make a half-empty display your convention surprise!

33–36. **Display shipping/handling.** Generally the responsibility of a single person. When using a display company, let it handle #28, #30, #32 and #34–36. They do it every day, know exactly how, and will save you *lots* of money.

37. **Setup/tear down.** Let your display company supervise, if practical. Keep house kibitzers away. Show personnel are *very* expensive and get paid by the hour.

38. **Follow-up.** 80 percent of leads found at trade shows are never followed up! Put in place a system to make sure yours are. If yours are not because of lack of personnel, see the chapters on telemarketing, direct mail, and broadcast fax.

14 | Moving a Project from Camera-Ready Art Through Film, Printing, and Distribution

FILM SEPARATION AND PROOFING

Almost all modern printing begins with a "prepress," prepublishing process that changes type and pictures into a computer "digital" format that lets you see them on a computer monitor. Rather than moving type and illustrations the old-fashioned way, by "cutting and pasting," your designer and film house do it with the click of a mouse.

Film preparation begins with one or more of three kinds of materials:

1. *Camera-ready art.* All the type and illustrations with instructions on how they are to be combined to create an ad, catalog page, brochure, and so on.
2. *Electronic file.* Some or all of the materials to be printed that are prepared on a computer. Type is practically all "set" this way. Adding illustrations requires specific kinds of equipment and skills.
3. *Digital photography.* Studio-quality photography using special new cameras that produce computer-compatible images rather than film.[1]

Whichever process or combination is used, the final image is transferred onto a film and from there to a printing plate from which the actual printing is done. If colors are to be used in printing, there are two options:

1. Select from or have the printer create a special color. Thousands of such colors exist.
2. Print by one of several color systems in which all printed colors are a combination of just four inks. "Process printing," which uses the four "process" colors, is the best known such system.

It is the job of the filmmaker (known as a "color separator" or "service bureau") to create the films from which the printing plates are made. Use color separators[2] for anything in full color or otherwise complicated. Use a lower cost service bureau for

---

[1]For current capabilities of this evolving system, see the article "Camera Man" in *Pre* magazine, March 1996.

[2]Such as Tukaiz, Inc., of Franklin Park, IL (800) 543-2674, who helped bring us up-to-date in this section.

routine one- or two-color projects . . . but let the color separator quote on that, too. What follows tells how this is done.

INSIGHT 80

Discuss the capabilities and limitations of their separation system with your film supplier *before art or photography is assigned.* It's a lot easier and cheaper than attempting to fix the product after it is delivered.

From Final Art to Film

"Final art" is everything that is given to the color separator to produce the film. To reproduce something in color, the filmmaker begins by separating the original image into its four process colors. For instance, an ad or catalog page that is reproduced from a combination of type, drawings, photographs, and slides is quite typical. Each of these preliminary scannings must be correctly sized, then positioned onto the final film. There are three ways of doing this:

1. *Special process cameras.* Comparatively little used today, these cameras have a series of filters that "see" full-color art as shades of red, yellow, blue, and black and prepare film for each. A page to print in black, or one color, uses one filter only.
2. *Laser scanners.* This more-sophisticated method of seeing and separating the original art for printing became widespread in the 1970s. This quickly became the primary way of preparing film for printing.
3. *Digitized color separation.* In the 1990s, computerized film preparation has revolutionized the "prepress" (preprinting) process. Computer-prepared type and art, plus laser-scanned elements, are digitized onto a single computer image. The images are brought onto an oversize high-resolution viewing screen and positioned as called for on the original design. Here, clients, artists, designers, and others can see the page(s) before film is made.

At this stage, *anything* can be changed at the click of a mouse . . . copy, position, color, size—anything! This latest process has huge advantages over previous systems:

- Work done by the digitized system can be seen as "work-in-progress" on a high-quality computer screen.
- The same computer that does the color separation can be used for on-the-spot major and minor retouching. There is no need to wait for final film and its proofing before errors are corrected.
- Film created from a digitized format can always be duplicated or modified to its original fidelity. There is no "second-generation" copying loss. Every "copy" is, in fact, another "original."

- The computer-stored images can be used or modified for any promotional activity: brochures, ads, slides, transparencies, and billboards and other out-of-home promotions. Anything. Instantly.

Many design studios also produce computerized final art and film. Although not quite as technically advanced as a color separator, they are excellent for many individual ads, flyers, and brochures. For major projects such as catalogs or sophisticated art, the color separator is the answer.

Creating the Original

In preparing film for one or more colors, each color must end up on a single piece of film, which is then used to make the printing plate. But that film can seldom be made from just one camera shot or laser scan. Each of the preliminary shots must be put into position and contacted onto the final film. It is not at all unusual to have a dozen or more scans to create the film for each page that will actually be used in printing! Since a few projects still combine older existing film with modern laser-scanned or computer art, traditional stripping and scanning is necessary. However, as explained in the chapter on catalogs, both these processes are essentially obsolete. Although they still *can* be done, the advantages of ditigized film creation and duplication outweigh possible cost savings for most advertisers.

INSIGHT 81

For clarity and legibility, *always* mark your original art "SHOOT ALL TYPE AS LINE." Without this instruction, type may be screened routinely, giving it the appearance of a series of fuzzy dots rather than continuous lines. Your color separation filmmaker knows this but is not permitted to avoid it without your instructions!

Stripping

In stripping (the trade term was "work ups"), the filmmaker takes two or more pieces of film and tapes them together. Magazines, which get film for advertisements from dozens of different sources, are an example. We can think of this as "film pasteup." Stripping can also be used to move elements closer together or place them further apart once they have already been transferred to film. It is page makeup using lithographic film.

Contacting

Contacting involves two different processes: "composing" (creating) a final film through a series of exposures for each color, or copying that film at some later time.

Contacting for new generations. The final film used for the printing plate is known as the first-generation film. If contacted (copied) from an existing film, the result is second generation. Second-generation film is used when the first generation may not be cut for repositioning or is not available, but a copy is. This frequently happens when the original film is part of another project and must be maintained in its current form. However, a copy can usually be made through the contacting process. If that copy must be transferred once again by contacting, the film becomes third generation. Ask which generation a particular film is, because each contact will lose some of the fidelity of the original. Think of it as a copy of a copy of a copy, and so on: The more generations, the further removed is the film from the original source. However, the more careful and talented the film house, the less is the loss overall. Expect a loss of 2 to 4 percent per film generation. That's hardly noticeable until the third or fourth generation, but, especially in full-color work, it's definitely a factor thereafter.

One of the major benefits of computer-stored, digitized art is that it will always produce an "original" film. There is no loss through second- or twenty-second-generation film. Every use produces first-generation results.

Ownership

Specify on your purchase order *your* ownership of the digitized art (CD-ROM, disk, etc.) as well as the film upon payment. This does not require you to take physical possession of the film unless you want to do so. It does, however, give you complete freedom to use and move your film as you wish.

Proofing the Film Before Printing

Once the film is ready for printing, it is used to make one or more prints for a final check. The sample that is checked is called a *proof*. For catalogs and other material that will be folded, the filmmaker provides at least two kinds of proofs for the same project.

Color Proof

When two or more colors are to be printed, a color proof shows how the printed piece will look and how it compares with any original art or photographs. This comparison is not checked on the computer screen. To show what the finished piece will look like, this proofing is done on standard proofing paper or, through the new "waterproofing," on the same paper on which the project will be printed. The comparison to the original art and design should be made under industry-specified controlled lighting of 5,000K, which sounds unnaturally bright but is actually the intensity of typical workplace lighting. The purpose of the controlled lighting is to give specified, uniform conditions for comparisons, rather than the random light sources that are available wherever you happen to be. Your film-maker will have such a light source.

For multicolor projects, it is quite common to begin with a *random proof*. This shows, to size, the illustrations and photographs only, before they are placed into position. These are viewed and corrected for color density and detail. Any substitution or other change at this point is less costly than after everything is in place. After corrections are made, a second random proof is done only if the changes are major. More often, the second proof shows everything in position, that is, as it will appear in print. This proof is checked again, both for the specified corrections and for any other changes and corrections that may still be needed. Most often, none of the latter are needed, and this is the proof that goes to the printer.

INSIGHT 82

Accidents can happen any time anyone works with film. Don't just check for your corrections—check *everything*. But don't change anything unless *absolutely* necessary. The process is costly and requires equally careful checking every time.

The proof is accepted, dated, initialed, and marked "OK for printing" or "OK as corrected." (*Note the difference!*)[3] It becomes the guide against which the project is checked while it is actually being printed. In reviewing proofs, be mindful that "what you see is what you get." Do not give your approval until you are satisfied with what you see!

Of course you will let your print production and art departments take the lead in proof checking and approvals. If such departments are not available, use your design source. It is *their* area of *expertise*. It is *your* area of *responsibility*.

Single-Color Proofs and Folding Dummies

Where only one color will be used in printing, the color chosen and the sophistication of design will determine how closely the proofing must match the printed piece. An exact proofing match of a specific color (or something as close as the filmmaker can provide) is more costly than a routine monotone, but like multicolor proofing, it is the only way to *know* what you will see when you print.

The folding proof is produced in one color on the actual stock or on paper that is thin enough to fold easily. The proof is folded or formed into the exact shape and format of the final printed product. It is this folded proof that lets you see how facing pages actually look when all the elements are present and that lets you check whether all those elements are the way they were specified.

Always check the following elements on folding proofs:

- ☐ Are all pages present and in consecutive order?
- ☐ Do elements that run across the center of facing pages (across the gutter) line up?
- ☐ Does the index or table of contents reflect where the elements are? If not, which one is wrong?
- ☐ Do all the elements work together? (Do the materials fit into envelopes? Are items that bind together the proper size and shape? Etc.)

---

[3]Typical "as corrected" notations will indicate that a color is to be slightly darker or lighter, that something has been removed, that a number or letter has been changed, and so forth.

☐   Are comparable elements positioned properly?
☐   Are all page numbers (called "folios") in the same spot?
☐   Is the use of page or section headings consistent? If not, was this deliberate?
☐   Do all cross-references check out?
☐   Do the captions match the pictures? Are both in the right place?
☐   Is all mailing information present and accurate?
☐   Is all ordering information present and accurate? Telephone numbers? Addresses? Legal and self-protection requirements (e.g., "Printed in USA," "Prices subject to change," etc.)?

This is your final chance to see the job as a whole before printing. Take the opportunity to *check everything.*

A Continuous Process

The preparation of film for use in advertising or printing and the printing itself are so interrelated that we shall treat them as continuous, with the film checklist and the notes that follow a part of the basic information. Whereas in other chapters checklist notes are supplemental, here they are a significant part of the text.

The proof delivered by the color-separator film house and accepted by the printer carries an implied guarantee that the film will produce what the proof shows. Many printers inspect all film and proofs carefully before agreeing to accept the film. Once accepted by printers, any problem in producing what the proof shows is to be solved by them and the supplier of the film, not by the client. (And not as Hahn took upon himself in Chapter 5.) Be mindful, however, that the printer is matching a proof, not original art! The time to settle questions concerning the artwork is when it is first seen by whoever makes the film. If the filmmaker does not forewarn you about how art will actually reproduce and suggest ways of doing it better, he or she may be the wrong person for the job. Note that certain colors or inks probably cannot be matched in standard process printing. They simply will not reproduce as seen. So warn your colleagues. And for the sake of your printer's sanity and yours, do not try to "fix" it on press!

NOTES ON THE FILM PREPARATION CHECKLIST

Unlike notes on most other checklists, these notes are not *a supplement to the material presented in the chapter. Rather, they are an integral part of the chapter.*

1. **Project manager.** The direct technical supervisor. If the client has no one in this capacity on staff, use the person or studio that prepared the camera-ready art.
2. **Tentative schedule.** The schedule prepared before the film house is selected. This is generally done at the very beginning of the project, during its planning stages. For anything complicated or more than a few pages, have a color separator give a ballpark *time* estimate to help your

PREPRESS FILM PREPARATION CHECKLIST

Project Title _____   Date _____

Project Description _____   Project # _____

_____   Checklist # _____

Overall Supervision By _____   Deadline _____

Budget _____ Completion Date _____   Start Up Date _____

	ASSIGNED TO	DUE	IN	MUST APPROVE	BY DATE	IN	INFO COPY ONLY	SEE ATTACHED
1. Project Manager	_____	__	☐	_____	__	☐	_____	☐
2. Tentative Schedule	_____	__	☐	_____	__	☐	_____	☐
3. Start-up	_____	__	☐	_____	__	☐	_____	☐
4. Supplier Selection	_____	__	☐	_____	__	☐	_____	☐
5. Final Schedule	_____	__	☐	_____	__	☐	_____	☐
6. Completion	_____	__	☐	_____	__	☐	_____	☐
7. Film/Printer Contact	_____	__	☐	_____	__	☐	_____	☐
8. Prefilm Art Check	_____	__	☐	_____	__	☐	_____	☐
9. Prefilm Final Art Check	_____	__	☐	_____	__	☐	_____	☐
10. Random Proofs	_____	__	☐	_____	__	☐	_____	☐
11. Final Proofs	_____	__	☐	_____	__	☐	_____	☐
12. Dylux Sample	_____	__	☐	_____	__	☐	_____	☐
13. Delivery	_____	__	☐	_____	__	☐	_____	☐

planning. The separator probably can't estimate costs without more facts.

3. **Start-up.** The date the color separator can begin processing materials and, if different, when the final piece of art will be delivered. (Note that if illustrations or photographs have been delivered without specifying their final sizes, the color separator cannot begin working on them.)

4. **Supplier selection.** If you are new to the field or to the geographic location, here are workable suggestions for selecting a film supplier.
   - Find out whom your company or organization has used in the past. Don't change without a reason.
   - Call several printers in the area and ask for their recommendations.
   - Ask the nearest local direct marketing association. To find it, call the Direct Marketing Association in New York at (212) 768-7277. Ask for the "DM Clubs and Association Network."
   - Ask the promotional director of some local businesses.
   - Check the Yellow Pages under "Color Separators."

   For simple one- or two-color projects, almost anyone recommended should do. So shop for price and schedule. For full-color or complicated projects, call first to learn the kind of work the various suppliers do. (Think twice before having a podiatrist do brain surgery or a brain surgeon look at your feet.) Get references. Check! Get samples. Give your final candidates written specifications, including deadlines.

5. **Final schedule.** Prepare a schedule that you, your color separator, and your printer can meet to get the project done on time. If all else fails, negotiate.

6. **Completion.** The date the client is responsible for approving the final proofing. Be sure to allow for at least two proofings on *everything.*

7. **Film/printer contact.** Film must be prepared to match the printer's need. Choose your printer as early as you do the film house, and have both agree on how the film is to be delivered (for instance, as 4-, 8-, or 12-page units). But first, ask other printers how their film is normally supplied, and ask color separators how their film is normally prepared. In case of conflict, get the cost of fixing the difference before film work is assigned. Your higher priced supplier may turn out to be a pleasant surprise.

8. **Prefilm art check.** The color separator should check the drawings, paintings, and other original art so as to foresee problems in duplication and to discuss their solutions. (It is sometimes better to begin with a color photograph, rather than with the original.) Also, the color separator should select the most reproducible photograph or transparencies when several are available. Often, the choice is between contrast and detail. In printing, the printed photographs and drawings are called halftones because they are made up of dots of various sizes lined up in rows, with from 65 to 300 dots per inch. The fewer the dots, referred to as line, screen, halftone, or any combination of the three ("65-line screen," "120-line halftone" etc.), the less detail can be shown. But specific lighting and camera settings also control results. Without instructions, color separators tend to work for a middle ground. For advertising and promotional purposes, we almost always prefer high contrast. When numerous illustrations will be used, have the separator shoot and proof samples in a range of modes before you make a decision on which to use.

For rapidly disappearing letterpress printing and for rougher stock newspapers, 65- to 85-line halftones are standard. In general commercial offset work, 120 to 150 dots are typically used. Two hundred- to 300-line reproduction is used only in the highest quality printing, almost always to show detailed illustrations to exceptional advantage. For any advertisement or for your own commercial work, check on the maximum number of lines *the printer can use.* Each printing press works best at a specific line value. Know what that is, and make certain that no finer screening is ordered from the filmmaker. Fewer lines may give you less of an impact, but it is never a *printing* problem. On the other hand, over 10 percent more than the maximum number of lines for a particular press tends to produce random ink blots that reduce rather than enhance detail.

9. **Prefilm final art check.** Except on the simplest of projects, do not just ship a final art copy boards to the film house. Rather, take your artist or art director with you to meet with the color separator or service bureau and go over *each* instruction. Ask the filmmaker to point out potential

difficulties in making the film *or in printing,* as well as costs not covered by the estimated total. (Marking type for more than two colors is a typical problem—not for the filmmaker, but for the printer. Often a two-color substitute can be found after the difficulty is noted.)

10. **Random proofs.** When transparencies are the art against which proofs are compared, they are generally placed on a "light box," which illuminates them as if they were projected onto a screen. *No printed proof can possibly match the intensity of the colors this produces!* Visualize the originals that the transparencies show, and make *that* the basis for judging.

INSIGHT 83

Color separators expect to do two random proofings for advertising agencies, but only one for most other clients, and quote accordingly. Specify your likely needs when you describe the project, and have those needs reflected in writing in the quotations.

---

11. **Final proofs.** Final proofs show the project as it is to be printed. The corrected illustrations are in position, and everything should match what was asked for on the copy boards checked in #9. Make sure to:
    - Compare the corrected illustrations against the previous version, using the uniform lighting source.
    - Check the proof against every instruction given on the copy boards. Literally check them off to make certain that none are missed.
    - Make a final inspection of every color, to be certain that no obvious errors were made. (For instance, green will turn into blue if yellow has been erroneously located on the film.) If the color of the products is important, have someone who knows about colors check with you. We often see what we expect to see—especially the tenth time we look at it!

Full-Color Proofing

Six types of proofs are possible for most full-color projects. If you are unfamiliar with any of them, ask to see a sample of all six ways, with the cost difference for each. The six types of proofs are:

A. *Digital on-screen proofing.* The only proofing system that permits as-you-watch retouching, changes, and corrections. It is followed by ink on paper "hard copy" for on-press checking.

B. *Waterproofing.* A new (1995) Dupont process that proofs regular process colors on the stock on which the project will be printed, no matter how thick or thin, dull or shiny; even on plastics and cloth. The first proofing process other than actual printing that can show a project on two or more different stocks before stock is ordered.

C. *Match print.* This closely matches what will be printed. It is not as popular as it should be, probably because many clients prefer the flashier Cromalin.™

D. *Cromalin.* This is the most accurate proofing for non-"process color" printing. It produces a very high-gloss surface that can be somewhat deceptive in its feel as a printed piece.

E. *Color key.* This technique results in layers of film, one showing each printing color, positioned on top of each other to reflect what happens in the actual printing process. The colors are slightly muted through effects of the film itself. This was the original color proofing process and is the least expensive of the color systems available.

F. *Reading or Dylux™ proof.* In this technique, proofs are used to make the samples described in #12, for a final check of all copy, and for the positioning of all illustrations. Depending on the colors used, this proof can be made from just one or two of the four colors used in printing.

Two-Color Projects

In many two-color projects, single-color "reading proofs" are adequate. Where only the color of the type is affected—for instance, red headlines or blue handwriting—color is often indicated as a grey, less dense image that is still easy to read.

Illustrations

Where illustrations are to be shown as "duotones," that is, in two colors, one of which most often is black, at least a color key should be used for proofing. The two ways of achieving the final color have quite different effects:

- **Fake duotone.** The illustration is printed in the darker of the two colors and then covered with a light layer, or screen, of the second color. This is the easier way to print and is less expensive for film.

- **True duotone.** A halftone image is made on film for both colors and is then printed with all the care used in full-color projects. True duotones require specialized knowledge and skills by the film house. The technique does not simply use the same film for each color. To give instructions to the film house and to help check results, you need an art director who is familiar with the process.

12. **Dylux™ sample.** This is the *only* preview of how the final project will look in its actual size and with all pages or elements in proper order. All other proofs are presented with wide margins for notations and can be very deceptive. (Dylux is a trade name, and your printer may use a different process. Check for nomenclature.)

 Everyone with whom you work will have a near heart attack when you dare to fold or cut a Cromalin to see what a page actually looked like, although it was never what they thought they had seen in the untrimmed version. (Cut very carefully with a sharp razor, and you can tape it back together almost like new. Remember, we give you absolution: "Hey! It's not a sacred relic! It's just a proof!")

13. **Delivery.** You are responsible for providing the address of the destination. Let the color separator be responsible for shipment or delivery to media and printers. The last thing you want to hear is "It was perfectly fine when you picked it up." So don't!

ON WORKING WITH YOUR PRINTER

Hahn's first full-time job, at age 16, was as a printer's helper at a company that prepared the newspaper advertisements used in Chicago by Montgomery Ward. The preparation of the ads and the printing itself were essentially unchanged from the way Johann Gutenberg had set type and printed his Bible five hundred years before. Individual letters, cast in lead, were selected from a large wooden tray that held the alphabet in specific compartments whose locations one had to learn, much as one learns a touch-typing keyboard today. Once composed, or set, type was locked into a frame with metal wedges. Ink was applied, paper placed on the inked type, and a roller moved over the paper, pressing it just hard enough to produce printing. This method, called *letterpress,* had grown in sophistication, speed, and applications for five centuries and is still the way printing is done in much of the world today.

Other Methods of Printing

In the United States, two newer methods, *offset* and *rotogravure,* now do almost all commercial printing work. Both have two major advantages over letterpress:

1. An easily handled printing plate replaces the heavy and bulky metal type, and CD-ROM or other computerized systems replace the need for storing film. Thus, storage for reprinting that once took a warehouse can now fit into a closet!
2. Illustrations are produced photographically or digitally rather than through the metal etching process required by letterpress. This makes possible practically instant transformation from final art to printed piece.

Even newer methods of printing are now in research, development, or use. Computerized systems that can personalize direct mail will undoubtedly do the same for advertisements printed in magazines and home-delivered newspapers. The same teenager who helped set metal type, ten years later ran an office-sized offset press as part of his first job in advertising. Nothing about printing has surprised him since.

NOTES ON THE PRINTING/BINDERY CHECKLIST

Unlike notes on most other checklists, these notes are not *a supplement to the material presented in the chapter. Rather, they are an integral part of the chapter.*

PRINTING/BINDERY CHECKLIST

Project Title _____   Date _____

Project Description _____   Project # _____

_____   Checklist # _____

Overall Supervision By _____   Deadline _____

Budget _____   Completion Date _____   Start Up Date _____

PRINTING	ASSIGNED TO	DUE	IN	MUST APPROVE	BY DATE	IN	INFO COPY ONLY	SEE ATTACHED
1. Printing Budget	_____	___	☐	_____	___	☐	_____	☐
2. Start-up Date	_____	___	☐	_____	___	☐	_____	☐
3. Completion Date	_____	___	☐	_____	___	☐	_____	☐
4. Project Manager	_____	___	☐	_____	___	☐	_____	☐
5. Tentative Schedule	_____	___	☐	_____	___	☐	_____	☐
6. Supplier Selection	_____	___	☐	_____	___	☐	_____	☐
7. Final Schedule	_____	___	☐	_____	___	☐	_____	☐
8. Paper	_____	___	☐	_____	___	☐	_____	☐
9. Inks/Colors	_____	___	☐	_____	___	☐	_____	☐
10. Varnish	_____	___	☐	_____	___	☐	_____	☐
11. Shipping	_____	___	☐	_____	___	☐	_____	☐
BINDING								
12. Bindery Budget	_____	___	☐	_____	___	☐	_____	☐
13. Bindery Start-up	_____	___	☐	_____	___	☐	_____	☐
14. Completion Date	_____	___	☐	_____	___	☐	_____	☐
15. Project Manager	_____	___	☐	_____	___	☐	_____	☐
16. Schedule	_____	___	☐	_____	___	☐	_____	☐
17. Folding	_____	___	☐	_____	___	☐	_____	☐
18. Binding	_____	___	☐	_____	___	☐	_____	☐
19. Shipping Dates & Methods (skids, cartons, etc.)	_____	___	☐	_____	___	☐	_____	☐
20. Postage	_____	___	☐	_____	___	☐	_____	☐
21. Reports	_____	___	☐	_____	___	☐	_____	☐

1. **Printing budget.** The portion of quoted or estimated costs allocated to printing, even if printing and binding are given to a single supplier. You will want this figure for future comparison shopping. Be mindful of probable savings in getting a printing-binding "package" price.

2. **Start-up date.** When the project will actually go to press. Dates materials must be received by the printer are covered in #7.

3. **Completion date.** When the *printing* portion of the project is to be done. Any bindery work that is to follow is checked off in #12 on.

4. **Project manager.** When in-house technical expertise is available, use it, always asking to be a spectator *permitted to learn.* When printing decisions are thrust upon you before you feel quite ready for them, ask the

printer to be your guide. Never involve yourself in how-to questions! Remember the client's magic words: "I know what we have to achieve. I couldn't begin to tell you how to get there."

5. **Tentative schedule.** This schedule is generally prepared at the beginning of the project, before suppliers are chosen, and helps guide in their selection. Some flexibility must be built in, depending on the complexity of the project.

6. **Supplier selection.** Follow the same procedure as that suggested for selecting a film supplier on page 319 and then add the following considerations:

   • **Sheet or web printing.** Sheet-fed printing uses precut individual sheets. Web printing uses paper taken from huge rolls. Web printing almost always prints on both sides of the paper at the same time, with folding continued as part of the same printing process. Commercially, web printing is used for larger quantities—generally, no less than 25,000 for printing one or two colors and 50,000 for full color.

     Sheet-fed printing has many advantages of its own. It tends to be much more flexible in quantity, number of pages to be printed, size of the pages or printed sheet, stock to be used, and number of suppliers than does web printing. The "quick print" shops found almost everywhere are sheet-fed printers, as are commercial printers in smaller communities.

   • **Check for the right printer for each job.** No one printer can do everything! Visit the plants you asked for quotations. If you are unfamiliar with anything you see, ask. If the plant is not spotless, leave.

7. **Final schedule.** Prepare a schedule that you and your color separator, printer, bindery, and distribution supplier can achieve to get the project done on time. If all else fails, negotiate. Remember to differentiate between how and when!

8. **Paper.** Selecting paper, or "stock," is one of the most critical aspects of any printing project. There are literally thousands of different stocks, many available in a variety of thicknesses or "weights." The lower the weight, in units of pounds, the thinner the stock. Thus, paper used in most office copy machines is 50-pound offset, or 50# stock, which means that 1,000 25" × 38" sheets weigh exactly 50 pounds. To keep

---

INSIGHT 84

Before making a final decision on paper, get stock samples and dummies—that is, actual-size samples—from the paper merchant or printer. Have *them* label each paper type and weight. Include that sample stock when you order. Let your order read: "80# cover and 70# body *as per samples herewith*" if you don't want 70# cover and 80# body and want no excuses for getting them confused.

life from being too simple, different kinds of stock use different weight criteria, but each is consistent within itself and shows thinner to thicker (light to heavy weights) as smaller to larger numbers.

Buying Paper Yourself

Paper and other stocks can be purchased through the printer or, for large jobs, directly by the client from wholesalers or paper mills. If you are inexperienced in purchasing paper or judging among suppliers, get expert help. Merchants are listed in major cities' Yellow Pages. Information is available from your advertising or direct marketing organization or trade publications in the graphic arts.

Here is a short checklist for purchasing paper:

Paper Supplied by Printer

- ☐ Availability
- ☐ Cost
- ☐ Alternative comparable stocks, including their availability and cost

Paper Supplied by Client

- ☐ Minimum order required
- ☐ Cost of specified paper and comparable stock
- ☐ Delivery schedule and guarantees
- ☐ Storage and handling
- ☐ Responsibility for quality
- ☐ Insurance
- ☐ Alternatives if delivery or quality fails

Many organizations and companies purchase their own paper. Others take advantage of their printers' house stocks, purchased in huge quantities at equally huge discounts. But *when only one stock will do, allow enough time for its acquisition.* Paper can seldom be manufactured overnight, no matter who orders it. If it's not on hand, it must wait until the manufacturer's production schedule says it's ready to be produced.

There are many types of paper, including the following:

- **Cover stocks.** These are heavier papers used for catalog covers and similar projects.
- **Offset or matte papers.** These have a duller finish, though not necessarily less white, than that of the glossy alternatives. Most books and newspapers are printed on offset stock.
- **Enamel papers.** These are glossy papers used in many magazines and promotional mailings and on book jackets and other retail packaging. Printed on enamel, color illustrations achieve more sparkle, and even black-and-white illustrations seem to have more life. Enamel papers range from having a lesser gloss, used where materials have to be read as well as seen, to having practically mirrorlike finishes, called "chrome coats," where attention-getting ability is the major criterion.

- **Textured stock.** Few things are as underused as textured papers to give an immediate impression of elegance and good taste. Their very touch conveys prestige. Perhaps a fear that textures will cause difficulties in reproduction is why they are not more used. However, this fear is most often groundless, whether reproducing type or illustrations. Ask to see printed samples, and then be pleasantly surprised at how little more it costs for this added impact.
- **Colored stock.** The more popular offset stocks tend to be available in dozens of colors, at a somewhat higher cost than white. Most enamel stock, unless specially prepared by the paper mills, is white only.

Advantages and disadvantages of color. The major advantage of colored over white stock lies in its being different—in its standing out from the majority of paper people look at. The disadvantage lies in the way printing on color mutes type and illustrations, especially photographs. (Since many art directors are interested in how something looks, rather than how easily it can be read, be especially mindful of this problem.)

Fortunately, there is a solution that produces both unmuted illustrations and color stock: printing the color and leaving the areas to be illustrated white. To do this, you need merely instruct the filmmaker to match a particular light color or use a "screened," light tone of one or more inks that are already part of the job. The process is quite simple and adds little to the overall cost of printing. For example, you can mark the final art, "Screen entire background 20% blue, but drop (remove) color behind all illustrations." This not only gives your illustrations their maximum visibility, but also frames them in color for even more impact.

9. **Inks/Colors.** One of Hahn's favorite memories is of Don Eldredge, then a Rand McNally vice president, screaming at an art director who had just shown him a proposed layout, "This is the last time I'm going to tell you. There is no such color combination as black and blue!" Eldredge knew exactly what colors he wanted, why he wanted them, and what their effect was likely to be in the marketplace. So should you! Before agreeing to radically different colors, ask to see a few samples using those inks on your kind of paper. Quite often, even the person making the suggestion is surprised.

   In addition to the five-color presses discussed in #10, many new presses can print even more colors in a single "press run." This permits combining four-color process with metallic and other colors for special effects and at comparatively low costs. If unfamiliar with everything new in the field work with a printer's reperesentative who will keep you up to date.[4]

10. **Varnish.**[5] Varnish on paper has the same results as its use on wood: protection, durability, and special visual effects.

---

[4]Donald Ladin of Sunrise Printing (847-928-1800) has been Hahn's expert for such new state-of-the-art projects.

[5]Much more expensive plastic coatings are possible but almost always unnecessary.

- **Protection.** Touching unvarnished printing, especially on enamelled, glossy stock, tends to leave fingerprints on the paper. The darker the ink, the more obvious the fingerprints will be. Catalog covers are the most common example. Adding an inexpensive, easily applied coating of varnish totally eliminates this problem. Many four-color (full-color) printing presses have a fifth-color unit that can be used for this purpose. More often, varnish is applied on a single-color press, after the ink has dried. Both methods are effective. Using the latter, however, permits an actual fifth color in the printing. Few of us are able to resist that temptation.

- **Durability.** Fingerprints are far from being the only danger to unvarnished printing. Scuff marks, caused by pieces rubbing against each other during shipping, can make anything appear used or damaged, much as if you were asked to accept a new car with a blotched paint surface. We have seen thousands of presentation folders thrown out because their printing buyers had not known about press varnish. You do. Use it!

- **Special effects.** Varnish can be glossy or dull. No explanation will be as effective as seeing the difference, so ask your printer for samples. Either will give protection. More important is the use of "spot varnish," which adds a striking gloss to a portion of the page, usually its illustrations. In trade terms, "spot" can be any size and any quantity, as long as it does not cover the whole page. Here, too, seeing is much better than describing, so ask several printers for examples and costs. Comparatively few of them have a wide range of samples.

11. **Shipping.** Many printers have their own bindery departments. Those with major mail order clients may also have an in-house lettershop. This can eliminate the time and cost of one or two shipping and handling moves: from the printer to the bindery and from the bindery to a mailing service. In getting quotations, factor in all these variables. We have always been willing to pay slightly more to keep everything under one roof—with one supplier held responsible.

12. **Bindery budget.** Find out the bindery portion of the estimated or quoted costs, even if printing and binding are given to a single supplier. You will want this figure for future comparison shopping. Be mindful of possible savings through a printing and binding "package" price.

13. **Bindery start-up.** Start-up does not necessarily or often occur the moment printing is done. Be there, or ask to see the first completed pieces. Show them to the lettershop as a final safety check.

14. **Completion date.** Specify what "completion" means: the day a job is finished at the bindery or the day it is received at the next destination, usually the letter shop mailing service. Go for the latter.

15. **Project manager.** Costly outside creative direction should not be needed here. Do-it-yourself management again comes into its own.

16. **Schedule.** Whether work is done by the printer or contracted with a separate bindery, get a schedule that shows the following:

- The time and cost (if any) for shipment from the printer to the bindery.
- The time and cost of specialized outside services, such as die-cutting or embossing, before bindery work can begin. Have the print shop run those portions first. They can be finished outside while the rest of the printing is being completed.
- The time and cost of all standard bindery work.
- The time and cost (if any) from the bindery to the lettershop and all other destinations.

17. **Folding.**[6] Before ordering folds on pieces that are to be mailed, especially if they will be placed in an envelope, show them to the bindery and to the lettershop. Almost any fold is possible; some, however, may be very expensive because they cannot be made by a single run through the folding machines at the bindery. Your lettershop will tell you if a folded piece can be handled by their automated equipment. Some folds can't! Don't lock in your paper-folding ingenuity without assurance from both the bindery and the lettershop.

18. **Binding.** For multipage promotional pieces, such as catalogs and brochures, there are three binding or fastening options:[7]

    - **Press glue.** Pages are glued together at the spine as they are folded. When printers have this equipment, and unfortunately few do, it is an excellent—and inexpensive—way of binding 24 or fewer pages.
    - **Saddle stitch.** Pages are folded and stapled together with a metal fastener through the spine. For thicker saddle-stitched projects, allowance must be made in filmwork and printing to have uniform-sized pages. To get an immediate view of the problem, fold several dozen same-sized pieces of paper in half, and then look at the front. The "v" formed by the folding becomes more exaggerated with each sheet you add.
    - **Perfect binding.** This is the system used on most paperbound books. Where thickness permits (different binderies have their own minimums), perfect binding is the method of choice for appearance and ease of printing. Where it is used, it produces a flat spine that should be imprinted as if it were a book. The trade magazine *Pizza Today* prints a highlights index on its spine—an ingenious application for catalogs and other perfect-bound pieces. Many perfect bound catalogs are filed vertically, on bookshelves, rather than in filing cabinets.

19. **Shipping dates and methods.** Discuss with your lettershop, warehouse, and other bulk destinations how they want their shipments sent to them—in cartons, on skids, and so on—and how each unit is to be marked. Get their instructions in writing. Discuss this with the bindery before you approve. If the bindery suggests a better way, let the bindery people discuss it with the people at the destination. As always, don't pretend to an expertise you do not have. But learn and get it!

---

[6]A variety of folds available through most printers and lettershops is shown on page 64.

[7]A variety of binding options is shown on page 154.

20. **Postage.** How much postage and other shipping costs must be paid in advance? Where? When? How is the proof of mailing or shipping documented and recorded?

21. **Reports.** In a brief form, reports are for management. A more detailed version is for do-it-yourselfers. Give yourself time to review such reports at a later date. All too often, they are done, filed, and forgotten. Remember a critical difference between a professional and an amateur: Where a professional has, say, 10-years' experience, an amateur has 1 year's experience 10 times.

ON WORKING WITH YOUR LETTERSHOP

Lettershops began as mail-handling services that could print your letter and reply card or order form, address the letter on the bulky mechanical systems then in use, insert the pieces into envelopes, often by hand, seal the envelopes, and deliver them to the post office. Many lettershops maintained and housed their clients' mailing lists, because their sheer bulk and weight, and the cacophony involved in creating or correcting individual metal addressing plates, made them unwelcome elsewhere. Today's lettershop[8] is still your partner in getting your mailings stuffed, addressed, and delivered. But what a difference the computer age has brought to you and to them! The Lettershop/Distribution checklist that follows will help you both in evaluating potential suppliers and in scheduling their responsibilities—and yours—once they are selected.

Three-Column Format

The Lettershop/Distribution checklist is not complete in itself, except for the simplest of mailings. Its purpose is to guide you through at least one preliminary and final planning meeting with your lettershop. Additional checklists and schedules will be needed for creative design, printing, acquisition of mailing lists, and your in-house handling of responses and their evaluation. Make liberal use of the third column, "SEE ATTACHED." Where possible, use the other checklists in this book. Where none exists, use them as models and make your own.

Evaluating the Lettershop

The type of work lettershops do has remained fairly consistent since our first edition. *How* they do it has changed dramatically for the better. Before planning your promotion, arrange a visit to several lettershops that handle your quantity mailing, plus a multimillion unit mailer, if yours is much smaller. Ask for a guided tour to learn what is now possible and practical.

Figure 14.1 give an overview of the savings that are possible. But the free 1996 Postal Service guide to rates and procedures, *Max It!*, is too important to do them justice by attempting to condense them into our book.

---

[8]Such as Lee Enterprises in S. Holland, IL (708) 596-7900, who helped bring us up-to-date in this section.

SERVICE GRAPHICS, INC.

This quick reference guide provided by Service Graphics

July 1996 — Reclassification Rates

First Class — Postal Rate

Letters, Flats and Sealed Parcels

	Postal Rate
Regular	
Single Piece	32.0
Presort	29.5
Rate for Additional Ounce	
Letters/Flats	23.0
Automation (Presorted & Barcoded)	
Basic	26.1
3-Digit	25.4
5-Digit	23.8
Carrier Route	23.0
Basic Flat	23.0
3/5-Digit Flat	29.0
Post Cards	
Regular	
Single Piece	20.0
Presort	18.0
Automation (Presorted & Barcoded)	
Basic	16.6
3-Digit	15.9
5-Digit	14.3
Carrier Route	14.0

Business Reply Mail

Annual Permit Fee	$ 85.00
Basic Service:	
Cost per piece—First Class Postage	+$ 0.44
Account Fee Service:	
Annual Accounting Fee	$ 205.00
Cost per piece—First Class Postage	+$ 0.10
BRMAS:	
Annual Accounting Fee	$ 205.00
Cost per piece—First Class Postage	+$ 0.02

Sizes

Card	Max. 4-1/4 x 6	.0095 thickness, double max.
	Min. 3-1/2 x 5	.007 thickness, double max.
Letter	Max. 6-1/8 x 11-1/2	1/4" max. thickness
	Min. 3-1/2 x 5	.007 max. thickness
Flats	Max. 12 x 15	3/4 max. thickness
	Min. larger than 6-1/8 x 11-1/2	over 1/4 thick

Standard Mail — Regular Rate

Letter (for pieces weighing 3.3087 ounces or less)

		Destination Entry Rates		
Regular Subclass		Bulk Mail Center	Sectiontal Center Facility	Destination Delivery Unit
Presort:				
Basic	25.6	24.3	23.8	N/A
3/5-digit	20.9	19.6	19.1	N/A
Automation:				
Basic	18.3	17.0	16.5	N/A
3-digit	17.5	16.2	15.7	N/A
5-digit	15.5	14.2	13.7	N/A
Enhanced Carrier Route Subclass				
Basic	15.0	13.7	13.2	12.7
Basic automat.	14.6	13.3	12.8	12.3
High density	14.2	12.9	12.4	11.9
Saturation	13.3	12.0	11.5	11.0
Non-Letter				
Regular Subclass				
Presort:				
Basic	30.6	29.3	28.8	N/A
3/5-digit	22.5	21.2	20.7	N/A
Automation:				
Basic	27.7	26.4	25.9	N/A
3/5-digit	18.9	17.6	17.1	N/A
Enhanced Carrier Route Subclass				
Basic	15.5	14.2	13.7	13.2
High density	14.7	13.4	12.9	12.4
Saturation	13.7	12.4	11.9	11.4

Non Profit

Letter and Non Letter (for pieces weighing 3.438302 ounces or less)

		Destination Entry Rates		
Non-Automation		Bulk Mail Center	Sectiontal Center Facility	Destination Delivery Unit
Letter size:				
Basic	12.4	11.2	10.6	N/A
3/5-digit	11.1	9.9	9.3	N/A
Carrier route	8.6	7.4	6.8	6.3
Saturation	8.3	7.1	6.5	6.0
Non letter size (flats):				
Basic	17.5	16.3	15.7	N/A
3/5-digit	16.1	14.9	14.3	N/A
Carrier route	12.8	11.6	11.0	10.5
Walk sequence 125 piece	12.6	11.4	10.8	10.3
Walk sequence saturation	12.1	10.9	10.3	9.8
Automation				
Letter size:				
Carrier route	N/A	N/A	N/A	N/A
Basic zip+4 (2.5oz. limit)	11.7	10.5	9.9	N/A
3/5-digit zip+4 (2.5oz. limit)	10.7	9.5	8.9	N/A
Basic barcoded	10.6*	9.4*	8.8*	N/A
3-digit barcoded	10.1*	8.9*	8.3*	N/A
5-digit barcoded	9.3*	8.1*	7.5*	N/A
** Letter-size pieces over 3 ozs. subject to addtional standards (DMMC810)*				
Non letter size: (flats)				
Basic zip+4	N/A	N/A	N/A	N/A
3/5-digit zip+4	N/A	N/A	N/A	N/A
Basic barcoded	14.9	13.7	13.1	N/A
3-digit barcoded	14.3	13.1	12.5	N/A
5-digit barcoded	14.3	13.1	12.5	N/A

Figure 14.1 In addition to merge/purge, note the huge savings available through a variety of mail handling options. Discuss this with your in-house or mail handling services! This superb postage chart, based on July 1996 rates, was prepared by Service Graphics (630-941-2899), a Chicago-area printing and direct mail company.

WARNING! WARNING! WARNING!

Before doing any in-house or outside lettershop mailing, get *Max It!*, the 1996 Postal Service guide to rules, regulations, and *savings* under the 1996 guidelines. It's easy to understand and *free* from your Post Office. Depending on when you read this, ask for the current updates, if any. There are huge savings possible. Do not mail without learning how!

For your evaluation, visit prospective suppliers while they are working. Note especially the degree of supervision they operate with, the relationship of supervisors to line workers, and the esprit de corps in the shops. Lettershop work demands unflagging attention to detail by *everyone* involved. Look for that first. Where it exists, the rest is likely to follow.

NOTES ON THE LETTERSHOP/DISTRIBUTION CHECKLIST

Unlike notes on most other checklists, these notes are not *a supplement to the material presented in the chapter. Rather, they are an integral part of the chapter.*

1. **Discussion of project specifications.** Your lettershop can be an unexcelled source of *free consultation* on the mechanical aspects of direct mail. Involve it in your preliminary planning. If you are not a direct mail pro, tell the lettershop people! Ask for guidance in mechanical and postal specifications that will help your more detailed planning as you proceed. For lowest mail-handling costs and postage, envelopes must be of a certain size, with flaps in a certain position, larger materials must be folded in certain ways, and addressing, whether printed or on labels, cannot be affixed to specific areas of the envelope. Your lettershop can be invaluable in helping you plan. See Figure 14.2 for standard sizes, but do not plan to use *any* envelope before discussion with your lettershop! Even if you are a pro, the one way to keep up in this volatile industry is to ask.

2. **Dummy copy for estimate/quotation.** Show your dummies—samples of the exact size and stock you plan to use—to the lettershop. Discuss with them possible cost-saving changes and get estimates or quotations. Estimates are just that—an *approximation* of what the project will cost. *Quotations* demand *exact specification* of every item on this checklist.

3. **Date mailing is to get to recipients.** The date mail *must* be received by the recipients controls all your decisions. Tie-ins with scheduled events or traditional promotion times are obvious examples. Fourth of July sales are announced in June. Seed catalogs arrive in January. Every business product has its own season, and some bloom all year long. Do not, without careful testing, mail anything out of season. The reason everyone in your industry mails at the same time is . . . because that's when everyone decides what to buy.

LETTERSHOP/DISTRIBUTION CHECKLIST

Project Title _____   Date _____

Project Description _____   Project # _____

_____   Checklist # _____

Overall Supervision By _____   Deadline _____

Budget _____ Completion Date _____   Start Up Date _____

SUBJECT	PLANNING	FINAL	SEE ATTACHED
1. Discussion of project specifications	_____	_____	_____
2. Dummy copy for estimate/quotation	_____	_____	_____
3. Date mailing is to get to recipients	_____	_____	_____
4. Scheduling	_____	_____	_____
5. Quantity to be mailed	_____	_____	_____
6. Source and type of lists	_____	_____	_____
7. Merge/purge and other list control	_____	_____	_____
8. Type(s) of addressing	_____	_____	_____
9. Personalization–wanted/required	_____	_____	_____
10. Class of mail (first/second/third/fourth)	_____	_____	_____
11. Date(s) printed materials must be at lettershop and how delivered (skids/cartons/etc.)	_____	_____	_____
12. Printing and bindery work to be provided by lettershop	_____	_____	_____
13. Date mailing list(s) required by lettershop	_____	_____	_____
14. Outgoing mail permit(s)	_____	_____	_____
15. Incoming mail permit(s)	_____	_____	_____
16. Postage amount(s)	_____	_____	_____
17. Date(s) postage is required	_____	_____	_____
18. Lettershop charge(s)	_____	_____	_____
_____	_____	_____	_____

ELEMENTS OF MAILING	QUANTITY	SUPPLIER	ID#
Self-Mailer			
Outgoing Envelope			
Reply Envelope			
Reply Card/Order Form			
Letter			
Flyer/Brochure			

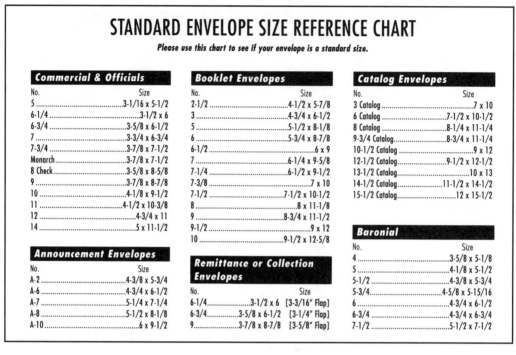

STANDARD ENVELOPE SIZE REFERENCE CHART
Please use this chart to see if your envelope is a standard size.

Commercial & Officials

No.	Size
5	3-1/16 x 5-1/2
6-1/4	3-1/2 x 6
6-3/4	3-5/8 x 6-1/2
7	3-3/4 x 6-3/4
7-3/4	3-7/8 x 7-1/2
Monarch	3-7/8 x 7-1/2
8 Check	3-5/8 x 8-5/8
9	3-7/8 x 8-7/8
10	4-1/8 x 9-1/2
11	4-1/2 x 10-3/8
12	4-3/4 x 11
14	5 x 11-1/2

Announcement Envelopes

No.	Size
A-2	4-3/8 x 5-3/4
A-6	4-3/4 x 6-1/2
A-7	5-1/4 x 7-1/4
A-8	5-1/2 x 8-1/8
A-10	6 x 9-1/2

Booklet Envelopes

No.	Size
2-1/2	4-1/2 x 5-7/8
3	4-3/4 x 6-1/2
5	5-1/2 x 8-1/8
6	5-3/4 x 8-7/8
6-1/2	6 x 9
7	6-1/4 x 9-5/8
7-1/4	6-1/2 x 9-1/2
7-3/8	7 x 10
7-1/2	7-1/2 x 10-1/2
8	8 x 11-1/8
9	8-3/4 x 11-1/2
9-1/2	9 x 12
10	9-1/2 x 12-5/8

Remittance or Collection Envelopes

No.	Size
6-1/4	3-1/2 x 6 [3-3/16" Flap]
6-3/4	3-5/8 x 6-1/2 [3-1/4" Flap]
9	3-7/8 x 8-7/8 [3-5/8" Flap]

Catalog Envelopes

No.	Size
3 Catalog	7 x 10
6 Catalog	7-1/2 x 10-1/2
8 Catalog	8-1/4 x 11-1/4
9-3/4 Catalog	8-3/4 x 11-1/4
10-1/2 Catalog	9 x 12
12-1/2 Catalog	9-1/2 x 12-1/2
13-1/2 Catalog	10 x 13
14-1/2 Catalog	11-1/2 x 14-1/2
15-1/2 Catalog	12 x 15-1/2

Baronial

No.	Size
4	3-5/8 x 5-1/8
5	4-1/8 x 5-1/2
5-1/2	4-3/8 x 5-3/4
5-3/4	4-5/8 x 5-15/16
6	4-3/4 x 6-1/2
6-3/4	4-3/4 x 6-3/4
7-1/2	5-1/2 x 7-1/2

Figure 14.2 Standard envelope size chart by Service Graphics (630-941-2899), a Chicago-area printing and direct mail company.

4. **Scheduling.** Based on your "must be received" dates, work through this checklist with the lettershop. Most suppliers will have standard cost, expedited, and EMERGENCY schedules and rates. Note that your lettershop has no control over your outside suppliers. Item #11 especially will demand its own schedule. Try for the lettershop's standard time line. Not only does it have the lowest costs, but if anything does arrive late, it has built-in time for expedited or emergency action. If you begin on the fastest track and something goes wrong, how can anyone make up the time?

5. **Quantity to be mailed.** The total quantity of your mailing is not the only question to be decided here. Will you test? If so, what quantities and what potential rollout? Different equipment and planning may be needed for different-sized lists. Can your lettershop do both economically? If not, should you try to find a different shop that can or use two suppliers? If two shops are used, who will supervise the second—your primary lettershop or you? There are lots of questions. *Now,* in the planning stage, is the time to get answers.

6. **Source and type of lists.** If anything more than simple affixing of labels is required, discuss with your lettershop what it can do, how much it costs, how long it takes, and how the list must be supplied to make it all possible. Before agreeing, contact your list sources to see whether they can meet those needs and at what cost. Do not pretend to

expertise you do not have. Let lettershops speak with sources of lists and translate for you.

7. **Merge/purge and other list control.** The operations here are computer generated. They cannot be provided economically—if at all—from printed lists already on labels. Before any of these operations are specified, give your lettershop a contact at the location of each list source and let the lettershop determine what is *possible.* You must decide what is *practical.*

- **Merge/purge.** A way of eliminating duplicate addressing when using more than one list. Merge/purge is a computerized system that can save you money on postage and on mountains of printed material. But it does have a price. Check on its possible savings versus mailing to duplicate names. Check it in an area that would get a lot of mail and see how much you would save. You do not actually have to mail anything! Just run the test lists through the merge/purge system, and compare before and after totals.

- **Merge only.** It is often less costly to create a single large list (without purging duplicate names), than it is to handle several lists individually. Although this list will include all the duplicate names, it may qualify more of your list for postal presort discounts. Merge only definitely is less expensive *as a system* than merge/purge.

- **Test selected items.** The *nth* name, zip code, or other selection from larger lists may be less costly when done by a lettershop rather than the list source. Let both quote, but get *all* costs involved.

- **Coding of source list.** If the lists are delivered uncoded, it still may be possible to code them. Check.

- **Presort and zip code qualifications.** Sorting from alphabetical order into zip code, combining for individual mail carrier delivery, and refining into zip code plus four, or plus six bar code, generate substantial savings. The bar code on an increasing amount of mail permits automatic sorting by the Post Office. It is refined to individual mail carrier routes in block-by-block (or floors of larger buildings) street number order. Not every mailing needs this much sophistication, but find out what your lettershop can do, the costs, and savings in postage. (See Figure 14.1.)

8. **Types of addressing.** You can address on labels, simulate typewriter or handwriting, and address onto envelopes, reply forms, or letters that show through windows. There are lots of options, different requirements, and costs. Know *why* as well as *how* if you decide to test.

9. **Personalization.** Practically everyone loves to see their name in print, no matter how obviously it is mass produced. New computer technology is making personalization increasingly more versatile and less costly. Learn what your lettershop can do and what they will need—and charge—to do it. Test.

10. **Class of mail.** Check with your post office, as well as your lettershop, on the requirements and costs for different classes of mail. Then find out

whether your list sources can supply what's needed. You may need postal permits, or you may be able to use the lettershop's. Most *business* mailings will produce essentially the same results no matter how they are mailed, but don't take it for granted. For *your* mailing, . . . test. Believe the numbers.

11–13. **Deliveries to the lettershop.** Determine the specific dates by which outside materials must be received by the lettershop to maintain the dates and costs that were quoted. On-time delivery is *your* responsibility for printing, bindery work, and mailing lists. Some lettershops can provide printing or binding in addition to mailing services. Consider outside shipping and handling in your costs. Find out the lettershop's capabilities, especially in regard to personalizing materials you might not otherwise give that special touch.

14–15. **Mail permits.** New mail permits may be required, depending on where and how you mail your material. Check with both the post office and the lettershop at the beginning of your planning, and then incorporate the permit numbers into your printing. Certain preprinted permits may simulate an *undated* first class meter. Let your lettershop be your guide.

16. **Postage amounts.** Make out your check to the postmaster rather than to your lettershop. It must be deposited in its entirety at the post office. A refund of any overpayment requires a written request, while underpayment *by any amount* may cause refusal of the entire mailing. If you mail regularly from the same post office, establish a bulk rate account there, and always deposit a bit more than you think you'll need. For a one-time mailing only, ask your lettershop how best to handle the postage. Deposit postage at the post office before it receives the mailing. If a check accompanies the mailing and there is any question raised about it, the mailing may be refused.

17. **Dates postage is required.** Deposit checks at the post office several days in advance of the mailing, to give them time to clear. (A cash payment may require references!)

18. **Lettershop charges.** *Any* change between what your lettershop saw for estimating and what it actually receives may change costs. Get samples to the lettershop so it can confirm or requote prices in advance of the actual mailing.

INSIGHT 85

Code *every piece of every mailing,* whether that piece changes within the mailing or not. Place the code where it can be seen (on the outside, not the inside of the brochure). Ask the mailing service where the code must be placed. It's the best—and often the only—way of getting the right pieces into the right envelope addressed with the right list. Code reply cards and order forms *on the ordering side.* For test mailings, copy each reply (that's why you put it on the ordering side) before it goes to the order fulfillment department. Use those copies to check any computer analysis reports. This time, don't believe the numbers. Check!

15 | Finding the Right Advertising Agency[1] and Other Promotional Resources

The selection of an advertising agency is based on one of four circumstances:

1. You have never had an agency and are convinced that you need one now.
2. Your previous agency has resigned.
3. Your previous agency has been or will be fired.
4. You wish to evaluate your current agency against other resources.

The process suggested in this chapter works equally well for an external or in-house advertising agency, an advertising department, or any other advertising or promotional resource.

INSIGHT 86

The most frequent reason for the "failure" of an advertising or promotion campaign is a client's refusal to continue a multistep program when success planned for step six has not yet been reached at step four. Don't plan steps if only the long jump will do!

THE JOB DESCRIPTION

No matter what the urgency of your need, precede the search with a job description as carefully considered and detailed as one for an executive vice president or other senior officer.

- Put in writing *exactly* what the job involves, including an objective basis for evaluation.
- Specify what you, as a client, will contribute to help make the desired results happen. Your agency, as well as you, needs assurances of resources to get the job done.
- Detail the compensation—how much you will pay.

---

[1]If all else fails, call 847-866-9009 and ask for Fred!

Of course, the job description is just a beginning. You and your more likely candidates must discuss it—often phrase by phrase—until there is agreement not only on what it says, but on what it means. For example, every such description contains the words "assist with marketing." But what is "assist"? What is "marketing"? How does one get compensated for marketing?

COMPENSATION

Begin with the budget. Everything that follows will be determined by the dollars available for it. Agencies and other promotional resources—whether they admit it or not—are structured to work within specific budget ranges. Those handling accounts of $50,000 or less probably could not provide the service demanded by clients spending $500,000 or $5 million. A $50,000 account represents one-half of one percent of its billing to a $10-million agency. It means a 10 percent increase to the one billing $500,000. Find the right-size pond in which to swim.

INSIGHT 87

An advertising agency is a business. Unless there are overriding reasons to the contrary, put your account where your financial contribution is meaningful to that business's success. You certainly don't have to be the biggest fish in their pond; just be one that they'll *know* is gone if you're landed by someone else.

MAKE FIGURES MEANINGFUL

Differentiate between your advertising and promotion budget and your agency budget. To the client, $100,000 for direct mail is detail enough. For your candidate agencies, the critical facts would be $80,000 for *client-purchased* film, printing, and postage, with $20,000 for agency copy, art, and supervision. Think of your possible client-agency union as an arranged marriage where compatibility will matter beyond anything else. Of course you want to feel comfortable with your mate from the very beginning, so put that in the job description, too. But always remember that you have a *business* relationship, with mutual profitability as its only likely continuing bond.

WHAT ADVERTISING AGENCIES CAN DO

Advertising agencies excel in the ability to tell a story convincingly in a variety of media, address that story to its most appropriate audience, and get that audience to take some specific action based on what they have seen, or heard, or both. Where the product or service is new, different, or simply superior, the descriptive job is comparatively simple. It's making oneself seen and heard through the competitive clutter that calls on all the agency's creativity. Any of us can tell you that something is bigger, better, faster, cheaper, safer, or healthier. It's getting our audience to pay attention, believe what we say, and do something about it that becomes difficult.

The difficulty is compounded when you and your competitors' products or services are essentially the same. It grows even more so when even the client recognizes that the problem lies in the product or service itself, yet advertising is assigned to provide the sales solution. And advertising often does! The storyteller becomes mythmaker and the customer, believing the myth, makes it come true.

In evaluating potential agencies or services, know which client description you match, and then evaluate their proposals against your need. Beware of brilliant solutions to the wrong problem. Beware of any solutions until the problems are agreed upon.

AN OBJECTIVE BASIS FOR SELECTING AN AGENCY

Any competent agency can produce innovative and pictorially striking concepts. But even when competing products are essentially the same—e.g., hamburgers, beer, women's jeans, men's athletic shoes, telephone service, credit cards . . . the list is endless—creativity alone is probably not enough. Rather than asking for speculative *creative* presentations, pay the competing agencies to research the reasons for the advertising problem, and then make that the basis for a competition among them based on their proposed solutions.

Do what many of the most successful direct marketers do: Recognize that you do not know what may work until you try it. Within specified parameters of good taste, good policy, and good law, give each of your finalists a chance with its solution to its analysis of the best way to reach your audience. Any good media-buying service can work with you in structuring a fair trial. If budget is a problem, limit your search to just two finalists. And if you must select one only, take comfort in the fact that they are almost all competent and practically everyone else does it that way, too. The fact that they are wrong as often as right is what makes the "agency business" so competitive . . . and so much fun!

Index